CLASSICS IN ANTHROPOLOGY
Rodney Needham, *Editor*

KINGS AND COUNCILLORS

Arthur Maurice Hocart 1883–1939

A. M. HOCART

KINGS AND COUNCILLORS

An Essay in the Comparative Anatomy
of Human Society

Edited and with an Introduction by
RODNEY NEEDHAM

Foreword by
E. E. EVANS-PRITCHARD

THE UNIVERSITY OF CHICAGO PRESS
Chicago & London

A. M. Hocart's original text was first published
in 1936 by the Printing Office Paul Barbey, Cairo

International Standard Book Number:
(clothbound) 0-226-34566-1; *(paperbound)* 0-226-34568-8
Library of Congress Catalog Card Number: 71-101297
The University of Chicago Press, Chicago 60637
The University of Chicago Press, Ltd., London

To

E. G. H.

Contents

Foreword ix
Editor's Introduction xiii
Preface 3
Abbreviations and Bibliography 7
1 Rules of Evidence 11
2 The Witnesses 28
3 Opening the Case 30
4 Nature 41
5 The World 60
6 The Good 72
7 Centralization 81
8 The King 86
9 The Estates of the Realm 102
10 The Law 128
11 War 156
12 The Church and the State 162
13 The Commander-in-Chief 180
14 The Priest 190
15 The Revenue 202
16 Public Works 215
17 Temples 226
18 Idols 238
19 The City 250
20 Heaven and Earth 262
21 Summing Up 291
Additional Notes 300
Appendix 303
Index 305

Foreword

HOCART WAS an industrious student, prolific writer, and in many respects an original thinker, but he does not appear to have had as much influence on the anthropology of his time as one might therefore have expected. There may have been many reasons for this. He was shy and reserved and some found him awkward and difficult also. I did not do so. Then his close association with Perry and later with Raglan, neither very critical in their contributions to the subject, gave the impression that somehow he was in a backwater, outside the mainstream of social anthropology. Also, he never occupied a chair till he had one at Cairo at the end of his life, and consequently was not able to influence students by personal contact as well as by his pen. There may have been other reasons, among them what some may regard as a rather arid style and a slightly testy, or at least a non–suffering-fools-gladly, tone in his writings.

Whatever may have been the reasons for a seeming failure at the time, it was Radcliffe-Brown and Malinowski who attracted more attention with their talk, which now appears naïve, about functional interpretation of social phenomena. Neither, however, made any serious attempt to base their claims on anything that could be called a systematic use of the comparative method, and neither could in any case have used it as Hocart did, for neither was a scholar and Hocart was. He had a knowledge of history that they lacked and he, unlike them, could go to the original sources, for he had a good knowledge of Greek, Latin, Sanskrit, Pali, Tamil, and Sinhalese as well as of modern European languages.

His idea of functional interpretation was, if I understand him correctly, to compare the manner in which social activities of one sort or another are carried out in societies of different types, e.g., Arunta, Winnebago, Jukun, ancient Greece and Rome, the Hebrews, the ancient and modern Egyptians, ourselves. The same function may take widely divergent forms, though Hocart regarded it as axiomatic that there is always a tendency for function to determine structural form. So settlement of disputes by feud and in a court of law are functionally comparable; likewise are a professional man in our society earning money to buy in the market goods to maintain his family and an Australian aboriginal hunting kangaroos to maintain his. This treatment makes it interesting for students in that they learn to see fundamental similarity beneath a diversity of institutional forms and to appreciate that the form they are familiar with in their own culture is only one of many possible modes of organizing social activities; and I think this book must have grown out of lectures to the author's students at Cairo. It is evident that the conclusions derived from comparative analysis will depend on the criteria of classification. If one classes whales with fish and bats with birds one is not going to reach the same conclusions as one would if one classed both with mammals. So we have to bear in mind that Hocart's analysis is based on the sort of functional classification that zoologists use when they class whales and bats among the mammals.

I must here confess that personally I have not found that, granted his method of functional classification, his technique of analysis, rather loaded with conjecture, is one that I would wish to follow. I find his anatomical analogy unenlightening, and his use of words like "identity" and "equivalence" and his constant use of equation signs in this book confusing; likewise such statements as "the king is the sun." But this is a personal reaction, and it should be borne in mind that when Hocart speaks in such terms he does so in functional or symbolic senses, in the senses that in certain situations one thing can be substituted for another.

Having said that, I must add that I am not saying that Hocart's analytical technique is not the right technique or one of the right techniques but only that it does not appeal to me. It may appeal more to others. What I find more valuable than the dissection of a custom, the breaking down of it into elements, which does not for me make it more intelligible (though this procedure is perhaps more fashionable now than it was in Hocart's day), is the sense of movement imparted by his use of history, a sense so often lacking in anthropological literature; also the implicit indication that everywhere the logic of the situation imposes on the actors in it what might be said to be, at least up to a point, an inevitable structural form; and also, as in Fustel de Coulanges' *The Ancient City*, the insistence that what we today regard as institutions established for their utility have as often as not a sacred origin. It is on account of these emphases, among others, that this book is well worth a reissue, and it is to be both hoped and expected that the new edition will bring to the attention of students the importance of Hocart's writings.

E. E. EVANS-PRITCHARD

All Souls College, Oxford

Editor's Introduction

It is not . . . government that man wants. . . .
It is life he wants.

A. M. Hocart

What life have you if you have not life together?
There is no life that is not in community . . . .

T. S. Eliot

I

ONE OF the most lively and grateful benefits of scholarship
is the immediacy of communication with remarkable men, and
very often with what is best and most admirable in them,
without consideration of time elapsed or any other distinctions
of circumstance. We are made members of an ideal community
in which the address of Aristotle or Kant, Descartes or Hume,
is a satisfaction more real than many things in the press of
actualities. When our resolution falters, or inspiration flags,
under the trials and distractions of commonplace affairs, these
clear voices and precellent talents restore the confidence that
there are yet ultimate values, of reason and humane concern,
to be worked for.

On the lesser plane of anthropology there have been few
men who have spoken to us with such clarity, arresting direct-
ness, and genial provocation as A. M. Hocart. Not many in
that subject have written with his intellectual candor and
displayed with so little self-regard the checks, turns, and processions of a mind at work. A classic might well have been
looked for from a thinker of his distinction, and the present
work now reissued in a series so entitled has indeed marks
of that quality; but it has not been accorded so prominent
a place in the professional literature, it has exerted no great
theoretical influence, and it cannot thus be said to mark a
point in the history of ideas. The intention of this new edition
is to claim that significance for it.

Kings and Councillors was originally published in Cairo,[1]
and it made little stir. It is true that Elkin, congratulating
Hocart on the accomplishment of "an erudite and brilliant

1. Printing Office Paul Barbey, 1936.

contribution to our understanding of man," judged him to have performed in it "a great service for all students of ritual, and . . . for all who are endeavouring to understand the relation of ritual to social order";[2] and that Hornblower paid the book the compliment of a respectfully long and careful review, if also a rather dubious one.[3] But elsewhere it was not given much notice, and its comparative rarity has since intensified its neglect. It is moreover in some respects a difficult work to comprehend, and it makes rather special demands on the concentration and synthetic capacity of the reader.[4] Its merits have hence remained unproclaimed, it is little cited, and it has not been embalmed in the textbooks, any more than the author himself has been thus commemorated.[5]

For the most part Hocart has been relegated to almost as obscure a position as *Kings and Councillors* has been. He is not to be found in contemporary directories or in the *Dictionary of National Biography*; and even Lowie's learned and judicious *History of Ethnological Theory* mentions him only twice, if approvingly.[6] His views form no part of the ordinary university syllabus, and students of social anthropology can gain their certificates of competence while ignorant of Hocart's very name. In a general purview he appears as a somewhat forlorn and idiosyncratic figure, out of the mainstream of anthropological thought. He spent much of his life away from England, and in that country he was vastly overshadowed by Radcliffe-Brown and Malinowski; his comparative and historical concerns were unfashionable in the heyday of functionalism; and for most of his career he held no academic post which could have served as a rostrum for the expression

2. A. P. Elkin, review in *Oceania* 8 (1937): 120–21.
3. G. D. Hornblower, review in *Man* 38 (1938): 154–56, art. 175
4. Less intent students may be advised to gauge what it is about by reading just the first three chapters and the last.
5. To take two representative examples, neither T. K. Penniman, *A Hundred Years of Anthropology* (London: Duckworth, 1935; rev. ed., 1952) nor J. H. M. Beattie, *Other Cultures: Aims, Methods and Achievements in Social Anthropology* (London: Routledge & Kegan Paul, 1964), so much as mentions this or any other work by Hocart.
6. (New York: Rinehart, 1937), pp. 199, 237.

of his ideas.[7] Yet he had after all carried out extensive field research in the Pacific, before the First World War, and in Ceylon; he had some two hundred publications to his credit, including five books published during his lifetime;[8] and he enjoyed the professional respect of such eminent personages as W. H. R. Rivers and Marcel Mauss. By the ordinary standards of estimation, therefore, he was certainly not a negligible figure, and there is this justification at least to re-examine what is his most systematic and challenging monograph.

There is another consideration, too, in including this book in a series of "Classics in Anthropology." To bring forth again a work which is an undisputed classic is doubtless a commendable pedagogical service, though there may be some risk that the editorial assessment will verge on the supererogatory; and to make available once more a work of note which has happened to fall out of print or circulation is a very convenient enterprise of a practical kind. But to revive a slighted or unknown work is a venture which promises a more marked and original instruction, and it may contribute more emphatically to the history of ideas; for if it is useful to establish the pedigree and credentials of ideas which have become firmly accepted, there is no less interest in examining the merits of other notions which were not so accommodated, and to conjecture the reasons for their neglect. There has to be some assurance, of course, that the arguments were worth considering in the first instance, but in Hocart's case this is hardly a debatable issue. In latter years, moreover, his views have been adduced by a number of leading anthropologists, and these would be unlikely to bestow their regard where it was not due.

Lévi-Strauss has found Hocart's work relevant to his own on such varied topics as dual organization, reciprocity, caste,

7. For the influence which such a position may confer, properly or not, see Leslie A. White, *The Social Organization of Ethnological Theory*, Rice University Studies, vol. 52, no. 4 (Houston: William Marsh Rice University, 1966).

8. See *A Bibliography of Arthur Maurice Hocart* (Oxford: Blackwell, 1967), by the present editor (hereafter cited as *Bibliography*).

cross-cousin marriage, the role of wife-takers in marriage contracts, and alternate generations; on structural analysis and linguistics, emotion and concepts, the analysis of ritual, and feudal systems.[9] Dumont ranks Hocart as one of the immediate masters in the field of Indian studies, and ascribes to him the very inspiration by which he thinks these studies should be directed; while in his own superlative work on caste he pays repeated tribute to the quality of Hocart's perceptions and stresses how much is owed to him in the comprehension of the system.[10] Fortes, referring to "that neglected pioneer," writes that "Hocart's analysis of coronation ceremonies (1927) has not, to my knowledge, been superseded as an attempt at a comparative and generalising study of ceremonies of this type," and he generously declares that the conclusions to his own inquiry into installation ceremonies are "No more, perhaps, than confirmation for the thesis in Hocart's study."[11] Other social anthropologists, too, have written with patent admiration of Hocart's "creative, synthesizing imagination," his "complex and contrary mind," and his intelligence;[12] his brilliant essay on kinship systems[13] has been of decisive relevance to modern theoretical debate, and the analysis of

9. C. Lévi-Strauss, *Les structures élémentaires de la parenté* (Paris: Presses Universitaires de France, 1949), pp. 89, 166 n. 1, 490, 500, 542, 584 (cf. English rev. ed., *The Elementary Structures of Kinship*, ed. Rodney Needham, trans. J. H. Bell, J. R. von Sturmer, and R. Needham [Boston: Beacon Press, 1969]); *Anthropologie structurale* (Paris: Plon, 1958), pp. 38, 228, 263, 346.

10. Louis Dumont, *La civilisation indienne et nous: Esquisse de sociologie comparée*, Cahiers des Annales, 23 (Paris: Colin, 1964), pp. 90–97, 108; idem, *Homo hierarchicus: Essai sur le système des castes* (Paris: Gallimard, 1966), index; see also references idem, *Une sous-caste de l'Inde du Sud: Organisation sociale et religion des Pramalai Kallar* (Paris and The Hague: Mouton, 1957). Cf. [D. F. Pocock], "A. M. Hocart on Caste—Religion and Power," *Contributions to Indian Sociology* 2 (1958): 45–63.

11. Meyer Fortes, "Of Installation Ceremonies," *Proceedings of the Royal Anthropological Institute*, 1967, pp. 5–20.

12. Pocock, "Hocart on Caste," pp. 45, 59, 60.

13. A. M. Hocart, "Kinship Systems," *Anthropos* 32 (1937): 345–51; reprinted idem, *The Life-giving Myth* (London: Methuen, 1952), pp. 172–84.

prescriptive alliance has been illuminated by what has been called his "characteristic insight."[14] It has been found, furthermore, that university students very readily respond to Hocart's intellectual virtues and even to his expository quirks, and that they are specially stimulated by the radical cast which he can impart to even the most particular or esoteric of questions.

At the present time the attention of social anthropologists is turned more than ever to the scrutiny of their own categories of description and analysis, the premises with which they operate, and more rigorously to the perennial issue of how best to come to terms with the distinctive features of alien cultures. In this renewed examination of the conceptual foundations of the subject, Hocart's intransigent genius, uncomfortable and unfashionable though it was previously found, may prove to have a singular and invigorating effect.

II

Arthur Maurice Hocart was born on 26 April 1883 at Etterbeck, near Brussels.[15] He came of a French family said to be traceable to Domrémy, birthplace of Joan of Arc, where a Hocart is reported to have been living in the time of the Maid. A descendant removed from there to Guernsey, in the Channel Islands, where Hocart's forebears acquired British nationality. His grandfather, James Hocart, was born on Guernsey; he was a high church clergyman, but became a Wesleyan Methodist. Hocart's father, also James, was born in France, at St. Pierre, near Calais; he was a Wesleyan minister, but became a Unitarian.[16] These last two were both men of active intelligence

14. See editor's *Structure and Sentiment* (Chicago: University of Chicago Press, 1962), pp. 37, 97.
15. *Register of Exeter College, Oxford, 1891–1921* (Oxford: Blackwell, 1928), p. 79.
16. Information by kind courtesy of Hocart's sister, Mlle E. Hocart (private correspondence, 17 March 1966). Marcel Mauss writes that Hocart came of old Norman stock (introduction to A. M. Hocart, *Les castes* [Paris: Musée Guimet, 1938], p. b). The name Hocart does not appear in Albert Dauzat, *Dictionnaire étymologique des noms de famille et prénoms de France*, 3d ed., rev. by Marie-Thérèse Morlet (Paris: Larousse, 1951), though there is a form Hocquart (p. 333, s.v. "Hoquet").

and wide learning. James Hocart the elder published considerably, in French and in equally exact English, on a variety of religious questions. James Hocart the younger followed his example, and with a serious eclecticism; he wrote, for instance, a book on the pagan origins of monasticism, another about Jews, and a forthright but calmly analytical paper on the obstacles to Protestant faith in Belgium.[17]

A. M. Hocart was educated at the Athénée d'Ixelles, Brussels, at Elizabeth College, Guernsey, and at Exeter College, Oxford. He matriculated at Oxford University in October 1902 and was a classical scholar of his college. He gained the Richards Prize in 1904 and a second in classical moderations in the same year. He graduated in 1906 with second-class honors in Literae Humaniores (Greek, Latin, ancient history and philosophy), and later studied psychology and philosophy for a time at the University of Berlin.[18]

In 1908–9, with the aid of a senior studentship provided first by Exeter College and then by Jesus College, Oxford, he did ethnographical research in the Pacific, as a member of the Percy Sladen Trust Expedition to the Solomons, in close association with W. H. R. Rivers, who found him "a disciple after his own heart."[19] Upon the recommendation of A. C. Haddon he was then appointed headmaster of the Lakemba school, in the Lau Islands, Fiji, a post which he held from

17. James Hocart the Younger, *Le Monachisme* (Paris, 1903); idem, *La question juive: Cinq conférences avec un appendice sur la charité juive* (Paris: 1899); idem, "The Struggle against Catholicism in Belgium," in *Liberal Religious Thought at the Beginning of the Twentieth Century*, ed. W. Copeland Bowie (London, 1901), pp. 126–34. The works of both the elder and the younger James Hocart, incidentally, are run together, without separate attribution, in the catalog of the Bibliothèque Nationale, Paris, and probably therefore in the catalogs of other libraries also.

18. *Register of Exeter College*, p. 79; E. E. Evans-Pritchard, obituary notice of A. M. Hocart, *Man* 39 (1939): 131, art. 115.

19. W. H. R. Rivers, *The History of Melanesian Society*, 2 vols. (Cambridge: Cambridge University Press, 1914), 1: vii; R. R. M[arett], obituary notice of A. M. Hocart, *The Stapledon Magazine* 9 (June, 1939): 289. Rivers announced (*Melanesian Society*, 1: 234) a joint work on the Western Solomons, to be written in collaboration with Hocart, but it never appeared, doubtless because of the war and then his own death (in 1922) not long after the war's end.

1909 to 1912 and which permitted him to acquire a profound understanding of Fijian culture.[20] In the latter year he received from Oxford University a graduate research scholarship in order to carry out investigations in Fiji, Rotuma, Wallis Island, Samoa, and Tonga.[21] In the spring of 1914 he was back at Oxford, where he registered for the diploma course in anthropology, but there is no record of what instruction he received and he did not sit the final examination.[22] He is reported to have deputized in 1915 for Wm. McDougall, then Wilde Reader in Mental Philosophy,[23] and in Hilary Term of that year he delivered lectures on "Problems of Anthropology."[24] From 1915 to 1919 he served in the Oxfordshire and Buckinghamshire Light Infantry; he fought in France, where he was mentioned in despatches, and reached the rank of captain.

After the war he was appointed Archaeological Commissioner for Ceylon. As preparation for the post he was first sent back to Oxford in order to study Sanskrit, Pali, Tamil, and Sinhalese.[25] He read Sanskrit with A. A. Macdonell, who in 1905 had been one of the initial members of the Committee for Anthropology, the body responsible for the organization of anthropological teaching at the University of Oxford and for the administration of the Diploma in Anthropology which was initiated in 1906.[26] It has been said that Hocart also had some contact with Tylor, though if this is so it must have

20. G. K. Roth, review of A. M. Hocart, *The Northern States of Fiji* in *Man* 53 (1953): 95–96, art. 148.
21. Evans-Pritchard, Hocart obituary.
22. Register of students for the Diploma in Anthropology, University of Oxford.
23. S. Paranavitana, obituary notice of A. M. Hocart, *Journal of the Ceylon Branch of the Royal Asiatic Society* 34 (1938): 264–68 (see p. 264).
24. "Papers of the Committee for Anthropology" (University of Oxford), Bodleian Library, shelfmark: Hyp. K, no. 106.
25. Paranavitana, Hocart obituary, p. 265.
26. "Papers . . . ," no. 10. Another member of the committee was Hocart's tutor, L. R. Farnell, Fellow of Exeter College and Lecturer in Classical Archaeology, who had also been a signatory (in company with Tylor, Marett, Balfour, McDougall, and others) to the "Memorandum on the Position of Anthropology in the University" ("Papers . . . ," no. 1), which led to the establishment of the Diploma as the first academic qualification at Oxford exclusively in anthropology.

taken place when he was an undergraduate, since Tylor died in 1917; and the same source has it that he worked at Cambridge "près de" Frazer, Haddon, and Rivers.[27] In any case, he was then sent to India as well, presumably on his way to take up his appointment in Ceylon, in order to study Hindu and Buddhist monuments and the methods of their conservation.[28]

On January 24, 1921, he assumed charge of his department in Colombo. He found it in poor condition, and had to work almost single-handed to restore matters. Much of his time had to be devoted to the preservation of ancient monuments which were in urgent need of attention, but he managed nevertheless to maintain an energetic program of exploration, registration, and publication. In the field he was invariably punctual and conscientious, and he was present right through any excavation; in his long journeys, armed only with a cane, through forests which were the habitat of wild elephant, leopard, and buffalo, he was "utterly intrepid."[29] He put the results of his predecessors' work into print,[30] and also founded and edited Section G, devoted to archaeology and ethnology, of the *Ceylon Journal of Science*. He was "prepared to undergo any hardship to accomplish the task that had been undertaken" but he taxed himself too severely and was forced by dysentery to go on home leave in July 1925. After his return to Ceylon he had a near-fatal relapse, and was ill and absent from duty from 13 October 1928 to 9 January 1929. He was retired, as medically unfit to serve, on 11 September 1929.[31] In 1930 he married Elizabeth Graham Hearn, who had nursed him during his illness and to whom he later dedicated *The Progress of Man* and *Kings and Councillors*.

In the next few years he was occupied with writing and with lecturing at University College London, where he was an honorary lecturer in ethnology and worked in close asso-

27. Mauss, introduction to Hocart, *Les Castes*, p. b.
28. Paranavitana, Hocart obituary, p. 265.
29. D. T. Devendra to editor, 16 October 1968.
30. See Needham, *Bibliography*, items nos. 51 and 78.
31. Paranavitana, Hocart obituary, p. 267; D. T. Devendra to editor. See also D. T. Devendra, *The Story of Ceylon Archaeology* (Colombo: Archaeological Society of Ceylon, 1969), p. 7 and passim.

ciation with G. Elliot Smith and W. J. Perry. He examined for the University of London, and from 1932 to 1934 was a member of Council of the Royal Anthropological Institute, but he had no secure position.[32] In 1934, however, he was elected to the chair of sociology at the Fuad I University of Cairo, in succession to E. E. Evans-Pritchard; and in the following year he was awarded the high distinction, the title of which must have been especially valuable to him, of the Rivers Memorial Medal, for field work in Melanesia, Polynesia, and Ceylon.[33] At Cairo he continued to publish, and he initiated and supervised ethnographical investigations in Egypt, until he contracted an infection in the Fayoum and died, at the age of fifty-five, on 9 March 1939. His remains are buried in the British military cemetery at Cairo. Mrs. Hocart died on 2 May 1947. All of her personal belongings had been destroyed in a Nazi air raid, and with them her material remembrances of Hocart. There were no children.

The tragedy of Hocart's early death was fortunately mitigated, from a scholarly point of view, and his memory better secured, by the exceptional efforts exerted for his sake, and for the preservation of his work, by his friend, intellectual congener, and literary executor, the late Lord Raglan. At what must have been a very considerable cost of time and labor, the latter placed articles in journals, wrote a preface to *Caste* (1950), brought out a collection of Hocart's papers (*The Life-giving Myth*, 1952), edited the manuscript draft of *The Northern States of Fiji* (1952), and compiled for publication as a book (*Social Origins*, 1954) a number of notebooks which Hocart had left in a very incomplete state.[34]

Those who knew Hocart were to speak of him in terms

---

32. Since the parties are dead, it may be permissible to mention the report that Hocart applied for the chair of social anthropology at Cambridge but suffered a great setback to reasonable and encouraged hopes in seeing it given to another. The reason, it is said, is that doubt had been felt that his health was robust enough to bear the strains of the appointment. It would be invidious to suggest any direct comparison, but it seems indisputable that social anthropology at that university, and more generally the course of the subject in Britain, would have been markedly different had Hocart been elected.

33. *Journal of the Royal Anthropological Institute* 65 (1935): iv.

34. Needham, *Bibliography*, pp. 34–36; see index under "Raglan."

of great respect which were clearly not conventional, and he was by all accounts a man of truly scholarly disposition and unusual gifts. He made a practice of consulting Sanskrit, Pali, Greek, and Latin sources in the original tongues, and was a fine practical linguist with some fourteen or fifteen languages at his command.[35] This latter facility must have aided him in his ethnographical researches, the published results of which demonstrate him to have been a sympathetic and effective investigator with a resolute capacity to think with the ideas held to by the people he was trying to understand. ("What *we* think has nothing to do with the matter, but only what the people we are studying think.")[36] Evans-Pritchard has judged him to have had a very clear understanding of the methodology of science and of the place of theory in research. "In his writings he was unbiased by personal considerations and allowed himself to be guided solely by the facts. He was always a courageous critic of what he considered pretentious and slovenly work."[37] Paranavitana, a former colleague of Hocart's in Ceylon, has also stressed his "free and unbiased mind";[38] and correspondents have more recently recalled, decades after their acquaintanceship with him, their admiration for his penetratingly analytical intelligence, his erudition, and his warmth. In his only academic appointment, at Cairo, he was immensely popular among his colleagues, very successful as a teacher, and his students were "devoted to him."[39] He could on occasion be plain-spoken, it is remembered, and even peremptory, but it appears that he was essentially a reserved and withdrawn man;[40] and it was the late Lord Raglan's opinion that "the absence of that recognition

35. C. R. H. Taylor, "The Hocart Papers in the Turnbull Library," *Journal of the Polynesian Society* 59 (1950): 269–72 (see p. 269).
36. Below, p. 217. (Future page references to the present work will be given in parentheses within the text of the Editor's Introduction.)
37. Evans-Pritchard, Hocart obituary.
38. Paranavitana, Hocart obituary, p. 268.
39. Lord Raglan, foreword to A. M. Hocart, *Kingship*, abr. ed. (London: Watts, 1941); Evans-Pritchard, Hocart obituary, p. 131.
40. See the frontispiece portrait, in which an initially rather commanding impression quickly gives way, it may be thought, to the signs of an uncertain inner tension.

to which his talents and attainments entitled him was due as much to his retiring disposition as to the unorthodoxy of his views."[41]

There is no doubt that Hocart's thought is bold, unpredictable, and quite out of the run of the usual academic style. A man who can serenely declare that "the first kings must have been dead kings"[42] is obviously not much concerned to pander to received ideas. Nor, in this case, is he being pointlessly contrary.[43] What counts for him is the evidence, and then the inferences which it seems plausibly to permit, whether the conclusions agree with a currently fashionable doctrine or whether they sound absurd. Hocart was not bothered by fashion or by apparent absurdity, but was interested only in what seemed to follow from the facts; and the positions to which he thought these led were commonly quite unexpected. His trenchant theoretical views were often unconventional to the point that they seemed actually to court rejection, and in fact, as Evans-Pritchard has observed, his originality did not commend itself to a very large body of students, though "even those who most strongly disagree with them are forced to acknowledge their brilliance."[44]

Very clearly, however, Hocart was not preoccupied with the prospect of any present and general agreement with what he thought. He certainly wanted to change people's minds, but it was typical of him that he would make no concessions, even in the matter of presentation. He often wrote in a staccato style, yet traced his arguments merely elliptically; he constantly offered shocks to conventional notions while demand-

41. Foreword to Hocart, *Kingship,* abr. ed. (cf. Needham, *Bibliography,* item no. 196).
42. *Social Origins,* p. 77.
43. He could, however, sound a perverse note, as for instance when he observed, in a scholarly monograph, "We may never know how Paleolithic man was organized, and for my part I do not care if we don't" (*Les castes,* pp. 253–54; English trans., *Caste* [London: Methuen, 1950], p. 150), an admission which just could not have been true of someone with so curious and speculative a mind. Cf. also the later observations (below, pp. 14–15) on the social organization of Neolithic man.
44. Evans-Pritchard, Hocart obituary, p. 131.

ing transitions of thought for which the grounds were not sufficiently laid; and he resorted to tersensess and allusion where a plainer and more evidential exposition would have made a more convincing case. For him the idea was the thing, and once he had stated it, usually with a revelatory lucidity, he tended to leave it in a form which could appear unduly simple or even dogmatic. His characteristic vehicle of expression, and that most suited to his mode of thought, was the essay, often brief and incisive, commonly enigmatic and inconclusive, but full of "useful and important ideas."[45] His books, also, such as *Kingship* (1927), proceed on an episodic and veering course, and even about Fiji he wrote no formally composed monograph.

But he did write one book, published when he was a confident and vigorous fifty-three, of a far more comprehensive and integrated kind. This was *Kings and Councillors,* his most extensive investigation and the most consequential in its argument. Unlike Hocart's other monographs it is not confined to the study of one intricate institution, such as a temple or kingship or caste; instead, it analyzes some very general features of human society, and it draws upon evidences taken from around the world. In these respects it is a piece of work which most readily permits, on a major scale, an assessment of Hocart's distinctive approach and his predominant interests.

III

The topic is the origin of government, a question so fundamental that it has occupied political philosophy in the west

45. G. C. Homans, review of A. M. Hocart, *The Life-giving Myth* (London: Methuen, 1952) in *American Anthropologist* 55 (1953): 747. This collection of problematical essays, incidentally, is perhaps the best general introduction to Hocart's thought. (See 2d ed., edited with a foreword by Rodney Needham [London: Methuen, 1969].) When, however, Professor Homans says that "some of the ideas, such as the relation of myth to other aspects of the social system, seem to have been stated earlier and more effectively by other anthropologists," he seems not to take into account the fact—which is not clear from the listing of the original places of publication—that the essays were written over a period of more than twenty years. That on the common sense of myth, for instance, dates from 1916.

for more than two millennia. That a twentieth-century anthropologist should have anything novel to add to so protracted a debate might seem improbable, but the first interest of *Kings and Councillors* is that this is in fact what Hocart tries to do. The ambition might seem too high, and the implicit comparison with illustrious predecessors too partial, for such a venture to command any hopeful attention; but Hocart was always drawn to the fundamental and the universal, and the very scope of large and ultimate questions appealed especially to his faculty for looking at things anew and with a "penetrating idea."[46]

In the course of the philosophical tradition two chief sociological theories of the origin of government had contended with each other.[47] One was that government had been established by main force, and that its offices and forms were instruments of control and exploitation found convenient by autocrats. The other was that men had perceived the necessity and the advantages of government, and had come together to institute a social contract which would give effect to the general will for a settled regulation of their affairs. Central to each of these doctrines was the importance of the law: in the former it served the power of the ruler; in the latter it secured justice in the mutual accommodation of men's rights. But both views long had in common the twin premises (a) that government in some form was essential, and (b) that law was indispensable to an ordered social life.

Hume, however, turned a radical scrutiny on the issue, and in a direction which for us leads straight to the grounds for Hocart's position. Hume at once denied the origin of government in a subjugation internal to a society, and also the fact and the philosophical foundations of the original contract. According to him, the first rudiments of government arose "from

46. A. N. Whitehead, *The Function of Reason* (Princeton: Princeton University Press, 1929; Boston: Beacon Press, 1958), p. 45: "The power of going for the penetrating idea, even if it has not yet been worked into any methodology, is what constitutes the progressive force of Reason."
47. Excluding, that is, the deistic argument, which ascribed the institution of government to what Hume called the "concealed and universal efficacy" of God.

quarrels, not among men of the same society, but among those of different societies." Men will launch themselves against other societies, in order to gain their riches, with less compunction than they would dispute among themselves when they depend so much upon each other; but a foreign war necessitates a government and a stricter application of the laws than is customary in peace. A verification is to be found in the example of the American tribes, where men never pay submission to any of their fellows except in time of war, when their leader enjoys an authority over them which he loses after their return from the field. "This authority, however, instructs them in the advantages of government," and teaches them to have recourse to it whenever they are led to forget the interest they have in the preservation of peace and justice. Hence "all governments are at first monarchical," and republics arise only from the abuses of monarchy and despotic power. "As war cannot be administered by reason of the suddenness of every exigency, without some authority in a single person, the same kind of authority naturally takes place in that civil government, which succeeds the military."[48] As for the doctrine that lawful government is founded on an original contract, or consent of the people, as Locke had affirmed, this plainly leads to "paradoxes repugnant to the common sentiments of mankind, and to the practice and opinion of all nations and ages."[49]

Two features of Hume's argument are of special interest here. One is that after setting out the philosophical basis for his position, both on absolutism and on the original contract, he resorts for decision to matters of social fact: the American Indians make his own case, while classical history and the examples of other nations confute Locke's. The second feature leads further. Hume's American tribes "live in concord and amity among themselves without any established government," and this he finds perfectly understandable; it is only the increase in riches and possessions which could, he thinks, oblige men to quit this early condition. He asserts, indeed, against

48. David Hume, *A Treatise of Human Nature*, bk. 3: *Of Morals* (London, 1740), sec. 8.
49. Idem, *Essays, Moral and Political*, 3d ed., rev. and enl. (London, 1748), pp. 289–307: "Of the Original Contract" (see p. 307).

the long Aristotelian tradition, that "The state of society without government is one of the most natural states of men. . . ."[50] So one of the chief assumptions upon which the rival doctrines of government had been predicated was summarily rejected, and with ethnographical support. It may be stressed that Hume is not asserting merely that mankind can exist, by "the conjunction of many families" or by any other means of informal aggregation, without government, but that organised human society is a natural state prior to the institution of government. He does not, however, challenge the complementary assumption, namely the indispensability of law. "Tho' it be possible for men to maintain a small uncultivated society without government," he writes, "tis impossible they shou'd maintain a society of any kind without justice." By this he means the observation of laws concerning possession, free transference of rights of ownership, and the performance of promises. It is from this last type of law, Hume argues, that the original obligation of government can be derived. In sum, government is not necessary, and in certain conditions of society it may in fact not exist, but where it has been established it is originally and essentially a jural institution.

This preamble gives us an excellent background against which to set Hocart's thesis. His case is that government is the result of social activities already carried out before the differentiation of administrative status and function: "We shall see all the functions of government discharged among peoples without government" (p. 30). There is no government, in our sense of the word, among peoples like the Fijians because there is no need for any: "If, however, we look more closely at such societies we shall discover that nevertheless the machinery of government is there ready to govern, if governing is required. There is, so to speak, a governing body before there is any governing to do" (p. 31). But what is this organization doing before it is turned to the work of governing? Hocart's answer, very briefly, is that it is an organization for ritual, i.e., for the quest of life. "This ritual organiza-

50. Hume, *Treatise*, bk. 3, sec. 8. Hocart evidently forgets Hume when he attributes to philosophers, rather tendentiously, the view that "man invented government to get out of anarchy" (below, p. 128).

tion is vastly older than government, for it exists where there is no government and where none is needed. When however society increases so much in complexity that a coordinating agency . . . is required, that ritual organization will gradually take over this task" (p. 35). The functions now discharged by king, prime minister, treasury, public works, etc. are not the original ones; they may account for the present form of these institutions, but not for their original appearance. "These were originally part, not of a system of government, but of an organization to promote life, fertility, prosperity by transferring life from objects abounding in it to objects deficient in it" (p. 3). Only gradually has the scope of this organization become enlarged, and its functions modified, until it has become a centralized means of organizing the activities of society.

The aim of *Kings and Councillors* is to outline this evolution from ritual organization to government. Like Hume, Hocart assumes and observes that the formal institutions of government are not always necessary; but, unlike the philosopher, he does not make the sociological assumption that the origin and the purpose of government are jural. Possessions and promises are not fundamental in his view; their importance is secondary to the real end of corporate existence. The prime value of social life is not society but life.

IV

The argument of Hocart's monograph is clear, and there is no need to rehearse it, but some critical appreciation of so unusual an enterprise seems called for. To carry this out properly would demand a conspectus of all of Hocart's work, as well as extended reference to political philosophy and much else. Such an assessment is not practicable here, but there are certain salient points in the argument which can be more commodiously dealt with.

The first necessary consideration is the attitude in which the book should be approached. No investigation outside the natural sciences can be rigorously exact, and it is always a question how literally any anthropological thesis should be interpreted. In Hocart's case in particular it is a matter of special importance to determine how large a tolerance should reasonably be conceded to his arguments. He could be designedly extreme, sometimes farfetched, and perhaps outrageous on occasion, just so long as he jolted people's thoughts, and some readers may be inclined to respond to certain of his flat assertions with a feeling of affront. It should be kept in mind, therefore, that in most of Hocart's writings there are many things, as Sir Thomas Browne excellently forewarned of *Religio Medici*, "to be taken in a soft and flexible sence . . . "; and it may be well in coming to *Kings and Councillors* also to be prepared to grant the author a pretty wide latitude. Hocart is always worth taking seriously, even when he is apparently most extravagant, but participation in his thought can demand at times a rather indulgent suspension of critical judgment. It is a useful precept, then, simply to take the argument as it comes and to postpone objection until its cumulative effect has been weighed.

The reception of the argument when this book first appeared was hampered, in the eyes of one reviewer at any rate, by the suspicion that so total a reliance on ritual origins argued a lack of rational objectivity in the author. Thus Hornblower wrote that we may distinguish "a kind of mysticism" which may have caused Hocart to abjure the methods of Tylor and his successors.[51] Depreciation of this kind is perhaps less likely today, when there is an efflorescence of interest in all forms of symbolism, but a charge so specifically brought, and one bearing on choice of method, needs to be taken into account. What is the evidence for the alleged predisposition? The critic deposes that "the author's mysticism is traceable in many of his ideas," and he presents as an exhibit Hocart's reconstruction of the origin of the city, which he states as: "The city has not been developed for the purposes of defence, marketing or sociability, but because it is the royal seat (pp. 244-5)." But this charge is incorrectly drawn up. What Hocart says at the pages cited is that merely practical reasons do not suffice to explain the origin of the city: there may be no need for a center of distribution or co-ordination, and people do not

51. Hornblower, review in *Man*, p. 155; cf. below, p. 3.

congregate out of a general impulse or in order to work. "Population first condenses round the centre of ritual" is what he claims (p. 251). The center may be a camp, a village, or a town; and if the condensation is round a king or a cathedral it is called a city. As far as defense, marketing, or sociability is in question there is no real resemblance among these types of settlement, but they do have in common the general feature that they are symbolic constructs. The form may be apt for defense, but this is not the cause of the form; there can be markets, but even these commercial utilities may be numbered and located by symbolic considerations; and although people congregate there the sociability may be circumscribed by ideological factors which have nothing to do with gregariousness. From camp to city the settlement is not simply a social aggregate designed for practical convenience, and continuing because of the security and the services that it provides. It stands for something other than itself, and its original purpose has to do with that conception. The root idea is the procuring of life by means of ritual, and the locus of ritual is the center around which the population condenses. Ultimately there may develop a city, with a king and a queen standing respectively for parts of the cosmos to which the city as a whole corresponds,[52] but it is not Hocart's argument that the city developed merely because it was the royal seat. Nor does he

52. Cf. Werner Müller, *Die heilige Stadt: Roma quadrata, himmlisches Jerusalem und die Mythe vom Weltnabel* (Stuttgart: Kohlhammer, 1961). In Hocart's personal copy of *Kings and Councillors* he has written (on the leaf facing present p. 259 f.) a passage from G. C. Homans, "Terroirs adonnés et champs orientés: Une hypothèse sur le village anglais" (*Annales d'histoire économique, et sociale* 8 [1936]: 438–48), illustrated by a sketch of a quadripartite village plan, on the connections between daily life in medieval England and "un grand cycle cosmique" (p. 448). Cf. idem, *English Villagers of the Thirteenth Century* (Cambridge, Mass.: Harvard University Press, 1941), pp. 100–101: the village plan is "evidence of the scheme according to which the northern peoples conceived their world. . . . Their cosmology took a part in the day to day work of their lives. The very way they plowed their fields was determined by their philosophy." (It would surely not be suggested, incidentally, that this fine work of scholarship was inspired by any kind of mysticism.)

maintain that ritual considerations are paramount and practical advantages secondary; e.g., man does not cling to a symbolically square city when it is "dangerous tactically" (p. 257); "Strategic necessity, or the ground, eventually destroys the shape of the city . . . " (p. 261).

Similarly, Hornblower states that "temples have been raised by the author to a very mystic plane," whereas all Hocart has done is to demonstrate (ch. 17) that a temple is not only an abode of a god but is also a replica of the world.[53]

Now it might easily be responded that this individual critic is mistaken in these particulars, but that Hocart could still remain open to the reproach of "mysticism," but it is harder to see what substance could be given to the reproach. As the reader will subsequently find, what Hocart is doing is to discern in various forms, offices, and instruments of government a symbolic element so marked as to seem essential and hence original.[54] This symbolism is not primarily an adjunct to practical administration but is the expression of a quest for that without which there could be neither kings nor councillors, neither cities nor temples, and that is life itself. To isolate certain common forms and principles of symbolism is scarcely to be mystical; and to argue that the purpose of that symbolism is to secure life is not to display an invalidating aversion from reason and evidence. There is, moreover, a helpful parallel to be drawn here, in specific connection with the origin of the city. Hume declares that "Camps are the true mothers of cities";[55] i.e., that men came together and submitted themselves to authority for the purpose of making war, and that this led to the establishment of civil government and the formation of cities. But it will not therefore be inferred that Hume had a bellicose temperament which caused him to seek his explanations in the bloody practice of warfare. Hocart says

---

53. Cf. Lord Raglan, *The Temple and the House* (London: Routledge & Kegan Paul, 1964), esp. chaps. 14–17.
54. Cf. M. Fortes and E. E. Evans-Pritchard, eds., *African Political Systems* (London: Oxford University Press, 1940), pp. 16–22, on mystical values and symbols associated with political office.
55. *Treatise*, bk. 3, sec. 8.

that ritual is at the origin of cities, and this does not make him a mystic.[56]

V

It may be thought a far more serious question, however, whether "life" is exact enough as a term of explanation, and whether it is not too undifferentiated a notion to serve as the focus of ritual.

In assessing an anthropological theory a crucial test is to gauge the degree to which its terms correspond to the alien concepts which it is intended to make intelligible. Hocart has described as "disastrous" the results of forcing the customs of non-European peoples into "the familiar categories of religion, state, family, medicine, etc.;[57] and the interpretative progress of social anthropology has been marked largely by its increasingly effective scrutiny of such notions as god, soul, gift, marriage, and so on. We have every reason, therefore, to be on our guard when a theory places so total and ultimate a reliance on the sole concept of "life."

There is a special reason to be alert, moreover, in the parallel case of the conception of death. Hertz showed, in a classical essay, that death is not a simple and obvious natural fact, but is the object of collective representations; these representations are neither simple nor unchangeable, and each culture adds to the organic event a complex mass of beliefs, emotions, and activities which give it a distinctive character.[58] Rivers later made the same point, with particular reference to the Melanesian word *mate*, which is commonly rendered as "dead" but is also used of a person who is seriously ill and

56. There emerges, however, a curious contrast between the theories of these similarly liberal and radical thinkers which has an interest of its own. For Hume, government originated in the physical dealing of death; for Hocart, it began in the symbolic acquisition of life. But perhaps the former view will be accounted practical, after all, and the latter mystical just the same.

57. *The Northern States of Fiji*, Occasional Publication no. 11 (London: Royal Anthropological Institute, 1952), p. 25.

58. Robert Hertz, "Contribution à une étude sur la représentation de la mort," *Année sociologique* 10 (1907): 48–137; English trans., idem, *Death and The Right Hand*, trans. R. and C. Needham with an introduction by E. E. Evans-Pritchard (London: Cohen & West, 1960).

likely to die, and often of a person who is healthy but so old that from the native point of view if he is not dead he ought to be.[59] As Hocart, who worked with Rivers in recording these facts, phrases it, *mate* covers "all degrees of diminished vitality from weakness due to hunger, fatigue or sickness to complete extinction."[60] It is a standard precept of ethnographical investigation, hence, that the conception of even so universal and inescapable a matter as death can never be taken for granted. Why, then, should we accept a theory that is so simply premised on the concept of life? If conceptions of death are so variant, perhaps conceptions of life also are so disparate as to render Hocart's reconstruction of that primal value unlikely or invalidatingly imprecise.

Hocart recognizes of course that an uncritical assumption will not do, and that "we must look at man's conception of life." He does not in the event make a very narrow examination on this score, but he gives a useful enough indication of what he has in mind. It is "a concept of life, fertility, prosperity, vitality" p. 32) of so unelaborate a kind that all existing peoples everywhere can be reckoned to subscribe to it. In other words, what is really in question is not the precise definition or formal theory of the state of being alive, but a fluid and highly inclusive notion of well-being and an abundance of everything that is accounted desirable (cf. p. 202). A better word for this notion than the English "life" is the German *Heil*, the scope of which corresponds well to the extremely generalized concept that Hocart proposes.[61] His investigation

---

59. W. H. R. Rivers, "The primitive conception of death," *Hibbert Journal*, 10 (1912): 393–407; reprinted idem, *Psychology and Ethnology*, ed. G. Elliot Smith (London: Kegan Paul, Trench, Trubner, 1926), pp. 36–50. Rivers does not cite Hertz's paper, and it is something of a question whether he knew it or not, though it is certain that he was familiar with the works of other French sociologists, such as Durkheim, Mauss, Lévy-Bruhl, and van Gennep.

60. *Social Origins*, p. 86; cf. idem, *The Progress of Man* (London: Methuen, 1933), pp. 136–37.

61. Cf., e.g., Hans Schärer, *Die Gottesidee der Ngadju Dajak in Süd-Borneo* (Leiden: Brill, 1946), pp. 142–44; English ed., *Ngaju Religion*, trans. Rodney Needham (The Hague: Nijhoff, 1963), pp. 126–28.

therefore is not confined to any special definition of life, or to any particular cultural concept, but calls upon an aspect of experience and a type of value which are recognized by all men. "Keeping alive is man's greatest preoccupation, the ultimate spring of all his actions."[62]

If this idea in turn sounds too simple, we can turn for assurance to the testimony of an ancient, literate, and acutely analytical civilization. For the Hebrews, namely, the possession of life (*hayyim*), in the sense merely of physical organic life, is felt in the whole of the Old Testament to be "an absolutely unqualified good, in fact the highest good."[63] And it is not without sound reasons that anthropological works have constantly dwelt on "fertility cults," that ethnographers invariably report or encounter symbolic and other procedures intended to procure fertility and the preservation of life, and that the museums are full of fertility charms and life-enhancing "medicines." Furthermore, if so imprecise a concept as "life" as Hocart adduces seems too simple to serve in any exact analysis, we may be encouraged by the theoretical fecundity which utterly simple propositions may sometimes have. A man of the caliber of Whitehead did not waste his brains on trivial and simplistic formulations, and he was not doing so when he argued something so apparently simple and obvious as this: "The art of life is first to be alive, secondly to be alive in a satisfactory way, and thirdly to acquire an increase in satisfaction."[64] For Hocart, the art of life as conceived and practised by the generality of mankind has been expressed

---

62. *The Progress of Man*, p. 133. Hocart, pitiably, was never in the position to realize for himself that for perhaps the majority of human beings the really dominant concern is not just to keep alive but to keep their children alive and safe.

63. Rudolf Bultmann et al., *Life and Death*, Bible Key Words from Gerhard Kittel's *Theologisches Wörterbuch zum Neuen Testament* (London: Black, 1965), pp. 1, 2.

64. *Function of Reason*, p. 8. Cf. also the particularly apt assertion by a Nobel laureate, Professor George Wald: "The only point of government is to safeguard and foster life" ("A Generation in Search of a Future," address at the Massachusetts Institute of Technology, 4 March 1969, as reported in *The New Yorker*, 22 March 1969, p. 30).

in the "technique of life-saving" which he calls ritual (pp. 33, 34).

This introduces another defense which Hocart could well make to criticism of his premise of life. He argues that ritual techniques have a common scheme, and that the organization of ritual developed into the organization of government. All he needs to do initially, therefore, is to establish this common aspect, without reference to the conceptions of life or well-being which inspire the performance of the ritual. These conceptions may well vary from one society to another, but conceptual variations would not affect the significance of the demonstrated similarities in the ritual.

There is, too, a curious feature of the comparison of conceptions of life and death, and one which also argues for Hocart's undifferentiated definition of life. This is that in practice the understanding of a concept of life usually does not present to an ethnographer difficulties comparable with those relating to death. Such a finding is logically unexpected, for the distinctive contours of a concept of death would seem to entail their counterparts in the complementary concept of life, but, interestingly enough, this appears generally not to be the case.[65] There is no doubt that conceptions of life may be complex and that they vary in different cultures and change also over time;[66] but on the whole there does commonly seem to be a contrast between a relatively patent and apprehensible conception of life and a more obscure and perplexing conception of death. One reason for this contrast readily suggests itself. We have our being in a life that we know; we are struck down into a death that we can only surmise.

VI

There are ample and diverse grounds, therefore, to accept Hocart's vital premise, vague and simplistic though it may at

65. For example, understanding the concept of *matai*, "dead," among the Penan of the interior of Borneo is an intricate business, similar to the case of the Melanesian *mate*, whereas grasping and analyzing the concept of *murip*, alive, encounters nothing like the same difficulties.
66. For an excellent survey of Biblical notions, which constitute the most instructive case we have, see Bultmann et al., *Life and Death*.

first appear, and to concentrate on how he makes his case. Let us begin with his evidence.

He is at pains to adduce reports from practically all over the world (a notable omission being South America), but this span inevitably has some effect on the presentation and testing of the argument. Hocart himself realized, as he later wrote, that numerous gaps were inevitable;

> but the aim was as much to point out the gaps as to fill those that had been found. It [*Kings and Councillors*] was an attempt to show how small things might lead up to big things; but in order to do so the smallest had to be omitted lest they bewilder the reader. It was necessary to cut down the evidence to the bare minimum so that the general ideas might stand out.[67]

This is a reasonable explanation, but Hocart's use of sources has attracted comment on other scores. Hornblower asserted that "the authorities are not always happily chosen," and maintained that Hocart had relied for his Egyptian information on publications that had been superseded.[68] More recently, Pocock has observed, in connection with Hocart's work on caste, that he "draws his evidence promiscuously from a variety of ancient [Indian] texts of very different periods."[69] Homans, more generally, finds that the ideas in Hocart's essays "are not backed with sufficient evidence;"[70] and indeed it is an apt epithet that Hutton employs when he writes that these essays are "suggestive."[71]

Hocart's work on Fiji, and especially his demanding monograph *The Northern States of Fiji*, proves how keen an eye he really had for evidence, and how fervent was his constant concern for an exact record of ethnographic facts as seen by the people studied; but in his more comparative writings his

67. *Les castes*, p. vi; cf. *Caste*, pp. ix–x.
68. Review in *Man*, p. 155.
69. "Hocart on Caste," p. 49.
70. Review of Hocart, *Life-giving Myth*, p. 747.
71. J. H. Hutton, review of Hocart, *The Life-giving Myth*, in *Folk-lore* 63 (1952): 244.

sourcework can sometimes be called into question. As far as the present book is concerned, one can easily see that to deal with eight large areas and with forty-two peoples or civilizations (including the Chinese, the English, and the ancient Greeks) must preclude a thorough exploitation of the body of evidence on each. Nevertheless, there is in most instances such a gap between the authorities cited and the total available that the reader cannot help wondering whether the author has adduced the best evidence, and also whether he could possibly have mastered enough of any particular field to be able to judge such a matter or to go for what was essential. This is of course a perennial difficulty in literary research,[72] and there can be no set of rules or standards for resolving it, but all the same Hocart often cannot be seen to have gone far enough into the published evidence to make a satisfactory case. For example, Radin's monograph on the Winnebago is certainly excellent, and the evidence it provides is apt and clear; but it does not seem probable that all of the other titles (prior to 1936) in four columns of the standard bibliography could be irrelevant.[73] Also, the principle by which certain societies are called upon is not always well observed. The secondary witnesses which are cited in support of the main testimony are said to be "mostly near neighbours" of the witnesses-in-chief (p. 29), with the implication that when evidence on a point is lacking for a certain society it will be supplied from a culturally similar, and perhaps related, nearby society. But the secondary witnesses for the Aranda, for example, are not all strictly qualified to offer testimony on these counts: the Kaitish might be reckoned as neighbours, though distant, but the Warramunga are at an added remove northwards; the Dieri are a long way to the southeast; and the Wikmunkan, described merely as "further north" than the Aranda (p. 42, cf. p. 59), are actually hundreds of miles away

---

72. For a salutary illustration, see A. van Gennep, *The Semi-Scholars,* ed., trans., and with an introduction by Rodney Needham (London: Routledge & Kegan Paul, 1967), pp. 32–36: "The Research Topic."
73. George Peter Murdock, *Ethnographic Bibliography of North America,* 3d ed. (New Haven: Human Relations Area Files, 1960), pp. 187–89.

to the northeast and almost as far from the Aranda as it is possible for them to be and still remain on the same continent.

These considerations do not undermine the relevance to the main case of the facts thus cited, but it would have been more encouraging to see either a more strict adherence to the criterion of evidence enunciated or, by another criterion, a rather more determined search for decisive and comparable ethnographic data.

The sources on the ancient civilizations must be judged by the specialists, and it can only be reported here that in spite of certain incidental doubts and criticisms (such as those quoted above), Hocart's researches and his reliability have not in general been called into question. He relied upon good advice (p. 4), and he was unusually well fitted to take advantage of it. His two chief areas of interest, moreover, both in this book and throughout his work, are India (with Ceylon) and Fiji; he had a scholarly access to the evidence on India, combined with years of residence and research in Ceylon, and he was by any reckoning an authority on Fiji. In these crucial respects, therefore, it would seem (in the absence of detailed refutation by better judges) that Hocart's evidence can for the most part bear the weight of argument that he puts upon it.

VII

The method that Hocart employs is a more difficult matter, and here we may concede no soft and flexible sense.

Always very conscious of the methodological aspect of his investigations, Hocart was explicit in stating the procedure he followed, and frequently drew comparisons between other approaches and his own. It is an inference from the general emphasis which he places on method in all of his writings that it is for this, as much as for his conclusions, that he would have wished to be appreciated. More than this, indeed, for whereas he often recognized the preliminary and uncertain character of his conclusions, and presented his theoretical reconstructions as tentative and corrigible results, he was consistently definite in his methodological statements.

In *Kings and Councillors* he provides the most extended and integrated example of the application of his method; its premises are clear, the procedure is well-defined, and the conclusions are decisive. His contention is that rituals are rigorously logical and that it is possible, by means of a correspondingly formal approach, to analyze them into simple formulas. His paradigm is geometry, his ideal a natural science: "It may be that some day the comparative history of culture will proceed by a series of deductions as in Euclid or a text-book of physics . . ." (p. 21). In the analysis of the Fijian theory of agricultural gods, similarly, "it is only by advancing, after the manner of Euclid, from one proposition to another, that we can trace them throughout the structure of the state."[74] His expository idiom, too, is often formal; e.g., in trying to define the character of a mythical figure "we must draw lines from at least two points to converge on the point we are seeking" (p. 17).

Two crucial and recurrent terms in the argument are "principle" and "structure," and the latter term has a special importance. The working hypothesis of the present work is that "a common structure is proof of common descent" (p. 81). It is necessary, therefore, to determine what he means by structure and what theoretical predispositions associated with this term we should look for in his analysis.

The chief point to make is that Hocart's conception of structure, unlike his formal idiom, is not relational or abstract. When he introduces the term, he does so, revealingly, by way of a zoological parallel; and when he urges that in cultural studies we must penetrate below the surface, he explains that we must "dissect" the structure (pp. 81–92). When he thus dissects Agni and Hermes, however, what he does is no more than to make a comparison by listing their defining characteristics side by side. This does indeed show a close agreement between the two figures, but it does not lead to the conclusion that "the resemblance lies, not in the surface, but in the structure" (p. 17–19). The term structure here denotes merely a general resemblance such as makes it probable that two or

74. Hocart, *The Northern States of Fiji*, p. 13. Cf. his observations, in an essay first published in 1939, that the ideas behind Brahmanic sacrifice are "worked out in a manner more akin to Euclid than to the mystics" (*The Life-giving Myth*, p. 55).

more cultural facts are radically connected, either directly or by common descent from some earlier form. Not geometry, but palaeontology, is the prototype of this method.

But even this is only partly true, for an anatomical structure is articulated in a way to which a list of attributes of a fire-god bears no orderly similarity. Hocart in this instance distinguishes the superficial from the structural merely by degree of outer resemblance, not by systematic correspondence, by visible components rather than by relations. It is noteworthy, too, that he speaks of the "organization" of ritual, not of its structure. When he compares rituals, he does so merely under the descriptive headings of purpose, ownership, initiation, communion, etc. (pp. 46–47), i.e., by means of an assortment of overt features, not by reference to an abstract analytical construct.

The point of these observations is by no means to argue for a real definition of "structure," or to criticize Hocart for not anticipating some more modern conceptual or verbal fashion.[75] It is in order that he shall not be thought to say, simply by the employment of the word structure, something that he does not say. That is, he might be taken to propound or to follow one method of analysis, whereas in fact he consistently adopts another.

The term that better defines his approach, as is proclaimed on the very title-page, is "comparative anatomy." What he looks for in ritual is its "skeleton" (p. 46); the peoples examined in a comparative study should be compared "limb for limb" (p. 28); "government . . . is the nervous system of the social organism" (p. 30); "there is a striking analogy between this evolution of human society and that of the body" (p. 38); "whenever we try and understand, we shall find ourselves thinking of society as a vast body, and of the body as a small society" (p. 68);[76] and so on. The biological cast

---

75. Cf. Jean-François Revel, *La cabale des dévots* (Paris: Pauvert, 1962), p. 71: "Aujourd'hui on rencontre structure à chaque page, là où 'machin,' 'truc,' ou 'chose' iraient aussi bien. . . ."

76. Cf. Mary Douglas, *Purity and Danger: an analysis of concepts of pollution and taboo* (London: Routledge & Kegan Paul, 1966): "Just

of Hocart's imagery is made especially clear in the telling passage where he wishes to show that the brahman and the Greek herald are "homologues": "We cannot be content with superficial resemblances, but must probe into the innermost structure. . . . Here is the comparative anatomy. . . ." (p. 194). The two offices, moreover, are said to have undergone a "divergent evolution" (p. 195) from a common type. Correspondingly, Hocart opens his case with the premise, adopted from neuro-anatomy, that in government as in the nervous system "function precedes form" (p. 30), while a biological notion of function, also, is one which marks the entire course of his argument (see index, s.v.).

In sum, the predominant idiom to which Hocart resorts is not that of geometry and logic; it is organic and evolutionary.

VIII

This much of an exposition has been necessary in order to establish the chief terms in Hocart's analytical vocabulary, and to distinguish in his approach two quite different methodological paradigms. The above comments may thus serve to preclude certain confusions in the interpretation of the argument; but the "organic analogy" has come in for such a variety of disapprobation[77] that it may be well to defend Hocart's argument against some of the more damaging imputations.

It has been asserted, for example, that to conceive of societies as something like organisms leads to the serious error of treating society, or an institution, as a physical entity, and particularly as a living thing, such as a frog or a jellyfish, which can be put on a table and dissected. It is entirely doubtful, of course, whether anyone who has seriously thought about

---

as it is true that everything symbolises the body, so it is equally true . . . that the body symbolises everything else" (p. 122; cf. pp. 115, 163–64).

77. The most determined account of the "grave limitations" of this "dangerously misleading" analogy is to be found in Beattie, *Other Cultures*, pp. 11, 56–60. (This textbook attracts special attention on such a score not merely because it is recent but because its author claims [p. xi] that it represents the current theoretical standpoint of the majority of British social anthropologists.)

society has ever fallen into quite so daft a reification, or whether indeed it is possible even to conceive so substantial a likeness between a society and an organism. The image of dissection, however, could lead to the misapprehension that Hocart committed this improbable error. In fact, he did nothing of the kind. What he is expressly concerned with is society as a concept, an abstraction from people's observed behaviour, and particularly as a conception in the minds of people in quest of life. Men, according to Hocart, sought the good life, and in doing so they effected a purposeful adaptation of their communal life by reproducing in their government the various departments of nature as they conceived them (p. 298). The object of the investigation is thus a cosmic conception, not an entity of any kind; the social adaptation is the product of human purpose, not of blind evolutionary strife; and the resultant order is one of social, not organic, function.

Since no scholar (least of all, it should be specified, Durkheim) has actually said that societies are "things" like organisms,[78] it is difficult to know what other awful mistakes to look for; but at least it is clear, next, that Hocart did not commit the compounded error which is alleged to have followed from the initial organic analogy. This is the assertion that society has "needs," whereas, of course, it is people, not societies, that exist and have needs. Once again, it is dubitable whether any anthropologist, even Malinowski, has ever thought that a society could literally have needs. It is not clear, either, what connection is supposed to obtain between the organic analogy and a theory of needs, or in what sense the term "need" is to be construed, though it is plain that to employ an organic analogy does not entail subscribing to a sociological theory of needs in any sense. In any case, whereas Hocart does resort to the analogy, he does not write of needs, and his argument does not depend on any theory of this sort.

A third respect in which an organic analogy is held to conduce to error is the supposed implication that societies, taken

---

78. Cf. Beattie, *Other Cultures*, p. 56.

as empirically given aggregates, are or should be harmoniously integrated. Views of this kind have, it is true, been held in anthropology, but they are not at all entailed by the analogy. There is thus no logical ground to impute them to Hocart, and in fact his argument contains no such assumption. On the contrary, Hocart is at some pains to recognize the significance of contradictory statements in ethnographic reports, and he maintains in effect that "harmonious integration" is not to be expected:

> Those . . . who make living societies the basis of their study learn that a perfectly consistent picture cannot be true, because one system appears before the old one has decayed, so that the old and the new always overlap. . . . For the student of living forms therefore a contradiction points to a change-over (p. 276).

This latter observation introduces the answer to the concluding item in this catalog of alleged conceptual blunders, namely the assertion that the organic analogy provides no means of understanding change. Now this is an odd criticism, though it has in fact been confidently published, for it is a celebrated fact—upon which, after all, the entire theory of natural evolution is premised—that organisms do change, so that it might even be expected that an organic analogy would be precisely appropriate to the study of social change. The basis of the criticism, anyway, is that many societies are far from being harmoniously integrated systems, and that their complexity and the multiple stresses and strains which they show could not thus be adequately comprehended in so restricted a frame of reference. Social institutions can change rapidly, they break down and are replaced by new ones, and these changes cannot be understood, it is concluded, by means of an organic analogy. Here again there is simply no specific connection between the idiom of the analogy and the analytical difficulties which are said to follow, so we should not be surprised to find that Hocart's position, in spite of his idiom, is quite the converse. His view, which is surely the more sensible, is that societies as (*nota bene*) "living organisms" are "continually changing and adapting themselves, ever in a state of transition between two states" (p. 276).

We need not dwell on the attitude of mind which may inspire such criticisms, or on the acuity of thought which can discern in the analogy so gross a collection of disadvantages, for we have seen that Hocart at any rate is safe from them. But in the face of such definite pronouncements, which may be attributed some authority, it is prudent to secure the argument of the present work by suggesting two possible sources of confusion which may have prompted the rejection of organic analogy.

The first is a misunderstanding, or at least a suspicion, of the role of metaphor. The positivist view is that there is no place in a social science for any but the most strictly defined terms of description and analysis, and that metaphor introduces instead a vocabulary and a range of inappropriate considerations which can only mislead. This is plausible, but rigid. A more liberal view, and one not tendentiously premised on the idea of a social science, takes better account of the intricacy of the circumstances. All thought is hard, and understanding other people's thought is worse. In attempting to communicate or to interpret, we need to have free recourse to all the means of apprehension and expression that language can provide. To speak of a centralized government as the nervous system of a society, and to reconstruct the origin of the institution in terms of the evolution of tissue differentiation (p. 30), need conduce to no error; i.e., there is nothing in the device of metaphor which (like an illicit process in a syllogism) leads formally to a wrong inference. The effectiveness in the implicit analogy resides in those points of resemblance which are seen to be apt, and in suggesting further possible resemblances which will then be assessed by the same standards of aptness. There is nothing in metaphor as such to impair the critical sense; but it can, by adducing exotic connotations, frame new conjectures which may prove useful. It is always easy enough, after all, to draw back from a bad idea once you have seen that it will not work; the real difficulty is to conceive an idea in the first place, and this is something that the imaginative incitements of metaphor can well lead to.

The second obstacle is the more serious, but also more easily removable. It is a philosophical confusion about the nature of analogy and the kind of inference that it permits. We may take as illustration a methodological injunction which firmly warns us not to suppose that "societies are something like organisms; they are not, and to suppose that they are may lead to serious error."[79] If this assertion were right it would gravely undermine confidence in Hocart's judgment, and it would of course abolish the force of this particular analogy in his argument. But it is mistaken, and on two chief counts.

The first is that resemblances are not given; they are conceived. It cannot therefore be said that societies are, or are not, objectively like organisms. All that can be proposed is that in certain particulars, abstracted for the purpose of the comparison in question, a qualified resemblance may be posited. Whether the features thus related are or are not alike depends partly on how they are defined and partly on the analytical context. It would not be plausible to assert flatly that a society was "like" a frog (though, really, who has ever said that it was?); but it is entirely justifiable to propose that in some particular respects certain resemblances between the two can be conceived. The likeness may or may not be admitted, but this is a question of critical judgment, not phenomenal identity. A resemblance, once conceded as an analytical premise, may or may not lead to serious error; but this once again is a matter for critical judgment concerning the particular inference that is drawn. In numberless respects societies can very well be said to be like organisms. Everything hangs in the first place on the contingent factor of just what is said. But how it is said is also important, and this brings us to the second mistake referred to.

This is the assumption, a fundamental misapprehension, that an organic analogy depends on a degree of direct resemblance. But it is not the function of analogy to establish that kind of resemblance. The similarity, as Kant has best stated, is rela-

79. Ibid.

tional: "Analogy . . . does not mean, as the word is commonly taken, an imperfect similarity of two things, but a perfect similarity of relations between quite dissimilar things."[80] Relations, in turn, do not subsist phenomenally; they have to be posited. It is in this analogical sense that it may validly be said that in certain respects a society is indeed like a frog.

We can easily conclude, therefore, that whatever the defects and errors in Hocart's argument, his reliance on an organic and evolutionary analogy is not in principle among them.

IX

Now that we have examined Hocart's methodological premises, his main concepts, and his expository idiom, we are in a position to consider a more technical matter which is central to his approach. His "Euclidean" procedure, namely, is intended to make it possible to advance logically from one formulary proposition to another until the organization and the intention of a ritual are understood. The propositions in question are framed as elementary equations, and the method of deduction is correspondingly simple.

The typical form of a transitive analysis by Hocart is:

$$a = b$$
$$c = b$$
$$\therefore a = c$$

This method attracted particular attention when *Kings and Councillors* was first published. Hornblower was dubious: "The finality assumed in such equations seems on the face of it too rounded off, too neatly pigeon-holed, to be convincing. . . ."[81] Elkin, on the other hand, thought that Hocart had well pointed out "the rigour of ritual logic and the significance of ritual equivalence."[82] We, in our turn, need especially to form an opinion on the crucial notion of equivalence if we

---

80. Immanuel Kant, *Prolegomena zu einer jeden künftigen Metaphysik die als Wissenschaft wird auftreten können* (Riga, 1783), p. 176 (§ 58); cf. English trans., *Prolegomena . . .* , trans. Peter G. Lucas (Manchester University Press, 1953).
81. Review in *Man,* p. 154.
82. Review in *Oceania,* p. 120.

are to grasp the alleged ritual logic and the appropriateness of Hocart's method for analyzing it. Here are the chief contentions underlying his argument.

Equivalence is "the basis of imitation," which is itself the most fundamental thing in ritual: "The ritual turns on the fact that one thing can be made equivalent to another. . . . If you cannot act on A by acting on B there can be no ritual" (p. 45; cf. p. 64). "This identification is . . . no mere mysticism, but a practical technique: A = B, ∴ all that accrues to A will accrue to B" (p. 50). "The ritual establishes an equivalence that was not there. If it were there already there would be no point in having a ritual" (p. 69). "In all rituals there may be more than one thing equivalent to another" (p. 233). "Ritual equivalence nowhere consists in material identity, but in sharing a common spirit, life, or whatever you may choose to call it. It is that common spirit that is ritually important: the bodies are merely means to get at it. By effecting this equivalence men are enabled to control whatever has been allotted to them" (p. 58). Vedic ritual provides an example: "The participants are deliberately seeking to establish an identity between man and the ritual objects, between ritual objects and the world, and so between man and the world, a kind of creative syllogism" (p. 64).

This, in summary, is Hocart's doctrine of ritual action. It will be noted, however, that in two of the passages quoted he states that the ritual is intended to produce, not an equivalence, but an identity. This is a point of uncertainty which can be seen in other of Hocart's writings also. At one place he writes that "Between identity and equivalence a very fine line is drawn. . . ."[83] Idolators appear to address their worship to stones, and thus to identify the stones with their gods, whereas they simply make the stones equivalent to the gods.[84]

83. *The Life-giving Myth*, p. 36. The essay from which the quotation is taken, viz., "Turning into Stone," was posthumously published in 1948; there is no indication when it was written or therefore what place it occupies in the sequence of Hocart's thought.
84. Hocart continues that they worship "rather . . . something that resides in the stones." Doubtless some peoples may do so, but it is worth remarking, as a nice detail in the history of ideas, that a subtler

Elsewhere, however, he declares that in studying Fijian institutions we must take our start from "the fundamental principle that the god and his material representation are completely identified."[85] Yet in his last published observation on the point he writes: "It is not so much the degree of resemblance that matters as resemblance in one vital particular"; and he also introduces explicitly the further idea that "in addition to the idea of equivalence, there is the idea of power."[86]

In the present book, moreover, the issue is not made clearer by the fact that he uses the equation sign for two very different purposes, viz.: to indicate a homology, such as Brahman = Kerux (p. 21); and to indicate a symbolic equivalence, such as principal = objective (p. 47). In interpreting his argument in this respect, therefore, we are faced with a compound difficulty made up of terminological inconsistency, conceptual unclarity, and notational confusion. A prudent construction to put upon the matter is to adopt Hocart's last explication, which is also that which better corresponds to the facts, and to take it that equivalence, not identity, is what is at issue.[87] Equivalence may be established in any particular whatever, without consideration of degree of resemblance. This acceptation accords with Hocart's actual practice, moreover, in the present work. The value of the equation sign can be illustrated best by a crucial translation that he makes in examining a Pawnee ritual. A priest draws a circle, and according to the ethnographer "The circle represents a nest. . . ." But when Hocart puts the facts into a formula, he writes: "circle = nest" (p.

interpretation of religious symbolism was proposed long before by the genial Emanuel Swedenborg in *Vera Christiana Religio* ([Amsterdam, 1771], p. 153; English trans. *True Christian Religion*, 2 vols. [London, 1781], 1: 279 n. 205): images were set up by the ancients "not with any intention to worship them, but to serve as a Means of recollecting the celestial Things signified by them."

85. *The Northern States of Fiji*, p. 13.
86. *Social Origins*, p. 24.
87. Not a startling recommendation, but we can can judge what people think only by the words they use; and if, by using words indifferently, they give us a choice of interpretation, we have to make the choice and know on what grounds we do so.

227). In other words, the equation sign means "represents" or "stands for" and is to be read simply as indicating a symbolic equivalence.[88] Dumézil has indeed defined the import of a symbol as "equivalence without identity,"[89] and this is precisely what is at issue in Hocart's analyses. Although he refers to science and logic, he is actually concerned with very general features of symbolic association.

This conclusion may be unexceptionable, but it does not quite meet the theoretical expectations encouraged by the allusions to geometry and physics. The frequent use of equational formulas lends an appearance of scientific exactitude to the demonstration, but once these devices are translated back into their true values the argument is seen to be conducted in empirical rather than in abstract terms. At one point, in fact, Hocart stresses "how important it is to keep in mind the meaning of the equivalences" (p. 52); and although this is a salutary reminder never to lose sight of the ideas and associations that are to be understood, it nevertheless imposes a connotative factor which would be out of place in a strictly formal analysis.

As for the alleged revelation of "the rigour of ritual logic," one may wonder what exactly the issue is, what comparisons are called for, and what consequences are to be awaited. This phrase of Elkin's is not merely, as it could perhaps have been, a rather unconsidered reviewer's gloss of a complimentary kind, for it echoes Hocart's own words: "Those who have

88. An incidental curiosity is that the equation sign, which now looks so obvious and even indispensable, was not devised until 1557, by Robert Recorde, *The Whetstone of Witte* (London, 1557). Even then, it it did not appear again in print until 1618. It was more generally recognized in English mathematical works in 1631, but in 1638 Descartes was using it to stand for $\pm$, and in 1670 it was employed as a decimal point. It did not become fully established in Europe, mainly due to the influence of Leibniz, until the beginning of the eighteenth century. The mathematical idea of equality can however be traced, under one sign or another, as far back as an Egyptian calculation of 1700 B.C. (Florian Cajori, *History of Mathematical Notations*, 2 vols. [Chicago: Open Court Publishing Co., 1928–29], 1: 298–309.)

89. Georges Dumézil, *Les dieux des Indo-Européens* (Paris: Presses Universitaires de France, 1952), p. 117.

never sat down to analyze rituals in their smallest details, do not realize the rigour of their logic, and so they will merely say I am being ingenious" (p. 55). The implications of this passage, however, are dubious. There are no degrees of rigor in logic; there are only degrees of rigor in the extent to which a case is presented in logical terms. Where a demonstration purports to be logical in character, it is either valid or invalid. The question is not whether the logic of rituals is rigorous, but whether rituals are inspired by logically coherent doctrines of thought and action. To this question Hocart has already, in effect, given his answer when he writes: "All theories are conceived and worked out by thinkers" (p. 232). To the extent that such thinkers must conform to certain canons of reason, if their cogitations are to qualify as doctrines or theories, they think logically and their products will have a systematic and coherent character which can be logically analyzed.[90]

This conclusion may not seem to claim much, but if we recall the contemporary anthropological theories of primitive religion it will be realized that Hocart's advocacy of the logical character of ritual ran counter to some very prominent and well-established ideas. One such was the view, often connected with the name of Lévy-Bruhl, that primitive man was "irrational," and that his thought did not conform to western criteria of logic. From Hocart's allusions to conceptual confusion and to an inability to make distinctions (p. 57), the inference is that he believed this to be Lévy-Bruhl's thesis and intended to oppose it. If so, he was mistaken, for there is no part of his own argument, touching on the logical, with which Lévy-Bruhl's theory conflicted; but to the degree that he shared an ignorant misunderstanding about Lévy-Bruhl it is likely that he had him in mind.[91] A more certainly identifiable opponent was Marett, and there is convincing evidence in other of Hocart's

90. Cf. idem, *L'héritage indo-européen à Rome* (Paris: Gallimard, 1949), p. 36. "Si primitif soit-il, l'homme, du moment qu'il pense, pense par systèmes. . . ."
91. See E. E. Evans-Pritchard, *Theories of Primitive Religion* (Oxford: Clarendon Press, 1965), p. 17: "Lévy-Bruhl's books . . . have time and again been grossly misrepresented by persons who, I am sure, have read them either not at all or not with diligence."

1

writings as well that he stressed the logic of ritual in express opposition to Marett's assertion that primitive religions were the product of "a single universal feeling, namely a sense of awfulness. . . ."[92] In an essay on "Ritual and Emotion," which was published in the year of his death, Hocart made a masterly case against the conviction that ritual is essentially emotional. Here he pointedly declared that "ritual is not a disease," and that even if it were "a disease of religion" it would still need to be studied. He did not cite any dissentient authority to whom his argument was directed, but any interested reader would have known that only a few years earlier Marett had published a paper entitled "Ritualism as a Disease of Religion."[93] In the posthumously published *Social Origins*, also, he again attacked "the mistake of deriving clear-cut ideas and detailed rites from vague emotions."[94] In particular, he quotes the complete passage from which the assertion about awe is extracted above; and although he does not give the source, it is a matter of no great knowledge or industry to discover that it was Marett's position which he thus had a special care to disintegrate.

There is, then, a real issue at stake in Hocart's emphasis on logic; there are quite contrasted interpretations of ritual to which his approach can usefully be opposed, and the theoretical confrontation with these views, which still exert their influence, has methodological consequences for the study of symbolic action.

X

The topic of Hocart's method, however, has not yet been quite covered. There remains to be considered a definitive feature of his argument which is of crucial interest and importance. The method of equivalences which we have been examining possesses the same ambiguity as we have seen in the use of

92. R. R. Marett, *The Threshold of Religion,* rev. ed. (London: Methuen, 1914), pp. 19–20.
93. A. M. Hocart, "Ritual and Emotion," *Character and Personality* 7 (1939): 201–10 (reprinted in *The Life-giving Myth,* pp. 53–65; see p. 63); R. R. Marett, "Ritualism as a Disease of Religion," *Folklore* 45 (1934): 310–16.
94. P. 7.

the equation sign: in one application the internal logic of separate rituals is analyzed; and, in the other, structural homologies among a number of rituals are determined in order to trace common descent. Correspondingly, Hocart resorts to the examples of two different sciences in order to characterize his argument: on the title page he calls it an essay in the comparative anatomy of human society; but in the preface he states that the method applied is that of comparative philology (p. 4).[95] He is interested not only in distinctive functions but also in the evolutionary process of differentiation. The best description of his work, and one which avoids distracting considerations introduced from other fields of inquiry, is that it is "the comparative history of culture" (p. 21).

This is an aim which, since the vagaries of the British diffusionists and the predominance of empirical functionalism, has in many anthropological circles aroused intense distrust. There have admittedly been reasonable grounds for suspicion, and we need therefore to be quite clear about where Hocart stands in relation to the more extreme theories with which his own may otherwise be classed.

When *Kings and Councillors* was first published, Hornblower went so far as to relate its argument to the so-called "heliolithic" theory, which "attributes the most important features of culture to the influence of ancient Egypt,"[96] i.e., to the rather extreme ideas of G. Elliot Smith and W. J. Perry. He reported that "this theory has greatly influenced our author," and adduced as evidence the fact that the thesis centered on mankind's great quest of life. "This is the quest," he concluded, "that the 'heliolithic' school has put forward as the great stimulant for culture-migration."

Now it is true that only a few years previously Hocart had been associated with these prominent diffusionists at University College London, and that in the book under review he acknowledged the guidance of Perry in American ethnog-

95. Cf. A. M. Hocart, *Kingship* (Oxford: Clarendon Press, 1927), which is "an attempt at applying to customs and beliefs the methods that have been so successful in the study of language" (p. v); see also *The Life-giving Myth*, p. 234, and *Social Origins*, p. 4.
96. Review in *Man*, p. 155.

raphy; but neither these circumstances nor the historical intention of his argument justified the prejudicial imputation of
their views to Hocart. Nevertheless, as Evans-Pritchard has
written, Hocart "became identified, quite unjustly, with the
University College school of Elliot Smith and Perry, whose
theories were considered by most anthropologists of the day
to be uncritical to the point of extravagance."[97] So far as Hocart is remembered at all, it is probably with them that he
is still linked today; but, as Evans-Pritchard continued, "it
was with their method rather than with their conclusions that
he was in sympathy." His working principles, though, were
distinct from theirs, and his concerns were quite different.
As the late Lord Raglan has pointed out, he "does not suggest
that the focus of diffusion lay in any one country such as
Egypt, or indeed that it need always have been the same."[98]
Hocart himself proclaimed, thirteen years before Hornblower's
review, his belief that "civilization is one," but he bluntly
rejected Perry's derivation of that civilization from Egypt:
"Why an author should wish to trace all civilization to Egypt
one fails to see. The argument fails to convince."[99] It is necessary, therefore, to define what Hocart's position really was.

As usual, he does at least three things at the same time
without distinguishing among them, but his premises at any
rate are clear and eminently sensible. To begin with, "The
great superiority of the historical method is that it assumes
nothing which we do not know actually to occur."[100] Next,
"If I can suggest a theory which is simple, which is reasonable, and which does not invoke a single process that cannot
be shown actually to occur, I shall have achieved at least
something."[101] His guiding principle is "to formulate simple
ideas that fit a large number of facts which formerly seemed

97. [E. E. Evans-Pritchard], review of Hocart, *Social Origins*, in *The Times Literary Supplement*, 7 October 1955, p. 591.
98. Raglan, Foreword to *Social Origins*, p. viii.
99. A. M. Hocart, review of W. J. Perry, *The Children of the Sun*, in *Indian Antiquary* 55 (1925): 119–20 (see p. 120).
100. *Social Origins*, p. 4.
101. *The Life-giving Myth*, p. 66 (from the essay "The Origin of Mono-theism," first published in 1922).

unrelated, . . . particularly the finding of recurrent structures or patterns" in rituals, myth, and social organization.[102]

These latter uniformities are so distinctive, and resemble each other so remarkably closely, as to prompt the hypothesis that they are divergent forms derived from a common original. Just as it is possible for comparative philology to reconstruct the development of English *father*, Latin *pater*, Greek *pater*, Sanskrit *pitar*, Old Irish *athir*, etc. from one Indo-European root (p. 16), so it should be possible to trace variant but probably related social institutions as well back to their earlier common form. There is nothing inherently implausible about this proposal; e.g., "The hypothesis that the pyramid wherever found was derived from a common centre is a perfectly sane one, in no wise different from the hypothesis that all variants of the word *mater* were derived from a common original." Yet it is the kind of investigation which both historians and anthropologists tend to repudiate. The resemblances of customs and beliefs in distant parts of the world are indeed often recognized as striking, but unfortunately the idea that institutions have spread from a common center has become mixed up with "curious complexes, involving the lost continent of Atlantis, or the missing tribes of Israel," and these have created a prejudice which is far from having died out. "One of the chief obstacles in the way of applying to customs the comparative methods which have worked so well in language is the fear of being taken for a crank." The historians and classicists have in the main steadily opposed every attempt to enlarge the boundaries of their traditional scholarly concerns so as to include the whole world. "Greece, Rome, and modern Europe have a history; we do not know the history of other countries, and reason as if they had none."[103]

Since we have for the most part no direct evidence, and since moreover evidence of this sort may fail to explain anyway, we should resort to circumstantial evidence, the value of which has been mistakenly decried. To reconstruct history

102. *Caste*, p. ix. Cf. "It is the aim of science to reduce as many facts to as few principles as possible" (*The Life-giving Myth*, p. 144).
103. *Social Origins*, pp. 8–9.

on such a basis may not supply proof, if by proof we mean direct evidence, such as actually seeing something happen.

> But proof does not consist in seeing: it consists in providing so complete an explanation of the disjointed evidence of our senses that no better alternative can be thought of. Some day an alternative may be found; but in the meantime our hypothesis, if it is any good, will have helped us to further conquests: that is all that really matters (pp. 26–27).

An excellent example, finally, of Hocart's practical and undogmatic attitude is the following, on the evolution of ritual:

> We have set out to reconstruct the history of thought, and we cannot afford to neglect any possibly fruitful hypothesis. We shall adopt the obvious hypothesis of common origin and see where it will lead us.[104]

These sound and modest precepts form the basis of Hocart's various attempts to reconstruct the comparative history of culture. But he did not put them to the service of a typically diffusionist aim of plotting migration routes. On this point he made himself particularly clear, and it alone should have been enough to dissociate him from his more precipitate colleagues. Too often, he thought, a comparison of customs leads to "nothing more than a discussion of migrations, which soon cease to arouse interest"; and he criticized his old teacher, Rivers, for putting into his work much more of "mere migration" than was good for anthropology. He found Elliot Smith's migrational diffusionism "too drastic," and regretted that the fight for the acceptance of diffusion had laid "too much stress on migration."[105] His most definite statement of his viewpoint is to be found in his observations on the movements of peoples in the Pacific:

> Those who wish to disentangle all these movements in detail are welcome to attempt it. To us the task seems unprofitable, if pursued for its own sake. Of migrations

104. Ibid., p. 15.
105. Ibid., pp. 10, 11.

there is no end, for man is always on the move, and he who sets out to trace them all is undertaking a catalogue which is never complete, and which expands without adding to science. Migrations only interest us in so far as they are necessary to an understanding of the way culture is built up or destroyed. . . ."[106]

Hocart is thus content to comment on the fact that over a large part of the world kings are divine, "I have no hesitation in believing that all the varieties of this doctrine, wherever they occur, are derived from the same original source. . . ."[107] He offers no suggestion where this source may be; the similarities alone demonstrate, for him, that there must have been a common source, and that is good enough. Similarly, though in more detail, he compares the licensed behavior of the uterine nephew in Fiji and among the Thonga of southeastern Africa, who have, he says, classificatory kinship systems of the same type: "I have no hesitation in believing that . . . these peoples derive their kinship systems and the customs associated with them from a common source."[108] And, he asks challengingly, "Why not?" Once again, however, he supplies no indication where the source may be, but is content to draw the inference and leave it. Doubtless he had his ideas on both these questions, but it was not relevant to the problems he was really concerned with to publish speculations about migration routes. Also, he must have been conscious of the fact that to do so would be likely to divert attention into historical minutiae and away from his analyses and from the lessons he wished these to furnish.

Nevertheless, in order to understand the distribution of similar cultural facts, and to explain the changes involved in their dispersion, it is necessary in the end to establish certain general lines of migration and divergence. An historical connection which was of constant concern to Hocart throughout his

106. *The Northern States of Fiji*, pp. 6–7. Cf. below, p. 291: "It is not the purpose of the comparative anatomy of society to reconstitute the past in all its details, but to sum up growth in formulae."
107. *The Life-giving Myth*, p. 29 (from an essay, "Flying Through the Air," first published in 1923).
108. Ibid., p. 196 (from an essay, "The Uterine Nephew," first published in 1923.)

career, and which is of some special relevance to the thesis of *Kings and Councillors,* is that which he infers between India and the Pacific.[109] We cannot, he maintains, derive Fijian culture from that which is mirrored in Vedic literature, but both can be derived from a common original which in India has been battered by successive invasions but which has been better preserved in the isolation of the Pacific.[110] But this hypothesis is still not demonstrated or supported, as it might have been, by conventional historical evidences and the tracing of paths of influence. The case rests on a comparison of customs, and it is on the similarities thus established that Hocart bases his belief that "in the Pacific Ocean we find a culture which is closely connected with the archaic culture of India." He has a number of reasons for holding this view. To begin with, he writes, "I should myself require nothing more in the way of evidence than the identity of the kinship system used by the [South Indians] and the Koro Sea tribes of Fiji." The system referred to is a two-line ("Dravidian") prescriptive terminology combined with "cross-cousin marriage, unmodified by any other principle," i.e., a symmetric system of prescriptive alliance.[111] He considers the case for the independent origin of this system, and then adds a further evidence. If the system had been invented independently in India, Fiji, and America, is it likely, he asks, that "all three should have had the same idea of prescribing opprobrious language between cross-

109. Ibid., pp. 234–39 ("India and the Pacific," first published in 1925).
110. Cf. Hocart, review of Perry, *Children of the Sun,* pp. 119–120: "The successive waves [of civilization] that have spread in early times across the Indian Ocean and across the Pacific have received their impetus from one centre."
111. The South Indian system is standard, best described by Louis Dumont, "The Dravidian Kinship Terminology as an Expression of Marriage," *Man* 53 (1953): 34–39, art. 54; idem, *Hierarchy and Marriage Alliance in South Indian Kinship,* Occasional Papers no. 12 (London: Royal Anthropological Institute, 1957). For the Fijian system referred to, see Hocart, *Lau Islands, Fiji,* Bernice P. Bishop Museum Bulletin no. 62 (Honolulu, 1929) and idem, "Kinship Systems," (pp. 345–51; reprinted in *The Life-giving Myth,* pp. 173–84); cf. idem, *The Northern States of Fiji,* p. 49, on "the beautiful symmetry of the Lauan system." It is worth repeating, by the way, that when *Lau Islands* was published, "considerable alterations were made without reference to the author" (Lord Raglan, preface to *The Northern States of Fiji,* p. v).

cousins?" Other significant similarities of the kind are caste ("every important feature of the Indian caste system finds its parallel in Fiji"), divine chieftainship (in which respect "Ancient India and Fiji had the same religion"), fire-walking, and suttee. Fijian culture is "the more archaic," but the connection with that of India is thought to be sufficiently established by the resemblances, which incidentally Hocart admits to have merely picked up while following other paths of research. We shall return below to a consideration of this kind of inquiry. For the moment, this example (the connection between India and Fiji) serves well to illustrate the rather vague way in which he indicates the supposed sources of similar customs, and the type of evidence that he thinks appropriate to the demonstration of historical connections. How little of a conventional historian he was is shown, however, by the facts that he nowhere published a systematic comparison and interconnection of such cultural facts, and that he never said where he thought the archaic original of any institution was. Even in his work on caste, which could have been expected to come nearest to a demonstration of this sort, he deliberately abstained from historical proof of a more directly evidential nature:

> In the present case our aim is not to describe the social organisation that flourished in such and such a place at such and such a time before our records begin, but to explain the characteristics of living societies, and this we can do without reconstituting any particular society.[112]

His aim is to discover the "main principles" upon which the hypothetically original form of society was presumably based, and to accumulate "an increasing number of formulae" to account for subsequent offices and other individual features.

112. *Les Castes*, p. 253; English edit., *Caste*, p. 150. In this he had good philological precedent. Cf. Georges Dumézil on the realization, by students of the Indo-European language family, that "l'important n'était pas de reconstituer un prototype, ni de s'attarder sur la partie invérifiable des évolutions, mais d'en expliquer comparativement les parties connues" (*Mythe et épopée*, vol. 1: *L'idéologie des trois fonctions dans les épopées des peuples indo-européens* [Paris: Gallimard, 1968], pp. 9–10).

This more abstract kind of investigation leads us finally to the most general aspect of Hocart's comparative history of culture. This is his attempt to reconstruct the origin of all government and to trace the process of differentiation which results in the various modern forms of administrative organization. Since this is the substance of the present book, there is no need to go further than we already have done into the specific features of his argument. We need only stress that the investigation, based as it is on world-wide evidence, takes even less explicit account of primary locations or routes of migration or processes of diffusion. The evidence is circumstantial, the argument inferential, the analysis systematic. As a reconstruction of factors operating over a long and irrecoverable past, it is history of a kind, but one without dates, events, or personages. It is, one might say, a structural history.

XI

The test of all these conceptual and methodological positions is of course how well they serve to render intelligible the types of social facts to which they are intended to apply. Let us quickly consider this issue under a number of criteria of increasing generality.

As far as the analysis of individual rites is concerned, Hocart never published an analysis which adequately exemplified his scientific aims. Suggestive though his ideas may be, his empirical analyses are commonly brief, superficial, and elementary. In his own day, professional anthropologists such as Malinowski and Evans-Pritchard were producing studies of ritual which far surpassed his in range of evidence and precision of investigation.[113] A little later, in Oceania, Hocart's field of most intimate personal knowledge, Raymond Firth published a superb account of the ritual of life in Tikopia, a study which owed nothing to Hocart and had perhaps little to learn from him.[114]

113. B. Malinowski, *Coral Gardens and Their Magic*, 2 vols. (London: Allen & Unwin, 1935); E. E. Evans-Pritchard, *Witchcraft, Oracles and Magic among the Azande* (Oxford: Clarendon Press, 1937).
114. *The Work of the Gods in Tikopia*, 2 vols., Monographs on Social Anthropology, no. 1 (London: Lund, Humphries for the London School of Economics, 1940); cf. 2d ed., with new introduction and epilogue (London: Athlone Press, 1967).

More recent analyses of the ritual of kingship, in particular, demonstrate even more plainly how far Hocart's work has been outstripped; e.g., T. O. Beidelman's exemplary analysis, in the African field, of Swazi royal ritual,[115] and J. C. Heesterman's profound monograph on royal consecration in ancient India.[116] Fortes's study of installation ceremonies, which draws most directly on Hocart's work, relies simply on the "general framework" proposed by him, and the value of Hocart's example is schematic rather than incisively analytical. This kind of value still subsists in the present work (e.g., ch. 5), and it can be helpful in embarking on a new analysis to have some expectation of the personages and events commonly to be found in a ritual, but for our present-day investigations there seems to be little in the way of more technical direction to be gained. Certainly it is an achievement, as Fortes writes of Hocart, to have shown that "installation ceremonies have much the same structure, use similar procedures, and serve broadly the same ends in all societies,"[117] and in this respect Hocart may be thought to have rendered a scholarly service similar to that performed by van Gennep in establishing the framework of transition rites.[118] But as far as the scheme is concerned, what he has provided is an empirical generalization, and it is only after this point (i.e., once the regularities have been discerned) that the real problems can be posed. For Hocart, the problem was posed simply by the resemblances, and answered by his presupposition that a basic uniformity was the result of evolution from a common and unique origin; but this case has still not been properly argued.

The historical reconstruction of an archaic form of organization has nevertheless received some authoritative approval. Mauss entered a caution about the necessity of "good *historical* proofs, contemporary with the facts of borrowing and diffu-

---

115. "Swazi Royal Ritual," *Africa* 36 (1966): 373–405.
116. *The Ancient Indian Royal Consecration*, Disputationes Rheno-Trajectinae, ed. J. Gonda (The Hague: Mouton, 1957).
117. Fortes, "Installation Ceremonies," pp. 5, 8, 19.
118. A. van Gennep, *Les rites de passage* (Paris: Nourry, 1909); English ed., *The Rites of Passage*, trans. M. B. Vizedom and G. I. Caffee (Chicago: University of Chicago Press, 1960).

sion," i.e., he demanded direct evidence of a kind which Hocart had argued to be unnecessary (ch. 1); but he still found it possible to conclude that the comparison of kinship in Fiji and in South India was "legitimate and natural":

> A great part of these civilizations and these peoples, and particularly techniques of cultivation and the arts, originated in southcentral Asia. Although the details of these institutions are not yet historically certain, the essence of the thesis is probable and exact, and there are grounds for relating the social and political structures of India, especially kingship, to those of Polynesia.[119]

As for *Kings and Councillors*, specifically, Mauss found that it made understandable a number of even classical facts, particularly those relating to social class.

More recently, and with greater scholarly weight, Louis Dumont also has subscribed to Hocart's thesis. After a comparison of Fijian with Indian facts, he concludes upon

> a likely hypothesis on the origin of the system, namely that pre-Aryan India had a system closely related to that of Fiji, as Hocart claimed.[120]

More generally, Hocart had proposed schemes of the evolution of government in which an egalitarian or complementary organization of social functions gave place to "a vertical hierarchy" (p. 292); and Dumont, correspondingly, conjectures for India a process, beginning with the Vedic period, in which the king was subordinated to the brahman and a "strict hierarchy" developed.

Hocart's reconstruction, therefore, in both cultural and systematic respects, is thought by excellent judges to be not only respectable but also probably correct in its main features.

119. Introduction to *Les castes*, pp. d–e. For undeclared reasons, this introduction was not reproduced in the English ed., *Caste* (1950) but was replaced with another by Lord Raglan; nor, incidentally, is it listed in Josef Gugler, "Bibliographie de Marcel Mauss" (*L'Homme* 4 [1964], 105–12).
120. Louis Dumont, *Homo hierarchicus*, p. 100 n. 32[h]. Cf. "In Fiji we get nearer to the parent system than in the oldest writings of India" (Hocart, *Les castes*, p. 132; English ed., p. 74).

The major sociological thesis of *Kings and Councillors*, finally, carries the most conviction. What Hocart argues is that there has been a systematic evolution of society from segmentary (p. 38) to centralized; from undifferentiated to specialized; from precedence to authority; from complementarity to hierarchy; and from representative to administrative. This is a coherent and general theory of the development of centralized social organization and ultimately of the state. Where Hocart presents documentary historical evidence (as he does when he readily can), his argument can be tested; where there is no such evidence, his argument is at least persuasive.

His more specific proposal, that government evolved from a ritual organization and was continually shaped by a predominant impulsion to secure life, is more dubitable but also more original and striking. Indeed, it is a prime achievement of Hocart that in *Kings and Councillors* he succeeded in propounding, after Aristotle, Locke, Rousseau, and Hume, a novel theory of the origin of government.

This theory has of course the advantage of a mass of ethnographical and historical information which Hocart's distinguished predecessors lacked, but where he makes a more creditable contrast is in his attitude to such evidence. In general, political theorists had worked out their views on government within the framework of familiar institutions, and their ideas on the origin of government had been largely a priori and normative.[121] Hocart's decisive step was to start from social facts, and to take them deliberately from societies of very different types and from far-flung regions of the earth. Anthropologists such as Tylor, and as far back as McLennan for that matter, had certainly called upon a similar range of ethnographical evidence in their schemes of institutional development, but Hocart made an advance on them in two respects.

---

121. Cf. Fortes and Evans-Pritchard, *African Political Systems*, p. 4: "We have not found that the theories of political philosophers have helped us to understand the societies we have studied. . . . Political philosophy has chiefly concerned itself with how men *ought* to live and what form of government they *ought* to have, rather than with what *are* their political habits and institutions."

In the first place, he began from his own observations in Fiji, and later in Ceylon, and then worked outward, as it were, and back into history from this solid base of personal knowledge. In the second place, unlike his forerunners in their reconstructions of the several origins of the classificatory terminology, the family, marriage by capture, sacrifice, and so on, he resolutely adhered to his stipulation that he would assume in his comparative history "nothing which we do not know actually to occur."

The ritual origin of government is a thesis which, however cogently inferred, cannot be directly tested; and in assessing Hocart's argument as an intellectual achievement we cannot strictly consider it as a demonstrated finding of a conventionally scientific kind. But this is not to say that it is impossible to form reasoned opinions on it or to refer its contentions to social facts. We can, for instance, estimate the probability of the conjectured origin by comparing it with other speculations of the kind. Is it good enough simply to assume, from current observation, that man is by nature, as Aristotle avers, a political animal? Locke and Rousseau thought not, but their own proposal of an original social contract does not respond much better to the demands of the case. If we are to look for a more constant factor, i.e., not for a hypothetical and singular event but for a general and continuing impulsion occasioned by the circumstances of social existence, then Hume's recourse to quarrels among men of different societies hardly procures much convinction. In this regard, Hocart's theory is on all counts more probable, beginning with its first premise, viz., that the object of ritual is not to express a sense of religious awe, nor just to propitiate fearsome powers, but is a practical activity intended to secure life. This does not impute to early man alone some latterly formulated orectic philosophy; it is a premise resting upon universal and reliable observation. Whether or not all ritual is so inspired depends partly on how the anthropologist decides to define ritual; but the world-wide existence of symbolic actions which are intended to acquire, preserve, enhance, and give life is not a matter of definition. These human intentions, and the standard procedures designed to fulfil them, do not in themselves entail the development of government; but once they are conceded to exist, the organizational consequences which Hocart has traced are not only possible but considerably likely. As he put it in a previous formulation:

> The early pioneers of thought . . . were not seeking to give themselves poetic thrills, but to abolish the uncertainty of existence by solving the eternal problem of the weather. To some extent they did succeed in abolishing that uncertainty, not in the way they thought by controlling the forces of nature, but by controlling themselves. . . .[122]

The quest of life, he says, is a social quest;[123] and social action necessitates organization. Co-ordination of actions conduces to the localization of authority in one status; the elaboration of a doctrine of life lays the grounds for a matching differentiation of functions; and so on by way of increasing differentiation, specialization, and centralization to the formation of the state with its complex apparatus of government.

Hocart's theory, then, is not an engaging scholarly fiction or an insubstantial novelty.[124] In its vital premise, working concepts, method, and conclusions it has good claims to be taken seriously as an original contribution to the ancient debate on the beginnings of government. It suffers, of course, from the defect that it is a unicausal theory, and in view of the great complexity of the circumstances it cannot be wholly right as it stands. But Hocart, in spite of the vigorous tone of his exposition, was a most sane and circumspect thinker, and he could certainly never have imagined that he was explaining everything. It should be enough that he has presented a coherent and quite impressive case for the recognition of

122. *Kingship*, pp. 56–57.
123. *The Life-giving Myth*, p. 52 (from an essay, "The Purpose of Ritual," first published in 1935).
124. One may contrast, for example, the marvellously intriguing but quite unpersuasive reconstructions proposed by Robert Graves in *Greek Myths* (London: Cassell, 1958), esp. pp. 11–23.

an important and perduring factor in the organization of men's affairs, a concern so powerful that it surely had some part in the development of society and its proliferating apparatus of administration.[125]

XII

This laudatory assessment of Hocart's enterprise might easily be elaborated, and in further respects than those cited here; but no amount of explication of the substance of the argument could shield it from the expectable rejoinder that its very aim is quite misconceived.

Evolutionary and historical reconstructions have fallen very much out of favor in social anthropology, and they have in some quarters been obdurately rejected as having nothing to do with the subject. The trouble with both of these approaches, according to an ordinary textbook view, is that

> their advocates went far beyond the evidence, as they were bound to do as long as their interest was directed to the remote past. . . . Arguments from man's present

125. Inferences from etymology are always hazardous, but it is perhaps worth remarking that the English word "government" is relatively recent in origin, and that it does not testify to any early inception of the idea of state-like administration. It comes from the Latin *gubernare*, to steer or pilot a ship (cf. *gubernaculum*, helm, rudder), which only transferentially signifies to direct, manage, conduct, guide, or govern (Lewis and Short). Similarly with the German *Regierung*, with its original connotation of steering. *Rex*, king, is also based on the same notion of moving or guiding in a straight line (cf. Skr. *rjúh*, straight; *rājā*, king). This metaphor does not itself express any explicit theory of government, such as one premised on contract or defense, and the possibility would thus seem to suggest itself that before the hypothetical formation of the institutions of government communal affairs were regulated by some more ancient conception than that of coercive administration. Dumézil, moreover, has established for the early Indo-European peoples a cosmological theory of dual sovereignty, based on an inseparable combination of the jural and the mystical (*Mitra-Varuna: Essai sur deux représentations indo-européennes de la souveraineté*, 2d ed. [Paris: Gallimard, 1948]), which can accommodate many of Hocart's views. This reconstruction takes us back only about three millennia, however, and Hocart would probably maintain that his own conjectures, derived as they are from a world-wide comparison, must relate to a very much older period.

to his past condition which are unsupported by good historical or archaeological evidence can never be other than merely speculative.[126]

The conviction fundamental to this declamation is that the past is "lost for ever," so we should not even think about it.

Now Hocart would surely have responded that this is a very dull dogmatism, and that it would be a blinkered view which could so cut off social anthropology from our human past and also from its own past as an academic discipline. As he actually wrote of this class of critic,

> The fact is when they say we can never know, what they really mean is they cannot see the way by which we can know, so they do not think anyone else can, which is rather an arrogant assumption.[127]

The answer to the reproach of going beyond "the evidence" is to be found in the course of Hocart's opening chapter. Evidence is not identical with direct (or with "good historical") evidence,

> for all history is of necessity a reconstruction, the degree of probability attending a particular reconstruction depending upon the evidence available.[128]

As for even material evidence, inscriptions can be untrustworthy, and if pots and pans do not lie, "that is because they do not speak"; archaeology can give us dates, but, Hocart asks, "what is the use of dates without facts to fit into them?"

---

126. Beattie, *Other Cultures*, p. 8. See also p. 242, on diffusionists going "beyond the evidence" in postulating a common source for cultural or social phenomena. On this issue, as indeed largely throughout his textbook, the author merely echoes some of the more didactic views of A. R. Radcliffe-Brown, at this point namely the dictum that "speculative history cannot give us results of any real importance for the understanding of human life and culture" (*The Andaman Islanders* [Cambridge: Cambridge University Press, 1922], p. vii).

127. "Evidence in Human History," *Psyche Annual* 13 (1933): 80–93; see p. 84. This article was reprinted, with alterations (the passage quoted, for instance, was deleted), as chap. 1 in *Kings and Councillors*.

128. E. E. Evans-Pritchard, *Essays in Social Anthropology* (London: Faber, 1962), p. 21.

(p. 14).[129] It is more difficult to know how to respond to the positivistic depreciation of the "merely speculative," for this is a question partly of intellectual temper and imagination rather than of method. Nevertheless, it is a matter of some consequence that we should be summarily enjoined to abjure any opinions reached by abstract or hypothetical reasoning, and to abstain even from the attempt to ascertain something by probable reasoning.[130] We need only conjecture (even though so intelligent an activity does fall under the critic's fiat) what would be the effects on our understanding of the world if this indiscriminate ban were submitted to. "The direct method is not only cumbrous, it fails to explain, and explanation is the end of science" (p. 22). If the republication of *Kings and Councillors* proves to exert any force in diverting students from that pragmatical confinement, it will be a satisfaction and an intellectual advantage that is much to be looked forward to.

But there still remains, for the present, the problem of accounting for a view about the past which is so opposed, and even hostile, to that of Hocart. A possible clue is furnished by the reference to diffusionists and evolutionists having their interest "directed to the remote past." This seems in fact to expose a basic misapprehension. Neither type of theorist has, in the history of anthropology, been interested solely in the remote past, but speculations of these kinds have always reflected upon the present. Hocart again states the position clearly when he describes the common end of anthropological factions as being ideally

> to understand the past as a preparation for the present, to explain the present as the outcome of the past, and perhaps even to conjecture the future from the lessons of both.[131]

129. It will be remembered that Hocart had been Archaeological Commissioner in Ceylon for nine years, and he was a skilled and scholarly archaeologist by practice; see, e.g., A. M. Hocart, *The Temple of the Tooth in Kandy*, Memoirs of the Archaeological Survey of Ceylon, 4 (London: Luzac, 1931).
130. *Shorter Oxford English Dictionary*, s.v. "Speculation."
131. *Social Origins*, p. 11.

It is surely this synoptic view that any student of culture should aim at, and whatever the certifiability of the evidence or the hazards of interpretation it is a feasible and ultimately inevitable enterprise. The fact that it was badly or uncertainly carried out at one stage in the development of anthropology is no reason not to do it at all.

A censorship which would delete historical reconstruction from the concerns of social anthropologists offers no advance in humane understanding, and if tamely suffered could only impede and frustrate the discipline in its proud and singular ambition as the study of man. Hocart's struggle for this ideal happened to run directly against the success of the monographical investigations of the inter-war years, and we can readily appreciate why he then had so little effect. But the intensive ethnography of Malinowski and his successors was no Copernican revolution in anthropological theory, a sempiternal triumph of good method and exact observation over everything that had gone before. It was an advance, an accretion to knowledge, but it did not preclude or supersede investigations of other kinds. The trouble, though, is that there is a tendency in anthropology to conceive types of explanation in all-or-nothing terms, and by an implicit criterion of absolute theoretical progress, so that careful and responsible opinions held by clever men only thirty or fifty years earlier become relegated to a limbo of unregenerate error. Some anthropologists therefore display, as we have instanced above, an apparent disregard for the history of ideas which corresponds to the current repudiation of cultural history. It is in order to counter such unprofitable attitudes that it may be well to look back, at a generation's distance, on Hocart's life work and particularly at the lessons of *Kings and Councillors*. Evans-Pritchard wrote in 1955: "Hocart's 'historical' approach is out of fashion, but fashions change."[132] We need not, however, wait upon fashion. Let us instead briefly review some of the grounds for a more decisive change of view.

The first requirement is to restore the universal purview of our predecessors, and this is crucial. Functionalist anthropologists have tended to consider human activity in a very

132. Review of *Social Origins*, p. 591.

shrunken perspective, not only with regard to comparative studies but also with regard to a long tradition of diffusionist work already done. British anthropologists, to speak only of them, generally go no further back than Elliot Smith, Perry, and Rivers when they consider diffusionism, and they are then understandably put off by the uncritical use of historical reconstruction for which these writers are well known.[133] But the central issues were posed much earlier, and in once-renowned publications which have lost none of their power of instruction.

Comparative ethnography was initiated in the eighteenth century, in France, by Lafitau and his successors such as Démeunier, De Brosses, and others of similarly impressive ability.[134] The theories of these writers—especially those relying upon scriptural authority—had not, however, the fundamental analytical interest which was to be brought out by the Germans in the following century. The perennial problems of the growth and transmission of culture are still better considered by reference to Bastian and Ratzel. Their names have little currency in social anthropology today, and their views receive scarcely any mention in the textbooks, as though they belonged to the Middle Ages of anthropological thought.[135] Yet it was they who effectively established and explored, with immense scholarly industry, the complementary explanatory traditions to which Hocart's work should be related. If *Kings and Councillors* is assessed in relation to contemporary works alone, it can appear outmoded and idiosyncratic, but it looks different if it is placed in a context where Bastian and Ratzel are dominant figures. It has to do with the greatest of all anthropological problems, namely the explanation of cultural resemblances: To what extent are similarities in customs, in-

133. There is much in their writings, nevertheless, which well deserves revival and reassessment.
134. A. van Gennep, *Religions, moeurs et légendes*, Troisième série (Paris: Mercure de France, 1911); Cinquième série (Paris: Mercure de France, 1914).
135. A recent exception is Lucy Mair, *An Introduction to Social Anthropology* (Oxford: Clarendon Press, 1965), in which Bastian and Ratzel are briefly considered, significantly, in the chapter "How Social Anthropology Developed" (pp. 17–18).

TABLE 1
Some Principal Works of the Period

1865   E. B. Tylor. *Researches into the Early History of Mankind.* London.

1878   R. Andree. *Ethnographische Parallelen und Vergleiche.* Stuttgart.

1884–85   G. A. Wilken. *Het Animisme bij de Volken van den Indischen Archipel.* Leiden.

1885–88   F. Ratzel. *Völkerkunde.* Leipzig.

1887   A. Bastian. *Die Welt in ihren Spiegelungen.* Berlin.

1890   J. G. Frazer. *The Golden Bough.* London.

1893   E. Durkheim. *De la division du travail social.* Paris.

1898   H. Hubert and M. Mauss. "Essai sur la nature et la fonction du sacrifice." Paris.

1900   W. W. Skeat. *Malay Magic.* London.

1903   E. Durkheim and M. Mauss. "De quelques formes primitives de classification." Paris.

1909   A. van Gennep. *Les rites de passage.* Paris.

1909   R. Hertz. "La prééminence de la main droite." Paris.

1909   R. R. Marett. *The Threshold of Religion.* London.

1910   L. Lévy-Bruhl. *Les fonctions mentales dans les sociétés inférieures.* Paris.

1912   E. Durkheim. *Les formes élémentaires de la vie religieuse.* Paris.

1912   A. C. Haddon. *The Wanderings of Peoples.* London.

1914   W. H. R. Rivers. *The History of Melanesian Society.* Cambridge.

1915   G. Elliot Smith. *The Migrations of Early Culture.* London.

1922   A. R. [Radcliffe-] Brown. *The Andaman Islanders.* Cambridge.

1923   W. J. Perry. *The Children of the Sun.* London.

1924   G. Dumézil. *Le festin d'immortalité.* Paris.

1925   M. Mauss. "Essai sur le don." Paris.

1936   A. M. Hocart. *Kings and Councillors.* Cairo.

1937   E. E. Evans-Pritchard. *Witchcraft, Oracles and Magic among the Azande.* Oxford.

1940   G. Dumézil. *Mitra-Varuna.* Paris.

1940   R. Firth. *The Work of the Gods in Tikopia.* London.

TABLE 2

COMPARATIVE TABLE OF SOME LIFE SPANS

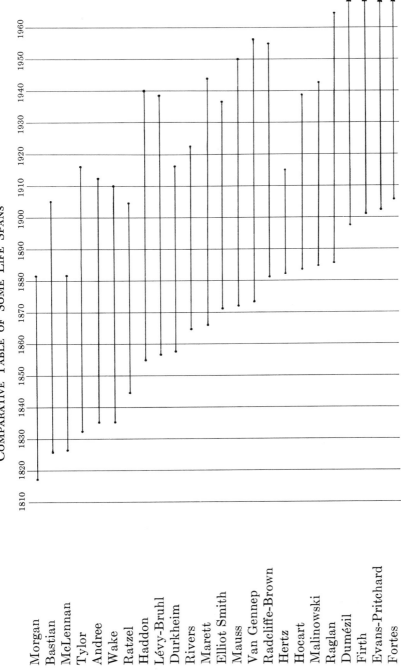

stitutions, and collective representations the products of spontaneous proclivities of human beings, and to what extent are they the results of historical transmission? This is an issue of absolute importance, and it has by no means been resolved. Indeed, in the nature of the case it never can be resolved entirely, and it is one of the worst consequences of the antihistorical functionalism which we have encountered that it gives a quite false impression of the significance of this enduring focus of theoretical concern. The student will be in a better position to judge the matter, and then to reconsider Hocart's intention, if he can be persuaded to take seriously the weighty and contrasting works of the pioneers.

Given the present neglect of Bastian and Ratzel, it may be helpful to make a brief statement of their characteristic views. Adolf Bastian (1826–1905) was the most prominent scholar, in the field of universal ethnography, to argue for the psychic unity of mankind. He maintained in great detail, drawing largely upon his own field researches in many parts of the world (a fact which is often overlooked), that the striking resemblances between cultures in far-separated places were the results of certain natural tendencies of the human mind which he called elementary ideas (*Elementargedanken*). Differences in the expression of these ideas were to be accounted for by the environment, by the stage of social development a people had reached, and by the autonomous elaboration of distinct ideologies (*Völkergedanken*) within cultural provinces. Bastian did not deny the influence of historical factors and the diffusion of ideas from one society or region to another, but for him the original and constant shaper of civilization was the natural proclivity of man to think in certain forms, and it was this tendency which explained the cultural resemblances.[136] An opposite view was propounded by Fried-

136. See, e.g., Adolf Bastian, *Die Welt in ihren Spiegelungen unter dem Wandel des Völkergedankens: Prolegomena zu einer Gedankenstatistik* (Berlin: Mittler, 1887); idem, *Ethnische Elementargedanken in der Lehre vom Menschen*, 2 vols. (Berlin: Weidmann, 1895), esp. vol. 2, on theoretical interpretation. For a clear exposition of Bastian's theory, see Richard Schwarz, *Adolf Bastians Lehre vom Elementar- und Völkergedanken* (Leipzig: Noste, 1909).

rich Ratzel (1844–1904), who was also concerned to explain the common features of culture in both "the highest and the lowest strata" of mankind. According to him, the explanation of these similarities is to be found in historical events. "Restless movement" is the characteristic of man, and in comparison with the strength and duration of this tendency, as he concluded in his once-famous aphorism, "the earth is small."[137] It is because of this continual wandering over the earth's surface, pursued over vast periods of time, that every habitable region is in fact inhabited, and that every institution, or "form of life" (*Lebensform*), however restricted its incidence, nevertheless has cognate forms in the remotest parts of the world. Human migrations have constantly been forced to turn back on themselves, so that they have repeatedly gone over their own tracks, perpetually following old routes and bringing about recurrent contacts and mutual influences between cultures. It is for this reason, Ratzel argued, that it can lead only to confusion to seek points of origin and routes of migration, and that the researcher should instead try to describe culture areas.[138]

These polar types of explanation were not mutually exclusive in the minds of their proponents, any more than they are so in fact, for Bastian and Ratzel each accepted premises held by the other. A practical combination of their views was actually soon demonstrated in the work of Richard Andree, a scholar who has fallen into an even greater obscurity. In his formerly standard works on ethnographical parallels and comparisons he brought together reports on a large variety of customs and ideas (e.g., omen birds, the evil eye, petrifaction, smiths, mother-in-law avoidance, personal names, possession, masks, circumcision, etc.) from a wide scattering of cultures, and he argued that these world-wide similarities corre-

137. Fr. Ratzel, *Völkerkunde*, 2 vols., 2d ed., rev. (Leipzig and Vienna: Bibliographisches Institut, 1894–95), 1: 9. (1st ed., 1885–88.)
138. Fr. Ratzel, "Der Lebensraum: eine biogeographische Studie," in *Festgaben für Albert Schäffe* (Tübingen: Laupp, 1901), pp. 104–89; cf. idem, *Anthropogeographie*, vol. 1: *Grundzüge der Anwendung der Erdkunde auf die Geschichte*, 2d ed. (Stuttgart: Engelhorn, 1899), pp. 113–204 (§§ 43–90): "Die geschichtliche Bewegung."

sponded so minutely that they demonstrated "the mental unity of man."[139] But he explicitly admitted, also, the facts of borrowing and inheritance of institutions from a common source, only in either case he demanded evidence of the process in question. What kind of evidence he had in mind was made crystal clear in his own study of the distribution of scapulimancy, the practice of divination from marks and formations on the shoulder blades of sacrificial animals. This custom is found all the way from Britain and Morocco in the west to the Bering Strait in the east, but is unknown in Africa (apart from the Muslim littoral in the north) and the greater part of south and southeastern Asia. Andree therefore opted in this case for a common historical origin, which in fact he placed among the Mongols of inner Asia.[140] It would not have occurred to him to discount the patent implications of such a circumscribed distribution, on the ground that direct evidence of dispersal was lacking, and his classical investigation is an excellent illustration of the case which Hocart was much later to make on behalf of circumstantial evidence.

This very brief retrospect on certain of Hocart's precursors serves first to relate his work to a well founded and responsible intellectual enterprise, rather than to his somewhat erratic associates at University College London. Seen against this background, *Kings and Councillors* can be better appreciated as a contribution to a great debate staged by German scholars in the nineteenth century and continuing, if sporadically, down to the present day.[141] It is notoriously true that Bastian no-

139. Richard Andree, *Ethnographische Parallelen und Vergleiche* (Stuttgart: Maier, 1878), p. vi; cf. the second series (*Neue Folge*), under the same title (Leipzig: von Veit, 1889).

140. Idem, "Scapulimantia," in *Boas Anniversary Volume* (New York: Stechert, 1906), pp. 143–65.

141. This is not to overlook Tylor, especially his *Researches into the Early History of Mankind* (London: Murray, 1865; new ed., abr. with intro. by Paul Bohannan, Chicago: University of Chicago Press, 1964), but the volume and the contemporaneous opposition of the works of Bastian and Ratzel make a more effective theoretical impact. They are perhaps less open, moreover, to the methodological objection which Hocart (p. 3 below) raises against Tylor.

where stated just what the elementary ideas were,[142] though he supplied abundant empirical indications, and that Ratzel similarly failed to demarcate his culture areas;[143] but the scope of their demonstrations and the confrontation of their modes of explanation produce together an enlargement of outlook which for us can have a decisive importance. This extended perspective permits a realization which is not merely historical but affects the very bases of judgment. It conduces, that is, to a readjustment of the scales of space and time against which the central problem is conceived. Bastian's case for innate mental operations cannot be assessed except by specific contrast with Ratzel's historical argument, and to make this comparison, in their universal setting, permits an appreciation of the situation which today appears rather foreign to social anthropologists. To accept, with Ratzel, that the earth is small, in comparison with the swarming explorations of man, can subtly but crucially change our view of the possibility of, for instance, an historical link between India and Fiji. To contemplate this connection brings also a changed estimation of the time scale, a switch to the view which is taken for granted by prehistorians but is foreign to the functionalists. It is a curious mental adjustment, this decision to adopt extended scales of judgment, but it can have large consequences. Once we adopt the premise that "the earth is not too big," as Ratzel alternatively phrases it,[144] and put it to ourselves that it is *only* some six thousand years since the birth of the great civilizations, and perhaps only thirty thousand or so years since man crossed from Asia into the Americas and into Australia, then Hocart's historical ambition, to speak of nothing else, can seem modest indeed and far more realizable.

An altogether excellent example of comparative history, and the kind of research to which social anthropologists might ideally turn, is presented by Georges Dumézil, whose admirable and voluminous works on the theory of the "three functions" have impressively established a new conception of

142. Schwarz, *Adolf Bastians Lehre,* p. 40.
143. Lowie, *History,* p. 125.
144. "Der Lebensraum," p. 104.

the integrity and continuity of Indo-European civilization.[145] Dumézil, like Hocart, had to work in the beginning against powerful criticism and prejudice from traditionalists who were not merely skeptical about such technical matters as philological points of argument, but were resistant to the very inspiration of the enterprise, namely the historical reconstruction of the ideological foundations of Indo-European society. As Hocart observed,

> It is strange . . . that there is no more determined opponent of the extension of the comparative method to other branches of culture [sc., in addition to language] than the comparative philologist. He is positive it will not work in religion or social organization (p. 16).

The best answer, as he continues, is not argument but example, and this in the event is what Dumézil has overwhelmingly presented, in a stunning array of scholarly researches,[146] which have abundantly proved that the kind of comparative history to which Hocart made his lesser contribution is indeed possible and revelatory. It is true that in this case there is a great quantity of evidence from a variety of literary and other sources, covering centuries of a great civilization, but the same method can be applied to other cultures as well. On a small scale, we may cite, to take only two modern examples, the comparative and historical reconstructions of the development of Pueblo Indian society, in the southwestern United States, by Eggan and by Fox.[147] These investigations demonstrate well

145. For a survey of the main lines of the investigation, see Georges Dumézil, *L'idéologie tripartie des Indo-Européens*, Collection Latomus, 31 (Brussels: Latomus, 1958); for bibliography and evaluations, see *Hommages à Georges Dumézil*, Collection Latomus, 45 (Brussels: Latomus, 1960); see also C. Scott Littleton, *The New Comparative Mythology: An anthropological assessment of the theories of Georges Dumézil* (Berkeley and Los Angeles: University of California Press, 1966).
146. For his own recent account of the course of his researches, and the parallel enquiries of his collaborators, see his *Mythe et épopée*, vol. 1: *L'idéologie des trois fonctions dans les épopées des peuples indo-européens* (Paris: Gallimard, 1968), pp. 9–25.
147. Fred Eggan, *Social Organization of the Western Pueblos* (Chicago: University of Chicago Press, 1950); Robin Fox, *The Keresan Bridge: a*

that schemes of migration, cultural transmission, and the origin and transformation of social forms can be validly worked out for a culture area which lacks most of the direct evidences of the past that are to be found in the Indo-European field. Another line of historical inquiry in anthropology which deserves special mention, and one which corresponds more expressly to the older idea of diffusionism, is that which has been so intriguingly pursued by Schuster. His distributional studies of joint-marks and of skin mosaics, to take two examples, give a new life to a branch of scholarship which academic fashion has tended to ignore but which in future will doubtless resume its proper place in social anthropology.[148] A similar interest is to be found, to give only one more illustration of this kind, in Kauffmann's studies of the distribution of the thread-cross in Asia and in Africa.[149] These works bring out with a special clarity, made possible by a far better quality and accumulation of evidence than was available in the last century, the compelling character of the problems posed by far-dispersed cultural resemblances. Hocart's particular regional interests are paralleled, incidentally, by the comparative and historical study of the diffusion of Indian tales, dating from as far back as the fourth century B.C., into Southeast Asia and eastern Indonesia,[150] and beyond into the Pacific.

In these and in many other regards it has been abundantly demonstrated that responsible historical reconstructions are

---

problem in Pueblo ethnology, London School of Economics Monographs on Social Anthropology, no. 35 (London: Athlone Press, 1967); cf. the present editor's analytical review of the latter work, in *Sociologus* 18 (1968), 86–87.

148. Carl Schuster, *Joint-Marks: a possible index of cultural contact between America, Oceania and the Far East,* Koninklijk Instituut voor de Tropen, Mededeling 94 (Amsterdam, 1951); idem, "Skin and Fur Mosaics in Prehistoric and Modern Times," in *Festschrift für Ad. E. Jensen* (Munich: Renner, 1964), pp. 559–610.

149. Hans E. Kauffmann, "Das Fadenkreuz," *Ethnologica,* n.s., 2 (1960): 36–69; idem, "Das Fadenkreuz in Afrika," *Paideuma: Mitteilungen zur Kulturkunde* 13 (1967), 76–95; idem, "Das Fadenkreuz, sein Zweck und seine Bedeutung, II," *Ethnologica,* n.s., 4 (1968): 264–313.

150. Rodney Needham, "Jātaka, Pañcatantra, and Kodi Fables," *Bijdragen tot de Taal- , Land- en Volkenkunde,* 116 (1960), 232–62.

not only possible but are indeed becoming more and more feasible as new evidence is uncovered and further connections emerge. This is not a question of opinion, but rests on a great deal of work actually done. It is all the more puzzling a task, therefore, to understand why even the most single-minded functionalist should wish to persuade students of social anthropology that cultural history should be none of their concern. Even a sociologistic definition of social anthropology encounters no great difficulty in this field, for it has been shown persuasively enough (as if it could really be doubted) that modes of social organization can be transmitted, just as can material techniques or symbolic motifs or legendary themes. It is true that in the past certain scholars have gone too far in treating institutions as though they were discrete objects such as the back-loom, the fire-piston, or the outrigger, without sufficient regard to their systematic connections with other institutions and their general context of significance; but there is no need, when assessing the feasibility of a sociological cultural history, to put the worst cast on the issue. For that matter, there is not any need, either, to consider only exotic cultures and alien institutions, for the recent history of imperialism provides a superfluity of precisely documented examples of the transmission of social philosophies and types of organization from Europe to parts of Asia, the Americas, and Africa, where they have been grafted on to a great variety of indigenous societies. The African examples cover a fairly short span of time, but the subjugation of India to a British government constitutes a more substantial test case, and the history of Indonesia presents an excellent experimental range of contacts and developments.

This last example leads us both territorially and temporally in the direction of Hocart's argument. Indonesia was greatly influenced, in religious and social ideas, by India over many centuries before the arrival of the Portuguese, the English, and the Dutch; and the history of this long cultural contact can, as Coedès and others have shown, be traced back to the beginning of the Christian era and even before.[151] This recon-

---

151. G. Coedès, *Les états hindouisés d'Indochine et d'Indonésie*, new ed.,

struction is marked by very different degrees of certainty or probability, according to period, area, and problem, but it is demonstrably a feasible scholarly task.[152] More than this, it is also an essential concern for the social anthropologist who works in this area, for here he constantly encounters traces of Indian institutions, or is at least very likely to do so. He must therefore be able to recognize them for what they are, and if he is to assess their significance he should be able to relate them to the more extensive cultural impact to which they partially testify. Such an obligation is particularly clear in the cases of mystical symbolism and cosmological ideas, in spells, ornamental motifs, sacred edifices, divinatory practices, the plans of cities, or the ritual of monarchy.[153] In this part of the world it is possible to be sure of the fact of Indian cultural influence, largely because of a great deal of research done by historically-minded students of civilization. In Fiji, however, and in other parts of the Pacific, there is no such certainty or clarity on the question of such influence—either from India or from a source common to India and Oceania—

---

rev. (Paris: Boccard, 1964); Paul Wheatley, *The Golden Khersonese: Studies in the historical geography of the Malay Peninsula before A.D. 1500* (Kuala Lumpur: University of Malaya Press, 1961); F. W. Stapel, ed., *Geschiedenis van Nederlandsch-Indië*, 5 vols. (Amsterdam, 1938–40).

152. It may be of some interest in this connection to report that the present editor, by academic title a social anthropologist, has over a number of years brought to a point of advanced compilation an historical and ethnographic study, focusing on the penis-pin and related matters, which attempts a reconstruction extending from India throughout Southeast Asia and Indonesia and as far back in time as the beginning of the Christian era. This circumstance confers no authority, but it does at least mean that the judgments on comparative cultural history which are offered here have been arrived at on the basis of much hard experience. It is easy to pontificate on sound method, and safer to abjure the uncertainties of speculation, but work yields a better instruction. "Qu'il n'y ait discussion des méthodes que de ceux qui trouvent" (Jean-François Revel, *Pourquoi des philosophes* [Paris: Pauvert, 1957], p. 119).

153. The literature is very extensive. See, for example, F. D. K. Bosch, *The Golden Germ: An introduction to Indian symbolism*, Indo-Iranian Monographs, 2 (The Hague: Mouton, 1960); H. G. Quaritch Wales, *The Making of Greater India*, 2d ed., rev. (London: Quaritch, 1961).

because in the main the work has not been done. And it will not be done, of course, until the problems of historical reconstruction in that region are taken more seriously by those with the best command of the ethnographical evidence, i.e., by the social anthropologists. They may find themselves unconvinced by Hocart, but he has at least made a case, and if his arguments are rejected the problems will still remain. When the ritual of Indian monarchy is firmly known to have existed (as in places it still does) in the states of mainland and island Southeast Asia, when a Hindu civilization flourishes on Bali and evidences of Indian ideology and symbolism can be traced through the eastern islands of the archipelago, there is surely every encouragement to look especially hard for whatever attenuated indications may have survived in cultures further to the east.[154] It is perfectly possible, naturally, that there are no historical connections to be established there, but we shall never know until we follow Hocart and try to find them.

The relevance of Southeast Asian studies to the issue of cultural history, and the necessity for a social anthropologist in that area to be in some regards a conventional orientalist, are considerations which may help further to understand the attempted refutation of comparative historical reconstruction. In addition to the rather doctrinaire opposition to conjectural history which is associated with the names of Malinowski and Radcliffe-Brown, and which Evans-Pritchard has done much to combat, the influence of the area in which anthropological critics have happened to work may also be of some importance.

A great deal of ethnographical research has been done, by British social anthropologists in particular, on societies in Africa which have little recorded history and whose diverse traditions have not been ordered, on any large scale, by scholarly collation. There is as yet, correspondingly, no equivalent of the Indonesian histories such as those by Coedès, Wheatley, and a number of distinguished Dutch scholars, works to which

154. For an early attempt to show symbolic relics of Hinduism in New Guinea, see D. W. Horst, *De Rum-Serams op Nieuw-Guinea, of het Hinduisme in het Oosten van onzen Archipel* (Leiden: Brill, 1893). The argument is rather unlikely in places, but at least it explores a possibility which will never be better determined unless such investigations are undertaken.

the social anthropologist at once turns when he embarks on his studies of that area. Admittedly, historical knowledge, both documentary and conjectural, is now being much improved in Africa, but in the formation of current anthropological attitudes towards the past the lack of the normal resources of historical research has apparently had a decided effect. A telling illustration of this is to be found in a recent symposium devoted specifically to history and social anthropology, in which the editor pleads for the mutual relevance of the two disciplines, and also for a modified concept of function.[155] The intention is laudable, but what is interesting is the presumption that there is not such a connection already, in other ethnographical provinces, and that social anthropologists have to be coaxed in the direction of history. The argument indeed makes a case for history in respects where no anthropological student of an historical civilization (e.g., India, China, Indonesia) would at all require persuasion, while on the other hand it urges an importance in the actual engagements and interests of people which any historian would take for granted. The very fact that there should be occasion for an argument of this kind, however welcome and useful it may in fact be, demonstrates a certain estrangement from history. This may be partially explained by a professional commitment to a functionalist doctrine, but it may also very well be the result of the concentration by anthropologists on the study of non-historical cultures. Evans-Pritchard himself is an outstanding proof that this is no absolute determination, but in general it may be thought that the Africanist preponderance among British social anthropologists, and the kind of societies in Africa which they have studied, may have had something to do with an attitude towards the past which is so opposed to Hocart's historical aims.

XIII

The above considerations have had to do with the reconstruction of particular cultural traditions, and it may well be possible to persuade all but the most doctrinaire that this is a rea-

155. I. M. Lewis, ed., *History and Social Anthropology*, A. S. A. Monographs, 7 (London: Tavistock, Publications, 1968), Introduction.

sonable activity. The better documented and the more distinctive an historical basis one starts from, moreover, the greater is the chance of making acceptable conjectures, and it should be possible to induce all but the most positivistic to see some interest in these hypotheses.

But there is another kind of reconstruction, which Hocart also attempts, namely that of an evolutionary or developmental scale which outlines the formation and subsequent changes of institutions and types of society. This common product of an earlier comparative method has become quite discountenanced by modern social anthropologists. As Evans-Pritchard has most clearly stated, the Victorian schemes amounted to little more than hypothetical scales of progress delineating necessary courses of development which could be reduced to general principles or laws; and "a combination of the notion of scientific law and that of progress leads in anthropology . . . to procrustean stages, the presumed inevitability of which gives them a normative character."[156] Happily, however, Hocart did not subscribe to any such absolute doctrine of social evolution. He does, it is true, speak of "stages" in the development of a coordinating system, but these are not presumptive or necessary; they have to be discovered, with the aid of records and comparative research, by working backwards from known forms of society. He also argues that specialization is the result of man's purpose, and the purpose is an aspect of a contingent conception of the good life; it is not necessarily progressive in any other normative sense. Hocart makes this clear when he writes that specialization gives a better immediate chance in the struggle for life, "whatever the *ultimate* effect may be" (p. 298). In other words, the conception and the process may thus both be inimical to the long-run survival or well-being of the society. This is no doctrine of progress.[157] More than this, there are in fact hints in this book that Hocart regarded the evolution he sketched as being actually detrimental to man's best interests. For example,

156. E. E. Evans-Pritchard, *Essays in Social Anthropology*, pp. 16, 17.
157. It is true that Hocart entitled one of his books *The Progress of Man* (London: Methuen, 1933), but that work is nevertheless equally free of the moralistic view in question.

specialization in an industrial society means that there is a fragmentation of a person's occupations, an excessive application to narrow tasks, a sense of frustration during work, and an immoderate recourse to compensatory satisfactions. "The pursuit of life is no longer a wide all-embracing exercise, but an alternation of limited reactions" (p. 298). In addition, the proliferation of offices and functions which Hocart seeks to establish is not regarded by him as a necessary process. On the contrary, as he wrote elsewhere in the same year, "When we come to think of it why should a custom develop in any direction at all? Why should it not stay as it is?"[158] Or again, "The real problem is not why customs persist, but why they ever change."[159] In this he supports Ratzel's view of the normally uninventive nature of man: neither a particular form of change, according to this view, nor change itself is to be taken as necessary. Finally, the course of social evolution which Hocart sketches is not intended to correspond to individual events. In outlining the "growth of the state," he carefully points out that the diagrams especially introduce a definiteness of detail which is certainly not in the evidence; and it may never be there, he continues, for "it is not the purpose of the comparative anatomy of society to reconstitute the past in all its details, but to sum up growth in formulae" (p. 291). In this preponderant respect Hocart thus entirely observes what Dumézil has argued are

> the limits of comparative method, in particular what ought to be its golden rule, namely that it permits the recognition and a clearer view of structures of thought but not the reconstitution of events.[160]

Far from continuing an outmoded evolutionism, therefore, Hocart expressly avoids those very aims and procedures which brought it into such discredit.

The focus of our examination has so far been on reconstruction, and the defence of Hocart has thus argued for Ratzel's

---

158. *The Life-giving Myth*, p. 140.
159. *Ibid.*, p. 219.
160. Georges Dumézil, *La religion romaine archaïque* (Paris, 1966), p. 8. By "structures of thought" he means here systems of ideas.

side of the debate; but the case for Bastian's *Elementargedanken*, or for their modern equivalents in "structuralism" has not yet been presented. There is no need to do so in much detail because in general the theoretical disposition of social anthropologists today is so decidedly in favor of synchronic analysis. But a reconsideration of Hocart's work, and of the "historical" tradition to which it belongs, raises a doubt concerning the grounds for this present commitment.

The structuralist tradition can be traced back certainly to the establishment of the *Année sociologique* at the end of the nineteenth century, and to the earlier writings of students of Australian section systems, i.e., back to the days of Bastian and Ratzel and even before. Yet it is at least a question whether there is not a curious contrast when the advances made by historical studies are compared with the attempts to formulate structural hypotheses. In spite of the current slump in historical or evolutionary reconstructions, a steady progress in knowledge and speculation continues to be made. With every investigation into cultural history, diffusionist explanations of cultural similarities in far-separated parts of the world become increasingly acceptable or at any rate plausible. But it may be argued whether any comparable progress has been made in the investigation of innate proclivities of thought, either as content, like the *Elementargedanken,* or as relational modes of representation, like that of opposition. The sociological and categorical analysis of institutions and of systems of collective representations has certainly been much improved in recent decades,[161] yet when any particular resemblance between cultures has to be accounted for it becomes evident how very limited, to say the least, is the explanatory power of structural comparison.

For example, Hocart takes as evidence of an archaic connection between India and the Pacific the presence of two-section systems in both South India and Fiji, a proof which would probably not be assented to by most social anthropologists today. Since that argument was written, in 1925, we have come

161. Cf. introduction to E. Durkheim and M. Mauss, *Primitive Classification,* ed. and trans. Rodney Needham (Chicago: University of Chicago Press, 1963), pp. xl–xliv.

to know of structurally similar or even identical systems in areas so remote from each other as Australia, the Himalayas, and South America, so that it would not seem at all probable, in the common view, that they should all be survivals from a common original form of society. Yet when we look for an alternative, non-historical explanation, there is nothing decisive to be adduced from the complementary tradition of structuralist research. There are intriguing hypotheses about certain features, both conscious and unconscious, of the mind, but it has never yet been explained why these should continue to manifest themselves in social forms among certain populations and not among others. This is not to say that there are no grounds for reasonable conjecture, specifically about the varieties and the distribution of two-section systems, but until these have actually been worked out in as much definite and convincing detail of demonstration as is the accepted standard in historical research, then it must be acknowledged that Hocart has been given no real argument against his own presumption. It is true that in this instance he himself does not work out an argument to prove a common origin, but the case is nevertheless plausible. Such connections have certainly been established, and over distances just as great, in other regards, so why should there not be an historical answer in this case also? If scapulimancy, why not prescriptive alliance? At present we just do not know the answer, but then we ought not to carry on as though we already knew the kind of answer that it would have to be.

So also with the rituals of kingship. Fortes agreeably confirms Hocart's conclusions that installation rites have much the same structure, use similar procedures, and serve broadly the same ends in all societies, yet he expressly adds that we need not follow him in attributing this basic uniformity to a common and unique historical origin. "Not common historical origins but common structural requirements . . . underlie these uniformities."[162] The occasion of this declaration (viz.,

162. Fortes, "Installation Ceremonies" p. 19. He mentions also certain "universal cultural resources for the expression of these requirements," but since they are by stipulation both universal and cultural they do not affect the structural point.

a presidential address) would have precluded a full analysis, but Hocart would doubtless respond, all the same, that until he had been shown just what these structural requirements were he had every right to maintain his own opinion.

Even if we were to take as a test case an institution which is far more general than either prescriptive alliance or installation ceremonies, a structuralist interpretation would be likely to encounter the same kind of check. For example, transition rites are practically universal, and their distribution and common forms would seem hardly explainable by the assertion that all civilization is one. Van Gennep maintained indeed that they had a necessary (i.e., logical) character, and that they exhibited a constancy and rhythm which permitted the formulation of a law; and this, he thought, rendered useless "those outworn discussions about the possibility of borrowings and migrations."[163] But the constancy and rhythm are features which can explain nothing until they have themselves been explained, and in spite of the abundant confirmation of van Gennep's tripartite scheme (i.e., his "law") by practically all ethnographers since, this has still not been done.

Finally, to demonstrate that an institution was indeed quite universal would not alone prove an innate basis in the mind, or make supererogatory an investigation into its possible evolution and its history. Hocart, after all, never denied the importance of discovering a common structure; he was a structuralist, all right, only for him "a common structure is proof of common descent" (p. 81). There are many sound arguments and demonstrations in favor of this principle of interpretation; but structural analysis will have to do very much better than it has done if it is to arrive at another kind of determination which will make as great an appeal to the understanding. In any case, historical research and conjectures about origins and courses of evolution can never be superseded by structural analysis or by the determination of innate mental characteristics. It will always be essential in comparative studies to begin with historical considerations—and only if these fail to supply

---

163. A. van Gennep, *Religions, moeurs et légendes: Essais d'ethnographie et de linguistique* (Paris: Mercure de France, 1908), p. 125.

an answer will it be justifiable to resort to other factors such as "fundamental structures of the human mind."

Nevertheless, as far as *Kings and Councillors* is concerned, some of Hocart's most interesting observations touch on features of thought, even if as usual he makes only rapid remarks. He proposes, for example, that there is a similarity between the evolution of the state and that of thought. In the development of the state the ritual and its imagery lose their prominence, and instead the function of kingship comes to the fore; this is given an abstract representation and, being no longer confined to its original setting, is extended to administrative offices and to other areas of social life. Similarly, in the evolution of thought and its expression man begins by putting together representations, and only gradually does he disentangle relations and modes, to which he eventually gives separate expression; but in expressing relations man has to make use of existing material, namely the representations, which are then purged of all substance and thus become the vehicles of abstractions (p. 154).

A related interest is to be found in Hocart's contention that "conscious purpose precedes the adaptation of behaviour, and the adaptation of behaviour is followed by adaptation of structure" (p. 299); in other words, that values and the ideas in which these are expressed have a constant primacy over social action and must therefore claim the first attention of the social anthropologist.[164] More specifically, also, and touching upon an issue which is very much to the fore today, there is Hocart's concentration (in ch. 20) on dual organization and the classificatory principle of dichotomy.

> This raises the question whether this dichotomy is traditional or innate in man, whether it is merely an old habit persisting age after age, or whether it does not lie deeper in human nature, as a law which it obeys in common with the rest of nature (p. 289).

The question is certainly fundamental, and Hocart's response is perspicacious. He concludes that perhaps it is a law of na-

---

164. Cf. the editor's "Terminology and Alliance," *Sociologus* 16 (1966): 141–57 (see esp. pp. 156–57); 17 (1967); 39–54 (see esp. pp. 47–50).

ture, "but that is not sufficient to explain dual organization, for dichotomy need not produce a pair, except fleetingly as a first step" (p. 289). The interest of the question has since been repeatedly demonstrated, in a substantial number of intensive analyses which have far superseded Hocart's explorations,[165] but his nagging doubt concerning the possibility of an innate proclivity of the mind which stops dead as soon as it has achieved an institutionalized form has yet to be decisively allayed. Dual classification, of all things, ought surely to decide the issue between culture history and mental structuralism, but even on this topic there is still no answer which would satisfy Hocart's forthright demands for proof.

XIV

There is, however, another kind of interest in this aspect of Hocart's work. At many points in his writings there are very marked similarities to the interests, style of thought, and conclusions of French scholars, chiefly the members of the *Année sociologique* school, whose enterprises—if not all of their sociological premises—he could be expected to have found particularly congenial, yet his failure to take advantage of their works is almost equally marked.

Marcel Mauss actually wrote of his "French sympathies" for Sanskritists and Indianists, "and also for the French sociologists."[166] But, as Pocock well observes, "Mauss's politeness here oversteps itself for it draws our attention to the astonishing fact that Hocart nowhere in his work [viz., *Les Castes*] makes any reference to Bouglé. . . ."[167] The sad, and curious, fact of the matter is that for the most part, in the generality of his publications and not only in his book on caste, Hocart either ignores the French investigators whose work was related to his own or he gives them a curt dismissal.

A prominent instance is that in *Kings and Councillors* he argues throughout for an evolution from segmentary to cen-

165. See, e.g., Rodney Needham, ed., *Right and Left: essays on dual symbolic classification* (Chicago: University of Chicago Press; forthcoming).
166. Introduction to Hocart, *Les Castes*, p. b.
167. Pocock, "Hocart on Caste," p. 45.

tralized forms of society (pp. 38–40, 83, 161), yet nowhere does he make any reference to Durkheim's *De la division du travail social* (1893). He deals at length with the symbolism of space (ch. 19), yet does not even mention the pioneering observations on this topic made by Durkheim and Mauss in their famous essay "De quelques formes primitives de classification."[168] In *The Progress of Man*, he stresses the "momentous" importance of exchange in the evolution of culture, but his references (which include *Argonauts of the Western Pacific*) make no place for Mauss's "Essai sur le don" (1925). In writing about the mind, he does mention Lévy-Bruhl, but only to ascribe to him, by an astounding misrepresentation, the thesis that "savages cannot reason."[169] Van Gennep, on the organization of rites, is noticed, but Hocart maintains against him that since all rites are transition rites there is no need to distinguish a special class of *rites de passage*.[170] Later, too, he attempts a sharper refutation, claiming that van Gennep's classification is pointless, that it stresses what is inessential and so obscures the real nature of the rites, and that the term *"rites de passage"* is identified with "a false psychological standpoint."[171] Finally, Hocart was very early acquainted with the work of Dumézil, whose book *Le Festin d'immortalité* (1924) he cites in his monograph on kingship;[172] but in his introduction to anthropology, where he again refers to the same work, he says of it, with a rather slighting stress, merely that it is an *"attempt"* and a "step in the right direction."[173]

The reason for this treatment of his French colleagues could certainly not have been an inadequate acquaintance with what they had done, for his French was perfect, he does cite some

168. *Année sociologique* 6 (1903), 1–72; English ed., *Primitive Classification.*
169. *The Progress of Man*, p. 27.
170. Ibid., p. 166.
171. *Social Origins*, pp. 36–37.
172. *Kingship* (1927), p. 63 n. 2.
173. *The Progress of Man*, p. 226. The assessment is not, however, as derogatory as it may appear, for Dumézil himself was to write of that period of his researches that neither the method nor the results were worth much, and that *Le festin d'immortalité* in particular was "quite unfruitful" (*Les dieux des Indo-Européens*, p. 39).

of them, and he was, after all, "a scholar, even if an erratic one."[174] There is nothing that erratic about his position, though, for the tenor of his comments and of his silences as well is pretty constant. Nor is the positivism of some of the French the reason, although he would have been out of sympathy with this philosophical stance, for there are many points in their work which he could nonetheless have related to his own without necessarily subscribing that inclination. There was in any case not such a consistency in them, nor such a trenchant division between the French sociologists and himself, for in his concern for the moral quality of social life they had one value at least in common. In *Kings and Councillors*, for instance, Hocart explicitly deplores as the "tragedy of our civilization" the fragmentation and narrowness of people's lives (p. 298), i.e., the decline from an earlier condition of total implication in social existence such as he had glimpsed in Fiji and clearly admired. Similarly, Marcel Mauss, in his essay on the gift, plainly decries the commercialization and individualization of modern economic society, and he concludes his sociological study of exchange with moral considerations bearing upon peace, well-being, and the enrichment of life.[175] It is well known, too, that Durkheim and his colleagues felt and expressed a concern with society which was by no means entirely detached and scientific.[176] The answer to Hocart's attitude has to be sought, it would appear, not in his ideas but in the circumstances of his life and in their effect on his character.[177]

It will be remembered that for almost the length of his career, and in spite of the unusual breadth of his experience and the volume and quality of his scholarly publications, Hocart held no academic appointment. He was by all accounts

---

174. E. E. Evans-Pritchard, review of Hocart, *Social Origins*, p. 591.

175. *Année sociologique*, seconde série, 1 (1925): 30–186; reprinted in Marcel Mauss, *Sociologie et anthropologie*, 3d ed. (Paris: Presses Universitaires de France, 1966), pp. 143–279.

176. Cf. E. E. Evans-Pritchard, introduction to Robert Hertz, *Death and The Right Hand*, p. 18 n. 2.

177. The editor, to his regret, has had no personal acquaintance of Hocart.

a truly modest man, and although he was obviously convinced of the rightness of his views his confidence rested on public argument and not on self-esteem. But it must have been galling for him, all the same, to have to remain outside the universities where his talents could have been best exploited and his ideas more effectively heard. It is true that in the twenties and thirties there were very few anthropological posts to be had in Britain, but there were some, and Hocart was not given one. There were in any case other academic possibilities; the title of the post was not important, but only the proper employment of an interesting man.

It is no wonder, therefore, that there should sometimes be a certain edge to Hocart's references to academics. With his mere allusion to "our intellectuals" (p. 35) a distance is created. In the social sciences, he asserts, the readiness to discuss a hypothesis with an open mind is "an uncommon virtue" (p. 4); historians "will not read anything that is not literature" (p. 21); and orientalists "are immersed in grammar and literature, and are not much interested in social organization" (p. 184). Elsewhere, too, we find the same ring to his observations: historians take no notice of "anything that is not dead and buried;"[178] "the sociological classifications of the schools" only prevent the student of Fijian customs from understanding what the people are talking about;[179] and for "specialists," of any academic kind, "one inaccuracy outweighs a multitude of sound ideas."[180] When he writes that a "forlorn hope must go forward to be shot down by the opposing forces of narrow specialism,"[181] it is clear under which banner he places himself and with what resignation he contemplates his own lot.

It would be a mistake to regard most of the above comments as merely personal responses on Hocart's part to his private situation, for some of them at any rate strike fairly home, but in a biographical setting they do appear nonetheless to betray a sense of justifiable grievance. It is not enough, then, for us to understand why he wrote as he sometimes did, or

178. *The Progress of Man*, pp. vii–viii.
179. *The Northern States of Fiji*, p. 25.
180. *Social Origins*, p. 11.
181. *The Progress of Man*, p. vi.

xci

simply to deplore that such a "man of ideas"[182] was not better encouraged to develop and to discipline his talents. It is to our own advantage, and to the potential benefit of scholarship, that we also take special care to extract and apply the lessons of Hocart's life. Without knowing more about the prevailing circumstances we cannot go far towards isolating the factors then at work, but it is clear that to a serious degree Hocart's remarkable abilities were wasted and diverted. Perhaps he could at times be an uncomfortable intellectual neighbour, but universities are not supposed to be shelters for the susceptibilities. He sometimes put forward theories which others were likely to consider wild, but the academics could surely have found arguments to temper his more extreme conclusions. If he was not familiar with the best sources, or relied on authorities whose judgment was less respectable than he knew, then they could have guided him.[183] Universities exist for the advancement of learning, but Hocart's case prompts some uneasiness on this score. His asperity towards academics is not only a clue to a certain feature of his writings; it is of graver importance as an indication of a tendency to decline from that high purpose.

If we ask ourselves what Hocart's reception would be today, or with how scrupulous a judgment of scholarly merit alone we should weigh the claims of an equally unconventional spiritual descendant, there are grounds for some faltering of confidence. It is a fact of common, if dismayed, observation that universities can on occasion, in their less reputable actions, find posts for dullards, placemen, and time-servers; favoritism, nepotism, and what might be called a perverted fraternalism are not entirely unknown; and the forms and institutions of higher learning may in these regards be twisted to discreditable personal ends having nothing to do with the teaching of knowledge or the prosecution of research. At worst, what should be a community of scholars may, it has

---

182. E. E. Evans-Pritchard, review of *Social Origins*, p. 591.
183. ". . . What are experts there for unless it is to guide the inexpert? If they are truly expert we are safe in sticking closely to their translations and commentaries; if we are not safe they cannot claim to be experts" (Hocart, *Caste*, p. 69).

been charged, sink into a "système . . . substituant au travail d'équipe la complaisance mutuelle, à la recherche collective la complicité dans le privilège."[184] Such lapses certainly occur, as we all know, and they are of course deplorable; but they are also readily understandable, and to a degree they must be reckoned normal and even acceptable. For it is a condition of the best intellectual work that it be done under as little direction, constraint, and surveillance as is reasonably consistent with the organization of academic communities; and this desirable liberty naturally gives play to laxity, or even to corruption, as well as to the exercise of original enquiry. The issue in any particular case, therefore, is how high a price in defection shall be conceded in order to preserve an invaluable freedom. Moreover, it is not always so plainly the dereliction of academic probity which is responsible for bad appointments, for universities may in good faith be taken in by "the highly polished minds of accomplished frauds,"[185] and we may be inclined to wonder whether even the proudest and most ancient institutions have managed wholly to preserve themselves from intruders of this kind. But these realizations still do not allay the doubts prompted by Hocart's case. We may grant that bad men do get appointed by universities, sometimes over the heads of better, and that such persons tend thereafter to engineer the admission of even worse; but this does not explain what flaw there is in our system which can compound such disgraces by also keeping out those who have shown themselves to be excellent. Hocart, after all, was no mute, inglorious Mauss, languishing unknown because he had neither the means nor the occasion to display his quality. He was a man of very pronounced capacities and of more than respectable published accomplishments, someone who Mauss himself thought had led "a fine scholarly career,"[186] but all the same he did not until practically too late receive a teaching position and the security to get on with his work.

184. J.-F. Revel, *Pourquoi des philosophes*, p. 57.
185. Guy Davenport, trans., *Carmina Archilochi: The fragments of Archilochos* (Berkeley and Los Angeles: University of California Press, 1964), p. 26 (fr. 62).
186. Introduction to *Les Castes*, p. f.

If such neglect were peculiar to Hocart's case the lesson would be sharp enough, but what is far more worrying is that he was preceded by others in a similar position, and their careers, taken together, seem to indicate a more serious and continuing defect in the organization of higher education. In anthropology alone there are three notable cases of the kind, covering the hundred years of its effective development and its establishment in the universities. They are well worth an apprehensive glance.

J. F. McLennan (1827–81), to begin with, was a most original thinker and an assiduous scholar. He wrote an early classic in anthropology, *Primitive Marriage* (1865), which in spite of the fact that it is mistaken at practically all points of its argument is now firmly established in the professional literature and forms an indispensable part of every student's education, and he also initiated the study of totemism and was responsible for numerous other investigations of solid worth and theoretical interest. He wished at one time to give up his legal practice in favor of anthropology, and he much desired a post at Cambridge. Lewis H. Morgan, when he visited England, approached Sir Henry Maine in this connection, and suggested that McLennan should be proposed for such an appointment. But it never come about, and the chief reason conjectured is that McLennan's very dedication to scholarly argument, as well as the boldness of his ideas, made him too contentious a character for an academic position.[187]

The next case is that of Charles Staniland Wake (1835–1910), a solicitor who over fifty years published a weighty series of books and papers which were, to claim no more, well up to the academic standards of nineteenth-century anthropology. In his chief work, furthermore, namely *The Development of Marriage and Kinship*, he cogently set to rights the opposed theories of such prominent figures as Morgan and McLennan, and he arrived at analytical positions which are

187. Editor's introduction, by P. G. Rivière, to J. F. McLennan, *Primitive Marriage*, new ed. (Chicago: University of Chicago Press, 1970). The academic world was not, however, uniquely purblind; Tylor later reported that the immediate and "natural" consequence of the publication of *Primitive Marriage* was to lose McLennan half his legal briefs.

of continued interest and theoretical relevance today.[188] He had every title, therefore, to the respect of his contemporaries in the universities, but they ignored him. While Radcliffe-Brown, for one, held a fellowship at Cambridge, Wake was reduced to the menial occupation of clerk in the Field Museum; while dons now long and duly forgotten were comfortably esconced in their colleges, Wake was dying in penury in a mean Chicago lodging house. It is not possible to make out why a man of such scholarly commitment and demonstrated attainments encountered so shabby a fate, but the fact remains disturbingly plain that Wake was shunned and abandoned by those whose avowed duty it was to nurture that subject to which he made his cogent and memorable contributions.

The third example is that of Arnold van Gennep (1873–1957). His treatment is even more dejecting. He was a man of quite outstanding intelligence, enthusiastic scholarship, and disciplined imagination; he worked with scarcely paralleled zeal throughout a long life; and he made a classical contribution to the study of society and collective representations with the publication in 1909 of *Les Rites de passage*. Yet, with one short exception early in his career, he was (as in effect it seems) resolutely kept out of any university appointment, and he was forced to waste his fine spirit making translations of other men's books and doing hackwork for publishers.[189] Although he did more for scholarship outside the universities than many professors had ever done in them, he was offered no fit employment and received little useful encouragement in his work.

Hocart's career is thus by no means singular, but it becomes only the more perturbing in its implications when it is considered against this background. It is a grim lesson of these lives that innovatory thought and dedication to scholarship are not always paramount in our universities; and it is an ur-

188. (London: George Redway, 1889; new ed., with intro. by Rodney Needham, Chicago: University of Chicago Press, 1967). The new edition contains, at pp. xliii–xlvii, an impressive list of Wake's writings.
189. See A. van Gennep, *The Semi-Scholars*, ed. trans., and intro. by Needham. Editor's introduction, pp. x–xi, xviii.

gent inference that we need constantly to be alert against the repetition of such damaging misprisals of the talented. Doubtless it is only in an ideal world that even a great university could always engage or retain only the clever and diligent, while sternly discharging the incompetent and the idle; but these four cases, in a series and within a relatively small subject, seem to indicate that something more than occasional errors of academic judgment has gone seriously amiss. If there is any continuing factor responsible, we shall not be in a position to bring about a general improvement until we have determined what it is. One clear feature common to the cases of McLennan, Wake, van Gennep, and Hocart, and what is perhaps the decisive factor as far as they are concerned, is that they were all mavericks. There is little doubt, at any rate, that the more staid, unoriginal, and unproductive members of any faculty would have been disagreeably affected by their vigorous incursion. But we, for our part, have to make up our minds whether we really want our universities to be universities or not. If we do, we cannot afford to repeat such deleterious rejections, and certainly not on such a petty ground. History, as well as conscience, teaches us that with each appointment we have the choice between making a university nearer to what it ought ideally to be, or permitting a further deterioration into complacent mediocrity.

Another lesson which we may draw from an examination of Hocart's life, and one which is more readily realizable, is to put our faith in exemplars rather than in institutions. If the organization of higher learning can operate defectively, at least there is no reason why our judgment of intellectual excellence should also be flawed. Hocart, for all his sad biography, yet survives his detractors and supplanters in the qualities which are to be found in his work. Admittedly, we cannot make a practical application of these virtues; we cannot become imaginative by appreciating his imagination, or clearsighted or bold or radical simply by remarking that he was all of these. But we can surely try to encourage a more liberal and fertile style of investigation in social anthropology by turning students, or at least those who are not already too set or malformed in their ideas, away from the banalities and shuffling compromises of the textbook, "cemetery of common-places, the crossroads of platitude,"[190] and more in the direction of those adventures of the mind such as Hocart exemplified and for which a university is the proper place. In social anthropology of all subjects, as he constantly illustrated, there can be no room for orthodoxy, for a predetermined conception of what questions may be asked, what interests are respectable, what analogies may be employed, or what must invariably be conformed to as sound method. The boundaries of explanation will never be charted except by launching uninhibited sallies and venturesome reconnaissances beyond them.[191] Problems will not emerge automatically from information, let alone from dim generalities about other cultures, but will be formulated only by genuinely curious questions about social life—and without such questions "we are in danger of falling into mere empiricism, one field study after another adding to the number of known facts, but uninspired and uninspiring."[192] As for all the injunctions, finally, about how research has to be done, there is little doubt that ultimately Hocart would have agreed with Marcel Granet that "La méthode, c'est le chemin, *après* qu'on l'a parcouru."[193]

In these respects Hocart presents an uncommon demonstration that originality and scholarship, imagination and proof, are not incompatible. It is true that not even his most devoted admirer would wish to claim that his results were always, or even usually, correct, but that is not the decisive test. It is clearly a hard saying for some, but it really is not crucial whether all of Hocart's ideas were right or not. In their literal acceptation, indeed, his theories may not fare much better now than they did when he first propounded them; for that matter, it is even possible that "Hocart himself did not take

190. J. F. Revel, *Pourquoi des philosophes*, p. 56. Revel's scathing description actually refers to modern French academic philosophy, but it attaches with some aptness to certain didactic exercises in social anthropology also.
191. Cf. C. S. Wake, *Development of Marriage and Kinship*, editor's introduction, pp. xvi–xvii.
192. E. E. Evans-Pritchard, introduction to R. Hertz, *Death and the Right Hand*, p. 24.
193. Marcel Granet, quoted in Georges Dumézil, *Mitra-Varuna*, p. 12.

some of [his] hypotheses seriously."[194] But they are nonetheless rewarding in their brilliant power to stimulate thought about topics of enduring interest and undoubted importance. In Hocart, challenge is the thing, not a safe consensus; the value of his work is determined largely by what we ourselves are capable of in our responses to his galvanic probes into the forms and evolution of human experience and into "the meaning of it all."[195]

The length and the varied character of this introduction, superficial though much of it has had to be, may have indicated something of the range of intellectual responses that Hocart can call forth; but in the end these analytical concerns are of far less significance than the temper of the man and the moral inspiration of the personal example that he set:

> Hocart was the ideal type of scholar. He bore profound learning lightly. . . . He did not acquire knowledge to advance himself, but because he had the true scientist's craving to understand the causes of things. . . . All who knew Hocart were struck at once with his entire freedom from any kind of pretentiousness, a quality he detested, and with his intellectual integrity and independence.[196]

These moving words, uttered by so eminent and well placed a judge, depict indeed an ideal, and to some of us at least they will appear the highest estimation of character that a scholar might ever hope for. But even such laudatory phrases are more than matched, in an exotic idiom, by the epitome recently pronounced by a former assistant of Hocart's in Ceylon: "Hocart was not a man but a Bodhisattva."[197]

XV

This edition has been prepared from Hocart's own copy of *Kings and Councillors*, kindly lent by the present Lord Raglan. The text and index have been reset, and the occasion has been taken to correct various misprints in the original, but no other

194. E. E. Evans-Pritchard, review of *Social Origins*, p. 591.
195. *Social Origins*, p. 10.
196. E. E. Evans-Pritchard, Hocart obituary, p. 131.
197. D. T. Devendra to editor, 16 October 1968.

editorial changes have been made. Hocart's copy is inter-leaved, and he has added in manuscript approximately 184 additional references and quotations in Greek, Latin, English, French, German, Fijian, and Arabic. These notes, however, are all intended to be confirmatory only, and since none of them changes the argument they have not been incorporated or otherwise taken into account.

The portrait photograph which has been placed as frontis-piece was made by Payne Jenkins, Tunbridge Wells, Kent, in July 1930, when Hocart was forty-seven years of age.

An appendix on parallels between Indian and Greek culture, bearing expressly on the argument of *Kings and Councillors*, has been taken from *Social Origins*, by permission of the pub-lishers, and has been inserted after the additional notes which follow the text.

The idea of bringing out a new edition of this work was first conceived in consultation with Professor E. E. Evans-Pritchard, who is especially thanked for contributing a fore-word. The project was warmly supported also by the late Lord Raglan. It gave him considerable pleasure that his old friend should receive this new recognition, and it was intended, be-fore his much regretted death in 1964, that he himself would collaborate in the undertaking. If it were customary to dedi-cate an edition, this one would be inscribed to him in vicarious gratitude for his many and selfless labors on Hocart's behalf.

Grateful acknowledgement is made to the following for their kindness in reading this introduction and for the benefit of their advice: Dr. J. K. Campbell, Professor Meyer Fortes, Pro-fessor C. von Fürer-Haimendorf, Dr. Francis Korn, and Dr. E. R. Leach.

R. N.

University of Oxford

Kings and Councillors

Preface

*Scientists delight not in abundance of material;
they rejoice only in the excellence of their
experiments.*
Jabir Ibn Hayyan

THE PRESENT work definitely abjures the method of Tylor and his successors, the composite picture made up of scattered fragments. It takes peoples as a whole, even as the zoologist studies his animals as a whole. Like the zoologist it dissects its specimens and lays bare the structure of different societies.

This intensive anatomy means limitation in extent. It is better to do a few societies thoroughly than a vast number superficially.

If we have the patience for this minute dissection, homologies will soon emerge which escape the collector of scraps. On the other hand apparent homologies turn out not to be homologies, but superficial resemblances. If we take these homologies one by one we shall be forced to the conclusion that the machinery of government was blocked out in society long before the appearance of government as we now understand it. In other words the functions now discharged by king, prime minister, treasury, public works, are not the original ones; they may account for the present form of these institutions, but not for their original appearance. These were originally part, not of a system of government, but of an organization to promote life, fertility, prosperity by transferring life from objects abounding in it to objects deficient in it.

It is only by degrees that this organization has enlarged its sphere of action and modified its functions till it has become what it is now, a machinery to coordinate the activities of the community.

There still survive many societies that have no regulating body to speak of, just as there are animal forms without a nervous system. These societies get on quite well without a government, as the animalcules get on without a brain or

3

nerves. There are other societies where one group gradually absorbs the ritual functions formerly discharged by all; that group is thus placed in a position to become the regulating organ, when such an organ is required: it becomes government.

This is a work of pure science, for pure science must precede applied science. But pure science inevitably must influence practice if it accustoms us to look at the societies we dominate, not as schoolchildren to be educated, but as organisms that have evolved along different lines from the same starting point, which are differently adapted, but not on that account less successfully adapted. We shall then come to think it just as absurd to Europeanize them as to insist on a dog always walking on his hind legs.

The method applied is that of comparative philology into which I was initiated by that remarkable man, the late Prof. Joseph Wright.

For the art of studying living societies I am indebted to the late Dr. W. H. R. Rivers, and for the means to Exeter and Jesus Colleges, Oxford, to the Royal Society, and to the Percy Sladen Trust.

I owe thanks to Dr. W. J. Perry for guidance through the literature, especially of America; but still more for being always ready to discuss a hypothesis with an open mind, an uncommon virtue in the social sciences.

Prof. H. J. Rose has ever been ready to put at my disposal his vast knowledge of the classics, and Mr. H. G. Richardson his equally deep knowledge of the Middle Ages.

To Prof. H. A. Harris I owe illuminating points of view in comparative anatomy.

If I have been able to include a few modern Egyptian facts after a short residence, it is due to the good offices of Major J. W. Macpherson, Mr. A. W. Wildridge, and Ali Ahmed Isaa Effendi. To the Egyptian Government I owe thanks for their generous assistance both in research and publication.

Mr. G. A. Cheshire has kindly read through the first version and made useful suggestions. My wife revised the second and has contributed topical instances, which are not the least important since it is the present we are seeking to explain. The final form is indebted to the criticisms of Lord Raglan.

Chapter 1 is reproduced with alterations from Psyche Annual for 1933 by kind permission of the editor.

The Greek, Latin, Sanskrit, and Pali texts have been consulted in the original tongue.

Abbreviations and Bibliography

Abbreviation	*Explanation*
Ait Br.	*Aitareya Brahmana.* Ed. Th. Aufrecht, Bonn, 1879. Trsl. by A. B. Keith in *Rigveda Brahmanas,* Harvard Oriental Series, Cambridge, Mass., 1920.
Anguttara	Pali Text Society's Publications.
Arunta, The	By B. Spencer and F. J. Gillen, London, 1927.
Ayscough	*The Symbolism of the Forbidden City,* by Miss Florence Ayscough, *Journ. Roy. Asiatic Soc., North China Branch.* 1933, vol. LXI, 111.
B.A.E.	Bureau of American Ethnology, Washington.
Bloch, M.	*Les Rois Thaumaturges,* Strasbourg, 1924.
Breasted, *History.*	*History of Egypt,* by J. H. Breasted, 2nd ed., London, 1912.
Breasted, *Records.*	*Ancient Records of Egypt,* by J. H. Breasted, 5 vols., Chicago, 1906.
Brih. Ar. Up.	*Brihad Aranyaka Unpanishad.* Ed. O. Böthlingk with German trsl., St. Petersburg, 1889. Trsl. by Robert Ernest Hume in *The Thirteen Principal Upanishads,* 2nd ed., Oxford, 1931.
C. J. Sc.	*Ceylon Journal of Science,* sect. G. (Archaeology and Ethnology), London, Dulau and Co., 32 Old Bond St.
Cult of the Dead.	*The Cult of the Dead in Eddystone Island,* by A. H. Hocart, J.R.A.I., 1922, pp. 71 and 259.
Daremberg et Saglio.	*Dictionnaire des antiquités grecques et latines.* Paris, 1873–1919.

7

Abbreviation	*Explanation*
Digha.	Pali Text Society's Publications.
Ep. Z. (*Epigraphia Zeylanica*)	(A record of Ceylon Inscriptions) issued by the Archaeological Survey of Ceylon, Clarendon Press, Oxford.
Forde	*Ethnography of the Yuma Indians*, by C. Daryll Forde, Univ. California Publications in Archaeology and Ethnology, vol. 28, p. 214.
Foucher	*L'Art Gréco-Bouddhique du Gandhara*, by A. Foucher, Paris, 1905– .
Gilbert	*Griechische Staatsaltertümer*, by G. Gilbert, Leipzig, 1881.
Gibbon	*Decline and Fall of the Roman Empire*, Bury's ed.
H.H.	*Homeric Hymns.*
Hako, The	*A Pawnee Ceremony*, by Alice C. Fletcher, 22nd Ann. Rep., B.A.E., Washington, 1904.
Howitt	*Native Tribes of South-Eastern Australia*, by A. W. Howitt, London, 1904.
Hymns A & M.	*Hymns Ancient and Modern for Use in the Services of the Church.*
Jataka	Buddhist Birth-Stories, ed. V. Fausböll, London 1875– . Trsl. edited by Cowell, London, 1875– .
Jochelson, W.	*The Koryak*, being vol. VI of the Publications of the Jessup North Pacific Expedition, Memoirs of the Amer. Mus. of Nat. Hist.
Joinville	Jean Sir de Joinville, *Histoire de St. Louis*, ed. N. de Wailly, 2nd ed., Paris, 1874.
J.R.A.I.	Journal of the Royal Anthropological Institute.

Abbreviation	Explanation
Kautilya	*Arthasastra.*
Kingship	By A. M. Hocart, Oxford, 1927.
Labyrinth, The	ed. S. H. Hooke, London, 1935.
Lau Islands	By A. M. Hocart, Honolulu, 1929.
Manu	*Manava Dharmsastra* or *The Laws of Manu.* Ed. J. Jolly; trsl. by A. C. Burnell and E. W. Hopkins; both in Trubner's Oriental Series, London, 1884 and 1887.
Meek	*A Sudanese Kingdom* by C. K. Meek, London, 1931.
Mhvs.	*Mahavamsa,* including the *Culavamsa,* (Sinhalese chronicle) ed. and trsl. by W. Geiger for the Pali Text Society, Oxford.
Muir, J.	*Original Sanskrit Texts,* 5 vols., 2nd ed., London, 1868–1874.
Nala	*Episode of Nala* from the *Mahabharata.* Ed. Julius Eggeling, London.
Native Gazette	*Na Mata,* official vernacular organ of the government of Fiji, Suva.
Nirukta	By Yaska. Ed. Rudolph Roth, Göttingen 1852. Trsl. by Lakshman Sarup as *The Nighanta and the Nirukta,* Oxford, 1920.
Northern Tribes	*of Central Australia,* by B. Spencer and F. J. Gillen, London.
Omaha	*The Omaha Tribe,* by A. C. Fletcher and F. La Flesche, 27th Ann. Rep., B.A.E., 1905–6.
Pollock and Maitland	*The History of English Law before Edward I,* by Sir F. Pollock and E. W. Maitland, 2 vols., 2nd ed., Cambridge, 1923.

9

Abbreviation	*Explanation*
Progress of Man, The	By A. M. Hocart, London, 1933. French trsl. Paris, 1935.
Quaritch Wales	*Siamese State Ceremonies*, by H. G. Quaritch Wales, London, 1931.
Radin	*The Winnebago Tribe*, by P. Radin, 37th Ann. Rep., B.A.E., 1915–1916.
Rgv.	*Rigveda*. Ed. Th. Aufrecht, Bonn. 1887.
Round	*The King's Serjeants*, by J. Horace Round, London, 1911.
Sat. Br.	*Satapatha Brahmana*. Ed. A. Weber as vol. II of the *White Yajur-Veda*. Trsl. by Julius Eggeling in S.B.E.
S. B. E.	*Sacred Books of the East*, ed. Max Müller, Oxford, 1882–
Skt.	Sanskrit.
Strehlow, C.	*Die Aranda- und Loritja-stämme in Zentral Australien*, Frankfurt, 1907– .
Temple of the Tooth	*The Temple of the Tooth in Kandy*, by A. M. Hocart, *Memoirs of the Archaeological Survey of Ceylon*, vol. IV, London, 1931.
Thurston	*Castes and Tribes of Southern India*, by Edgar Thurston, 7 vols., Madras, 1901– .
Vacant	*Dictionnaire de Théologie Catholique*, ed. A. Vacant, Paris, 1903– (unfinished).
Yorubas	*The History of the Yorubas*, by Samuel Johnson, ed. O. Johnson, London, 1921.

1· Rules of Evidence

Except I shall see . . . I will not believe.
St. Thomas

PROGRESS IN the understanding of man's evolution, especially his mental evolution, is being hampered by popular fallacies concerning evidence. The nature of evidence is the same in all walks of life. It is the same in the courts of law as it is in science; only in the courts the rules of evidence are not usually distorted by prejudice and fanaticism, as they constantly are in science, especially the science of man.

In the courts they distinguish two kinds of evidence: the direct and the circumstantial. If a witness actually saw the murder and describes it, it is direct evidence. But it is rare that a murder is actually witnessed. It is then necessary to note every circumstance: the state and position of the victim, clues as to time, the movements of the victim and of the suspect, their conditions and characters, to interpret all these data in accordance with the laws of nature, especially human nature, and to frame a theory which explains them all, and for which we can imagine no alternative. That is circumstantial evidence.

There is a popular, but natural, delusion that direct evidence is necessarily better than circumstantial, in fact that it is the only satisfactory kind of evidence. A learned judge in summing up a famous murder trial rebutted this opinion. He pointed out that direct evidence might be the weaker of the two: the witness might be lying or biassed; his memory might be at fault, or his imagination be playing tricks. Even two witnesses might mislead. There are countries where fifty eyewitnesses all telling the same story could not be trusted. On the other hand when a hundred little details which no man could have premeditated or arranged all point in one direction, and one direction only, the certainty is as great as is ever to be attained in human affairs. Probably no man has been hanged in the last hundred years on direct evidence unsupported by circumstantial. Many have been hanged on circumstantial evidence alone.

The historian as a rule shares the popular prejudice: he pins his faith to direct evidence, to the writings of eyewitnesses, to coins, to ruins. Circumstantial evidence he distrusts. He clings to his direct evidence as a timid sailor to the coast.

Astronomy is universally acknowledged to be one of the most exact of sciences; yet it is not afraid to venture into those remote ages for which we cannot hope ever to find direct evidence. Whereas the historian is afraid to discuss the growth of society through a paltry ten thousand years except he has documents for each step, the astronomer coolly reconstructs the history of the solar system for millions of years from observation of the present only. He sees nebulae, suns, dead stars; he supposes that all these represent different stages through which our own solar system has passed or will pass. He imagines a course of development which will explain all the existing facts. Time may modify his scheme, but it does not modify his method.

The geologists too have only the present to argue from; and they argue in the same way. They have perceived that different types of mountains and rivers represent different stages of growth and decay, and they use this knowledge to reconstruct the history of the earth.

Biology itself has achieved its most notable successes purely by the use of circumstantial evidence. A biologist has recently declared: "Evolution itself is accepted by zoologists, *not because it has been observed to occur* or is supported by logically coherent arguments, but *because it does fit all the facts* of Taxonomy, of Palaeontology, and of Geographical Distribution, and *because no alternative explanation is credible.*" Biology, unlike astronomy, has something like direct evidence in the shape of bones and imprints of extinct animals. This evidence is called palaeontology; but it is both inadequate and superfluous for the theory of evolution; it has supplied welcome confirmation or amendments, has filled in details, but was never indispensable to the main theory. The theory of evolution was not based on palaeontology, but palaeontology received the breath of life from evolution. Evolution provided a new use for fossils. It set men looking for them with greater zeal, because it gave them a worthier end than the mere collecting of specimens.

In no branch of biology has this been so much the case as in human biology. It had no palaeontology before Darwin. The first Gibraltar skull was discovered in 1848: it passed quite unnoticed. *The Origin of Species* appeared in 1859. It was not till men had become thoroughly used to the idea of man's descent from an ape-like creature that the skull was brought out of its obscurity, in order to become a link in the evidence. It was not the direct evidence of a man-ape that converted biologists. Rather, having been converted by comparative evidence, they set out to find direct evidence in the shape of fossil men in order to confirm their deductions and complete the confusion of their opponents. It took thirty-five years of *The Origin of Species* to set them really looking. Then Dubois went out to find the ape-like fossil and found it. Since then discovery has succeeded discovery, and the illusion of direct evidence has taken possession of the minds of anthropologists. One leading authority tells us that "for the *serious* study of race history those characters are of special value which can be distinguished in the skeleton, as we naturally know nothing about the skin and hair characters for prehistoric man save by the *risky* analogy from modern men." He forgets that it was on the "risky analogy" of modern species that Darwin and Wallace based their theory of evolution. They risked and they won; for in science faint heart never won fair lady.

Yet what has this direct evidence, all these fossil skulls, done in the end? They have altered details, but they have never converted a single opponent of evolution. Rather the voluminous controversies that have gathered round Pithecanthropus and Piltdown Man have eagerly been seized upon by the fundamentalists to discredit the whole theory of evolution.

It is among students of culture that faith in direct evidence is most firmly implanted. Of that kind of evidence there is such a generous store that it seems gratuitous to fall back on so inferior a substitute as comparative evidence. There are manuscripts, inscriptions, pots, buildings in such plenty that we may reasonably hope to learn all we want to know from them alone.

This naive faith in the evidence of our eyes is all the more remarkable as the nineteenth century and the first quarter of the twentieth have been largely spent by historians in discrediting that very kind of evidence on which they rely. Niebuhr led with an attack on the early Roman tradition which had been accepted without question. But the critics were not long content with demolishing legends: they were soon emboldened to attack the great names among historians. Thucydides was a contemporary of the events he recorded and an actor in some. His testimony had never been doubted. Yet the liberal Grote convicted him of being a biased Tory traducing the Greek democrats. Herodotus may be credulous, but his honesty has never been questioned. He based his narrative of the Persian Wars on the evidence of eyewitnesses; but scholars infected by the fashionable scepticism went to Marathon to see for themselves, and proved on the ground that his account of the battle was impossible, and some even proved to their satisfaction that the Persians, not the Greeks, had won the battle. Moral judgments have been reversed wholesale; heroes have been deposed, villains exalted. One wonders that after this orgy of scepticism any one should go on writing history at all. Many historians have thought to find more solid foundations in the hard material turned up by the spade. Inscriptions have been collected as a check on writers; but inscriptions are no more trustworthy than writings. They are seldom candid, and often inscribed by way of flattery or propaganda. In any case they usually refer to events which seemed most important at the time, but which do not help us in the least to understand the evolution of culture. Pots and pans do not lie; but that is because they do not speak. Their chief use, apart from throwing some light on crafts, is to give us dates; but what is the use of dates without facts to fit into them?

No wonder that in despair many have turned away from history as a game of pure conjecture. They feel like a judge in an Oriental court who, after hearing fifty lying witnesses, loses hope of ever fixing the right and the wrong of the case because his detectives have supplied him with no circumstantial evidence with which to check the statements. Those who still retain an interest in the history of man see no hope of ever tracing the evolution of his ideas, except in so far as they may be stamped on hard, imperishable things like bones or stones. They assure us that we shall never know the beliefs of Neolithic Men, because beliefs do not get petrified. We can touch skeletons, and so we can get some idea what their owners' notions of death may have been: but how can we ever know what their social organization was like, or their marriage and birth rites, which do not get solidified?

They should remember that Auguste Comte once cited as an example of the unknowable the chemical composition of stars. A few years later Kirchhoff applied spectrum analysis to the stars, and provided that very knowledge which Comte had just declared to be impossible. The fact is men do not think of proclaiming a discovery impossible until they begin to contemplate its possibility. It may be an augury that the discovery is at hand.

There is one branch of human history which has no direct evidence to build on, and no hope of any. That is comparative philology. No one expects that we shall ever recover documents containing specimens of that lost speech from which Latin, Greek, Sanskrit, English, and such languages, are descended. Writing was not adopted by its users till long after it had split up into languages very distinct from one another. Our earliest Greek inscriptions hardly go back to 1000 B.C., at the very least a millenium after this splitting up. This absence of all direct evidence has proved a blessing in disguise. It has forced linguists to drop the wasteful and ineffective frontal attack, to which archaeologists are addicted, for a more decisive and economical flanking movement. They have been driven to the comparative method.

That method is based on the existence of divergence: if a species has diverged in different directions, giving rise to a variety of new species, it must be possible to trace back their lines of divergence till they converge on one point, the hypothetical extinct ancestor. Every offspring reproduces its parent or imitates it, but with a difference, which is not the same in all the offspring. By comparing all the descendants or derivatives we can eliminate all the differences, leaving only what they have in common, and that is presumably what they hold from the lost original. We can never draw conclusions as to that original from one derivative only. If we confined our attention to the Northern Europeans only we could only imagine that primitive man was fair-skinned. Other races however have other colours, so we must attribute to primitive man some colour from which all the existing ones can be derived. If we only knew English we should believe that a man had never called the woman who bore him anything else but "mother." Other languages however call her *mutter, matar, meter,* and so on. We must derive all these variants from some form which accounts for them all.

The test of these assumptions lies in their results. While the believers in the direct method still dispute who were the Greeks, whether Zeus was once a powerful king or a natural phenomenon, where the Neolithic Folk came from, how the Piltdown skull ought to be restored, the conclusions of the comparative philologists are in the main so well established that the subject has fallen into stagnation because there is little to dispute about, and controversy is the life of science. No one now disputes that Latin, Greek, and the rest are branches of the same tree; no one questions the main characteristics of the parent tongue. A great many words have been identified in the derivative languages once for all. Thus there is no going back on such equivalences as English *father* = Latin *pater* = Greek *pater* = Sanskrit *pitar* = Old Irish *athir,* etc.

It is strange then that there is no more determined opponent of the extension of the comparative method to other branches of culture than the comparative philologist. He is positive it will not work in religion or social organization. The best answer is not argument, but example.

Let any one take up a dictionary of classical antiquities or mythology, and look up what the believers in direct evidence have done with Hermes. Scholars and antiquarians have variously explained Hermes as darkness, dawn, twilight, the wind, a god of the infernal regions, a solar god. All these suggestions unfortunately are incapable of proof by the direct method, because the true nature of Hermes was forgotten, it is evident, long before our records begin. We could go on piling texts upon texts and get no nearer to certainty. The suggestions remain suggestions. This battle of conjectures is characteristic of those who will admit nothing but direct evidence. They are like men trying to draw a line from a known point to an unknown one without any idea of the distance and very little of the direction. We must draw lines from at least two points to converge on the point we are seeking. Greece alone can never give us direction or distance. Let us take India as our second point.

We cannot read an account of the Vedic god Agni, that is Fire, without being struck by some resemblance to Hermes. Superficial resemblance however is not enough: it classes fishes with whales, swallows with swifts. As in zoology, so in cultural studies, we must penetrate below the surface and dissect the structure. Let us dissect Agni and Hermes in parallel columns.[1]

AGNI	HERMES
1. Is fire, and is born of the fire-sticks.	1. Inventor of fire and the fire-sticks (*H.H.*, IV, 111).
2. Is more particularly the sacrificial fire.	2. . . . .
3. As such he conducted the first sacrifice (*Rgv.*, III, 15, 14; V, 3, 5).	3. After inventing fire he holds a burnt sacrifice, necessarily the first (*H.H.*, IV, 115).

1. For Agni see: A. A. Macdonell, *Vedic Mythology*, and E. W. Hopkins, *Epic Mythology*, both in G. Bühler's *Grundriss der Indo-Germanischen Philologie*, III. — Satapatha Brahmana (*S.B.*), VIII, 6, 6; VI, 4, 4, 11; 5, 1, 12; V, 3, 1, 1; III, 2, 2, 12; *et passim*. — Rigveda (*Rgv.*), I, 1; X, 16.

For Hermes: Daremberg et Saglio, *Dictionnaire d'Antiquités Grecques et Latines*, s.v. *Marcurius*. — Hesiod, *Theogony*, 939; *Op.* 80. — Homeric Hymn (*H.H.*), IV. — Pausanias, IX, 22, 1; V, 27, 8; IV, 3, 3, 4; VI, 26, 5; II, 3, 4. — L. R. Farnell, *Cults of the Greek States*, V, 17; 22; 67.

Agni	Hermes
4. As such he both conveys the offerings to the gods, and partakes himself.	4. He "lusts after the rite of eating the sacrificial meat," but refrains and holds a sacrifice for twelve gods, of whom he is apparently one.
5. As such he is the intermediary between gods and men, their messenger.	5. Messenger of the gods. Intermediary between gods and men.
6. With the offerings he conveys the sacrificer (spiritually) to the gods; makes him one with the gods.	6. Conveys Herakles and Dionysos to heaven on apotheosis.
7. He is also the altar on which the fire was made.	7. A *hermaios lophos* was a heap of stones, regarded as an altar, ascribed to Hermes as a resort. (Scholia and Eustathius on *Odyssey* XVI, 471).
8. He is also the cremation fire.	8. . . . .
9. As such he conveys the dead to the underworld.	9. He conveys the souls to Hades and so is called "Escort of Souls."
10. Priest and chaplain of the gods.	10. Herald of the gods.
11. Threefold and three-headed (*Rgv.* I, 146, 1), because he dwells in earth, in the air, and in the sky.	11. Three-headed is found as an epithet.
12. One form of Agni is called "The Face" because he goes in front.	12. There is a Hermes Fore-fighter, and one called Army-leader.
13. As Face of the Army the general sacrifices to this Agni the Face.	13. The Attic generals sacrificed to this Hermes Hegemonios, army-leader.
14. He is carried in front of the moving tribe to purify the country before them.	14. "Hermes first purified the ways"; "he is the protector of those who go abroad" (Scholia and Eustathius).
15. Abounds in semen (*Rgv.* IV, 5, 2).	15. Has images with erect phallus (Herodotos, II, 51).

Agi	Hermes
16. Associated with the ram.	16. Associated with the he-goat and the ram.
17. Agni is cattle and bestower of cattle (*S.B.*, VI, 3, 1, 32: *Rgv.*, I, 127, 10).	17. Receives from Apollo the rule over cattle and all four-footed beasts. Is called "cattle-driving," "sheep-tending," (*H.H.*, IV, 134; 491 ff.; 567 ff.).
18. Bestows wealth.	18. Called "Giver of good things"; lucky finds are ascribed to him.
19.	19. Protector of traders and travellers. Same as 14.
20. Called "slayer of demons" (*Rgv.*, X, 87, 1), also "Slayer of Vritra" a demon.[2]	20. Called "slayer of Argus," a monster.[2]
21.	21. Invents the lyre and the panpipe.
22. Identified with the sun.	22. Some scholars have taken him for a sun god.
23. Kindled at dawn (*S.B.* II, 3, 1, 15), and so is called "waking at dawn" (*usharbudh*).	23. Some have thought him to be dawn.
24. Kindled three times a day.	24. Born in the morning he develops in three stages in one day.
25.	25. Called "leader of dreams."
26.	26. Chief of thieves.

∴ Agni = Hermes

They agree so closely even to small details that we must conclude the resemblance lies not in the surface, but in the structure. There is however on the right hand side an important blank: there is nothing to indicate what was the nature of Hermes. He invented fire, but is nowhere identified with fire. The word Agni, on the other hand, means fire, and his

2. For further details and parallels see below p. 56.

nature is clearly defined over and over again in the texts. We are faced with two alternatives: one is that in the parent conception he was a fire-god; the other is that he was not and the idea of fire was added in the Indian branch after it had begun to diverge from the Greek, that it was a reinterpretation of an original god who was not fire. We have no direct evidence to decide between those alternatives. There is no test but the usual one in circumstantial evidence: which assumption explains the facts? The second one explains nothing, but leaves us with a host of difficulties. The first one explains satisfactorily most of the characteristics of Hermes. It explains why he is an intermediary between men and gods, for the sacrificial fire conveys the offerings; why he conveys men to the gods, for the sacrifice brings the sacrificer into communion with the gods; why he guides the souls to the nether regions, because the cremation fire takes the deceased thither. To be the intermediary between gods and men is the same as being the priest or the herald. The sacred fire was in India carried before a migrating tribe, in Sparta before an army on the warpath. Hence Agni is the Face of the Army, Hermes the Forefighter. The association with cattle is more obscure; but cattle are the most important sacrificial victims; the sacrificial fire feeds largely on their flesh. The sun is fire, it is Agni in heaven, so it is not surprising Hermes should have been taken for a sun-god.

The argument is exactly the same as that which decides whether the lizard is more primitive in retaining four legs, or the slow worm in never having grown any. The first alternative commends itself because it explains the presence of rudimentary legs underneath the skin of the slow worm; the second explains nothing. Palaeontology by supplying direct evidence of the succession of types may confirm the deductions of the zoologist and fill in the details, but it is not necessary to the main conclusion.

A comparison of Agni and Hermes takes us no further back than the nearest common ancestor of both, which is only two or three thousand, perhaps four thousand years B.C. We can work our way further back by enlarging our field, by calling in cultures that may have diverged at an earlier period still, the Sumerian, for instance. We can bring in living cultures from remote areas. The Koryaks of Kamchatka recognize their fire-board, from which they make fire, as a god. He is an intermediary between gods and men, also god of the Koryak cattle, which consist of reindeer. The affinity is obvious.

We can enlarge our inquiry in other ways than in space. We can regard Agni and Hermes as just items in each of two systems, Indian and Greek culture, like a tooth or an eye in two species of the same animal genus. They are homologies in two allied cultures. We concluded that

$$Agni = Hermes.$$

We noted that

$$Agni = priest, Brahman;$$

and that

$$Hermes = herald, Kerux.$$

We can deduce that

$$Brahman = Kerux.$$

This homology has then to be put to the test by analyzing the nature and functions of the Indian Brahman and the Greek herald, even as we analyzed their gods. I will not carry out this analysis at this stage, but return to it when we need it, and in the meantime take it for proven.[3]

It may be that some day the comparative history of culture will proceed by a series of deductions as in Euclid or a textbook of physics, in this form:—

$$X \text{ is composed of A,B,C,D,E;}$$
$$Y \text{ is composed of A,B,C,D,F,G;}$$
$$\therefore \ X = Y.$$

And so on.

A treatise cast in that form would never be read as things are now. Physicists expect a chain of demonstrations. Historians are used to a discursive style, and will not read anything that is not literature. We must therefore compromise in this treatise and cast our argument into a fairly readable form without sacrificing too much of its rigour.

3. Below p. 194 f. [*See* Appendix. —R.N.]

The comparative method in our example of Agni and Hermes reaches its goal more swiftly and certainly than the mere examination of records. It will be found to be so in every case. Scholars, historians, archaeologists, all the believers in direct evidence as the only one admissible, are wont to pile Pelion on Ossa without ever reaching higher than pure conjecture. They never achieve in affairs two thousand years old the certainty which evolution has attained concerning developments that took place geological ages ago, and for which there is no direct evidence.

The direct method is not only cumbrous, it fails to explain, and explanation is the end of science. The grammarian who sticks to his Greek texts, who will not adventure into what he regards as the quicksands of the comparative method, may note the facts of Greek Grammar: he cannot account for them. He cannot, for instance, tell you why Greek so often alternates *e* with *o*, as in *legomen, legete;* the comparative philologist can by calling Latin, Sanskrit, and the rest to his aid. He can postulate certain rules of the parent language which will account for all the facts of the derivative languages, and to which he can see no possible alternative.

Direct evidence not only fails to explain; it may even suggest the wrong explanation; because it tells us only a fraction of the facts, while seeming to tell all. I have in mind a case from Fiji. I became acquainted there with a nobility, or royal family, if you like, which was divided into four clans, two of them alternating in the chieftainship, two of them out of the running. I was told exactly how it had been so divided, and why. It was not so very long ago, in fact within the memory of the oldest men. The original family, descendants of a chief who lived just before 1800, had grown too large. As it was assessed at the same rate as the small clans it was not bearing its fair share of the public contributions. Therefore the youngest branch, which we shall call D, was split off. Then as the remainder grew A was set apart. Of the remainder B was zealous in public affairs, C neglected them for private work. In order to compel C to pull its own weight it was cut off from B. Had I confined my attention to this one village, as scholars confine themselves to Greece, or Rome, or Egypt,

I might have rested content with this bit of local history, and taken this fourfold division to be a local accident. But the same arrangement of 4 clans, 2 qualified for chieftainship, 2 excluded, turned up in a neighbouring tribe, then in another. It became quite impossible to accept the first case as the pure accident it seemed to be on the direct evidence, any more than we could accept as an accident the shape of a crystal repeated in experiment after experiment. The fourfold arrangement was a pattern into which Fijian royal families till recently tended to fall. The number four was doubtless connected with the ritual use of four, as in feasts, cures, etc. This fourfold division crops up again in Central Australia, in Java, in India, and is there connected with the four cardinal points of the compass.[4] Evidently it is a very ancient pattern since it is common to peoples so far removed from one another. It certainly never originated in Fiji. Yet the direct evidence supplied by the members of one family would lead one to think that it sprang up locally in the nineteenth century by the decision of one or two strong and able men. Are we to reject their evidence as lying? Certainly not: it tells us the truth, nothing but the truth, but not the whole truth. It tells us of certain passing maladjustments, such as are continually occurring in any community; it tells us how they were readjusted; it does not tell us of the immemorial tradition that there should be four clans, and that any readjustment should restore or retain that primeval arrangement. Nor does it tell us that there was not a fourfold arrangement before the readjustment.

To understand this let us suppose that Europe has been swept by a barbaric invasion that has destroyed all records, and even wiped out our social organization from the memory of men. America has escaped: it still has records of its constitution dating back to its original promulgation after the War of Independence. The historian would eagerly seize on these records, and would explain triumphantly to the learned world how parliamentary government originated. We know he would be quite wrong, that parliamentary government is vastly older than the eighteenth century, that in fact it never originated,

4. Below p. 251 ff.

but evolved insensibly out of some other sort of assembly, that the American Constitution is merely a local modification of an ancient institution to meet local needs and satisfy philosophical theories which we can trace back through Rousseau, Locke, Hobbes, and right beyond them.

Again let us imagine that we have no records of any peerage before George I, that our earliest notice of any creation of peers is by that monarch. The historians would at once conclude that George I invented the peerage, and mistake his reasons for creating those particular peers for the motives that led to the institution of the peerage. It is as if a palaeontologist were to say: "Here is a Pleistocene skull; it is the earliest that has ever been found. Here then we are assisting at the birth of mankind." That would be absurd; yet that is exactly what the historians are continually doing whenever they lose the scent; they commonly jump to the conclusion that the scent started where they lose it, not that it may have faded out. The Greeks are especially to blame for this bad habit. They tell us that Solon or Lykurgus promulgated such and such a law, state his reasons, and give us to understand that is how the law originated. Our historians are too often content and look no further. They forget that it is possible to promulgate an old law again, possibly with amendments. Parliament has recently voted against the Sunday opening of theatres; but that is not the origin of Sunday closure. We know it can be traced back to the Hebrews. The recent Act merely reaffirms a modern application of a very ancient taboo. Absence of records means nothing: comparative evidence alone can decide. It so happens we have comparative evidence in the case of Lykurgus. We know that many of the institutions attributed to him existed in Crete. We can only conclude that they are much older than Lykurgus, that they go back at least as far as the nearest common ancestors of the Spartans and the Cretans. If these customs are included in the laws of Lykurgus it can only be that he reaffirmed or emended what he found already in existence. Tradition also says that Lykurgus imposed iron money on the Spartans, and gives his reasons. But iron money is very widespread, and not peculiar to Sparta. Comparative evidence makes it impossible to believe that it originated in Sparta. If Lykurgus did include iron money in his constitution he can have done no more than insist on its retention.

The historian who trusts exclusively to records never reaches further back than incidents which look like the beginning, but are really episodes in growth. Ask him, for instance, the origin of mendicant orders: he will ransack libraries for documents, he will produce a history of the Grey Friars, for example, beginning with St. Francis, their founder. He will think he has answered your question. But there is an epidemic of mendicant orders at that time: Crutched Friars ten years earlier in 1198 in Rome, Black Friars in 1206, White Friars founded about 1238, but derived from a community known to have existed in the East not later than the XIIth century.[5] Evidently mendicant vows were in the air. Neither St. Francis nor the founders of other orders invented them; they adapted them. They were not the authors, but the instruments of evolution. This evolution had started before their time. Where and when was it set in motion? Records can never tell us.

The comparative historian turns from them to living institutions. He finds in Ceylon a mendicant order sufficiently like those of Europe to warrant him in postulating a common origin. Here direct evidence comes to his aid. Texts, inscriptions, bas-reliefs, shrines enable him to trace Sinhalese monasticism back to Nepal about 500 B.C. They make it quite plain, however, that even that is not the beginning; that other similar orders were founded about the same time, one of which, Jainism, still survives in India. The Buddha, founder of the Sinhalese variety, was evidently, like St. Francis, merely working out a preexisting idea. The origin, like all origins, lies far beyond our records.

Records can do one thing, they can strengthen the comparative historian's hypothesis. They tell us of westward Buddhist missions as early as some 250 B.C. They bear witness that there was a considerable influx of Oriental ideas into Europe throughout the Middle Ages, including Buddhist legends. It is an admitted fact that the Christian Saint Josaphat is no

5. Vacant, s.v. *Carmes, Frères Mineurs, Frères Prêcheurs.*

25

other than the Buddha,[6] and that the episode of the basket in the Merry Wives of Windsor is depicted on a Buddhist bas-relief of the first century B.C.[7]

True there are no records of the spread of mendicant orders from India to Europe. Neither is there any record that the anthropoid apes spread to Borneo and to Africa from a common centre. We cannot *see* them spread and never shall. We may find a chain of fossil apes all the way from Malaysia to Central Africa, but that all these fossils have a common ancestor and that this chain is due to spread, all that is pure assumption.

There are minnows in the Thames. There are minnows also in the Severn. There is no communication between the two rivers, and minnows do not go out to sea nor do they travel overland. Does the zoologist conclude that God made one pair, male and female, and put it in the Thames, and another pair male and female, and put it in the Severn? No, he is convinced that all minnows in whatsoever river are descendants of a common stock, and that they must have got from one river to the other, or from a third fresh water to both. He may then seek for evidence how this took place. If he fails he does not abandon his conviction, but modestly admits he does not know enough.

Students of man, scholars, archeologists, and anthropologists, are less modest, less conscious of their limitations. If they cannot see a people or a custom move from place to place, they conclude that it did not. If you cannot produce a text recording a passing of peoples from the Old World to the New they declare no such passage ever took place. If they cannot see dolmens moving across the face of the world from somewhere to England, to India, to Africa, they declare it not proved, which for them is as good as disproved.

It is not proved, and never can be, if by proving we mean actually seeing it happen, or knowing some one who has seen it. But proof does not consist in seeing: it consists in providing so complete an explanation of the disjointed evidence of our

6. T. W. Rhys Davids, *Buddhism*, 115 f.
7. At Barhut. Foucher, I.

senses that no better alternative can be thought of. Some day an alternative may be found; but in the meantime our hypothesis, if it is any good, will have helped us to further conquests: that is all that really matters.

In Science, as in the courts, circumstantial evidence is not an inferior substitute for the evidence of eyes and ears: it is the very foundation of knowledge.

2* The Witnesses

Not Ethnology, but Ethnotomy.
With apologies to Cuvier

A POET may take the head of a lion, the body of a goat, the tail of a snake, one thing here and one thing there, thus compound a chimaera, and describe its ways. Not so the biologist: he may not confuse his species, but must analyze each separately and compare them organ for organ, tissue for tissue. No more can the student of language take one word from England, another from Java, a third from Terra del Fuego, and on the basis of this imaginary language discuss the origin and nature of speech. No, he aligns the whole vocabulary of Latin over against the whole vocabulary of Greek, of Sanskrit, of Persian, and so on, and compares them item for item, never mixing up his languages.

The anthropologist on the contrary has always preferred the licence of the poet. He wanders erratically through the world, culling a bull-roarer from the Yahoos, a god from the Chinchins, a dance from the Ping-Pongs, a spell from the Ba-noodles, and thus constructs a chimaera of his own, which he labels Primitive Culture, and which he proceeds to expound, to analyze, and even psycho-analyze.

It is obvious such a procedure can lead to no final results; for it is left to the caprice of each to include in his composite picture, or to exclude. Thus each one is at liberty to fashion his own Primitive Man according to his predilections, instead of surrendering to the facts, to be led by them wherever they lead.

As a contribution towards restoring discipline I would propose the following rule: that the student should keep throughout to the same peoples, and compare them limb for limb. This ideal is not always possible, because we have no complete picture of any culture but our own. But we must temper our rules with reasonableness.

Space will not allow us to call more than seven witnesses-in-

chief; but I shall summon them from all the quarters of the
globe, in order to satisfy the reader that the facts to which
they depone are not of local interest only, but world-wide.
I shall frequently have to eke out, or confirm, their testimony
with that of secondary witnesses, mostly near neighbours of
the seven.

These witnesses have been imposed by fate or chance, not
chosen because they promised to support any particular
theory.

TABLE OF WITNESSES

Area	Chief Witnesses	Secondary Witnesses
I. South Seas	Fijians	Eddystonians
		Rotumans
		Samoans
		Tongans
		Gilbert Islanders
		Banks Islanders
		New Caledonians
		Kiwai
II. Australia	Arandas	Kaitish
		Warramungas
		Dieris
		Wik-Munkans
III. North America	Winnebagoes	Mandans
		Omahas
		Osage
		Pawnees
		Yumas
IV. Asia, North East	Koryaks	
V. Asia, South	Vedic Indians	Siamese
	Hindus	Egyptians
	Sinhalese	Mesopotamians
	Tamils	Hebrews
V. Asia, East		Chinese
VI. Africa, West	Jukuns	Igbos
		Hausas
		Yauris
		Yorubas
	Africa, East	Langos
		Baris
VII. Europe, West	English	French
		Italians
		Romans
		Greeks

3· Opening the Case

For God is Life.

"Functions," says Kappers, "dominate forms; but, on the other hand, do forms which thus arise facilitate the functions, and bring them to perfections unknown before morphological differentiations occurred. In other words, special tissues are the result of activities already carried on before the tissue differentiation."

"And so, dealing with the origin of the nervous system, we may ask whether in animals in which nervous elements are not yet differentiated, such as Protozoa and Sponges, functions are found that are comparable to nervous functions, differing from them only in degree."

"Now this certainly occurs, since the principal functions of the nervous system: *reception, conduction, correlation* and *elaboration of impulses* are generally properties of protoplasm, and consequently, are present also in non-nervous tissue. . . . Thus, reflexes running over long distances are seen in animals without any nervous tissue."[1]

These words might be applied *mutatis mutandis* to government, which is the nervous system of the social organism. There too function precedes form, and form merely facilitates function and perfects it. Government is "the result of activities already carried out before the differentiation of men."

We shall see all the functions of government discharged among peoples without government, theft prevented and punished, murder avenged, international peace maintained, and war subjected to rules, the distribution of food and wealth arranged, without our being able to point to any particular body of men as regulating social intercourse. This is indeed to a great extent true of our own society: it is not governments that make the rules by which peace is kept or broken, prisoners

1. C.U.A. Kappers, *The Evolution of the Nervous System in Invertebrates, Vertebrates and Man* (Haarlem, 1929), 1.

taken or massacred, enslaved or released. Governments merely carry out the rules which society has made, and, as the temper of a society changes, so change the rules which the government has to apply. As for our food supply it has organized or disorganized itself with little control from the government, and we have not yet discovered the way by which government can successfully intervene.

Yet, when all is said and done, there is a difference between our social organization at one end, and that of the Antipodians at the other. *There* it is the individual who has to apply to his own case the rules handed on by the ancients; the rest of the community merely keeps the ring for him, or forms a reserve ready to support him if he is not equal to his rights. It is only in the performance of rites for the increase of food, wealth, or immunity that there is a marked regulation by the headmen. In this country the individual has abdicated his private revenge in favour of a body which makes it its business to avenge.[2] The rest of the community specializes in the production of food, or of wealth, or in warding off disease, or in amusing others or in one of innumerable occupations. A Fijian is his own farmer, judge, policeman, sailor, statesman, priest, dancer, and singer. An Englishman can be any of these, but not all.

There is then no government, in our sense of the word, among peoples like the Fijians, because there is no need for any. If, however, we look more closely at such societies we shall discover that nevertheless the machinery of government is there ready to govern, if governing is required. There is, so to speak, a governing body before there is any governing to do. If a man is needed to regulate the lives of the people, to be the supreme arbiter of right and wrong, there is such a person prepared to assume the responsibility: it is the king. There is another who will turn himself into a prime minister when the time comes. There is as yet no commander-in-chief, no chief specialist in strategy, but when strategy comes into being there is a court official to whom command of the army

---

2. This abdication is not an unmitigated blessing. The law often favours the unjust where violence would not.

will naturally fall. It looks as if nature had prepared the organization before it was needed, had anticipated the growth of the state.

But what was the machinery doing before it was turned to the work of governing? Was it just lying idle? We learn from biology to expect that when an organ appears it is to do something, not merely to await developments. It is difficult to believe that the structure of government was outlined to serve no immediate purpose, but merely to bide its time. It must have done something else before it governed, just as bones stored calcium before they were called upon to act as levers.

To understand the earliest work we find it performing we must look at man's conception of life. Long ago he ceased merely to live, and began to think how he lived; he ceased merely to feel life: he conceived it. Out of all the phenomena contributing to life he formed a concept of life, fertility, prosperity, vitality. He realized that there was something which distinguished the animate from the inanimate, and this something he called life.

How this happened and when, we will not speculate. It is sufficient that all existing races have this concept of life, and that it must therefore be at least as old as their nearest common ancestors, if it is not prehuman.

The difference between life and death was, and still is, supposed to be due to the presence or absence of a certain something, an entity, which has an existence apart from the material objects which it animates. Here again we will not speculate how the idea developed; we shall content ourselves with the fact that all living races think of life as a thing that departs from the body and leaves it a corpse. They commonly speak of life going out, or they may call it soul; some scientists speak of an entelechy, which sounds more profound, but explains no more.

Though we may refuse to speculate about the origin of this concept of life, we may be allowed to show that it is merely one instance of a very common mental process. Man observes that certain phenomena have something in common; he attributes their affinity to the presence or absence of some entity, which readily becomes in his thought a substance. Thus hot and cold have been conceived as elements which pervade matter, and it is fairly recently that scientists have reduced them to motion. Evolution is constantly spoken of as if it were a power pushing living beings forward. One author complains, and with justice, that instinct is usually conceived as a special psychic entity which drives the organism. The terms magic and religion describe certain activities of men, but we forget that, and speak of them as causes, talk of magic tyrannizing over the savage, of religion doping the masses, as if these abstractions had an existence apart from men. To think of life as a thing is then a perfectly normal process in all ages.

If life comes and goes it must come from somewhere and go somewhere. The more scientific among us carefully avoid the question where; but the greater part of mankind has not been so agnostic: they think they know in what objects life resides and into what objects it passes. Man has gone further: he has come to think he can *control* that coming and going. He has worked out a technique to the end of controlling it. None of us has so far the remotest idea how this confidence first established itself, or how the technique was first worked out. We can only note that, like the concept of life, the technique of life-giving exists all the world over. Everywhere man goes through prescribed forms of words and actions in the persuasion that he can thereby transfer life from one thing to another.

Of this the Winnebagoes supply one of the most transparent examples. Like all men they desire long life. They seek to prolong their lives by transferring to their own account the unlived days of those who have been cut off before their time. Thus they take the scalps of their enemies, not as trophies, but in order to gain life for themselves. When they have secured a scalp they hold a dance in order to transfer the unlived life of its owner to themselves. "The soul of the scalp still remained within it," says Mr. Radin in his description of the dance, "so they tried again to make it less powerful and to conquer it, for they knew that if they succeeded in conquering it all the life that was still coming to the possessor at his death would be obtained by themselves. . . . All tried to add some new life to their own."[3]

When an Eddystonian dies his image or soul departs. That image or soul is not left to go its own way so that it is lost to the community. It is caught and fixed in a ring, then placed in a skull house, there to benefit his living kinsmen and give them life and prosperity.[4]

We have a good example in I Samuel x and xvi, if we keep in mind that God is Life, and if we note the effects of the rite. Samuel makes the spirit of the Lord to come upon Saul, thus turning him into a king and causing him to prosper. Later Samuel transfers the spirit of the Lord to David, whereupon Saul is afflicted with an evil spirit, ceases to prosper, is defeated in battle and dies.

No matter how this technique originated, it exists and from that fact we take our start. It is variously called magic or religion. I prefer to call all its varieties by the name of ritual.[5]

We recognize them all as varieties of one kind, and we express that fact by grouping them all under that term ritual, just as we express the kinship of collies, terriers and hounds by calling them all dogs. We cannot halt there: we have to find out what it is that gives all these life-giving methods a certain family air. To that end we must analyze ritual after ritual, just as the anatomist dissects dog after dog to find out what dogginess consists in.

When we do so we shall find that this general resemblance is due to the extreme permanence of certain principles. These principles determine the structure, which is consequently as permanent as the principles.

It is not only the ritual that exhibits a certain structure, but also the society that practises it; for the ritual is a social affair, it requires the cooperation of many, and so society must organize itself for ritual. In this quest of life all the actors do not play the same part; they must, in virtue of the very

---

3. Radin, 381.
4. *Cult of the Dead*, I, 83.
5. I have given reasons briefly in my *Progress of Man*, 134.

structure of ritual, have different roles assigned to them. There is a president, for instance, there is a master of ceremonies, and others we shall learn to know. This ritual organization is vastly older than government, for it exists where there is no government and where none is needed. When however society increases so much in complexity that a coordinating agency, a kind of nervous system, is required, that ritual organization will gradually take over this task. It is this evolution from ritual organization to government that is to be roughly outlined in the following pages. But before we proceed to do so we must deal with one formidable prejudice that stands in our way.

Ritual is not in good odour with our intellectuals. It is associated in their minds with a clerical movement for which most of them nurse an antipathy. They are therefore unwilling to believe that institutions which they approve of, and which seem to them so eminently practical and sensible as modern administration, should have developed out of the hokus-pokus which they deem ritual to be. In their eyes only economic interests can create anything as solid as the state. Yet if they would only look about them they would everywhere see communities banded together by interest in a common ritual; they would even find that ritual enthusiasm builds more solidly than economic ambitions, because ritual involves a rule of life, whereas economics are a rule of gain, and so divide rather than unite.

It can hardly be said of many of us that our lives centre in the town-hall; but there are many whose lives centre in the place of ritual, the church or the chapel. Let us take the chapel since it is so modern. It is much more than a place where hymns are sung and sermons delivered, as my friend, Mr. G. A. Cheshire, will testify:—

> To many Nonconformists the local chapel is the centre around which life revolves. There are the elective offices to fill, the weekly round of meetings to organize and attend. Funds have to be collected to pay the Pastor, and for other overheads. Sunday Schools need teachers. Choir and organist have to be recruited. "Tea-Fights" involve cookery and catering. Total abstinence has to

be propagated, and an occasional intruding sinner saved. Foreign Missions supply occasions for dressing up and lantern slides. Probably there is a fund for the erection of a new building. The whole family finds work and interest. The young folk intermarry; some mutual trading is done. Doctrinal orthodoxy is assumed, and it comes to the surface only in an occasional and bitter discussion with a closely related sect. It serves to emphasize the esoteric nature of the cult. But the other activities alone are sufficient to confirm the view that "they are in the World, but not of it."

When the religious community is large enough it tends to form a closed economic system. I have known Methodists who thought it a duty to shop with Methodists, and it might be an occasion of mental conflict if the co-religionist did not give the satisfaction that was to be found in shops outside the fold. After all, true Britons think it a duty to buy British. It is merely a question of the degree to which the self-sufficiency of a group is carried. It does not go far with our sects because their commercial interests are so intertwined with those of the whole country that they have no inclination for complete autonomy, even if it were possible. They are scattered throughout the nation and are not territorially compact. In America, self-sufficiency has been carried farther, and a certain territorial unity is achieved. Sects are perpetually forming tiny states within the state with their own customs and organization, so far as they do not conflict with the rules of the greater state. Most of them perish like the mayfly, but some have been quite successful, and of these the Mormons are a notable example.[6]

It is a remarkable fact that none of the communities founded on purely economic theories, such as those of Fourrier, have ever achieved the slightest degree of permanence. Yet it is not so remarkable either. Economics are but a very small fragment of life, and the pursuit of wealth is not one that inspires much zeal for the common good. Look at our Empire. Com-

6. Ray Strachey, *Religious Fanaticism*, London, 1928. — The "Evangelical Johannean Church" near Potsdam had its own school, museum, fire-brigade and temple.

merce is not holding it together, but everywhere setting up barriers and causing friction. It is the last remnants of the royal ritual that hold it together. You cannot build a state on the narrow basis of prices and wages, but only on the widest co-operation for life. Ritual, as long as it retains its meaning, is a co-operation for life.

What is happening at the present day can very well have happened in the past. It is our purpose to show that it did happen repeatedly, and that our present state has developed out of an undifferentiated organization for life by differentiation, and by shedding some functions and acquiring new ones.

In the process of development that organization has had to remodel itself. In its primitive state it has a head but no master. The various families that join together in seeking life have an order of precedence, but not of authority; they may arrange themselves into first and last, but not into rulers and subjects. If there is to be government, that is, co-ordination of actions, there must be some to command and a majority to obey. Gradually then, as the regulation of conduct becomes the main interest rather than the control of natu.., we see the leader become the regulator; grouns once equal acknowledge the supremacy of one; a vertical arrangement takes the place of a horizontal one. He who began by leading ends by directing.

Round him cluster subordinate leaders who were once his seconds. It is this body which decides and disseminates its decisions throughout society. To disseminate them it must have underlings to convey the decisions to furthest parts. In this manner it insinuates its roots deeper into the mass and holds it together. We begin with lineages arrayed side by side, and end with a mass penetrated through and through with conducting filaments that have radiated from a centre.

This process is called centralization. It begins at the centre and spreads outwards. We can trace this gradual permeation in our own records. For instance, the king's justice, exceptional in Saxon times, gradually spreads its tentacles throughout the whole country. By the time of Henry III "the king's courts have fast been becoming the only judicial tribunals of any great importance." The royal judges, sitting in Westminster or touring the country, edge out the local seignorial courts. These "local courts are being starved, and this result we cannot ascribe altogether to the ambition or greed of the lawyers at Westminster. Of his own free will the small freeholder passed by his lord's court and the county court on his way to the great hall." With royal justice spread royal judicial inventions. The "attorney is no outcome of ancient folk-law; it is a royal privilege." It gradually extends to all. Even "the jury is connected with royal power. . . . The jury spreads out from the king's own court. To the last, trial by jury has no place in the ordinary procedure of our old communal courts."[7] The process can be observed by any civil servant in India; and there again it is of his own free will the peasant goes past his own local panchayat, or court of five village elders, to imperial judges.[8]

The present work will go much further back to take up this tale of centralization. We shall go back beyond the vertebrates, as it were, to the invertebrates. For there is a striking analogy between this evolution of human society and that of the body. In the history of the body we get at one end invertebrates and chordates, such as Amphioxus, which consist of segments placed in a line. In some worms the middle segments are so much alike that, if they were cut out, the anatomist could not put them back in the right order with any certainty. Each segment, though not independent, is self-contained: it may have its own muscles, nervous ganglions and dependent nerves, its own blood vessels, its own gonads; but all are linked up, so that every segment regulates itself in harmony with the rest. There is a slight differentiation due to position. The most differentiated part is the head. It is only *primus inter pares;* but, because it goes first and so is best placed to receive information, it exercises a general control over the body. Other parts are adapted to their position; the rear part has to close the procession.

At the other end of the scale are highly centralized animals

7. Pollock and Maitland, I, 203; 213; 40. Cp. II, 226 f.
8. Cp. F. F. Abbott and A. C. Johnson, *Municipal Administration in the Roman Empire* (Princeton, 1926), 204.

like ourselves. They no longer consist of almost identical and autonomous parts, but everything is under the control of a nervous system which radiates through the body. The head is no longer a mere *primus inter pares,* but the coordinating centre. All information has to be passed on through it to lower or higher centres, which give out the appropriate impulse to the periphery, except in purely routine work which the organs themselves can deal with. The food supply too all goes up to the heart, and is distributed from it. We are far removed from the organism in which every part takes in its own nourishment, and responds directly to any stimulus.

In the same way, out of a society of autonomous, but co-operating, parts there has evolved a society of specialized parts controlled from a centre. Each part used to be like each other and self-sufficient, except in the presence of common obstacles. Such common obstacles are droughts, disease, enemies that threaten the life of the whole. There are, in consequence, joint arrangements to overcome them. These arrangements are the communal rites. They first appear as rites interdependent, but to some degree autonomous; they grow into an elaborate organization centralized and controlled from above.

Centralization means specialization. Centralization can only be achieved by selecting different individuals to perform different tasks. In our own time we select the men best fitted by natural endowments, or rather we are supposed to do so. We are apt in consequence to assume that it has always been so, that nature has always automatically yielded a supply of individuals with varying abilities to cope with the varying tasks. That is supposed by some to be the origin of the Indian caste system: men born with a special gift for carpentry have become carpenters, and have handed on their craft to their sons; born smiths have entered the smithy, and their sons have followed.

When however we look into the facts we shall find that it is not so, that differentiation of function precedes differentiation of ability, and therefore is presumably the cause of it; that men have certain tasks assigned to them not on grounds of fitness, but because ritual theory requires it. The specialization of men, who are the tissues of society, is, to apply the words of Kappers, "The result of activities carried on before the tissue differentiation." Somehow or other these activities have resulted in new types, leaders, fighters, manual workers. Special abilities are the consequence of special tasks and not the other way round.

It is true that even in the least differentiated societies there is some differentiation of ability: one man is more skilful with the adze than another; one is more skilful with his tongue; but the differentiation is far less than it is with us: there are no poets who will only write poetry and will do nothing else; there are no boys who run away from home because the sea is their vocation. Every man in Fiji, for instance, does the same work as every other, and does not expect it to be otherwise. The only differentiation of function is in the ritual, and there it does not correspond to ability or character. The performers in the quest for life are not selected for their personal aptitude, but by heredity and the manifested will of the gods. Descent is the chief qualification. We might express it more generally and say it is the theory of the ritual, of which heredity is part, which decides the appointment.

How this differentation of function has led to differentiation of abilities is a problem which will better be discussed when all the evidence has been reviewed.

4ˑ Nature

We must judge the ancients in the light of their ideas and not of ours.

Fustel de Coulanges

ALL MEN wish to control nature in order that they may live. In this desire we British are no different from others. We differ only in having lost faith in methods to which most peoples on earth still look to give them a prosperous existence. It is not that we no longer wish we could make rain, for instance, but that, except in Alberta, we have given up trying because we know too much.[1] Others retain all the confidence of little knowledge, and are quite sure they can bend animals and plants, even the sun and moon, to their wills not by direct physical action, but by becoming one with them and so controlling the behaviour of things even as they control their own bodies.

If the Arandas wish to ensure an abundance of grey kangaroos, they first eat some of that animal's flesh in their camp. Then follows a dramatic performance. One actor. comes forward. He must be of a group closely associated with the grey kangaroo, in fact identified with it. The members of this group are equivalent to kangaroos for all intents and purposes. The ceremony is their exclusive property. The actor's body is painted across with a broad black band and feathered. He bears a bundle of *mulga* twigs on his head and has ornaments representing the tail, testicles, back, and heart of the kangaroo. A hole is dug in the ground about a foot deep. The actor throws himself into it, lies on one side, and begins to nod as in sleep. An elderly man then calls the young ones. They run round the actor, while men sitting close by sing a song which relates a myth. For the actor represents a very fat kangaroo that was a mythical personage, at once ancestor and god, whose adventures are related in the song. During the performance the old men open a vein on their arms and let

1. Cp. *Report of the British Association*, 1933, 41: "Western farmers have paid a 'rainmaker' thousands of dollars at a time to produce rain."

the blood flow on a flat rock where a grey kangaroo-ancestor-god rested. That causes many grey kangaroos to come forth from the rock (not in the flesh, of course). Some time after, it may be two months, the actor eats a little grey kangaroo, and so makes this meat free to all those who are not, like him, grey kangaroo men.[2]

Different families have different animals. There are kanga-roo-rat men, wallaby men, pigeon men, and so on. Others have plants, or anything in heaven or on earth which a man may wish to influence by ritual, even rain, thunder, the sun, moon, fruitful women. Further North the list includes such artefacts as bark canoes and spear handles.[3]

If we analyze these rituals we shall find certain principles to underlie them all.

They cannot be carried out by any one who chooses, but by a group that owns the appropriate ritual. Membership of that group is determined by birth. Among the majority of Australian Blacks it is a matter of descent. It is unfortunate that our Arandas are not in this respect typical, for they decide membership according to the place of quickening of the womb. In practice this comes somewhat to the same, since a family tends to remain in the district of its particular god. Anyhow there can be no doubt that membership by heredity is the more primitive custom, from which the Arandas have slightly departed. We shall frequently come across such departures, notably among ourselves.

For every ritual there is a leader, the head of the group to which the ceremony belongs, or else a deputy. The head is not always a man, it may be an inanimate object.

The head acts in the ritual just as the ancestor or god acted of old. A legend is told in connection with the ritual describing how he and his companions acted: as they acted so do their descendants. Thus one rain-making group has a legend that an old man blew gypsum about to make clouds. The clouds came down in the form of rain—men who keep going up to the sky and coming down again. The leader squats on the

2. Strehlow, III, 1, 13 f.
3. Ursula McConnel, *The Wik-Munkan Tribe,* Oceania, I, 182.

ground and, as the others sing, tries to rise, and gazes into
the sky in imitation of the cloud men of former times. He
also blows some down about in various directions: the down
represents the clouds; the effect is to make the rain fall.[4]

The performer himself is in the rain ceremony identified
with the clouds, for, sitting motionless, he allows his blood
to flow on to the ground from an incision; the blood represents
the rain; so we draw the inference that he represents the
cloud.[5] This inference is confirmed by what happens after a
rain ceremony: some man among the rain owners has a tooth
knocked out, the reason given being that it makes his face
resemble a rain cloud.[6]

*The performers are not content to imitate nature as it is,
but as they want it to be.* Thus they want the rain cloud
to stay and shed drops, so the impersonator of the cloud remains motionless and sheds blood. They believe that the rainbow stops the rain, so the Kaitish hide a shield on which
a rainbow is painted: the effect is to hide the rainbow in the
sky, so that it does not stop the rain.[7] To cause certain grubs
to multiply. Aranda performers enter a shelter of branches
which represents the chrysalis case. They sit inside fasting
and singing songs. Then they come out and eat, just as they
wish the grub to do. Thus by identifying themselves with the
grub they can make the grub do what they want it to do.[8]

In order to help the identification the actors must dress up
to be like what they represent. The make-up is not realistic
as it is among many other peoples that wear masks, skins,
or otherwise masquerade so well there is no mistaking what
they stand for. Here the ornaments have to be interpreted
before the part of the body they represent can be recognized.
In former days there seems to have been more realism, for
a myth tells us of an ancestor who could enclose himself in
an emu skin. The make-up varies of course according to the
thing it represents, but some sort of headgear, a belt, and

4. Spencer and Gillen, *Northern Tribes of Central Australia,* 291 ff.
5. Strehlow, III, 1, 132.
6. *Arunta,* 478.
7. *Northern Tribes,* 295.
8. *Arunta,* I, 148 ff.

body paint are among the most constant. The paint is human blood, or red ochre, which appears to be a substitute for blood. *They not only make themselves equivalent to nature, but make other things, particularly stones, to be so.* Thus to make rain a Kaitish headman pours water simultaneously on himself and on certain stones that represent the whiskers of ancestors. Thus the ancestors are represented twice over, by the headman and by the stones. We saw that in the grey kangaroo ceremony the performer represents ancestors who are kangaroos; but a rock is also equivalent to kangaroos, and is smeared with blood just as the men often are. Thus

$$man = animal \text{ or } plant = ancestor = cult \text{ } object.$$

The headman must first eat a little of his animal or plant; then those to whom it does not belong may partake. It is chiefly for the benefit of non-owners that the ceremony is held, for the owners can only eat sparingly, and in some of the other tribes not at all.

We saw that

$$headman = his \text{ } animal \text{ or } plant.$$

Therefore the headman should be *eating himself*, then the others be eating *him*. This sounds absurd. It might be taken to prove how illogical the so-called savage is, or it might be argued that men do not always carry their ideas to their logical conclusion, and it is inconceivable that the Aranda should do so in this case, when the result would be so palpably absurd. Yet we shall see that this conclusion lies at the basis of rituals of highly civilized peoples whom no one has ever accused of being illogical.

When we understand in what sense man and victim are identified the absurdity will disappear; for it is all due to our interpreting the identity as being one of bodies, to our thinking of the body of the man as the same as the body of the animal or plant. That is a misunderstanding. What the correct interpretation is we must leave to unfold itself as we proceed. In the meantime we shall note that the Aranda expresses this equivalence by saying the stone, or whatever it is, is "his other body."

Another essential of the ritual is the Word. Some form of words is necessary: formulae or songs. The songs are not for pleasure, but *contribute to the end in view,* the multiplication of animals and plants, the production of stones, or whatever it may be. They relate the myth of the ancestor who was, like the present headman, identified with the animal or plant. The myth describes the ancestor as performing exactly the same ceremonies with the same purpose. It contains, as it were, the precedent for the whole ritual. Its recitation is an essential part of that ritual. We can see the sense of it, even if we cannot as yet see how it came about: the word indicates what they are imitating, the ancestor-kangaroo, and it makes that imitation not mere play-acting, but *an act of creation.* The word does not merely *say* this man represents the ancestor and the kangaroo: it *makes* the two equivalent for all practical purposes.[9]

I wish most particularly to insist upon this equivalence which is the basis of imitation, which is itself the most fundamental thing in ritual. The ritual turns upon the fact that one thing can be made equivalent to another, and so that principle remains the most constant throughout the ages; for, if it drops out, the ritual loses its meaning, and the very reason of its existence. If you cannot act on A by acting on B there can be no ritual.

To sum up, these Aranda rites are acts of creation achieved by identifying the actors by the power of the word with the things to be created, and with the ancestor who created them in the past by the same means as are now used.

Animals propagate by sexual intercourse. *It is only to be expected that this creative act should figure in ritual.* In point of fact it plays a great part in Aranda ritual, not, unfortunately, in the ceremonies directed to a specific object, such as we are now considering, but in others which lie beyond our present purview. We have to note however the way in which they insist on the sexual parts in their decorations. It is quite

9. Hocart, *The Life-giving Myth,* in *Labyrinth,* 263.

clear too that they regard creation as a process of birth, for in the rain ceremony the performer wears on his stomach a disc which is the "womb of rain." We have to go elsewhere however to see this process of generation dramatically carried out.

The Kiwai of New Guinea have charms to ensure the capture of dugong. "Like so many other rites, some of these bear a sexual character. . . . The man . . . takes his wife with him to the bush, where they stop at a parting of the road. The woman takes off her grass petticoat and lies down at the fork of the road with her head towards the village. . . . The harpoon head and the cord, used for lashing together the poles of the harpoon platform, are placed on her body. . . . The man has connection with her. . . . The woman carries the 'medicine plants' and harpooning implements against her chest in the same way as she holds her child." The object is not the multiplication of dugong; for this no rites are necessary because the natives say the number of dugongs in the sea can never be exhausted. The object of this charm is to ensure good luck, that the harpoon may hit the mark. We must infer from the manner in which the woman holds the implement that it is reborn as the result of procreation.[10]

Our dissection has laid bare a skeleton of ritual which may be summed up in this manner:—

A. PURPOSE: increase of a living species, or improvement in the efficiency of an inanimate object. The thing which the ritual is designed to influence we may call the *objective*.
B. OWNERSHIP: 1) it is in the hands of a *group*, usually hereditary; 2) that group has a head whom I propose to call the *principal*. Some would call him priest; but that term in our language designates, not the person in whom the ritual centres, but a man who gravitates round that centre, not the president, but one who attends on him, and is an intermediary between him and the rest of the community.
C. IMITATION is the very essence of the ritual: it is because

10. G. Landtman, *The Kiwai Papuans of British New Guinea* (London, 1927), 127.

the objective can be imitated so as to control it, that ritual is possible. The principal is the person that imitates. He imitates because he is somehow identical with what he imitates. Thus

$$\text{principal} = \text{objective.}$$

He is identical however only because both are identical with a third, the ancestor-god :

$$\text{principal} = \text{god,}$$
$$\text{objective} = \text{god,}$$
$$\therefore \text{ principal} = \text{objective.}$$

This equivalence is not limited to the principal, but extends to the other participants in a secondary manner, of which we may not yet quite understand the mechanism; but in some cases they seem to represent the subordinate elements of the objective. Thus in the rain-ceremony, putting myths and ritual together, one gathers that the principal is the cloud, and his acolytes the drops of rain. In order to complete the identity it is necessary to dress up like the thing imitated, if that is possible. Things can be made to multiply, like human beings and animals, that is by sexual intercourse between the principal and his wife, or it may be between the secondary personages and women. This is called a SACRED MARRIAGE.

D. COMMUNION, FEAST, INVESTITURE: the objectives are mainly food. When they are, they are usually eaten as part of the ritual. This is not an ordinary process of eating, since the principal is identified with what he eats. The term for this is communion. If the objective is inedible all that can be done is to hand it to the principal. This is called investiture.

The whole proceedings are only effective by means of the E. WORD.[11]

11. I have here analyzed only those elements of ritual that are important for our present theme. For a more exhaustive analysis see my *Progress of Man,* pp. 140 ff.

It is to the imitation I chiefly want to direct the reader's attention, because it is this that will determine the part of each functionary in the state.

The Mandans, a Sioux tribe of North America, have a technique very like that of the Arandas.[12] The PURPOSE is to produce an abundance of buffaloes. We have unfortunately no details as to who the OWNERS are or who the PRINCIPAL. The IMITATION, on the other hand, is so patent that I have selected this ritual in spite of the important blanks in our account, which is that of an artist, not a scientist. The whole ceremony is a repetition of one taught by the First Man, one who escaped the Flood. It is opened by a man who impersonates him. The rest of the performers dress up as bull buffaloes, and imitate their ways as they dance. SACRED MARRIAGE: a man impersonates the Evil Spirit. Armed with a wooden phallus he mounts the bull buffaloes.[13] He is then pursued by the women, who seek to wrench the phallus from him. She who succeeds claims that "she held ꞌthe power of *creation,* and *of life and death* over them; that she was the father of all buffaloes, and that she could come or stay away as she pleased." At night there is an orgy of free love and a FEAST. WORD: the myth of the Flood is recited at the beginning.

Although the ceremony is primarily concerned with buffaloes, there are also dancers dressed up as grizzly bears, bald eagles, antelopes, swans, beavers, vultures, and wolves. We are not told what they are doing there, but it is evident that the whole ritual has a much wider purpose than the mere multiplication of buffaloes: it is a ceremony of creation, life and death, and the buffaloes are protagonists only because the tribe is so dependent on their flesh for life and death.

We saw at the outset that ritual is a pursuit of life. Specific objectives are singled out merely as means to that end. That end is not lost sight of, but is constantly indicated in the prayers. Thus the Blackfoot Indians make easy the capture

12. G. Catlin, *O-kee-pa,* London, 1867.
13. Such unnatural acts are not infrequent in ritual, and remain a puzzle, since they cannot create. Perhaps they are merely particular applications of the principle of inversion so characteristic of rites associated with death (*Progress of Man,* 181 f.). The Evil Spirit is death. But why is the Father of Buffaloes a woman?

48

of deer by dancing the dance of the black-tailed deer; but they pray "for food, success in all undertakings and protection against death."[14] So much do the owners of the ritual keep their minds on this ultimate purpose, that they sometimes forget the immediate one, the increase of the specific objective. Thus the Cree Indians hold a bear dance, to secure not bear's flesh, but the goodwill of the bears and their assistance in obtaining long life.[15] Some buffalo dances have as their purpose, not abundance of buffaloes, but the cure of the sick.

For evidence of COMMUNION we have to turn to tribes described more thoroughly than Catlin's Mandans. The dance is often followed by a hunt of the animal concerned, and then the feast consists of its flesh. Not always: in one turtle dance they eat, not turtle, but green corn, which is supposed to be turtle food.[16] The actors are thus imitating the turtle.

The Winnebagoes are divided into groups to which the name of clan has been applied. Membership of the clan is hereditary; in other words, it is a big family. Each clan is associated with an animal. "The clan animals are among the principal guardian spirits to-day . . . The guardian spirit is at present conceived as an immaterial being in control of animal species." (Why not call them gods?) The PURPOSE of the worship of these gods has nothing to do with the increase of the associated animal; it is "life and victory"; the people pray "to have sufficient blessings to guide us all safely through life." The OWNERS are the clan after whom the ritual is named, bear-clan feast, buffalo-clan feast and so on. There are other ceremonies owned by associations of peoples who have been blessed by the same class of spirits, not by families. These spirits are also commonly associated with animals: buffalo spirits, grizzly-bear spirits; but there are also nonanimal spirits, such as night spirits.

The PRINCIPAL never appears to be a man. There is no neces-

14. Clark Wissler, *Societies and Dance Associations of the Blackfoot Indians,* Anthropological Papers of the American Museum of Natural History, XI, 440.
15. Alanson Skinner. *Political Organization, Cults, and Ceremonies of the Plains-Cree,* ibid., XI, 531.
16. Alanson Skinner, *Political Organization, Cults, and Ceremonies of the Plains-Cree,* ibid., XI, 531.

sity for him to be one. The function of the principal is to represent the god; if a stone can do so, the stone can be principal, as it often is. In the snake feast of the Winnebagoes four snake skins are brought. They are "the representatives of the first four snakes Earthmaker (the Creator) made." It is in honour of these snakes that the host gives the feast. The ancestor-gods are here represented by the skins of their animal embodiments. In the bear-clan ceremony a headdress is the principal, even as with us the crown can represent the king in his absence, and royal honours are accorded to it, such as presenting arms. Among the Winnebagoes the place of the king at the head of the ritual circle is always left vacant by men. In the bear feast the offerings are addressed to the four ancestral bears created in the beginning; but turtle, sun, moon, morning star, fire, etc., after which no clans are named, are nevertheless represented, just as we saw other animals figuring in the Mandan buffalo feast besides the buffalo. IMITATION: the members of the clan are descended from the four animals after whom the clan is named. The host recalls that they are doing as their ancestors said. We can watch this imitation in the buffalo-spirit dance (one of these cult associations); the performers behave like buffaloes and eat like them. It is evident the people attach great importance to this imitation, for they constantly underline it. Thus the host in the ceremony of the Night Spirits says: "To-night you have tried to imitate your grand-fathers, you have tried to take the place of the spirits." In the war-bundle feast the guests are addressed, not once, but again and again, as "You who are sitting here impersonating spirits." Why do they impersonate the spirits? For very practical reasons which appear in the following remark: "If the spirits accept offerings of food and tobacco and buckskins, then afterwards those who have impersonated them will participate in the blessings that follow." By blessings are meant long life, victory, and success generally. This identification is thus no mere mysticism, but a practical technique:

$$A = B$$

∴ all that accrues to A will accrue to B.[17]

17. Radin, 340; 346; 487; 507; 521; etc. Cp. 481 note 89.

The theory of COMMUNION is distinctly stated: a worshipper reminds his ancestors that his grandfather used to extend to them "water from an animal whom you considered the same as our own body, and spirit food."[18] They are thus offering themselves to the ancestors who are themselves. What appeared absurd when ascribed to the Arandas is definitely stated by the Winnebagoes. There are two elements at this communion, solid and liquid, hot water and food, plus the usual tobacco of American ritual. These three substances are described as "life-giving material."[19] WORD: in the bear feast the host tells the myth of the ancestral bear. Speeches are made and prayers are spoken, all referring to the ancestors; the four clan songs are sung.

Dr. Radin has allowed his Winnebagoes to speak to us direct. The result is we have not long been left guessing how they conceive the identity of worshipper with objective and with ancestor. It is no stupid confusion, but a lucid doctrine. Worshipper and objective are alike representatives, vehicles, of spirits. We have heard repeated statements that the worshippers "take the place of spirits," that they are representatives of the animals concerned, that these animals are spirits which are conceived as immaterial beings in control of animal species. It is all clear enough: the same spirit infuses worshipper and animal, the spirit of the ancestor. Since they are the receptacles of the same spirit they are equivalent, interchangeable. The animal body is for the ancestral spirit equivalent to the body of the worshipper, just as in Australia. It is the spirit that is important as the motive power, and that is the same in both cases. The body is merely a vehicle, and which vehicle is used is of secondary importance: it may be a man, a skin, a crown, a stone, anything which the particular conditions and history of the ritual may indicate. All the different vehicles are interchangeable, so worshipper, objective, cult-object are all one.

We are now in a better position to understand this doctrine of identity when we meet with it again, notably among the Koryaks.

18. Radin, 330. Cp. 455, note 30.
19. Radin, 323.

Their great ritual is the Whale Festival. On that occasion a whale is killed, brought in, and entertained like an honoured guest, feasted with its own flesh, and so treated that its spirit is induced to come back as another whale which they will kill and eat. The specific PURPOSE is thus indicated; but there is a more general one expressed in the prayers, that of avoiding sickness during the coming winter and of averting evil spirits. The OWNERS are the whole village, but the minor ceremonies are in the hands of particular families. No man, so far as our account goes, represents the ancestor and receives worship in that capacity. The PRINCIPAL, the honoured guest to whom the whole ritual is addressed, is the whale, or rather the spirit of the whale present in its own body first, then in a wooden image which takes the place of that body when this is cut up. We see how important it is to keep in mind the meaning of the equivalences: the principal is only a man in so far as that man is equivalent to the ancestor; but other things may be equated to him, and then those things receive the cult. It is really neither the man nor the things that are the principal, but the ancestor god for whom they stand. In other Koryak rites we do find men impersonating the same spirit as the animal, and then we have IMITATION by men. At the bear festival a woman dresses up as a bear and dances. At the wolf festival a man puts on the skin of the wolf and walks round the hearth to the beating of a drum. A myth tells of magpie men, raven men, and fox men attending a whale festival, just as all sorts of animals join in the Mandan buffalo dance. The Creator himself is called Big Raven "who turns into a raven only when putting on a raven's coat." SACRED MARRIAGE: no hint. At the FEAST food is placed before the image as if it were the whale itself. The fireplace represents the sea to which it is returning. The image is fed with parts of the whale's body, and these parts also represent the whale.[20] The host burns some fat of the whale. WORD: when the whale is landed a woman puts alder branches and sacrificial grass into its mouth with an incantation: "The Creator said, 'I shall go and get a white whale for my children as food.' He

20. Jochelson, 72.

went and got-it. Then he said, 'I shall go for an alder branch.'
He went and brought a branch. He brought a branch for the
whale. Later, he again procured the same white whale: again
he brought a branch. Thus always he did, and thus always
he hunted." In other words the participants are merely repeating what was done by the Creator, "the first man, the father
and protector of the Koryak."

The equivalences are somewhat obscured, but they can still
be seen:—

whale = image; animal = performer; performer = creator
and ancestor.

In other rites too natural objects figure as principals and
as ancestors, for sacrifices are made to the sacred rocks, hills
and capes, and they are addressed as "grandfather."

It seems nonsense this idea of feeding a whale with its own
flesh; but the nonsense varnishes when we remember it is not
the bodily whale that is feasted, but a spirit which was lodged
in a whale's body and which is provided with a new abode
in the form of an image.

It seems equally strange at first that men should kill what
they regard as a benefactor and a god; but we must get used
to the idea because it is fundamental. A further instance is
therefore justified. Among the inland Koryaks the domesti-
cated reindeer takes the place which the whale occupies
among their maritime brothers. It is closely "connected with
the family cult. The reindeer is the bearer of luck, and the
protector of the family. . . . They consider it a sin to sell
any live reindeer. Reindeer that are sold carry away with them
the luck of the herd: therefore when selling their reindeer
for slaughter, the Koryaks do not part with them alive, but
kill them themselves. Under such circumstances the slaughter
of a reindeer that is sold is considered as a sacrifice to the
Supreme Deity, and can bring no bad consequences."[21] The
reindeer is the protector of the family; we jump to the conclusion that it is treated with respect. That does not follow: it
is lassoed, harnessed, whipped, and treated just as we treat
animals that we need, or rather worse. We shall never really

21. Jochelson, 492.

grasp the essence of ritual as long as we imagine that reverence for the principal, and for the god he or it represents, is a necessary part of it. The essential thing in worship is not reverence, but identity. There may be reverence; there often is; but there may be none. It all depends what the particular purpose may be: the principal is treated as the interests of the community may require: if killing is indicated he, or it, is killed.[22]

As in Australia, the objective, the thing to be influenced, need not be an animal, or even a natural object: it may be an artefact such as the skin-boat, which is "an important guardian of the family hearth." Jochelson uses the term guardian where some speak of totems and others of gods. This multiplicity of terms for the same thing merely obscures the fundamental likeness, and leads men to think the things are different because the names are.

Rain-making is very prominent among the rituals of East Africa and the Sudan. The Lango of the Upper Nile have two kinds of rain-making, one annual, the other occasional, whenever the rain fails.[23] So have the Arandas, since every specific rite of theirs is performed when there is need of the objective, and also annually.[24] Only in the case of the Aranda we have not been told what the need is, whether for water to drink only, or for water to vivify the whole creation as well as man; and thus we remain ignorant whether they have realized the connection between rain and fertility. The East Africans are quite familiar with the connection, and so the PURPOSE appears in the Lango litany as much wider than the immediate objective, rain. The prayers utter a wish that the food shall ripen, the women and children rejoice, and the young men sing. The OWNERS of the annual ceremony are the tribe, of the occasional one the clan. The man who bears the title of "rain-owner" should be the PRINCIPAL, but, unfortunately for us, he has no authority over the rain or the festival. The dancers also disappoint us, because they do not imitate

---

22. For an excellent example see *Yorubas*, 136 f.
23. J. H. Driberg, *The Lango* (London, 1923), 243 ff.
24. Strehlow, III, 1, 1 ff.

the clouds or the rain, but the animals associated with one of the four groups into which the performers are divided: elephant, leopard, rhinoceros, buffalo. Mr. Driberg however draws the obvious inference from the rain-owner's title that he once did control the rain, and is able to support his inference by pointing to neighbouring tribes where that personage enjoys great authority. Setting to work therefore on the Lango ritual, I arrived by a long process of deduction at the conclusion that the following equivalences once held good, if they do not nowadays:

$$\text{men} = \text{clouds,}$$
$$\text{trees} = \text{clouds,}$$
$$\text{frog} = \text{cloud.}$$

I will not repeat the process, because those who have never sat down to analyze rituals in their smallest details, do not realize the rigour of their logic, and so they will merely say I am being ingenious. It has, besides, become unnecessary to rely upon roundabout inference, since direct evidence was later found as I searched among other tribes of the Upper Nile. There the principle of IMITATION comes out very clearly. For instance, the Bari have nests of stones which bear the names of former rain-makers and are addressed thus, "My father, you were in your day a mighty rainmaker."[25] Thus rainmaker = ancestor = cult object. Mr. Driberg informs me that if the rain fails the Ateso of Uganda rip open their rain-maker because he is withholding the rain in his inside. Thus rainmaker = cloud. Since the above was written Dr. and Mrs. Seligman, after reviewing the evidence from the Bari, definitely assert that "dead rain-makers, rain-stones, and clouds are equated with each other. . . . Rain-stones are clouds . . . while clouds are rain-makers."[26]

The FEAST is represented by a goat and a ram killed and eaten at the end. The WORD is represented by songs and litany.

25. F. Spire, *Rain-making in Equatorial Africa*, Journ. African Soc., V (1905), 15 ff.
26. *The Pagan Tribes of the Nilotic Sudan* (Cambridge, 1932), 288.

The imitation is very clear in New Guinea rain-making.[27] The principal imitates the Creator who was a rain-maker. With his axe, which is still used in the ritual, the Creator cut a sago palm, and so created the neighbouring tribes, the sun, moon, stars, and clouds. The clouds were dry sago which he swept into the air. While he imitates the Creator the principal also behaves as he would have the clouds behave: he utters booming noises, strikes the trees with the axe, and spouts water from his mouth. He whistles: this is to imitate the wind. Then he goes through a pretence of making sago on a stone formerly used by the Creator. He now behaves as he wishes his people to be in a position to behave: he plays many parts, as is often the case. He has four stones, one identified with the wind from one quarter, the second stands for another wind, the third for the sun who was a woman of his tribe, the last for the moon, who was a man of the tribe. Thus

principal = ancestor-creator = cloud = his people.

The trees are painted black and Mr. Williams has come to the conclusion, quite independently, that they represent the clouds. These are thus represented twice over.

Though more immediately concerned with rain, this ceremony embraces the whole world. The myth describes a creation ritual of which rainmaking is only a part.

These living institutions help us to understand the obscurities of ancient texts. The Rigveda is full of references to the slaying of the serpent and the release of the waters. The slayer is Indra, the thunder-god, the Indian Thor. Sometimes he is Agni, the fire-god. He is praised as a mighty bull. The serpent demon is variously called Vritra or Sambara. We learn from the commentators that this demon is the cloud, but the clouds are mountains, so the demon is also a mountain. This cloud-mountain is cloven by the thundergod, "the sprinkler of waters," who thus releases the waters withheld by the demon, just as they may be withheld by the Ateso king. The rains

27. F. E. Williams, *Rain-making on the River Morehead*, Journ. Roy. Anthropological Institute, 1929, 379.

are cows which are thus set free. They are cows because milk is rain.[28]

African facts suggest the following explanation of Vedic myths. The bearer of the thunderbolt cleaves the cloudman in order to release the rains. These are ritually represented by cows which are milked as part of the ceremony. It appears from the hymns all this is part of a creation ceremony, for the slaying of the demon is followed by "bringing forth the sun, the sky, the dawn."[29]

The Greeks had memories of a similar ceremony, if we remember our initial equation Agni = Hermes. For Hermes slew a demon and thereby released the cow Io, daughter of an Argive river-god.[30]

Here are some equivalences as worked out for Egypt by Prof. A. Erman:—[31]

Sun $\Big\{$ = Horus eyes = sun-god's snakes = king's snakes =
Moon $\Big($ Crowns of Upper and Lower Egypt = Nechbet and
Buto (goddesses).

So vital are all these equivalences to the ritual that we must drive home their true nature, even at the risk of repeating ourselves. They do not proceed, as has often been alleged, from an inability to distinguish one thing from another, to keep separate identities apart, for they do not consist in identity of the body. If this has not yet been made clear, the Fijians will make it so.

28. *Rgv.*, I, 59, 6 taken with *Nirukta*, VII, 23. Cp. my detailed analysis of *Rgv.*, I, 32 in *C.J.Sc.*, I, 135. — *Rgv.*, I, 57, 6. — Mac Donell, *Vedic Mythology*, 10; 80; 111; 159. — *Rgv.*, I, 32, 11; I, 64, 5 f.; 166, 3. — *Nirukta*, II, 16.
29. *Rgv.*, I, 32, 4.
30. Pauly-Wissowa, *Real-Encyclopädie der classischen Altertumswissenchaft*, s.vv. *Io, Argus.*—Perhaps we are witnessing such a ceremony in a Maya fresco which represents a priest smiting with his stone axe a victim stretched out on the body of a fantastic feathered rattle-snake made of some material we do not know. Th. Gann and J. E. Thompson, *The History of the Maya* (London, 1931), Pl. XIII, p. 133.
31. *Hymnen an das Diadem der Pharaonen* (Berlin, 1911), 14.

There each clan has usually an animal. They call it by a word we may translate "spirit" or "god." They might by the hasty be described as worshipping dogs and birds; but, if we know them and their language better, we shall also hear them calling the dog or bird, the "body" of the spirit, or the "canoe" on which it "embarks." It may equally well "embark" or "jump" on a man. Then that man is for the time being identified with the god, and speaks as if he were the god. The Fijians were not so confused as to think that man and the dog were the same: they are equivalent only in so far as they are receptacles for the same spirit. It is just as inaccurate to dub these people animal or plant worshippers, as to say, as I have heard Free-thinkers say, that Roman Catholics worship a wafer.

The true principal in a Winnebago, or any Red Indian, ceremony is not the bodily bear or snake, but a spirit bear or spirit snake, that is, spirits of which the bear or snake body is only the visible token. "It is believed by the shaman," says Mr. Radin, "that the spirits are a *tertium quid,* neither animal nor man, but possessing infinite powers of transformation now into one, now into the other."[32] It is equally clear that in the Koryak festival it is the spirit present in the whale that is the guest, and not the whale.

Ritual equivalence then nowhere consists in material identity, but in sharing a common spirit, life, or whatever you may choose to call it. It is that common spirit that is ritually important: the bodies are merely means to get at it.

By effecting this equivalence men are enabled to control whatever has been allotted to them. Things are not allotted on grounds of character, ability. A man is not detailed to take charge of kangaroos or buffaloes because he was born more skilful in imitating the gait of the kangaroo or the buffalo than others. The right to impersonate is a family heirloom. The hereditary principle may break down: then the right has to be acquired by apostolic succession.

Each family is in charge of one or more species, but it is responsible for its charge to the whole community. The spe-

32. Radin, 437.

cific rite is part of a system embracing the whole of man's welfare, a system which we have called a creation ceremony. The Aranda ceremonies at first sight seem to be an exception: they are performed quite independently of each other at the times of the year appropriate to each species. Increased knowledge however dissipates that exception: all these specific ceremonies are rehearsed together about November as part of a great festival, of which the making of boys into men is the central feature. Each specific ceremony, besides, presupposes a tribal system of which it is but a part, just as each variety of mechanic presupposes a factory into which he fits. The kangaroo men are not multiplying kangaroos for themselves, but for those who do not own the ceremony. They themselves eat sparingly. It is for the others they are working, just as a smith does not forge primarily for himself, but for the rest of the community.

Of tribes further north than the Arandas Miss U. M'Connel remarks: "It is generally recognized that though a clan has hunting rights over its own area, the control of the food supply by 'increase' ceremonies is not for its own benefit alone, but causes abundant supplies in other areas. Not only so, but it is generally understood that areas specially rich or unique in raw materials should send out word to relatives in other clans when the supply is ripe for consumption. The clan in charge must always initiate the first and ritualistic 'taking' of food, after which all are permitted to tap the supply."[33]

These ceremonies are then parts of a tribal scheme for the increase of all that is necessary to life.

33. *The Wik-Munkan Tribe*, Oceania, 1934, 334 f.

5' The World

We carry within us the wonders we seek without us: there is Africa and her prodigies in us.
Thomas Browne

THE RITUALS we have considered so far specifically notice each item that helps to make up the total of prosperity. It is possible to treat them all as a whole called the world. Prosperity can be achieved not piece-meal, but by one all-inclusive rite. The episodes lose their autonomy and are merged into one all-embracing conception of welfare, the life of the world.

Rites based on this conception may sometimes seem very different from those in which the species are summoned, as it were, by name. Yet when we penetrate beneath the surface and dissect the integuments and map out the structure, we shall find there is no change in fundamentals. The equation

principal = objective

remains throughout: all that changes is the scope of the objective. When each thing is treated separately the principal is in each case equivalent to the particular thing treated, animal, plant, stone, cloud, or whatever it may be. When the world is treated as a whole he is the world.

There is no hard and fast line between the types: one has evolved into the other, so that it may be difficult at times to decide to which chapter we should assign a ritual.

The ritual which formerly absorbed most of the enthusiasm of the Fijians, and still does, was not the cult of the gods, but the ceremonial that surrounds a chief. To the casual observer it appears as nothing more than ceremonial; but he who analyzes it soon discovers it to be much more than that. It is a ritual with as practical a purpose as any we have met so far; but that PURPOSE is no longer specific: it has not as objective one item; it goes straight for the whole of nature so far as it contributes to the life of the people. The following prayer, which I obtained in a Christianized form, will show the range. When the great chief entitled the "Lord of the

Reef" is installed they pray: "The offering of the chiefly *kava*, that you may live, you noble youths. Let the fields resound, the land resound. Exalted be the Father and Son whom we worship. Let the fish come to land; let the fruit trees bear; let the land prosper. May you all live; let the work of God grow. May our land be blessed; may your soil be blessed." This generalized character is not due to Christianity: the old heathen prayers were equally all-embracing, and in those days of warfare included a prayer for victory.[1] OWNERSHIP: the Fijians are grouped into tribes or states numbering from a few hundred to several thousand souls. The ritual is the ritual of the state. Each tribe is divided into clans, corresponding more or less to the Roman gens. Each clan has its own god, and the god's animal, if any; but the clan ritual is not directed to the increase of that animal: it has the same purpose as the state ritual, of which it is just a minor edition. The PRINCIPAL is the chief or king. It is usual to call him chief, because we think of a king as ruler over millions; but a Fijian high chief has as much right to be called king as Agamemnon or Odysseus, and his title, *Tui*, is the same as that of the sovereign whom we recognize as King of Tonga. Under him are the heads of villages and clans whom I shall distinguish as headmen or chieftains. They preside over the village or clan ritual, or, failing them, the next senior member of their family presides. All these titles, of chiefs and chieftains, run in families. IMITATION: "In the olden times," said a Fijian to me, "it was the chief who was our god." "Only the chief," said a subject of the Lord of the Reef, "was believed in: he was by way of being a human god. Spirits were only useful in war; in other things no." The term for god is *vu*, "stem," "ancestor." This ancestor is often represented by a stone. Thus we get

king = ancestor-god = stone.

The chief is also entitled "The Prosperity of the Land." We thus see how a great enlargement of the scope of the ritual

---

1. A long text is given by D. Hazlewood in his *Fijian Grammar*, p. 62.

has altered nothing in the fundamental principle

head of the ritual = objective.

The objective is prosperity, so the principal is prosperity, abundance. SEX does not appear either realistically or symbolically. The WORD is never absent; there are always prayers and formulae. The myth however does not figure in them. There is an abundance of myths explaining ceremonial traditions; but they are told apart from the ritual. FEASTS are the culmination of every ceremony. The solid part consists of pig, man, fish, and roots: the liquid is kava, the root of *piper methysticum*, pounded and strained in water. They are usually accompanied by gifts of artefacts, such as whale's teeth, mats, bark-cloth, so that all forms of wealth are represented. Feasts are not consumed by the people who prepared the food, but like the artefacts are gifts to another group which forms a vis-à-vis. In big feasts the contributions are pooled and shared out again.

There is no mention of the universe or its parts in Fiji, except for the land and its prosperity. In the neighbouring islands of Tonga the king is called the Sky. He is then identical with the sky, as he is elsewhere with animals and plants. In its structure the Tongan royal ritual is so like the Fijian that they must be considered varieties of one species.

The Igbo king assumes the title of "the Sky."

The ritual of the Vedic Indian had become so complicated that it could only be acquired by years of learning. Yet these complications have not altered the main lines. The PURPOSE, stated with wearisome iteration, is still the same: to increase the supply of food and wealth, which is largely cattle, to ensure progeny, to ward off illness and untimely death, to thwart enemies. The first hymn of the Rigveda, addressed to the sacrificial fire, sums up these aims.

> Through Agni one may gain wealth,
> Also prosperity day by day,
> Far-famed, most rich in heroes.

The prose literature based on the Vedas is full of such explanations as that, by reciting such and such a verse, the sacrificer becomes "an eater of food, lord of food, with his offspring he secures eating of food."[2] As in Fiji the objective is not specific, but all-round prosperity and success. Different constituents of prosperity may be successively dealt with, such as food, cattle, health, sovereignty, but always in such wide categories, not single species of animals and plants, or artefacts. OWNERSHIP: tribal and class. EXCLUSIVENESS is very strong. The ritual is confined to those in communion, heathens are identified with the demons and excluded; not only heathens, but all those besides that have not been initiated, the artisan classes, such as barbers, charioteers, huntsmen, etc.; also women. The nobles, priests, and farmers are alone qualified for ritual. Yet there are occasions when even the uninitiated have to play a part, and without a wife the principal cannot officiate. The rule is stated thus: "For she, inasmuch as she is his wife, is half of himself. Therefore as long as he does not find a wife, so long he is not born, for so long he is not complete. But in finding a wife he is born, for then he becomes complete."[3] In other words, through the ritual he is reborn, but he cannot achieve this without a wife, a "better half." The PRINCIPAL is termed the "Sacrificer." He varies in rank according to the ceremony, for the ceremonies are graded. There are those that are held by heads of families; there are royal ceremonies over which the king presides, or by which a nobleman becomes king; there are super-royal ceremonies culminating in the "Imperial Consecration," as we may term the Horse Sacrifice, which makes a king into a Universal Monarch, or Emperor. IMITATION: the principal stands for the god Indra, the wielder of thunder; but he may be other gods besides. The king is Varuna too, who keeps order in the world, and Brihaspati, the priest of the gods, and others whom I need not enumerate. Among these gods there ever recurs one Prajapati, "Lord of Creatures," who is the Universe, "everything here," as the texts put it. Thus the king is equivalent to the whole world inasmuch as he is the World Spirit, and also is the several gods who preside over the several parts of the World, such as the Guardians of the four or the

2. *Aitareya Brahmana,* I, 6.
3. *Satapatha Brahmana,* V, 2, 1, 10.

eight quarters of the globe. All these gods are also identified with objects used in the ritual. Thus Prajapati and the Fire-god, Agni, are identified with the sacrificial mound or altar. It follows logically that the principal is one with the altar, and that conclusion is actually drawn. Thus we have the explicit permission of the texts to say

principal = god = world = altar,

and everything is interchangeable with everything else. This feature has evoked the scorn of our modern rationalists, because they have not grasped the point of the ritual: it is to make one thing equivalent to another so that by acting on one you can act on another, just as the Koryak makes the image equivalent to the whale, or the European peasant makes his statue represent the saint, in order that he may reach his spiritual objective through a material representative. Without these equivalences there would be no point in the ritual; in fact, when they atrophy the whole system withers, as it has done among the religious liberals of Europe. The Indians were perfectly aware of these equivalences. It was a conscious system which had its technical terms. Thus we are explicitly told that "in respect of divinity" the sacrificial fire is the same as the sun; "in respect of the self" or the "spirit" (*atman*) it is the sacrificer's breath. "In respect of the ritual" the sun is the same as a gold disc which is placed under the altar.[4] The participants are deliberately seeking to establish an identity between man and the ritual objects, between ritual objects and the world, and so between man and the world, a kind of creative syllogism. The principal is equated to the altar, part for part; on the other hand the altar is equated with the world, the lower layers of bricks being the earth, the topmost the sky, and so on. Thus the principal becomes a microcosm which corresponds point for point with the macrocosm, eye with sun, ear with wind, feet with earth, and so on. At the same time, the gods are identified each with his own animal, as in the specific rituals; Varuna, for instance,

4. *Satapatha Brahmana*, X, 4, 1, 22 f.; 5, 2, 5 f. The terms are *adhidevatam, adhyatmam, adhiyajnam.*

64

with the horse, but there is no sign of any ritual to increase the supply of horses or of any specific objective.

It is no material identity the Indian seeks: it is not identity with the sun which he strives after, for it is not the sun he worships, not the moon, nor lightning, but the being[5] in the sun, the being in the moon, the being in the lightning. By the worship of all these beings he acquires their qualities and powers; he becomes equivalent on earth to sun, moon, lightning and the rest.[6]

We are given very precise information how this identity is achieved: it is by being reborn.[7] The king at his consecration is dressed in robes that represent the womb and the placenta from which he is to be reborn. In order to complete his identification with the world he is given a mace which stands for the thunderbolt; a gold disc is placed on his head to represent the sun. Sex runs right through the ritual, but only symbolically, except in the horse sacrifice, where the SACRED MARRIAGE is carried out in the flesh.[8] Generally the ritual act is described as an act of carnal intercourse.[9] Procreation is indeed the prototype of creation. The very word for creating means literally "to eject," "emit,"[10] and the creation of the world is conceived as a seminal effusion from which develops the whole.

It is in the myths that creation by sacred marriage is best preserved; for in practice it seems to have been generally toned down to a symbol. A legend from the end of the old Brahmanic period tells us how in the beginning the spirit "was as large as a man and a woman in embrace. He split this self in two. Hence there came into being husband and wife. . . . He had connection with her. Hence men were generated. She considered: 'How is it he has connection with me after generating me from his own self? Come, let me hide.' She became a cow; he became a bull. He had connection with her. Hence cattle were generated." She changed successively

5. *Purusha:* male, spirit, world spirit.
6. *Brihadaranyaka Upanishad,* II, 1.
7. *Kingship,* 77 ff.
8. *Sat. Br.* XIII, 2, 9; 5, 2, 2. — Muir's *Sanskrit Texts,* IV, 171.
9. E.g., *Ait. Br.,* I, 1.
10. *Srj.*

into a mare, a goat, a ewe, etc., "and in this way he created all that exists here as pairs down to the ants."[11] We seem in this myth to have got right back to specific rites, but there is this difference that all species are the creation of one being and not of a number of specialists.

In a late form this creation is thus described:— The creator "absorbed in meditation emitted from his own body the various creatures; he emitted even the waters in the beginning, and in them infused seed."[12] Here the consort is omitted, but in early conceptions the sky is the male infusing semen in the form of rain into the earth. The principal is the whole world, but he is also more particularly the sky, while the "other half of himself," his consort, is the earth. With her he creates. We can now understand why woman, though excluded from most of the ritual, is absolutely indispensable. In modern Hindu worship the sacred marriage is still carried out with images. The WORD has attained to supreme importance, as one might expect in a ritual which has passed into the hands of specialists in reasoning. At every step of the ritual a myth is told to explain the procedure. For instance at one point the sacrificer has to take three steps carrying a pan containing the sacred fire. The myth is told which I here render in simpler language than the original: "The god Prajapati by taking three ritual steps produced creatures . . . In like manner by taking three ritual steps the sacrificer produces creatures." The myth is not told merely for edification or amusement; knowledge of it is essential for the success of the ritual, and the myth over and over again ends with a formula like this: "Whoever knows this will become a consumer of food," in other words will not lack food.[13] The ritual is accompanied by the word in three forms: hymn, sacrificial formula, chant, the "Three Vedas." These are not mere requests for favours or expressions of thanks or reverence, like our forms of words; they are spells with creative force: "By Speech is this All made."[14] The hymns put vigour into the gods and

11. *Brihad Ar. Up.*, I, 4, 1.
12. Manu, I, 8.
13. *Sat. Br.*, VI, 7, 4, 1; I, 6, 3, 17.
14. *Ibid.*, VIII, 1, 2, 9.

the world, just as the Aranda hymns put it into specific objects. Offerings of cakes, butter, gruel, animal victims, succeed one another. The principal is identified with the victim, and the victim with the god,[15] so that we get the unfailing equation

Principal = offering = god,

and the principal eats of his own flesh. COMMUNION is in two kinds, solid and liquid. The liquid is *soma,* pressed from a plant which has not been identified. It is called also ambrosia,[16] that is elixir of immortality. Soma is also the moon, a royal god, one of those with whom the king is identified, so that logically the king drinks himself.

Our information about Indian ritual is so full, and, coming from the inside and not from foreign observers, is so valuable, that we must dwell upon it somewhat. The ceremony of creating the world will illustrate the principles.[17] It is prefaced by the myth of the creation. Then comes the actual performance. The principal seeks for a lump of clay which represents semen. He places it with a lotus leaf which stands for the womb. Water is poured on, and foam is produced, because in the beginning water was created, then foam, then earth. From the clay is prepared a four-sided pan which is the universe with its four quarters; the bottom is the earth, the lower part of the sides the air, the upper part the sky. Fire is put into the pan which now represents the sun. The principal, on this occasion impersonating the god Vishnu, holds it up, and makes three strides by which he mounts successively earth, air, sky. And so it goes on, and, as it goes on, it renovates this real world for the benefit of the sacrificers; it puts vigour into animals, puts milk into females, provides the body with head and limbs, organizes society, making the commons subservient to the king, etc., etc. Being the spirit of the universe, the king controls the universe.

The idea of macrocosm and microcosm is found at an earlier date in Babylonia. The analogy of man and the universe was

15. *Ibid.,* II, 5, 1, 7; V, 2, 1, 2 ff.; *Taittiriya Brahmana,* III, 9, 17, 4.
16. *Amrita.*
17. *Sat. Br.,* VI.

known to the Stoics and to the Chinese.[18] The doctrine that "man is a universe in little, and the universe a man in great" was a favourite with Jewish thinkers, especially the Cabala.[19] It descended to Paracelsus. Lately Sir Francis Younghusband has tried to reconcile it with modern science by supposing that "just as a germ-cell bears upon it the impress of its parents . . . so would terrestrial life bear upon it the impress of mother universe. And further, just as from an examination of the germ-cell, we would be able to form an idea of the leading characters of the parent . . . so would we from an examination of terrestrial life be able to gain a knowledge of its parent the universe."[20]

The fact is human thought is unable to get away from the idea of worlds in little. The science of physics has not got away from it; on the contrary it is more wedded to it than ever. Only its microcosm is not man, but atoms, units so tiny that an infinitude of them go to make up a man. When it tries to conceive the invisibly small it can only do so on the analogy of the visibly immense, as bodies revolving round each other like the stars. We cannot get away from this trick of thought in the present work: whenever we try and understand, we shall find ourselves thinking of society as a vast body, and of the body as a small society.[21]

The doctrine of man the microcosm is met with as a philosophy, more especially as a mystical philosophy. The conclusion is commonly drawn that it has never been anything but a philosophy, the property of a few thinkers, and never had an influence on society at large. On the contrary, it has played

18. H. Ritter und L. Preller, *Historia Philosophiae Graecae*, 8th ed. (Gotha, 1898), 499. — M. Granet, *La Pensée Chinoise* (Paris, 1934), 24.
19. *Jewish Encyclopaedia*, s.v. Microcosm.
20. *The Destiny of the Universe*, Hibbert Journal, XXXI, 165.
21. Cp. *Presidential Address to the British Association*, 1933 *Report*, pp. 15 f. — Hobbes' *Leviathan*, especially frontispiece. — Science is supposed to have begun with the Greeks; but viewed in relation to the whole evolution of man, they appear merely as ants adding a few grains of sand to a mighty heap. Brilliant and wonderful as they may have been, they merely emended and carried further doctrines much older than themselves, notably that of the microcosm, which itself grew out of very early theories of life-giving.

a great part, as we shall see, in the process of centralizing society. For the ancient Indians it was much more than a philosophical speculation, a brilliant idea, a plaything of the mind; it was just as much a working theory as our theories of electricity. The equation *man = universe in little* was not a fact from which deductions were made; but a goal to reach. Man *is* not a microcosm; he has to be *made* one in order that he may control the universe for prosperity. The ritual establishes an equivalence that was not there. If it were there already there would be no point in having a ritual; man would merely have to behave as he wished the world to behave, and there would be no needs of words, of altars, and other methods of effecting the identity.

Babylonia yields fragments so obscure that they chiefly serve to show how impossible it is to understand the direct evidence of ancient times without the clue of living forms. This much seems certain, that every year a festival was held at which the myth of the creation was repeated; the king in a triumphal procession took the part of the god; he and his consorts were identified with most of the important heavenly bodies; but he was also identified with a tree pillar, and the same ritual was carried out on the tree and on the king. Once again

king = god = world = cult object.

A picture of the sacred marriage has recently been unearthed. On a monumental stela at Tel-Asmar (which is the ancient Eshunna) "we see in the centre a couch with bull's feet, like the royal couches of the Early Dynastic period in Egypt, covered with a fleece upon which two people are lying. An officiating priest stands at the foot of the bed."[22]

The whole festival ended with an orgiastic celebration. The word is of great importance.[23]

It is Greece that has supplied us with the technical term "sacred marriage." In the Eleusinian mysteries it is alleged

22. *The Times*, 10th July 1933.
23. S. H. Hooke, *The Babylonian New Year Festival*, Journ. Manchester Egyptian and Oriental Society, XIII, 29. — Id., *Myth and Ritual* (Oxford, 1933), ch. III.

that "they enacted the union of Deo or Demeter and her daughter Pherephatte, alias Kore. Just before the love-embraces in the mystery, Aphrodite of the Sea arises somehow from some models of genitals. Then comes the bridal hymn for Kore, and the neophytes sing an accompaniment: 'I ate from the timbrel, I drank from the cymbals, I carried the dish, I entered the bridal chamber.' They enact the birth-pains of Deo." There is drinking of gall, and apparently a dance of men dressed as goats, common elements of ritual.[24]

The Jukuns have a Festival of the "Booths of Menstruation."[25] The PURPOSE is indicated in a prayer for good crops, health, progeny, immunity from disease and wild animals. The PRINCIPAL is the king. IMITATION: one might apply to him the same words as the Indians apply to Prajapati, that "he is everything here," for he is addressed as "our crops," "our rain," "our health," and "our wealth." "All Jukun chiefs, however minor, are regarded as being in some measure incarnations of deity." The king is "an earthly image of the plurality of the gods," and the greatest gods are the sky-god and the earth-god. The king is also "He of the Moon." He is referred to as the *jô* which means "god," "spirit," "sacred things" such as offerings to the god), "rites." Thus

king = world = gods = cult objects.

He is the same as the offerings; it follows he must be eaten. He is merely repeating what his ancestors did. The element of SEX is indicated in the name of the festival, but the meaning of it is obscure. The WORD is represented by prayers. One of these expresses the ancestral character of the rites. Two officials go to a mound of sand raised at the base of a tree where the former kings resided, and call on each former king by name, saying, "The King has come to Puje to observe the customs of his predecessors." Note as in Babylonia the connection of king and tree. FEAST in two kinds: food and

24. Psellus, *Quaenam sunt Graecorum opiniones de daemonibus*, 3 (ed. Migne), quoted by Otto Kern, *Die Griechischen Mysterien der klassischen Zeit*, (Berlin 1927) 71; and bowdlerized by Jane E. Harrison, *Prolegomena to the Study of Greek Religion*, 569².
25. C. K. Meek, *A Sudanese Kingdom*, 144.

beer. Beer, like the Greek ambrosia, "is the food of the gods, and when the king drinks beer he not only receives the same nourishment as the gods, but actually feeds the gods immanent in his person."[26]

I think I have kept my promise that enlarging the objective would not affect the structure. The objective is the world, and the principal is the world. We now come to an almost greater change in objective: the benefits from being material will become spiritual, but even this revolution will leave the fundamentals unchanged.

26. *Ibid.*, 153.

6˙ The Good

Hail the Sun of Righteousness.
Hymn A. & M.

SOME THREE thousand years ago Indian ritual was, as we have seen, frankly bent on the good things of this world; and the union of the sacrificer with the world and all its parts was a means to wealth and health. By 500 B.C. a great change had come over religious thought: wordly welfare was considered an unworthy aim; spiritual elevation became the goal of the religious leaders. The objective of the preachers is still welfare, but welfare is differently conceived: it is to a large extent identified with goodness. It is better to be good than to be healthy and wealthy, and so a ritual which leads to goodness takes the place of a ritual that only gives material prosperity.

India has not been unique in undergoing this transformation. A tendency to cast the sober hue of morals over all seems a recurring phenomenon in the life of civilizations. As they get older, they exalt the spirit higher and higher above the flesh, till at last the flesh becomes a thing to be ashamed of, bodily wants are tolerated as an unfortunate necessity, not enjoyed. Ritual has either to conform to the fashion or perish. At first, ritual falls into discredit, because the moralists, being intellectuals and individualists, are hostile to a materialistic and intensely social ritual. In the end however the ritual saves itself by adopting the new moral tone.

The causes of these ethical movements are not known. They have generally been accepted without question as stages in the evolution from low to high. As a matter of fact they seem to herald the fall of civilizations. The more decadent a people, the higher the moral tone.

However it lies outside the scope of this work to discuss the *causes* of these ethical movements; we have to accept them as *facts,* which go under the name of Buddhism, Christianity, Islam, philosophical Hinduism, Confucianism, and the rest. Their rituals we may label "ethical rituals."

72

It is a long way from a rite that ensures abundance of buffaloes or wheat to one which confers "holiness and pureness of living." Yet the ritual has travelled all that way without losing its fundamental constitution, as analysis will show.

The proper course would be to take Christian worship in its earliest recorded form, so as to get nearer to origins. I shall however take it as it was left by the Reformation in order to show that even a great revolution (great to those who see it from a short distance) changes little in the principles of ritual, however much it may affect its spirit. Our antiquarians need not then lament so over the loss of ancient documents, or spend quite so much time on their recovery and elucidation, since living tradition preserves so much. At the very outset, in the PURPOSE, we are confronted with one important transformation. It is still Life, and welfare; but by life is meant something different from mere bodily health. The prayers are mostly for spiritual benefits, "that the rest of our life hereafter may be pure, and holy; so that at the last we may come to his eternal joy," to live hereafter "a godly, righteous, and sober life." It is moral welfare then that is the prime object. Yet material benefits are not disdained. There is a prayer "to comfort and succour all them, who in this transitory life are in trouble, sorrow, need, sickness or any other adversity." The prayers for the king are among those that retain the old material purpose best. Such a one as "Grant him in health and wealth long to live; strengthen him that he may vanquish and overcome all his enemies" is hardly to be distinguished from a Vedic, or even a Fijian, prayer. On occasion there are prayers for rain, fair weather, in time of dearth and famine, in time of war and tumults, plague or sickness; but note how apologetic the Church is for concerning itself with such material blessings, and what excuse it makes: "Increase the fruits of the earth by thy heavenly benediction; and grant that we, receiving thy bountiful liberality, may use the same to thy glory, the relief of them that are needy, and our own comfort." These things are asked for mainly as a means to do good. In the matter of OWNERSHIP our ritual is evidently not primitive for it belongs to the Church, not a hereditary body, but one including all those that have been properly initiated, "confirmed," as we call it. In practice membership is more or less hereditary. The Reformation, too, though generally represented as an advance, has in some ways returned to a more primitive state; it has made the Church once more national, and has restored to the dignity of PRINCIPAL a hereditary king. He is no longer frankly identified with the deity; he is "the human symbol" of "the divine power." His office embodies the belief that all power is derived from God. "The continuity of kingship" symbolizes "the eternal dominion of God."[1] Thus with that convenient word "symbol" we evade the clear issues which other nations have faced naively and answered in the straightforward equivalence

King = God.

It is not always the "savage" or "primitive" that is illogical, nor is logic a mere matter of reasoning: it depends even more on moral courage.

We can hardly say now that we worship God through the king. We worship God directly, and He is the real principal. God is everywhere in the world, but he is not the world, except for the Pantheists. That is not such a great advance as may seem at first sight; for, though the Indian Prajapati may be spoken of as "everything here," he is not really the world of matter, but only the *atman,* or spirit, the life, of it. This spirit is worshipped immaterially by Protestants; but in the Roman Catholic Church it may be present in the material form of the host.

The actual king has been pushed into the background, so there can be no human representative; but the worshipper still feels that the royal dignity best expresses his reverence for the deity:

His the sceptre, His the Throne.

It is still a king that is worshipped, though his human embodiment has been reduced to a symbol.

As always divinity is not confined to the principal, but all

1. Jubilee broadcast, *The Times,* 13th May, 1935. The whole is worth reading as the latest exposition of divine kingship.

the worshippers have some divinity. As there is only one God, they cannot be different gods, but the same as the king and everybody. Further, the purpose having become "spiritual" there can be no realistic IMITATION, but only imitation in the spirit. Christ as the Head of the Sacrifice is, as we say, both Principal and offering:

> Thou on Earth both Priest and Victim
> In the Eucharistic Feast.

The worshippers are in a mystic sense united with him: "We dwell in Christ and Christ with us." Since Christ and worshipper are one it follows that the worshipper is also in a sense the victim: "And here we offer and present unto Thee, O Lord, ourselves, our souls and bodies, to be a reasonable, holy, and lively sacrifice unto Thee." And again:—

> Yea the very nails that nail Him
> Nail us also to the Tree.

The worshipper's life too should be a constant Imitation of Christ. As more closely representative of the deity than his subjects the king has to set them an example of this imitation, and the greatest claim that is made for him at a jubilee is that he has been an eminently Christian king, that is one who has exemplified the Christian virtues.

So fundamental is this imitation that it persists unabated in those sects that have reduced ritual to its simplest expression. Whatever they may discard, they keep the imitation. Let us attend a meeting of healing and prayer in the very heart of London, that stronghold of scepticism and rationalism. We shall see thousands crowding at the doors, seeking to be healed in body as well as in mind. They bring their physical ailments to Albert Hall just as the Fijian brought his to the temple of the clan. The preacher will tell us how this purpose is to be achieved. "If you would be healed, you must be identified with Christ." They strive earnestly after that identity which is consummated when the preacher lays hands upon them. Then they feel "the outpourings of the Holy Ghost," and sink overwhelmed to the ground.

But to return to our Church ritual. The ancestral character

of the deity does not attach to the second Person of the Trinity, only to the first, who is the Father of all mankind. That is only in a spiritual sense, but the spiritual grows out of the literal. He is also the Creator. Ethical theology has obscured, but not obliterated, the primeval equivalences

worshipper = ancestor-creator = world = cult object.

The SACRED MARRIAGE has been refined, like everything else, into pure metaphor, if one can call metaphor what, after all, is more than a picturesque figure of speech. It is a mystic marriage of the Church with Christ. The congregation is therefore requested to come to "such a heavenly Feast, in the marriage-garment required by God in the Scripture."[2] The COMMUNION, it will be seen, is conceived as a FEAST, it is described as a banquet, but it is a far cry from a South Sea Island feast, which is frankly a rich repast, the more the better. The communion has ceased to be a meal, it is spiritual food, "heavenly bread" and "living waters" for "the thirsty soul." There are, besides, "alms and oblations," which are offered to the Church or the poor, no longer presented by one group, and distributed by the other among its members. Christ is himself the WORD, and the Mass is mainly the word: its verbal repetition is sufficient when the full ritual is impossible. The myth (I use the term in its original sense of sacred story) is repeated as an essential part of the word. The Mass is a daily repetition of the sacrifice related in the myth. On special occasions other episodes are recalled, such as the Birth, the Ascension. St. Paul[3] goes right back beyond the Passion to the Creation and the Fall. The Anglican liturgy merely alludes to the Fall; but hymns refer more explicitly to the Flood:

> He, Who once in righteous vengeance
> Whelmed the world beneath the flood
> Once again in mercy cleansed it
> With his own most precious blood.

Hymns, chants, prayers no longer have the compelling, the creative, power they had of old. That is inconsistent with God's

2. Cp. I *Corinthians*, VI, 16 f.
3. Cp. I *Corinthians*, XV, 21 ff. and Burial Service.

omniscience and omnipotence, so the use of prayers has even to be apologized for: God knows "our necessities before we ask, and our ignorance in asking," therefore petitions are to be fulfilled only "as may be most expedient for them."[4]

The contrast between the Christian and the other rituals we have analyzed so far lies, not in the structure, but in the point of view. Everything has taken a moral turn, everything is refined almost out of recognition, "sublimated" to use a favourite expression of contemporary psychology.

India had, as we saw, preceded Christianity in this sublimation. Only Buddhism is more pessimistic and negative. Life is evil, and so true immortality consists in not living; it is nirvana, extinction. The PURPOSE of the modern Buddhist ritual is, in theory, not a long life and a prosperous one, but escape from the pain of the world by living a good life.[5] It is a change we express by saying the aim is spiritual, no longer material. Everything has to be reinterpreted to fit the changed point of view; everything becomes edifying symbolism. Thus the lamp no longer represents the material sun, dispeller of night, but the saviour who brought spiritual enlightenment, and lighted the way to salvation. The religion is pacific, so everything that is not pacific has to be eliminated, the sword, for instance. There is much talk of victory, but it is victory over ignorance and evil. These ethical religions all tend away from heredity. This is a necessary consequence of their individualism. The OWNERS of the Buddhist ritual are therefore no longer hereditary; they cannot be, since the clergy is celibate; yet they speak of a "heredity of master and pupil." Only men of good caste are allowed to officiate at the Temple of the Tooth, and only members of the farmer caste can officiate at any of the shrines owned by the Siamese sect: there is thus some real heredity as well. The PRINCIPAL is not a man, but a relic, or a statue, or a tree, representing the Great Man, the Buddha. The king is very far from having been eliminated, though he has been thrust on one side. The cult is a palace

4. The *Hymns Ancient and Modern* quoted are: 103; 313; 316; 322; 324; etc.
5. *Temple of the Tooth*, ch. V.

cult, and the king is regarded as a future Buddha. The priest-hood IMITATE the life of the Buddha: they wear the same clothes, observe perpetual chastity, do not eat after the sun has passed the meridian, and are supposed to beg like him. The Buddha is a model for the laity as well, but of course their imitation is tempered by the attachments of this world. Thus the worshippers imitate the principal, but the principal himself imitates former Buddhas. His prototypes are not his ancestors however, as in the older ritual, for a Buddha re-nounces the world, and has no successor after the flesh. Imi-tation of nature there is too, but only in metaphors and in symbols. Such titles as "Lord of the World," "Sun of Righteous-ness," "Sakyan Bull," all remind us that the principal once controlled the physical universe by impersonation. He is now controller of thoughts, of good and evil. This spiritualizing appears everywhere, in the SACRED MARRIAGE, which has been toned down to the waving of lights by two old women; in the COMMUNION, which consists of material things, food and drink, but which are presented symbolically only, and good conduct is regarded as a higher offering. The WORD is not a compelling force, but consists of praises of the moral leader and his moral law. Forgiveness is asked, not for errors of ritual, but for moral faults. There is no allusion to precedents in the stanzas recited at the service. The myth seems to have dropped out; but if we attend the special Wednesday service we shall hear singers chant the myth of the coming of the sacred relic to Ceylon. Yet after all this condemnation of matter, the ser-vice ends with a prayer in the good old spirit: "let the god rain in due season who promotes the welfare of the crops." The masses may repeat the moral precepts mechanically, but for them Buddhism really means worship for life, that is pros-perity, health, and a more fortunate lot when they are reborn on earth.

After all the ritual has much the same meaning for the Chris-tian masses. The Italian peasant who places his lottery ticket underneath the altar cloth so that it may be blessed has much the same end as the Vedic Indian or the Winnebago. We need not go as far as Italy. In our own middle classes, at least among the women, there is a conviction that an unbaptized child will not thrive bodily. The Roman Church ascribes to its last sacrament a healing virtue, though it be only secondary and not always operative.

The fact is that ritual can never be confined entirely to moral regeneration; for the spiritual and the material cannot be divorced, and all attempts to do so end in failure. Our Church is compelled to recognize that "the fruits of the earth" are necessary to the Glory of God, and the Lord's Prayer contains a petition for daily bread.

The Chinese religion belongs to the ethical type. In fact the Chinese seem to revel in moral sentiments, and everything in their religion is given a moral turn, at least in the official religion. The Emperor's connection with the sky remains very clear: he is still the Son of Heaven, but he has become etherealized; he is "the personification of Yang, the Positive Essence, which it must be remembered comprises light, strength and all the so-called masculine elements of Nature"; on the other hand "His Consort is looked upon as the personification of Yin, the Negative Essence, to which pertain all feminine qualities." A text says, "Hearken to the Son of Heaven in regard to the tenets for men; hearken to Her-who-is-his-equal in regard to the compliance required of women. The Son of Heaven directs the inherent principle of the Yang essence; She-who-is-his-equal regulates the Yin qualities." He is constantly compared to the sun, she to the moon; yet she evidently has been the earth also, for, whereas the Emperor's personal palace is called "the Palace of the Cloudless Heaven," hers is "The Palace of Earthly Peace." The rule that the principal must have a consort persists; for "the Son of Heaven is to His Consort as the sun is to the moon and as the Yang essence is to the Yin, so they are essential to each other and she perfects the whole." Hence, between the Emperor's and the Empress' personal palaces there is a small building of which the name is variously translated "Hall of Fusion and Permeation," "Heaven and Earth Vigorous and Productive," "Hall of Imperial Marriage Rites." Miss Ayscough thinks the last "is far too concrete. . . . ; it suggests that actual marriage rites take place in the Hall; this is not so. The name is entirely figurative, and refers to the moment when the descending Vital Force of Heaven meets and is fused with the ascending Vital Force of Earth, at which moment, on the fifteenth of the Fifth Month, all things are completely permeated with life." Anyhow it is the sacred marriage, whether actually carried out, or merely imagined.[6]

There is not a religion more permeated with the moral tone than Islam. It is consequently ultra-monotheistic. It becomes difficult under the circumstances for any one to be identified with God. Identity is therefore toned down and the reason given for many acts of worship is that "they bring near to God." That is especially the case on the mystic side. A foremost modernist of Egypt confesses that in his childhood "Magic and sufism . . . became one thing, and its aim, prosperity in life and propinquity to God."[7] Always the good life by union with the deity.

6. Ayscough, 121 ff.
7. Taha Hussein, *An Egyptian Childhood* (London, 1932), 109.

7· Centralization

Thou shalt have no other gods before me.
Exodus xx, 3

WE TOOK our stand at the outset on the working hypothesis that a common structure is proof of common descent.

At once we can make a step forward. It follows that whatever these rituals have in common was part of the hypothetical primitive ritual from which we suppose them to be all derived. The general structure which recurs over and over again must have been characteristic of the parent ritual: the quest of life, the exclusive ownership, heredity, the principal, the imitation, and equivalences, and so forth. We can then instruct our palaeontologist, the archaeologist, to seek confirmation. What he can produce at present is exceedingly meagre. There are drawings of the Upper Palaeolithic. Their meaning is uncertain but they can best be explained by assuming that there existed a ritual, of which the PURPOSE was to increase, or make easy, the capture of game; that it involved IMITATION of the animal hunted by a PRINCIPAL, who dressed as an animal and danced.[1] It is possibly the SACRED MARRIAGE that is depicted on a stone at Laussel in the Dordogne.[2] Perhaps we shall be able to interpret these fossils of art better some day, when we have prepared ourselves by a thorough analysis of modern rites. At present it is all conjecture, because the archaeologists are trying to get on without help from the student of living forms.

So far so good; but what about the points in which these rituals differ?

We distinguished three main types:—one in which nature is distributed among families; one in which the whole world is concentrated in one principal; and a third which is a variant of the second and in which everything is moralized. What is the order of development?

1. G. H. Luquet, *L'Art et la Religion des Hommes Fossiles*, (Paris, 1926). Eng. trsl.: *The Art and Religion of Fossil Man*, (London, 1930).
2. Luquet, *L'Art et la Religion des Hommes Fossiles* (Paris, 1926), 127.

The last named type, the ethical, is also the latest. We have direct evidence that it consists of older and more materialistic rites transfigured.

In these ethical rites the particular is completely swallowed up in the general, and in consequence they are the most highly centralized. The god is everything, and so these cults are generally monotheistic or pantheistic; there is no room for subordinate deities. The king is consequently the repository of all power; and when he goes it passes to an oligarchy. Whether monarchical or republican, the state whose religion is ethical can tolerate no state within the state, no local autonomy. Ritual and administration are standardized. They tend to overflow the national boundaries and to assimilate the nations around: they proselytize and annex.

Since these ethical cults are centralized and latest, we shall expect the oldest to lie at the opposite extreme of centralization. Now the least centralized are those in which nature is dealt with piecemeal. They are so little centralized that the episodes can be detached and performed separately, as we have seen it done. In fact sometimes the myth is the only evidence we have that they belong, or have belonged, to an all embracing creation ritual. They can indeed become completely detached. There is good evidence of this in Babylonia. A charm for toothache has been found there which begins by reciting the creation myth. The Malay tin-miner's charm is merely the Indian creation myth continued down to the appearance in the world of tin.[3] They are evidently fragments from the creation ritual.

It is possible to detach certain parts of the Anglican or the Fijian service as abbreviated forms for special occasions, but these extracts are not made to deal with some special department of nature such as tin; they are merely the essentials for use when there is no time for more. You can abridge the royal ceremonial of Fiji, but you cannot take out one part to treat yams, another for toothache. The episodes are no longer juxtaposed; they are interlocked.

3. R. Campbell Thomson, *Assyrian Medical Texts*, Proc. Roy. Soc. Medicine, vol. XIX, sect. History of Science, 59. — W. Skeat, *Malay Magic* (London, 1900), 265. — Hocart, *The Life-giving Myth* in *The Labyrinth*, ed. S. H. Hooke (London, 1935) pp. 266, 272 ff.

In all the periods covered by our records we see centralization making steady progress. It has set-backs; there are periods of breaking up; but when they are past, centralization resumes its upward course, and the world is now beyond doubt more centralized than it ever was.

If we come down from general considerations to the dissection of rites we find our presumptions confirmed. In the general rituals there appear features which can only be explained as survivals of a successive creation which takes item by item. There is an obvious reason why Aranda ancestor-gods should be identified with this or that animal, plant, or thing. There is no reason that we can see why one Fijian god should enter a hawk or another a dog, for they have nothing to do with the increase or control of hawks or dogs, but only with general welfare, and the rites are the same as any other. In the same way the witch-cult of England retained animal gods, chiefly goats or cats, although the purpose appears to have been quite general, and not specially connected with goats or cats.[4] The Greek rites were universal enough, yet their gods had animal forms which seem pointless, unless we suppose that they once belonged to specific rites. The most centralizing ceremony of Ancient India was the horse-sacrifice: it was the highest rung of the ritual ladder; it raised the sacrificer to be the overlord of minor kings. Consequently he was very much this Universe, this All, but he was identified with the world through the intermediary of a sacrificed horse whose parts stood for heaven and earth. All over the world we find highly specific characters attached to the universal god. The Koryaks call their chief god Strength, The-One-on-High, Thunder-Man. Some identify him with the sun. Like so many other gods he is the Universe, more especially the sky, and still more particularly the sun.[5] All food is abundant as long as he looks upon the earth, but no sooner does he turn away than all is disorder. He has a son Cloud-Man, and a daughter Cloud-Woman. He is not the creator, but, according to some traditions, produced the creator, who bears the name of Big-Raven, and is the ancestor

---

4. Miss Margaret Murray, *The Witch-cult of Western Europe*, (Oxford, 1921).
5. Jochelson, 24.

of the Koryaks, the Big Grandfather. This god "turns into a raven when putting on a raven's coat." Plainly there were once dances in which the creator masqueraded as a bird. There are also traditions of a Sun-Man, a Moon-Man, a Star-Man, a Wolf-Man, a Grass-Woman, and finally Stone-Hammer people who are stone hammers turned into men, a whole list of human beings identified with animals, plants, celestial bodies and artefacts. Even Christianity has not completely lost all specific features, though the species has been sublimated into a symbol, the Lamb of God.

Finally, rituals that treat the world as a whole nevertheless retain myths describing successive creation. Of this Genesis I is an example.[6]

These facts are best explained if we suppose that the creation rite made up of specific rites is earlier than that which seeks welfare in a more generalized form. In that early form the head of every cult represents one or more specific objects. As one of these headmen absorbs the rest he becomes a universal god, but he retains traces of his original nature.

How can one headman absorb others? The things of this world are ranged into two groups, heaven and earth. The interaction of the two gives prosperity. This dualism we shall find everywhere, so we can only conclude it belongs to the earliest strata we can as yet distinguish. All the rituals we are passing under review seem to go back to a creation ceremony in which the world is divided into two camps.

He who takes the part of the sky in the ritual must necessarily lead the denizens of the air, and contain them also, since they are in the regions above. In the same way the representative of the earth must lead and contain the earthy. All that is necessary for centralization is that the minor personages should become increasingly merged in their leaders. They cease to have an independent existence; they no longer control a specific object. The king controls all. They can only assist the king, or imitate, on a smaller scale, what the king does, if the king is not there to do it.

The sky not only absorbs all its denizens, but even proceeds

6. *Kingship*, chap. XVI. — Cp. above p. 65 f.

to invade the realm of earth. That is chiefly because the sky is the abode of the sun. The sun's role as the author of all life receives increasing recognition in the ritual. When our records begin he is already supreme, and for the earlier stages we are dependent entirely on comparative evidence. We can however observe in our records his further advance from supremacy to complete monotheism, as preached by Akhenaten and Julian, amongst others. All life is concentrated in his heavenly representative, the sun-disk; and so all power is concentrated in his national representative, the king.

It is as universal life-giver that the sun is all-important. It is his function that matters, not his visible form. The visible form is therefore dropped, and God becomes a function of the universe. Inevitably the king ceases to represent a thing; he no longer copies the attributes of the sun-disk, its roundness, its effulgence, knowingly. He is expected only to carry out in society the same functions which God exercises in the universe.

All this may sound metaphysical, but the sequel will show we are not dealing with metaphysics, but with practical politics.

The whole struggle of monotheism v. polytheism is meaningless as long as we look upon it as a conflict of philosophies. What does it matter whether there be one God or many? Because by abolishing minor gods you abolish minor sovereignties: monotheism means monarchy; polytheism means polyarchy.[7]

7. "Since the day that I brought forth my people out of the land of Egypt I chose no city among all the tribes of Israel to build an house in, that my name might be there; neither chose I any man to be a ruler over my people Israel."

"But I have chosen Jerusalem, that my name might be there; and have chosen David to be over my people Israel." II *Chronicles*, VI, 5 f.

"Thou knowest how that David my father could not build an house unto the name of the Lord his God for the wars which were about him on every side, until the Lord put them under the soles of his feet." I *Kings*, V, 3.

8· The King

THE PRINCIPAL of the ritual, if he is human, is the head of the community. In a small tribe of low degree we call him the headman; in more advanced or larger communities we call him the king. Sometimes we hesitate between chief and king. Our use of these words is rather arbitrary: we translate the native word one way or the other, according as the state kept by the principal comes near to *our* idea of a king, or falls short of it, and our kings keep very great state. Such a distinction is one of externals, of pomp and circumstance, whereas we are trying to get at the inner meaning. If a distinction is to be made it must be based on the whole structure, because the structure reflects the meaning; not on an accident such as the extent of square miles ruled, or the size of the civil list.

There is, of course, no fundamental distinction between headman and king: both are merely varieties of the principal; both are equivalent to the objective, and so behave as they wish it to behave. Since however rituals vary in scope and spirit, so must the attributes of those that take part in it. If

principal = objective,

it follows as the night the day that every change in the objective involves a change in the principal. In a rite that embraces the universe he will be something different from what he is in one that is limited to a species, or else the fundamental equation will break down. We have seen it does not: in a specific rite the principal is the species, in a universal one he is the universe. The anatomy of kingship will bear this out.

There is a dearth of information about Australian chiefs.[1]

1. Spencer and Gillen actually reported at first there were no chiefs. It was Strehlow who discovered them, but he was not sufficiently interested in them to tell us much.

All we know about the Arandas is that to each ritual objective there corresponds a principal identified with that objective. There also appear to be chiefs above these headmen, but we know nothing about them. When actuality fails us we turn to myths as reliable accounts of a state of society that once existed.

They tell us of a supreme god, Altjira or Ngambakala, who lives in heaven. There are besides specific gods, *altjirangamitjinga*, who are kangaroo-men, emu-men, and so forth. We have a sky-chief then with a number of specific headmen beneath him. This sky-chief includes in himself the spirits of unborn men. He must contain souls connected with all kinds of other objectives. What is inference here will be more clearly expressed elsewhere.[2]

All we know of the nature of the Winnebago chief is that he comes from the Thunder-bird clan, and is presumably identified with the Thunder-bird, which is the thunder conceived as a bird. His clan is descended from Thunder-people who went about smiting the earth with clubs.[3] He is apparently specific. Again we turn to the myths for a picture of the past. There is a supreme god called Earthmaker, because he made the earth. The departmental spirits were appointed by him. He "made many good spirits and he put each one of them in control of powers with which they could bless human beings." He is present in all men, and so is a universal spirit: "Into your body," say the guardians of the four quarters to men, "he has placed part of himself." He is very like the Indian Prajapati, the universal god, as will be seen if we place them in parallel columns:—

PRAJAPATI	EARTHMAKER
Called Father, Father of Gods and Giants. Begetter of the earth.	Called Grandfather.
Creator.	Creator.
Alone in the beginning.	Alone in the beginning.

2. Strehlow, I, 1, 1 ff.
3. Radin, 207 ff.; 287.

PRAJAPATI	EARTHMAKER
Is Agni, the fire-altar and sacrificial fire.	Is the sacred fire in the centre of the hut.
Is everything here.	Is present in every man.[4]

The Koryaks appear to have no supreme chiefs. All we know is that there is someone in charge of each household cult. Their myths however depict a society headed by a being who is at once the Universe and what it includes, the sun and the thunder, the whole and the parts.[5]

Thus over specific headmen the myths show us a supreme chief who is the universe. Since the universe includes all its parts, the divinity of this chief or king must perforce include the divinities of all his headmen. This doctrine suggested by the myths that

the king = the sum of his chieftains

is actually realized in the Fijian state.

The Lord of Tokatoka on the Lower Rewa was a thoughtful chief. He explained to me that all the gods of the several clans that made up his tribe were sons of God-of-the-Land. One-tooth was his son, but he was also the same as God-of-the-Land. "All these names belong to him," he continued, "Iranamalo is prayed to in one temple, Tora in another, Iranatora in another. The names of the three are the names of God-of-the-Land. These are all my names. I am called Iranamalo, Lord, God-of-the-Land, Tora, Iranatora, Iranasau.[6] For each of these names there is a priest. If I order a war the people go and make offerings to the small temples and say to the god, 'Be gracious, your namesake says. . . .', meaning the chief, because he bears the names of the gods." In short his people recognized a tribal god whose sons were clan gods, but were included in him; in the same way the chief is the supreme god and includes all the others; he is the whole and the parts.

4. *Ibid.* 212; 213; 215.
5. Above p. 85 f.
6. *Ira* is the pronoun 3rd plural. *Iranasau* = The Chiefs.

Nowhere is this more explicit than in India. The Indian king is not one, but many gods. He is compounded, among others, of the eight great gods who guard the points of the compass, the Moon, Fire, the Sun, Wind, the gods of wealth, of water, and of death.[7] The text that says so is late, but his composite nature is equally clear in Vedic times. Then he is first and foremost Indra, the royal god, the wielder of thunder, eagle-like. But he is also Brihaspati, the priestly god, and so on. He is the universe, but he is also the sun and the thunder-god. He is the whole and the parts.

Europeans and Semites seem to have carried furthest the process of absorption of all gods by one. When the gods are reduced to one the king must perforce cease to be a compound of deities. He may, like the Pope, be a compound of offices, Bishop of Rome, and Pontiff over all the bishops; or like the Kaiser who was at the same time King of Prussia, coequal of other German kings, and emperor over them all. But since the god they all represent is always the same, whatever the office, there can be no pluralism in godhead. James the Sixth of Scotland did not acquire a new divinity by becoming James the First of England. It is otherwise in India and Fiji: there, to hold a particular office is to be a particular god; to unite several offices is to unite several gods. It may be a survival of this that Roman Catholic princes are given at baptism the names of a whole string of saints and of the Virgin Mary, such as Francois-Joseph-Marie, and so on, while princesses receive the names of male as well as female saints. The explanation now given of the custom is that it places them under the protection of all these divinities.

We can thus distinguish two types of kings: kings who include in their divinity the divinities of their chieftains, and kings who are one indivisible and only god, and whose chieftains consequently cannot be different gods, but only dimmer reflections of the same god as their liege. These monotheistic kings belong to the ethical rites, for monotheism, centralization, and moralization go very much together. Must we recognize a third type of society in which there are no kings, that

7. Manu, V, 96.

is overlords compounded of the deities of their vassals, but only heads of families or clans, all coequal, and each in charge of certain objectives, none responsible for the whole? Aranda, Koryak and Winnebago societies seem to answer this description, but we know too little about them, and besides their myths lead us back to kings who were compounds. Perhaps we may throw some light on the subject if we leave it aside and turn our attention to another problem, which is to fix the genetic relations of the two types we know actually to exist. Did the indivisible god and king result from the fusion of many vassal gods and chieftains, or contrariwise has an indivisible god been broken up into parts? The previous chapter favoured the first hypothesis; can an analysis of the king's nature lend it further support?

If the king represented nothing which is not represented separately by one of his vassals the question might still remain in doubt. But, as a matter of fact, the king always represents certain objectives which are peculiar to him. He is therefore a specific chieftain as well as a universal monarch. He is closely associated with animals that are peculiar to him.

In Ancient India Indra is constantly described as a bull among men, an epithet that has been preserved by Buddhism and applied to the Buddha. Indra is also compared to an eagle. Buddhist scriptures describe the king or emperor as a lion; at his accession he roars like a lion; he sits on a lion throne, and dies on a lion couch.[8] The Buddha inherits all royal attributes, and so is hailed as the Sakyan lion. The kings of Ceylon are actually descended from a lion.[9] In the great horse sacrifice which raises the king to the highest dignity, makes him an emperor, he is identified with the horse according to the rule

principal = victim,

just as in a specific rite, only this rite no longer aims at the multiplication of horses.[10] Buddhist writings and art abound

8. Hocart, *C.J.Sc.*, I, 118 f.
9. *Mhvs.* VI.
10. *Taittiriya Brahmana*, III, 9, 17, 4.

in cobra kings who could assume human or serpent shape at will. They still survive in Chota Nagpur, "Little Cobra City," whose kings are descended from cobras and wear over their heads a hood of cobra heads, thus preserving the fundamental rule of ritual that the principal imitates the ancestor-god.[11] Such cobra-kings are still impersonated in Ceylon by masked dancers.[12] From India eastwards there exists a close sympathy between the king and the state elephant who usurps the place which the lion and the bull hold further west. There can be no doubt that the white elephant of Siam is a kind of double of the king; for a new one has to be found at every accession, it is consecrated by the same rites as the king, receives titles similar to the king's, and the welfare of the king is wrapped up in the animal's.[13]

The palette of King Narmer, of the first Egyptian dynasty, represents a bull trampling on his enemies and knocking down forts. The Egyptologists interpret the scene as the king victorious over his foes.[14] In texts of the XVIIIth dynasty[15] he is still described as a bull, a lion, or a panther,[16] but he is also the sun; but the sun is his eye, so that he must be the sky or the universe as well. He usually appears however in ritual scenes in human form surrounded by persons who wear animal masks to impersonate the various gods who often have both a meteorological and an animal form. Thus Horus is the sun and a hawk as well.

Kingship and the lion are associated in Jacob's blessing: "Judah is a lion's whelp: from the prey, my son, thou art gone up: he stooped down, he couched as a lion and as an old lion; who shall rouse him up? The sceptre shall not depart from between his feet, until Shiloh come; and unto him the gathering of the people shall be."[17]

11. Ph. Vogel, *Indian Serpent-Lore* (London, 1926), 35.
12. O. Pertold, *The Ceremonial Dances of the Sinhalese*, Archiv Orientalni, II, 108 f.
13. Quaritch Wales, 273 ff.
14. Breasted, *History*, fig. 19.
15. Circ. 1500 B.C.
16. Breasted, *Records*, II, Nos. 80; 143; 660; 900.
17. *Genesis*, XLIX, 9 f.

This lionizing of the king is no mere fancy, not just a gross compliment to the king's might. The king of Uganda's gait "was the traditional walk of his race, founded on the step of the lion. The outward sweep of the legs was intended to represent the stride of the noble beasts."[18] The Ugandese were not concerned with dignity, but with carrying out a necessary imitation. We can therefore take quite literally the Indian traditions of kings roaring like lions at their consecration.

The Jukuns regard lions as "either the counterpart of living chiefs or as embodying the souls of dead chiefs."[19]

Our kings have long ceased to be identified with animals, but they use the same old animals as emblems, the lion, the eagle, the panther, but not the bull, because we despise cattle.

If we did not know the history of Germany we could still infer that the kaiser had once been a king coequal with the other sovereigns included in the empire, because besides being emperor over all he was also king of Prussia on the same level as the kings of Bavaria, of Saxony, and other heads of states. That inference would be correct. So from the fact that the king is both the world and certain objects in that world, we are bound to conclude that the king is a specific chieftain who has swallowed up his fellows. And just as the vassal states of Germany lost all remnants of independence in a final centralization, and so are being obliterated as meaningless, so the end of the centralization of cults has been monotheism, that is to say the boundaries between one department of nature and another have been obliterated, god and king have become a whole without parts, and the state has become absolute.

There are states where the king is still a sectional chieftain. The royal family in Fiji is not, as with us, a family soaring above all the commons; it is one of a series of families, the leading one, the *primus inter pares,* only very much more *primus* than is the case among the Winnebagoes and the Arandas. It is organized like any other, furnishes its quota

18. J. H. Speke, *Journal of the Discovery of the Sources of the Nile* (London, 1863), 292.
19. Meek, 186.

of statute labour and contributions on the same footing as the others. What distinguishes it, is that its head is also head over all.

This fact is stated theologically in India. The king is at once Indra and all the gods including Indra. He is Indra twice over: first, as a member of the nobility, Indra being the god of the nobility; secondly, as king, because Indra is king of the gods.[20] In other words the royal god is the god of the family from which the king has to be chosen, and the head of that family is identified with its god just like any other sectional chieftain. By his consecration as king the head of that family absorbs the gods of the other families, and so does his god. We have seen that this happens also in Tokatoka in Fiji.

It is as if in England Lancashire always supplied the king. Whoever was the chief of Lancashire would automatically be crowned king. The god of Lancashire would then be also the god of all England. As Duke of Lancaster the king would be the Red Rose, but as king he would be identified with every regional plant, the White Rose of Yorkshire, the Red Rose of Lancashire, the Leek of Wales, and so on.

But how can a king absorb all the deities? That is easily answered: if a man can be consecrated to become a lion-god, he can also be consecrated to become a bull-god, a rain-god, an earth-god, or any kind of god, without any limit, so long as he can make good some claim. We can watch the process of absorption taking place in the coronation of many kings.

At one stage of his consecration the Vedic king goes to the house of the general and makes an offering to the Fire-god whom the general represents. Thereby he makes that officer of state "bound to himself." Then the king goes to the chaplain's house and makes an offering to the priestly god with whom the chaplain is identified, and so makes the chaplain "bound to himself."[21] And so he successively appropriates the twelve court personages. We saw it to be fundamental in all ritual, but especially in Indian ritual, that the worshipper be-

---

20. Sat. Br., V, 4, 3, 14 and 7. — Hocart, C.J.Sc., I, 134.
21. Sat. Br., V, 3, 1. — Kingship, 113.

comes one with the god to whom the worship is addressed. When therefore the king goes and makes an offering to the peculiar gods of his queen and court dignitaries, he is identifying himself with those gods. He is primarily Indra, the royal victorious god, but he also includes the gods of other ranks. A myth expresses the idea very definitely: "Now those desirable bodies and favourite abodes which the gods pieced together, they deposited in Indra; — Indra indeed is he that burns yonder (the sun); but he indeed did not burn in the beginning; but as everything else is dark, so was he; by that energy (deposited in him by the other gods) he thus burns."[22] The "bodies" and "abodes" are the cult-objects, the insignia of the gods, as we gather from other passages.[23] These they all assign to Indra; with the combined energy they contain the sun shines. The principal in this myth is Indra, and so he is Indra in the ritual; though many take part, he alone receives the offering of milk, because as Indra he includes the other worshippers. The myth is merely a precedent which the principal is re-enacting. When we are told that "Indra is all the deities; the gods have Indra as their chief,"[24] we are to understand that the king is all the deities, and the chieftains have the king as their head.

Ancient texts are obscure because we often lack the key. The best commentary on this text comes to us from West Africa. The Ashanti have a king, but higher than the king is the Golden Stool. Obviously it was once a royal throne, but it has been exalted so high that none may now sit upon it. It is said to have fallen from heaven. The priest at the time declared that it "contained the *sunsum* (soul or spirit) of the Ashanti nation, and that their power, their health, their bravery, their welfare was in the stool." He collected hairs from the head and pubes, and a piece of the forefinger nail from the king, from every queen mother, and every chief, made them into a powder which he mixed with some "medi-

22. *Ibid.* III, 4, 2, 15. — The same myth is told in *Ait. Br.* I, 24, only there the principal is Varuna, another royal god. The significance of this will appear in chapter 9.
23. *Sat. Br.*, IX, 5, 1, 48.
24. *Sat. Br.*, III, 4, 2, 2.

cine," and with it smeared the stool. Now the hairs and nail parings contain the *sunsum* of the men, so he was really putting the spirits of all these notables into the stool. In the words of the Indian text "he deposited their desirable forms" with this heavenly deity, so that they held all their life, their welfare, from it.[25]

Something of the kind happened among the Koryaks. Each family (consisting of six to thirty people) has its own hearth; but during the whale festival, which belongs to the whole village, "families that are not interrelated bring into the house where the celebration takes place, wood, dishes, and sacrificial grass. They build a fire jointly and cook together."[26]

Siam belongs to the Indian world, its ritual is a branch of Indian ritual. After the coronation of a Siamese king, the minister for foreign affairs offers to the king all his military equipment and personnel; the master of the palace the palace with all its contents, and so every minister offers up whatever he is in charge of. The king immediately returns all these things to their respective ministers, enjoining them to continue their functions as before.[27] Thus they surrender all their powers to the king and receive them back from him. Let us remember that

$$\text{worshipper} = \text{god} = \text{cult-object.}$$

The insignia, or as the old texts call them, the bodies and abodes, are thus duplicates of the officials themselves. In depositing them with the king they are depositing that spiritual force which is in themselves as well.

The Fijians preserve the first part of this surrender. When the Noble Lord of Mbau is consecrated "all the chieftains in the house take off their turbans and the brassards on their arms." It is a general rule in Fiji that turbans are not worn in presence of the High Chief. We have no direct evidence of the meaning of this custom, but we saw that the head of

25. R. S. Rattray, *Ashanti* (Oxford, 1923) 289 and index s.v. *Golden Stool.* — In *Lamentations*, IV, 20, the king is "the breath of our nostrils." Cp. *Labyrinth*, 14 et passim.
26. Jochelson, 77.
27. Quaritch Wales, 88.

one tribe considered himself composed of the gods of all the subordinate chieftains.

We English preserve the second part of the rite only, the restitution of the insignia. The Peers remain bare-headed at the coronation until the king has been crowned; then they put on their coronets and caps, thus indicating that they hold their dignities from the king.

Both the surrender and the restitution are preserved by the Igbo of Nigeria in a manner which makes their meaning clear. When the new king is installed at Oreri "all the prayer sticks acquired from the previous king, when the members took title, become null and void and of no account. A complete new set must be obtained by bringing them into the enclosure of the king where a sacrifice is made to consecrate the new prayer sticks."[28]

We are thus led back to a state of society in which the king is the senior member of a number of coordinate divisions. Such a society can be represented by a series of segments in a line, the first one leading, and so exercising control over the rest. Our society is best figured as spheres revolving round a central sphere. Of families formerly coequal one has become supreme.

What has lead to this predominance?

The first impulse of the historian is to consult his records and to pick out some accident, such as the personal ascendancy of some masterful man, as the cause of this rise. This recourse to accident is a favourite device with those who trust entirely to direct evidence, for they never see the world as a whole. Thus Egyptologists try to explain the fusion of sun and hawk, and the predominance of this combination in Egyptian polity, as a political accident. They would put it down to the rising might of a hawk-worshipping town, for instance, followed by the rise of another sun-worshipping town, or vice-versa. A comparative survey however soon puts accident out of the question. It is not in Egypt alone that the hawk or the eagle is

28. All my information about the Igbo I owe to the kindness of Mr. M. D. W. Jeffreys of the Nigerian Civil Service. I have taken the liberty of translating the Igbo terms *eze* (king), *ofo* (prayer stick) and *ama* (enclosure).

linked with the sun, but in India too. The hawk is a royal
bird even in Lakemba. The lion and the sun are associated
in India, Persia, Abyssinia, as well as in Egypt. Are we to
believe that a mere political accident in a corner of Egypt
has bound nations to accept the combination of king, sun,
lion, eagle, for evermore? What accident did, accident can
undo, and we should have all kinds of animals rising to kingship with the rise of their votaries. If the dog family smote
the lion king and seized the throne, the dog would become
the royal animal: he never is. Royalty is limited to a small
number of animals all distinguished by strength, the lion, the
bull, the horse, the eagle, the cobra. Some are not used generally for food, but they are mighty in battle, and we must
conclude that their association with kingship is part of the
growth of royal warfare, of which more hereafter; that it was
a logical development, not an accident. In the same way it
is not every tree that is royal. In India trees of the ficus tribe
are preferred.

The fundamental thing about kingship however seems to
be that the king is identified with the sky, and amid the sky
with the sun. It is here then that we must look for the reason
why the embodiment of one deity should have been chosen
to lead, and then to rule, rather than the embodiment of other
deities. It must lie in the nature of the sky and the sun, or
rather in the beliefs about them. They must be conceived as
playing a predominant part in the universe. The nature of that
predominance will become clearer when we come to discuss
the functions of the king. For the present we must be content
with a rapid sketch of the evolution of the king's nature as
suggested by our handful of witnesses.

The king leads because the sky leads for some reason or
other. He can increase his superiority by adding new offices to
his original ones, just as a dictator can strengthen his dictator-
ship by collecting ministerial portfolios. He can add to the
office of sky that of sun-phoenix-lion, then that of thunder-
eagle-bull, or of morning-star together with whatever goes
with morning star. Insofar as these accumulations are accidental, the effects of a masterful character, they will not last,
but pass away with the masterful character; but insofar as

they reflect a steady process of centralization the effects will be permanent, and these offices will become indissolubly fused together. As this fusion proceeds the parts lose their autonomy; they are merged increasingly in skyship or sunship, till their individuality can no longer be distinguished: they become one indivisible whole, one God. Eventually the sun invades the earth also; the king absorbs his once equal partner the queen.

The queen's nature does not stand out as clearly as the king's. It takes a longer search to find out that she is usually the earth, or the moon, or both. But it is clear in India; and the Romans knew it, and identified Augustus with Jupiter, the empress Livia with Ceres.[29] More evidence will appear later.[30] The reason why the queen's nature is vaguer than the king's is that, like all the other officers of state, she has been absorbed into the king. She ceases to share with him the world. When *he* becomes the universe *she* is reduced to be only part of him.[31] The creation of Eve from Adam's rib is the result. In Hindu sculpture the idea receives literal expression in statues of the high god whose right side is male, and whose left side is female. The late Greeks, probably orientalizing, fused Hermes and Aphrodite in this manner, hence our word hermaphrodite. This absorption of the female by the male survives as mystic phraseology in Christianity: God is present everywhere, but he resides more particularly in heaven, leaving the earth to his spouse, the Church.

It is to the outlying parts of the world that we have to go for clear evidence of the ancient dualism of sky and earth. Round the hub of the ancient world, as we may call the Near East, it is the sun that dominates everything, and blurs all details by his glare, till at last he obliterates himself in an abstract monotheism.

It may seem a roundabout way of centralizing government to let one god devour all the rest. It seems roundabout only

---

29. Daremberg et Saglio, s.v. *Apotheosis*, 326a. — A Ceylon king of solar descent was "the lord (or husband) of the young damsel, the land of Ceylon." He was directly married to the land. *Ep.* Z. IV, 65. Cp. *Kingship*, 109; 105 and 124.
30. Below p. 259 f.
31. Above p. 65.

to those who are still possessed by the idea that the primary function of a king is to govern, to be the head of the administration. We shall see that he is nothing of the kind. He is the repository of the gods, that is of the life of the group. He dispenses prosperity to that group, and to that group only. If he is to dispense it to any other group, he must become the repository of the gods, that is the life, of that group also. He does not become another god in order to govern another people, but in order to confer on them blessings as their god.

A concrete instance will perhaps help us to enter into a point of view so foreign to us. The people of Levuka in Fiji used to live in Mbau. They had to fly from it, and they came to settle in Lakemba. According to European notions they should have come under the government of the Lord of Nayau on whose territory they settled. But the chief of Mbau remained the Lord of Levuka, and, when one died, they went all the way back to their old home to instal his successor. When the king-makers tied a cloth on his arm at the consecration they addressed the people in these words: "Let the cloth be tied to be the cloth of your food, the cloth of your riches, also reverence him since he is your lord." He did not govern them, but he was their lord, because he was their dispenser of riches. At the same time they were navigators to the foreign potentate who had given them a new home; as chief navigator, their head sat in the kava ring, and took part in the ritual of which the Lord of Nayau was the principal. Thus they owed a double allegiance. It is not uncommon for a Fijian tribe thus to "go to" two suzerians, because it is just as possible to have two lords, as to worship two gods or two saints; the more the better. Expense is the only limitation.

We have done away with all that in Fiji, because it does not fit in with our political theory. We expect a chief to administer, that is to write letters, make returns, see that the villages are kept clean, and generally interfere with the routine once left to the clans. Two men cannot exercise this authority over the same territory. Inevitably the people of Levuka have come under that of the Lord of Nayau, they have become the subject of his letters and returns and inspections. The connection with Mbau has weakened with the weakening of the belief in the suzerain's supernatural power. All the dispensing of prosperity is now done with pen and ink.[32]

"What is the divine king to us?" exclaims the Youth Movement, "What have we to do with ancient superstitions? with dead things? Our eyes are on the future. The last vestiges of Divine Kingship were wiped out by the Great War." Were they? In 1933 I read of thanks being rendered "to God and his instrument, Adolph Hitler." A second instrument of God in the city of the Pope is scarcely possible; but the Fascist State claims infallibility, which is the substance of this new divine kingship. Austria is far enough removed from the Holy City to be free from rivalry. It has recently discarded a democratic republic whose Right proceeded from the people, in favour of a Right that proceeds from God Almighty. Moscow has abolished God, but the change is not as great as it may seem; for the philosophers have long reduced God to an Idea, and the Idea is still there, the final immutable Truth expressed in the infallible state.[33]

32. After all it was possible in Medievel Europe to have two lords. The case was common enough to be considered by English lawyers. In the XIIth century Glanvill says that "if a man has done divers homages for his divers fees to divers lords who 'infest' each other, and if his chief lord orders him to go in his proper person against another of his lords, he must obey the command, 'saving the service to that other lord from the fee that is held of him'." Later "Bracton fully admits that a man who holds land both in England and in France may be bound to aid both kings when they make war on each other; his liege lord he must serve in person, but none the less he must discharge the service due to his other lord." The state was not based then on the coordination of activities, so much as on service to the lord. Thus the Normans "regarded Normandy as a member of the state or congeries of states that owed service, we can hardly say obedience, to the king at Paris." (Pollock & Maitland, I, 301; 303; cp. 320; I, 66.)
33. "Just as the Roman Catholic considers the Pope infallible in all matters concerning religion and morals, so do we National-Socialists believe with the same inner conviction that for us the Leader is in all matters concerning the national and social interests of the people simply infallible. . . . For we love Adolf Hitler, because we believe deeply and unswervingly that God has sent him to us to save Germany." H. Goering, *Germany Reborn* (London, 1934), 79 f.

So far from having done with divine kingship we seem to be returning to it in a more virulent form. It is a harmless doctrine that God is life and that the king is the repository of that life. There are obvious dangers in a doctrine that God is infallibility and that the chief gunman is the mouthpiece of that infallibility. Its dangers are however less certain than those of anarchy. In turning from the chaos of beliefs and acts to absolutism, modern Europe is merely repeating the experience of imperial Rome, which welcomed back the firm divinity of emperors as better than the quicksands of party politics.

9· The Estates of the Realm

THE KING cannot alone cause increase. He must have the assistance of departmental principals, as we may call his chieftains. Each of these contributes his share to the general prosperity by causing increase in those things of which he has charge. The special duty of one is fire, of another cattle, of a third rain, and so on. It is possible for them to cumulate: fire and cattle went together in Greece, India, and Kamchatka.[1] In fact pluralism seems to have been the rule;[2] and indeed it would be impossible in a small community to find one principal for every conceivable element of prosperity.

The greatest cumulator of all is the king: he is everything. But it is evident that the more he absorbs the lesser powers the less need there is for departmental chieftains. As a matter of fact, it would seem that the specific rites gradually lost their individuality. Instead of a succession of rites each dealing with one group of objectives, an inclusive ceremony fertilizes the macrocosm as a whole through the person of that microcosm, the king. The chieftains do not however drop out as the result of this centralization, leaving the king to act alone. They remain as important as ever; in fact, they may be the real masters of the ritual, and so of the state; but they are no longer in charge of things; they are responsible for services. To make my meaning clear, let us take a concrete case. The cattle-fire-etc. chieftain ceases by degrees to be the man who causes increase of cattle-fire-etc., because the king can do that as he can do everything. This chieftain is transformed into the king's assistant, performing certain services, such as directing the ritual and speaking the prayers. The bear chieftain

1. Above pp. 18–19, 21.
2. This phenomenon is called "linked totems" by anthropologists when they find it among naked, or semi-naked, people. It is equally characteristic of Greeks, Egyptians, etc.

may continue to be known as the bear chieftain, but bears cease to be his chief concern: the duty on which he prides himself is the service he owes his lord, of going in front in war and migration.

All we know of the relations of Aranda headmen and the chief is that in one ceremony the chief is seen presiding; he sits facing the sacred pole; he is flanked on either side by his headmen. Behind the sacred pole lie the neophytes.[3]

About the chieftains of the Koryaks we know nothing, so we pass on to the Winnebagoes.

There the chief is also chieftain of his own clan, as well as chief over the whole. Every clan has its own chieftain in charge of a specific cult: the thunder-bird clan feast, the bear clan feast, the snake clan feast, and so on. No two cults are alike as far as their details go, and indeed they scarcely could be, since they must be adapted each to its peculiar objective. They are alike in their main features only. We have a plan of the bear clan feast: it is much the same as among the Arandas, except that no one sits at the top; the place of the supreme chief is vacant. At the lower end sit the women and children.

Besides being in charge of objects the chieftains have each a service to render in the general activities of the tribe. The Warrior clan is keeper of "certain tribal regalia." The Buffalo clan held the office of public crier who "was supposed to report to the chief early every morning and receive instructions." He "would then go all round the village making the chief's orders known." He seems to correspond to the Fijian "Sir Crier." The Bear clan were called soldiers and formed the vanguard.[4]

There is a remarkable similarity between Fijian and Winnebago organization. Both have a ceremonial of which the chief is the centre, and in that ceremonial each clan has a special function. The difference is that among the Winnebago the clan cult retains its specific character; the chiefly ritual is merely superimposed. In Fiji it has assimilated the clan cults.

3. Strehlow.
4. Radin, 219; 210; 226.

The Fijians sit in much the same manner as the Arandas at the central ceremony of their ritual, the drinking of kava. The high chief, who is also chieftain of his clan, sits at the head of the ring; on either side sit his chieftains, heads of clans. At the far end stands the kava bowl with its cord laid out to point to the chief. Behind the bowl sit huddled those who bear no title, even though they be great noblemen.

We have very full information about the clans which these chieftains represent. The tribe, so long as it has not absorbed other tribes, is a big family, for they acknowledge a common descent, and keep intermarrying so that they renew their relationship. Within that big family are smaller families, clans. The clan, however, is not altogether a natural family. A family, especially a reigning one addicted to polygamy, may grow to unwieldy dimensions and have to be split up; or it may so decay that it must be incorporated in another to make up numbers. The natural family may thus be larger or smaller than the clan. The clan is partly artificial: it is a family cut and trimmed and adjusted to one particular purpose, the feast. Contributions to a feast are assessed by counting, not heads, but clans. Thus the clan chieftains, who gather round the chief, will decide that each clan must contribute twenty yams and two bundles of fish, no matter what the size of the clan. Clans have therefore to be kept within certain limits: if one is too large, it is not doing its fair share; if it is too small, the burden is too great. Thus the clan system is an organization for the purpose of levying contributions; and also for distributing them; for the fast is divided, as it was collected, by clans.

The feast in Fiji, as throughout the South Seas, is an offering to the gods, whether unseen, or present in the chief. The South Sea Islander does not hold a feast just because he wants a good "blow out"; he holds one only when there is a death, a marriage, a royal consecration, an offering of first fruits, in short on all occasions where offerings are prescribed.

The social organization of the Fijians then is based on the ritual. This is expressed by the common term which I translate clan. It is *matangali*, from *mata*, eye, face, sacred land, temple. It is stated in plain terms by the learned chief of Tokatoka. He calls his clans *matambure*, that is "faces of temples," or

104

simply "temples," and he explains, "The faces of temples
are our clans, the temples where the various gods are served.
The tribes are one thing: they have a common descent; the
faces of temples are another: they are smaller; they are groups
of brothers with their several temples." The facts confirm his
definition: each clan has its temple; and the royal family of
Lakemba provides the exception that proves the rule: it is divided into four clans which have a common temple; but then
they always insist that their divisions are not clans, that they
form one big clan divided into four for purposes of contributions. The manner in which society gravitates round the temple is clearly illustrated by the tribe of Ndravuwalu in Kandavu. The clans of the commons all come together for a feast
under the leadership of a chieftain entitled the Lord of the
Grave or Tumulus.[5] When they are thus gathered together they
are known as the Temple,[6] because they own the god. Just
as each clan has a chieftain, and the whole tribe a chief; so
each clan has a temple, and the whole tribe a state temple[7]
of the chief god. Thus, as usual, the human organization reflects the divine, and vice-versa, since the two are one. Thus
a clan is usually named after the house of its head, but it
can also be named after the temple.

There is then a big temple for the state, and small temples
for the clans. The god worshipped in one of these temples
usually has an animal into which he enters. Round the Lakemban chief are grouped chieftains whose gods are respectively
a dog, a crab, twin *kaisevau* birds, and so on. It looks like
a collection of specific rites, even as among the Winnebagoes;
but inquiry does not confirm this first impression. There is
not one responsible for crabs, one for dogs, etc. Their functions
are to render certain services to the king. To understand the
nature of those services we must always bear in mind that
the king is the god or gods.

The extent to which kings and gods are interchangeable
is illustrated by the following fragment of Natewan history.

5. *Tu ni Mata.*
6. *Mbure kalou.*
7. *Mburenitu.*

This tribe was once independent. Now they are vassals to Somosomo, the capital of the King of the Reef.[8] "Of old they made offerings to the gods. Five generations ago a lady of the tribe of this great chief married into their own tribe. Since then the feasts are collected and sent to the Lord of the Reef." In other words the chief has supplanted the gods, and vassalage consists in adopting a foreign chief as god. The people of Namata did much the same thing. They are neighbours of Mbau. They once secured for their chief a lady from this most powerful state. Two sons were born of this union. Previously the best parts of the feast had been give to the gods. From that time on they were given to the sons of the great Mbauan lady.

It should always be remembered then, that it is a god who sits at the head of the kava circle. Beside him sits the herald or master of ceremonies. The Fijians round the Koro Sea call him the "Face of the Land"; but others by Face of the Land mean the sacred land, "the landing place of the gods, their entrance, where they come up." One tribe calls its herald the Lord of the Tumulus. He is then the man in charge of the sacred mound on which every temple and chief's house stands, and which crowns every grave.[9] He is a priest, the chief's priest. He directs the ritual addressed to the chief. His main business is to speak, and so he is sometimes called "the mouth of chief," or "the speech of the nobles." He is not appointed at random, but is the head of a clan to whom the title belongs.

In the same way every clan has its chieftain who is an official at court. They are often referred to as the Faces of the Land, the herald being the Great Face of the Land. They may indeed officiate instead of the herald, if he is not there. Each of them however usually holds his own special office. Some of these offices are to be found in all tribes, some are purely local.

There is, for instance, usually a chieftain of the Land, or Commons, as we may call them. His clan or clans are expected to be rough and energetic. The chief relies on them to make

8. *Tui Thakau.*
9. Hocart, *On the Meaning of Kalou,* J.R.A.I., 1912, 437; *Fijian Heralds and Envoys,* J.R.A.I., 1913, 109.

106

a special effort in war and in feasts. They assault anyone who fails in respect to the High Chief, and so form a kind of police. They, or a subdivision of them, form the vanguard in war.

Usually associated with the Commons is the Lord of the Village Green who with his men watches the collected feast on the green and assigns the portions. There is always a clan which dresses the chief's head, watches over his corpse, and buries him; it may be the same as the herald clan or a different one. In Vanua Levu there is often a "Sir Crier"[10] who proclaims the chief's wishes. I have only once come across a "chieftain of the dogs" whose men are the high chief's dogs and go everywhere with the chief, and bite any one who is disrespectful to him. One tribe has a Queen's herald; another a clan of Uterine Nephews,[11] whose duty it is to make feasts in emergencies only, as when visitors come unexpectedly to the chief.

The king is head of the ritual, the chieftains are his assistants. But there is an important difference between the ritual organization of the Fijians and that of the Arandas or the Winnebagoes. We saw that there each small group has its own peculiar cult which is not like that of the others except in structure; the tribal ritual is merely a confederation of these cults. In Fiji the chieftains are not the heads of rituals which can be carried out separately, but office-bearers in a great common ritual. The herald cannot carry out alone the duties he carried out in that state ritual. The clans are not distinguished by having different cults, but by having different functions in the common cult. Of course each clan has its own god, be it hawk, dog, crab, or what not, it has its own temple, and the chieftain is head of its cult; but the cult is not different from the others: it is the state ritual on a smaller scale. The herald in his own clan is the principal, and some junior plays the herald to him.

The rank of each chieftain and clan is determined by its function. They are classified into castes, royal caste or nobility, herald caste, vanguard caste, and so on. These castes have

10. *Ro Kathikathi.*
11. *Vusa Vasu.* Cp. below p. 110.

107

nothing to do with specialization in crafts. There is no such specialization in Fiji. All men do the same manual work. Here and there, it is true, among the bigger tribes, are to be found clans which look like specialists in some manual accomplishment: there are clans of carpenters, clans of fishermen, clans of navigators. But, in the first place, they are not an integral part of Fijian society; they do not belong to the original scheme of things, never being natives of the tribe, but foreigners attached to it. They have always come from elsewhere, it may be from as far as Tonga or Samoa. Secondly, they are only for the chiefs.

These carpenters, fishermen, and navigators do not ply their craft for pay. Such a thing as pay is unknown in Fiji.[12] A man does not go to a carpenter and order a canoe to be paid for on delivery; nor does he book his passage on a navigator's canoe. "Any one," says a Lakemban, "can build a paddling canoe, and there is no ceremony; but large sailing canoes are put into the hands of carpenters, and there are feasts at various stages of the construction." Technically the carpenters are superfluous. No doubt heredity and specialization increase their skill, but most tribes get on very well without them. They are chief's carpenters, not carpenters for the masses. A great chief likes to have them to build sacred canoes on which he sails, or with which he commemorates a dead nobleman, to build his temples or chiefly houses. They are required for the service of the god or the king, which is one and the same thing. Their work is punctuated with ceremonies from start to finish. Note how our Lakemban contrasts the absence of feasts at the building of private canoes with the succession of them when an official canoe is built. The carpenters have their own god, and the chief carpenter is his priest.

Every Fijian on the coast can sail; the passengers are the crew. The navigators are the chief's navigators, and sail the sacred canoes that convey him.

On the coast again every one can fish from childhood, and

12. There are a few exceptions among the fishermen. The men of Lasakau bartered fish, and the Levukans pots; but they were people apart. They also had ritual duties towards the tribe to which they were attached. The Lasakauans were fishers of men for human sacrifices.

most tribes get on without fishermen. "The fisherboys," a Fijian writes in the Native Gazette, "are vassals to the suzerain land. The various suzerain lands have fisher-boys. It is the duty of the fisher-boys to carry out the order to fish for turtle or for fish, as the order may come from the suzerain land." Such an order is not issued at random, but when a feast is to be held. The chief cannot just say, "Fish"; he has to send a man who holds the hereditary office of envoy to the fishermen. The envoy is sent with offerings, whale's teeth, which are presented to the Chief Fisherman. The Chief Fisherman takes them, prays over them in the usual style, then issues orders to his boys. But first he has to ascertain by divination where to fish. After the oracle comes a thanksgiving to the god. The leaders of the fishing party are called "the gods" or "spirits of the turtle." The Chief Fisherman's provisions are put into a sacred basket. He lies all night in the open with the turtle: is this the sacred marriage? There are many other observances which show that the Chief Fisherman is just as much a priest as the Herald or any chieftain. He is the owner of the turtle or the fish, and he is in charge of the ritual which ensures plenty of turtles. As a craftsman he is superfluous; as a priest he is indispensable. He is the principal in a specific rite of which the objective is the turtle. By analogy we conclude that the king's carpenter and the king's navigator are the heads of cults which have as objective some artefact, the adze or the canoe. Only this specific ritual has been drawn into the cosmic ritual of the Fijian chief, and it has become assimilated to it except for some minor observances such as I have recorded. The non-owners still have to make offerings to the owners and it is for them the owners work; but the parties are no longer owners and maternal relations as in Australia,[13] but owners and suzerain.

Pot-making is a craft pure and simple. Pots do not figure in ceremonials, and feasts are not cooked in pots. Therefore there is no potter caste and no king's potter.[14]

The technical castes retain that specific character which has

13. Below p. 190.
14. Contrast the priestly potter of India, below p. 116.

been lost by the other castes. They are still responsible for things, and their functions are based on that. They are however intrusive; they do not belong to the old Fijian scheme.

Since the Fijians specialize in duties, not ritual objectives, we might expect specialization in abilities, since the different office-bearers have to dove-tail into one another. Yet there is little specialization of ability in Fiji. The king's carpenter is not appointed because of his manual skill, but because he is the head of a family that holds the appointment. I knew a very skilful carpenter, and one who thought about his work and held as definite views about truth in art as Ruskin; but he was not king's carpenter, only an ordinary citizen who planted his yams and taro, and shared in the work of his clan.

In a small Fijian tribe it may be said that the court is coextensive with the people: the head of each family is an officer of the chief's. In larger tribes where one village is lord over several others the village headmen will have each his own herald and vanguard. West African states are vastly larger than the largest in Fiji. The king and his court are far removed. Each of his officers however has his own court, the members of which in turn have their own officers. The process can be repeated till the whole nation is permeated. These offices are as clearly ritual as in Fiji.

The Wukari division of the Jukuns contains families which hold hereditary offices. Here are some of them:—

1. The "Salt People," the present royal families.
2. Uterine nephews of the Salt People.
3. Another royal family whose head bears the title borne by the ancient kings of a ruined city.
4. The Ba-Vi who formally confer the kingship.
5. The Ba-Nando who carry out the burial customs of the kings of Wukari.
6. Descendants of a former king, but no longer having a claim to the kingship.
7. Potters *principally* employed in the manufacture of pottery.[15]

15. Meek, 66 f.

One division of the Jukuns is known as the people of the water. They are fishermen. According to Mr. Meek they are probably made up of Jukuns and non-Jukuns, who by a common occupation "in waters *controlled by the king* of Wukari, became fused together." Again it is round the king that these families revolve.

There are numerous important officials whose hereditary character is not stated, and we can only *infer*, that, like the others, they are heads of families that hold the title.

Among these there is the second king; there is the king's "younger brother" who "attends the royal rites each day, takes a prominent share in judicial work, in keeping the walls of the city and the fencing of the royal enclosure in repair." There is the royal diviner, corresponding, it would seem, to the Indian keeper of the dice.[16] On the other hand, hunting, which is technical enough to require long teaching, is not necessarily hereditary, but may be acquired by attaching oneself as a pupil to a hunting family.[17]

What are the personages whom Mr. Meek calls ministers or priests among the Jukuns? They are those who have parts assigned to them in the daily ritual of the king. The principal minister carries out the libations, and sees that the king is properly fed. Another sees to the cooking. A third sees to the washing of the king's dishes. A fourth keeps the enclosure in good repair.

"All Jukun chiefs, however minor, are regarded as being in some measure incarnations of the deity."[18] The priests are assimilated with the deity.[19] These chieftains are minor editions of the king. Thus "the king must always have a reserve of seed . . . He is the divine purveyor of corn, and when any new village chief or priest is appointed in outlying areas the first act of the local authorities is to send to the king for some of his sacred seed, of which the new chief or priest be-

16. Meek, 337; 339.
17. Meek, 414.
18. Meek, 121.
19. Meek, 133.

111

comes the local custodian."[20] Each officer of state has his own court which follows the pattern of the king's. It is with the Jukuns as with the Fijians: clan cults and organization have been assimilated to those of the king and country.

Mr. P. G. Harris describes to me the same state of affairs among the Yauri, further north than the Jukuns. "The village elders carry titles borne by the courtiers and councillors of the ruling houses. It is, in fact, just as if, should we say, the Mayor and the Aldermen of a small English town called themselves the King of So and So with his councillors the Duke of Norfolk, the Duke of Gloucester, the Duke of York, and so forth."

The Yorubas fill in some of the blanks left among the Jukuns. The following offices are stated to be hereditary:—

1) The "king celestial," moral overseer of the supreme king. We shall hear more of him.

2) The master of the horse. He has to die with the king.

3) The king's fathers, that is his admonishers.

4) The king-makers, the chief of whom is the celestial king.

5) The king's bards, cymbalists and drummers.

6) A family that carries out menial duties in connection with sacrifice.

7) Those "whose sole employment is to do all the needle and embroidered work for royalty. They are also umbrella-makers. The crown, staff, robes, and all ornamental beadworks, and workings in cotton, silk, or leather are executed by them." I give a full list of their productions, because it proves that their specialism is not imposed by the material in which they work, but by the purpose: they will work in any material that is needed for the king's regalia which are his ritual tools.

There occur besides the following offices of which it is not stated whether they are hereditary or not:—

8) The chief diviner, a kind of domestic chaplain.

9) The carrier of the king's remains to the mausoleum.

10) The palace surveyor, who washes the king's corpse.

20. Meek, 146.

11) The drummers.
12) The executioners.[21]

Mr. P. G. Harris has kindly allowed me to use his notes on Hausa blacksmiths. "Of all the arts and crafts of the Hausa States," he says, "perhaps the strongest and most respected is the craft of the blacksmith. This is expressed in the Hausa saying, 'The Chief, the Scribes, and the Smiths—these are the wielders of power,' and it is noteworthy that one or two of the most respected of titles existing at the present day mean literally 'Chief of the Anvil.' The anvil moreover is still the subject of the greatest veneration among those tribes which are still largely non-Mohammedan. To take two tribes at either end of the Hausa States as examples; the Kerri Kerri (to the East of Kano) swear upon the anvil the most binding of oaths of which they are capable, while the Arewa (to the North West of Sokoto) sacrifice to the sacred anvil which is kept in a grove of trees and which is said to move out in the open of its own volition to look at the sacrifice that is being offered." In other words the blacksmiths are in charge of a specific cult. They might be described as priests of the anvil. The anvil is their god.

There is of course a king's blacksmith. He is entitled "Sarkin Makira, or King of the blacksmiths, who lives at the headquarters of the Hausa State; he, by virtue of his position, is also the king's or chief's blacksmith." "As far as I know, he is not paid by the chief in any way except by gifts of, say, a horse now and then, meat at festivals, etc., but he has to hold himself in readiness to perform any of the chief's commands. He is also an ex-officio member of the Council on all matters concerning smiths. . . . He is expected to look after all the smaller or provincial 'King of smiths' when they come in to headquarters. He certainly holds land . . . I know of no special function in the royal ritual in which he takes part beyond the fact that he, or persons under his direction, makes all the kingly insignia such as sword, dagger, metal work for saddlery, etc." The king of the blacksmiths, we see, is much

21. *Yorubas*, 3, 42, 45, 57, 68, 70.

more than a man who forges: he is a court official who owes service to the king, because the royal ritual has need of metal insignia, and these have to be made by the men who hold the cult of which smithing is only a part.

Indian sovereigns likewise have their hereditary attendants and craftsmen. The process of copying the royal style has possibly been carried farther than in West Africa, and certainly than in Fiji. Simplifications of the royal court have penetrated right down to the peasantry who form the overwhelming majority of the inland population. In fact it is this popular version of the king's court that is best known to us under the name of caste system. Of the king's own court we know little, and, since kings have disappeared in Ceylon, it is too late to find out from them, and it is to the common people that we have to turn for information.[22]

In order to understand what our living witnesses are talking about we must possess the rudiments of the system, for they assume that much knowledge in their hearers. I shall sum up the system in Ceylon.[23]

The highest Sinhalese caste used to be the royal one, but since the annexation it has become extinct. The brahmans are also extinct. The highest caste to survive is that of the farmers. This aristocracy forms the vast majority of the inland population. These three castes, alive or extinct, are still known as the "good people"; the other castes are the "low castes." These comprise fishermen, smiths, washermen and barbers to the good people, tailors, potters, weavers, cooks, lime-burners, grass-cutters, drummers, charcoal-burners, washermen to the low castes, mat-makers, and at the bottom the untouchables. The same system prevails among the Tamils of North Ceylon, only the list differs a little in details. The word which we translate caste is in both languages *jati*, which means in Sanskrit birth, descent, family, tribe, genus. It is derived from the same root as the Latin *gens*.

Thus instructed we can now proceed to call our witnesses.

22. For the king's officers see D'Oyly, Sir John, *A Sketch of the Constitution of the Kandyan Kingdom* (Colombo, 1929), 132 ff., 140.
23. What follows is an abridgment of a paper on "The Basis of Caste in India," *Acta Orientalia*, vol. XIV, 203.

The first is a Tamil of the farmer caste. That does not mean that he farms; it only expresses his rank. As a matter of fact he is an official. He says, "The castes have a particular work to do for the cultivator (what I call farmer). This is how it is generally understood." Another Tamil giving evidence before a commission says, "The low castes were only service classes, such as washermen and barbers. Such low caste people in olden days were treated by their masters as their own children." These educated men have the advantage of being able to frame general definitions, but the disadvantage of leaving their definitions in the air. It is as well to bring them down to earth by consulting illiterate villagers. They are farmers, but lost in the jungle, and so unused to books and abstract ideas; they are forced to speak in concrete examples. "The people of Kadurupitiya (a neighbouring village) are drummers . . . They are like servants: when called they must come for dancing, festivals, processions. The farmers give the drummers food on a leaf, also cash for their hard work."

All our witnesses are agreed that the low castes are retainers of the farmers to whom they owe services, each according to his caste. The same view is expressed in old Sanskrit writings.[24] But what is the nature of these services? The drummer is purely ceremonial: he comes for marriages, deaths, temple worship, exorcism. He is referred to politely not as drummer, but as astrologer.

The European thinks of the barber and the washerman as men who ply a trade inherited from their forefathers; but that is not the native point of view. One of our witnesses says: "Practically on every occasion the barber and the washerman will have to be present. They are called 'the children of the family'." By "occasions" we soon find he means births, weddings, funerals, and other festivities. Thus at a wedding the washerman spreads cloths for the bridegroom to walk upon. Washermen and barbers sing his praises. The barber shaves him. It is the barber who carries the marriage necklace, the equivalent of our wedding ring. At a funeral the washerman dresses the dead man. The barber prepares the fire for the

24. Manu, I, 91. — *Vayupurana*, VII, 168 ff.

cremation, and conducts the person who lights the pyre three times round it. "He is," concludes my informant, "*like a priest on the cremation ground.*" So important are the priestly functions of the barber that in Travancore he is entitled "he who helps the souls," a kind of Hermes in the flesh.[25]

Whenever we discuss the functions of castes with the people themselves, we find that what is uppermost in their minds is the part the castes take in ritual. They do not, as we do, think of the barber as the owner of a barber's shop, or of the washerman as running a laundry, but as men who officiate in the ritual. They are minor priests. The same is true of the other castes. The smiths make statues of the gods, temple jewelry, wedding necklaces. Carpenters make temple cars, as well as household furniture. Potters officiate as priests in temples of village goddesses and of the elephant-headed god, make images, ex-votos, pots, which at weddings represent the gods. They claim to be a low order of brahmans.[26] The daily cooking of the household is done by the women of the family. The cook caste is only called in at weddings and other festivals of the farmer caste. The cook at the Temple of the Tooth is not of the cook, but of the farmer, caste; his scullion on the other hand is a cook and so are the night-watchers who have nothing to do with cooking. Our term cook is therefore a mistranslation, and does not express the caste. They are really ritual bottlewashers.

The caste called Balija in Southern India evidently hold much [the] same view of their organization as do the Fijians of theirs, namely that is a ritual organization; for their name means "born of the sacrifice," and they have a legend how their ancestor was created out of the sacrifice. This theory

---

25. Above p. 18.
26. The hypercritical rationalist, from the depth of his books, condemns this claim as an absurd forgery. But the potters wear the sacred thread like the brahmans, and no one disputes their right. They also claim to be creators like the brahmans, and that is why they are bone-setters. This creative function can be traced beyond the boundaries of India and farther back than our earliest Indian records. The Egyptian potter-god was already fashioning children in the womb about 1475 B.C. (Breasted, *Records*, II, No. 202). He had probably been at it many centuries.

of the origin of caste can be traced back to the Rigveda. Had we lost those ancient records we should still be able to collect specimens of that myth from the oral tradition of the twentieth century. The subdivisions of this Balija caste are called *bali*, which means offerings. In other words they are sacrificial units.[27]

As in Fiji and Nigeria, so in India, we have a king surrounded by specialists in various parts of the ritual, and every petty feudal lord, every village chief in fact, copies on a small scale the royal state. The minimum in Ceylon is barber, washerman, and drummer. In the old writings these feudal lords, kings, priests, and farmers, are alone admitted to the sacraments, and are identified with the gods. The serfs or artisans are excluded because they represent the demons. Mere priestly arrogance, the scholars say; an exaggeration existing only on paper, and not of any practical importance. But to the present day you can see drummers impersonate demons, and those who do are not allowed to officiate at a temple of the Buddha who has displaced the gods. Even those who officiate at temples do so in the courtyard; only men of the farmer caste officiate inside. It may seem monstrous that a whole class should be regarded as carriers of the demons; but the term demon is not a very good translation of the *asura* of the old texts. They are the equivalent of the Greek Giants and the Germanic Jotuns, not personifications of evil, but ritual antagonists of the gods, darkness against light, and darkness is just as necessary to the world as light, though we may not think it good. I shall therefore call these beings Giants.

Here is one point of difference between Fiji and India: in Fiji there is a dualism, as we shall see, but it is not so decidedly one of admitted and excluded. With one exception, the carpenters called *mataisau*, there is no exclusion of particular clans from the state ritual. Even in India the exclusion is not absolute, for the serfs have to be called in for some rites. The other differences are superficial. India has a much longer list of castes for the simple reason that specialism has been carried much further, and materials are more varied. There is no room

27. Thurston, s.v. *Balija Rigveda*, X, 90.

for washermen in Fiji, because barkcloth does not wash. There are no metals, so there can be no smiths. There are drums in Fiji, but they are not assigned to particular families.

The feudalism is not so perfect in India as in Fiji. Fijian heralds are heralds each to his own peculiar chief. The herald of Mbau is recognized as being of herald status all over Fiji; but he is attached to the Lord of Mbau only. This state of affairs had already ceased to exist in Northern India about 800 B.C.; for a king could select his own priest. Families were not attached for ever to the same king, but could attach themselves. That is not altogether unknown in Fiji. We have seen fishermen attaching themselves to strange chiefs. In the country parts of Ceylon farmer villages often have to send for barbers and washermen to come and dwell with them. Towns have broken down feudalism still further: they always destroy personal ties, and set men adrift. In the towns washermen wash, and carry out ceremonial duties for any one who hires them, and they have lost their position in the councils of the community. They are unattached and hold no lands as fiefs. The White Man only knows them as laundrymen.

We have enough details about the Persian system to know it was very closely allied to the Indian. Three aristocratic castes, priests, warriors, and farmers, contrasted with an artisan caste. In fact the Persian system is too like the Indian to teach us much. It is useful in proving that the system did not grow up on Indian soil. It also confirms the king as head of the system; for Darmesteter, in his translation of the Zend-Avesta, tells us that the king is the patron of the three aristocratic castes, and that his glory, or halo, is composed of the glory of all three. He too then is a compound.[28]

Our information about Greece is very meagre. Besides, the manner in which the whole problem has been approached places further difficulties in the way. The usual procedure is to set up a definition of caste based upon Indian practice, or rather a misconception of it; then to see how far the social systems of other nations fit into that definition. Of course they do not, since it has been specially framed for Indian condi-

28. J. Darmesteter, *Le Zend-Avesta* (Paris, 1892), I, 152 f.; 169.

tions. So the verdict is there is no caste in Greece, only classes. It is as if we defined a parliament as a House of Lords under a Chancellor and a House of Commons under a Speaker, looked round for other institutions answering to that definition, failed to find any, and so concluded other nations had only assemblies, not parliaments. We are not concerned here with definitions, but whether the structure of Indian and Greek society is so alike as to warrant us in postulating a common origin. I think Homer's few hints are sufficient to justify us in answering yes. His society is presided over by kings drawn from a royal caste. Their functions resemble those of the royal caste in India: to lead in war and to uphold justice. Their god is Zeus, the thunder-god, whose bird is the eagle; in other words he is the homologue of Indra. Some of their customs are identical with those of their Indian counterparts, such as the winning of brides by athletic and other contests.[29] They are surrounded by retainers, such as heralds and bards. The heralds are hereditary. Their status is so low compared with a brahman's, that, at first sight, we should never think they were the same; but we must remember castes sink and rise, and we shall later bring forward good reasons for thinking them homologues.[30] Their duties are purely ceremonial. There are goldsmiths: they appear at the sacrifice to gild the horns of the victim.

Egyptologists dispute the account Herodotos gives of the Egyptian caste system. Why dispute about ancient texts when there are living descendants of the disputed facts to study? There is no *rule* of heredity in a modern Egyptian village, but in *practice* every occupation is hereditary: blacksmith, potter, barber, mayor, etc. There is this difference with India that the title describes the work, not the lineage. The Egyptian *halaq* is a man who shaves and heals; the corresponding Tamil *ambattan* is a man of *ambattan* descent. Yet this contrast must be qualified. I have seen the tomb of a man whose grandfather was an engineer; the grandson was called Ali Ahmed, the engineer, though neither he nor his father ever plied that trade.

29. *Kingship*, 108 f.
30. Below p. 195.

These titles are thus in a state of transition between Indian
and English usage, and may throw some light on the origin
of our family names. We might express the different development of these three types of society by saying that in India
a fisherman is always a Mr. Fisher, but a Mr. Fisher is not
always a fisherman: he may be a lawyer, a shopkeeper, a cook,
anything that is not above or below the rank of the Fishers.
In England a fisherman may be a Mr. Fisher, but then it is
pure accident. In Egypt Mr. Fisher would be the descendant
of a fisherman, if not actually one himself.

Another difference with India is that the Egyptian village
functionaries do not hold lands in return for services. Some,
like the barber and the priest (*imam*), receive a salary from
the village in maize and wheat. The blacksmith, schoolmaster,
repairer of water-wheels, among others, receive such an annual
salary from their regular customers only. The potter is paid
piecework. The result is that the population of specialists is
much more floating than in Ceylon, as far as my very limited
information goes. In their divorce from the land they have
evolved farther than our early Middle Ages, as we shall soon
see.

Another result is that the work is more purely technical.
Nevertheless the barber cannot describe his work without
bringing in the family rituals. He gives first aid, heals scorpion
bites, circumcises, does cupping, issues certificates of death,
"decorates" the bridegroom, that is shaves his head, and generally smartens him up, and so is called decorator. Some years
ago near Cairo he still used to walk in the circumcision procession; but now he only operates. His ritual character is in process of decay. The *mughassil* retains it better: he washes,
dresses, admonishes the dead, and sees him into his last home.
It would not be inapt to describe him as "a priest on the
burial ground."[31] The so-called "schoolmaster," the *fiqih*, cor-

31. He certainly represents the ancient embalmer. He resembles the
Indian washerman; yet he has something in common with the Indian
barber. In favour of the first homology is the name, from *ghasal*, to
wash, and also the fact that his female equivalent is the midwife.
(H. A. Winkler, *Bauern zwischen Wasser und Wüste*, Stuttgart, 1934,
p. 128). Now in Ceylon the midwife is the washerman's wife. It is im-

responds to the Indian *guru*. He teaches the Koran, and dispenses charms.[32] He may also be the priest of the mosque.

In Egypt these craftsmen do not seem to be regarded as inferior and unworthy of marriage alliances with the peasants. The peasants of Homs and Hama in Syria, on the other hand, entertain the same feelings towards them as do their Indian equivalents. Blacksmiths, shepherds, barbers, millers, woolcarders and others are inferior to the peasants, and may as a rule marry only women of their own rank.[33]

The Medieval serjeanty was a tenure of land conditional on certain services being performed for the lord, just as in Ceylon potters hold lands of the farmers on condition that they supply pots to their lords. Among the serjeanties due to the king were such " 'as to carry the banner of the king, or his lance, or to lead his army, or to be his marshal, or to carry his sword before him at his coronation, or to be his sewer at his coronation, or his carver, or his butler, or to be one of the chamberlains of the receipt of his exchequer.' Some of the highest offices of the realm have become hereditary; the great officers are conceived to hold their lands by the service of serjeanty of filling those offices. It is so with the offices of the king's steward or seneschal, marshal, constable, chamberlain; and, though the real work of governing the realm has fallen to another set of ministers whose offices are not hereditary, to the king's justiciar, chancellor and treasurer, still the marshal and constable have serious duties to perform. Many of the less exalted offices of the king's household have become hereditary serjeanties; there are men holding by serjeanties to be done in the kitchen, the larder, and the pantry. Even some of the offices which have to do with national business, with the finance of the realm, have become hereditary; there are already hereditary chamberlains of the exchequer who do their service by deputy. . . . The king's sport has

---

possible to settle this homology until we have full details of the Indian washerman's duties by a dead body.

32. J. L. Burckardt, *Arabic Proverbs,* 2nd ed. (London, 1875), 158.

33. Kazem Daghestani, *Etude Sociologigue sur la Famille Musulmane Contemporaine en Syrie* (Paris, 1932), 19.

given rise to numerous serjeanties; men are bound by tenure to keep hounds and hawks for him, to find arrows for him when he goes a-shooting; and we cannot say that these are honorary or particularly honourable services: to find a truss of straw for the king's outer chamber when he stays at Cambridge, this is also a serjeanty. The carpenter, the mason, or the gardener who holds land in the neighborhood of some royal castle in return for his work holds a serjeanty. But again many serjeanties are connected with warfare. The commonest is that of finding a servant or serjeant (*servientem*) to do duty as a soldier in the king's army."[34] Serjeanties are held of nobles as well as of the king. "The abbot of Gloucester has tenants who spread his table, who hold towels and pour water on his hands. In the twelfth century the stewardship of the Abbey of St. Edmund's was hereditary in the family of Hastings, but was executed by deputy."[35]

An important difference between England and Fiji is that the Fijian serjeanty has nothing to do with the land. It is held by a certain family which appears originally to have been designated by the order of seniority. It does not matter what land they hold. Modern Ceylon represents an intermediate condition: only certain families are qualified for certain services, but a particular family only performs them for the particular village from whom it holds land. Thus only washermen wash, but washerman So-and-so washes for the village which has invited him and provided him with land. In England there are cases of serjeanties not attached to lands originally, and that was certainly the primitive usage; but the tendency was to make the service go with the land, and serjeanties came to be claimed not by descent, but in virtue of holding a certain manor. The serjeanty was hereditary in so far as the manor was, but it changed hands with the manor.[36]

The Middle Ages had gone far on the way to abolishing hereditary offices. "The prelates and barons seem to have followed the policy of their royal master and seldom permitted

---

34. Pollock and Maitland, I, 283 f.
35. *Ibid.*, I, 286.
36. Round, 44 ff.

substantial power to lapse into the lands of hereditary officers; the high steward of a monastery, like the high steward of the realm, was a man for pageants rather than for business. Still such serjeanties existed. The service of carrying the lord's letters was not uncommon and may have been very useful; the service of looking after the lord's wood was reckoned a serjeanty."[37] In the main however they were already then of a ceremonial character, and ceremony was no longer the serious business it is in Fiji. It is with us no longer the quest of life, but rather a psychological device to enhance the dignity, and hence the authority, of the lord. In time it ceases to do even that; it becomes an empty pomp which destroys authority instead of strengthening it. These ceremonial offices have been completely pushed out of the realities of the state by offices of a new type. The new ones are concerned entirely with that work of administration which has succeeded the old royal ritual as the instrument of prosperity.

The administrative body which thus prevailed was just as much of royal origin as the serjeanties it superseded. One set of king's servants ousted another. The victors were mainly the secretaries and the lawyers; the men who served with their brains squeezed out those who served with their hands.[38]

The old household offices, out of which our whole administration developed, reappear however at the coronation, while the new machinery which has supplanted it in ordinary life retires into the background. "Parliament it may be, now governs, or, it may be, the Ministry that Parliament has placed in power; but in the great act of the King's crowning Parliament has no part; Parliament and Ministry are still ignored, as they were ignored of old. On that day the King's Ministers are the ministers of his Norman ancestors; about him in the Abbey are the Steward and the Chamberlain, the Constable and the Marshal of England, though the Steward and the Constable are now revived for the day only to complete the picture of a dead past."[39]

37. *Ibid.*, I, 286.
38. Below, p. 294.
39. Round, 65.

Among those personages of a dead past the chamberlain may perhaps be identified with the Indian washerman. That may appear far-fetched until we read a petition presented as recently as 1901, while keeping in mind the fact that the Indian washerman's chief function is to provide clothes for ritual occasions, and that among his perquisites are the discarded clothes. The petition is to the effect that the petitioner may "have livery and lodging in the King's court at all times, and bring to His Majesty on the day of His Majesty's Royal Coronation His Majesty's shirt, stockings, and drawers: that your petitioner, together with the Lord Chamberlain of the Household for the time being may dress His Majesty in all his apparel on that day: and that your Petitioner may have all profits and fees thereunto belonging, viz. forty yards of crimson velvet for his robes against the day of His Majesty's Coronation, together with the bed wherein the king lays (*sic*) the night previous to the coronation, with all the vallances and curtains thereof, and all the cushions and clothes within the chamber, and also the night robe of the King wherein his Majesty rested the night previous to the Coronation, and likewise to serve His Majesty with water on the said day of His Royal Coronation and to have the basins and towels and the cup of assay for his fee."[40]

I annex a table of homologous offices in the English, Indian, and Fijian states. Some of these will require a chapter all to themselves, the king several chapters; but before we proceed let us sum up.

POSSIBLE HOMOLOGIES

ENGLAND	INDIA	FIJI
King' Serjeants[41] and other royal officers.	King's Jewels and other officers.	Faces of the Land.
Chaplain	Chaplain and Prime Minister	Herald (Great Face of the Land).
Constable	Army-leader	Vanguard
Marshal	Horsekeeper or Charioteer	. . . .

40. Round, 112.
41. For precedence of Serjeanties see Round, 122 f.

ENGLAND	INDIA	FIJI
Steward	. . . .	. . . .
Chamberlain	Washerman	. . . .
Usher	Doorkeeper	. . . .
Butler	. . . .	. . . .
Dispenser (cakes)		
Pantler (baker)		
Baker	Cook	House serfs
Waferer		
Sauser		
Turnspit, etc.		
Admiral	Fisherman in boats	Fisherman-Navigator
Tailor	Tailor	. . . .
Hunt Serjeanties	Hunters (Ceylon: Veddahs)[42]	. . . .
Barber-Surgeon	Barber	*Mbouta* or *Mbota*.

We start with an organization somewhat like this:

We end up with something like this:—

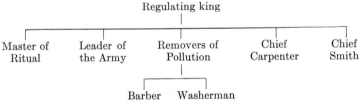

In a corner of Fiji we came across what looks like a transitional stage. The Chief of Ndreketi's body-guard behave like dogs, and it is in the character of dogs that they defend their lord.[43] Elsewhere in Fiji the animal character is wanting; the function is divorced from all impersonation; they are no longer described as animals, but as *mbati*, border.

The master craftsmen retain their character of chieftains in charge of things longer than the other functionaries, natu-

42. Hocart, *Yakshas and Väddas* in *Studia Indo-Iranica*, Leipzig, 1931.
43. Above p. 107.

rally since working with their hands is an important part of their duties, but by degrees they sink in the scale, and in Europe drop out of the court, as that court develops from a ritual organization into an administration. The removers of pollution follow the same course, and are now craftsmen. The other chieftains do not sink, but rise with the king. As the monarchy becomes a government, those who cannot adapt themselves to the change, fade into ceremonial attendants of the king; for ceremonial is merely ritual that has lost its reality. Such are the once mighty marshal and constable. The effective power passes into the hands of the clerks, in the old wide sense of the word.

It is a necessary part of this centralization that the brain workers supplant the manual workers at headquarters as the controlling body. The king's secretaries oust the king's serjeants.[44] In India the brahman, the holder of the Word, rises to dominance, while such castes as potters drop into the position of poor relations.[45] The Samoan master of the word has advanced beyond his Fijian compeer and got the country into his grasp. With every advance towards centralization the man who uses his hands is brought under subjection by the man who wields the word or the pen. The secretariat begins as the servant and ends as the master, as every executive officer in our dominions laments. It is inevitable. In a loose aggregate of small autonomous parts where every family must fend for itself, it is the man whose muscles are hard, whose hands are deft, and judgment sound that is valued most. There the man of brains counts only in so far as the brains improve the work of the hands and his good relations with his neighbours. But when the social activities have to be coordinated from a centre then it is necessary to pick out the pure brains, the men who specialize in thinking. For a thinker is really a man who spends his time making other people think as he does, and consequently act as he thinks.[46]

44. Above p. 123.
45. Above p. 116.
46. For the way in which the clerks have gradually bored their way from the centre through the whole feudal structure leaving only the shell, see de Tocqueville's *L'Ancien Régime*, especially Book II.

Vulgarization seems to be a necessary concomitant of this process of centralization. As everything is gathered up in one centre, as the court becomes a small group within the mass, that mass ousted from the royal circle proceeds to form its own courts copied from the central one. West Africa has carried this far, but Ceylon has perhaps carried it farther still. As feudalism decays, the serjeants to the minor personages are cut adrift from their lords. They cease to be manorial in order to become communal. That is the case in Ceylon: the country is still feudal in spirit, but the barbers and washermen of the countryside are not attached to a particular lord, but to the villages as a whole. In Egypt they have completely lost their feudal complexion. They are just specialists receiving a salary or a retaining fee from the village or those that employ them, or they may just sell their wares to anyone who will buy. Our own country has moved farthest away from the royal origins.

10· The Law

But with righteousness shall he judge the
poor, and reprove with equity for the meek
of the earth.
Isaiah, xi, 4

WE ARE SO used to being governed that we think it the most
natural thing in the world, something self-evident. Yet, from
Hobbes on, Moderns have always felt that some explanation
was needed, that man was not created governed, and that
he must at some time have acquired government. So philosophers sat down in a brown study to imagine how it came
to pass. They evolved history out of their own consciousness;
they wondered how they themselves could get on without
government, decided that they could not, that cessation of
government would mean anarchy, therefore, they concluded,
man invented government to get out of anarchy.

Had they had, like us, information from all over the globe,
they would have heard of numerous societies that have no
government, and yet are functioning quite well; rather better
in fact than we can boast of having done since 1914. Amongst
others the people of Tristan da Cunha were, until recently,
reported to have no government, but they did not live in a
state of strife. In fact it is said that two Da Cunhese who
were taken to the Cape begged to return to the peace of their
island home.

True it is that such societies cannot form big nations, maintain disciplined armies, lay networks of roads and railways,
or suffer economic crises on a colossal scale; but they can exist,
and quite successfully too, if success consists in surviving with
happiness. *We* cannot get on without a central government,
because our society is so vast and complex that some coordinating system is needed, for each one has to cooperate with
thousands whom he never sees, or even hears of. There are
societies where everyone is related to everyone else; they have
no need for a coordinating system. They work by mutual
understanding.

Such simple conditions still fill the greater part of our existence. We may be able to understand how ungoverned so-

cieties can work together, if we observe ourselves under those conditions. Take a shooting party of Englishmen: friends come together; one of them proposes a shoot, and the others agree. The time and arrangements are discussed; in the field stations are arranged; the guns work in harmony; the bag is brought home, and shared equitably, and all this by mutual consent without any one having been in command from start to finish. The men may be strangers to one another or mere acquaintances; but members of a hunting tribe are one family; they are born and bred together; they know one another by heart; they are loth to offend one another, because they cannot get away from one another. Even in agricultural communities the ordinary routine is carried on by mutual consent, not by command. In Fiji, for instance, the daily task of planting, fishing, house-building, is carried out by households, or clans, that is smaller or larger families inured to communal work from childhood. There is no intervention from above. The chief or king does not rule.

As a matter of fact we vastly exaggerate the importance of government in our own society. That is due in part to our histories. They still are concerned mostly with government. In our books we read all about the court intrigues and their petty consequences, and hear next to nothing of the vast silent, daily work of men and women, which is the real life of a nation. That daily routine is self-organized. The law of the queue, to take a small instance, is an unwritten law; it was not made by king and parliament, but is the outcome of a tacit understanding between total strangers very much imbued with respect for the traditional rights of possession. There is no law for street musicians, yet they are organized. A lawyer once pointed out to me that the law is quite inadequate to deal with the troubles that might arise in clubs; but such troubles never arise, and clubs carry on without the law, because the English are a clubbable people.

That spontaneous and incessant goodwill is not created by government, but on the contrary makes government possible. Without it government would collapse. The most government can do is to remove grit from the machinery.

Anyhow, whoever governs, it is not the king, but self-help.

Take the Aranda chief. "It is the totality of the old men that makes the important decisions, and exercises judicial powers. The headman, on the other hand, who is called *inkata*, is only a 'primus inter pares.'"[1] He does not keep the peace: no one does. Men will look on while women fight, and may, but need not, interfere. If two men are fighting the mothers and sisters of each try and shelter him.[2] Perhaps the greatest crime an Aranda can commit is to marry a woman of a prohibited degree; yet we are shown guilty couples often going about unpunished. Impotent society has to wait till an enemy party comes to demand blood for blood, then the wrong-doer will be betrayed to them as a scapegoat. Sometimes it will even invite another group to come and kill him. There is no haling before a judge: the only authority is public opinion. That opinion uses what means it can. Each man avenges for himself wrongs done to his property or wife. There is no anarchy on that account, because the community gives its moral support to the aggrieved. It favours justice by abandoning the wrong-doer to the avenger. In the gamble of private strife it loads the dice in favour of the just.[3]

Self-help is the backbone of order among the Omahas:—"Thieving was uncommon. Restitution was the only punishment. Assaults were not infrequent. When they occured they were settled privately between the parties and their relatives. In all offences the relatives stood as one. Each could be held responsible for the acts of another—a custom that sometimes worked injustice, but on the whole was conducive to social order. Running off with a man's wife or committing adultery was severely punished. In this class of offences the husband or his near relatives administered punishment. . . . A wife jealous of another woman who was attentive to her husband was apt to attack her with a knife. An assault of this kind . . . was seldom interferred with. If a man's wife died and left children, custom required that he marry his wife's sister. Should he fail to do so, the woman's relatives sometimes took

1. Strehlow, IV, 2, 1.
2. *Arunta*, 27.
3. Strehlow's description of the settling of crimes and torts should be read, IV, 2.

up the matter and threatened the man with punishment." If an injury was done to the person of another unintentionally "the act would be condoned by gifts made to the injured party or his relatives. Deliberate murder was punished by banishment. When the knowledge of such a deed was brought to the notice of the chief banishment was ordered, the offender was told of the decision and he obeyed."[4]

In Fiji I was long puzzled to find in the stories of bygone times that over and over again the High Chief did not intervene where my European preconceptions expected him to do so. Thieving went on, but the people did not complain to him. Instead they went to the priest, and got him to discover the thief, whom he did to death by catching his soul. A chief did not interfere in cases of adultery as a matter of duty, but only if induced by an offering, as one might propitiate a god. Against witchcraft the people devised their own protection. A murderous bully the people did not hale before the chief, but conspired to pray him to death, or met murder with murder. War might even go on between the chief's kinsmen and one of his vassal villages, and still his serenity continued undisturbed.

Self-help is the mainstay of West-African society as well. The Jukun king "as the head of the religious and social life, is the supreme court of appeal," yet the people can settle their troubles without him. "Normally," says Mr. Meek, "all cases of breach of law are settled in a lower court, viz. the court of public opinion which casts ridicule on one who fails to conform to the recognized standard of social contract, or which condemns him to a punishment by supernatural powers for a breach of some religious taboo . . . . The diviner, as the agent of supernatural powers, plays an important part in giving expression to the legal conceptions of the people."[5]

Hausaland supplies a good example how the people solve the problem of enforcing the law without having recourse to higher authority.

They have found means of punishing adultery purely by

4. *Omaha*, 213 ff.
5. Meek, 347.

self-help. "To fall out with the smiths," says Mr. P. G. Harris, "is indeed an unpleasant predicament and the smith craft is sufficiently strong to take the law into its own hands should anyone offend any of its members. What happens is somewhat as follows—an example taken from the writer's actual knowledge of the case. 'A' cast amorous eyes upon the wife of 'B', a blacksmith. 'E' caught the couple in 'flagrante delicto' one evening outside the town . . . . What happened to 'A' caused the best laugh that the neighborhood had had for years. On the market day a very small but very obscene image of 'A' in mud caricaturing all his worst physical characteristics was placed in the most prominent position in the market; behind it sat one of the smith-musicians beating his iron ring and singing a most execrable song all about 'A,' his parentage and his habits, real or fancied. 'A' managed to brazen it out for a week, but when the same thing happened on the next market day he packed up his belongings and fled the neighbourhood, never to return. Had he assaulted the musician, the next move would have been that his house would have been surrounded by the blacksmiths and the smiths' musicians of the town and neighbourhood, all dragging themselves along the ground like lepers and singing the same execrable song, until for very shame he left the neighbourhood or begged the chief of the blacksmiths (with suitable present and compensation to the injured one) to order a cessation of this shameful publicity."

Lawyers have ever had a horror of self-help. Specialists always believe in their own speciality as the universal remedy. As a matter of fact, self-help, in a healthy community, is often more equitable than the law, and it costs nothing. It is one of the chief defects of our highly individualistic society that such self-help as the Hausa blacksmiths use is no longer possible, because kin no longer stick together. It is only to be found in clubs, the army and the navy, where it works on the whole with far more equity than our royal courts, bound as they are by the letter of the law, and closed as they are to the million by expense.

Our medieval forefathers had to help themselves, for the king could do little too help them. The Anglo-Saxon king may have been, like the Jukun king, the supreme court of appeal, but his judicial functions "are very far removed from our modern way of regarding the king as the fountain of justice. His business is not to see justice done in his name in an ordinary course, but to exercise a special and reserved power which a man must not invoke unless he has failed to get his cause heard in the jurisdiction of his own hundred."[6] The people had to do the best they could for themselves before they had recourse to the sovereign; the hundred ran itself in England as the clan runs itself in Fiji. It was sufficient for all ordinary purposes; only matters extraordinary were dealt with by the king. "In so far as we can trust the written laws, the only topics of general importance were manslaying, wounding, and cattle-stealing." Even in such matters the king's jurisdiction seems to have depended very much on public opinion, for the court was not even "furnished with any obvious means of compelling obedience."[7] In its weakness the law was constantly compelled to fall back on outlawry. When it could not punish it resorted to much the same device as the Arandas: it left the wrongdoer unprotected; any one might slay him, he was a wolf.

The French king was still far from truly governing in the XIIIth century. Louis the Saint fought with his barons as one baron might with another. The doctrine that those who fight against the king are guilty of a crime expiable only by the axe or the halter is later.[8]

If the king does not govern it is small wonder that he is often dispensed with, and yet society runs on as usual.

Sometimes in Fiji no chief can be found who is *persona grata* with the spirits. They infer this from the fact as soon as a nobleman is consecrated he dies. The people of Lomaloma were convinced that this would be the fate of anyone who was installed before his hair had turned white. The Mbuans found that their chiefs died as soon as they received the salutation due to a chief. In such cases the throne remained vacant,

---

6. Pollock and Maitland, I, 40.
7. *Ibid.*, I, 37.
8. *Ibid.*, II, 505 ff.

and the state was administered by the chieftains. I have found no evidence that such tribes suffered anarchy. On the other hand, the chieftainship was often a case of recurrent disorder. One chief of Lakemba was known posthumously as "Died-in-Peace," because it was so rare for a chief to die a natural death. Yet chiefless tribes, undeterred by this spectacle, were eager to get a chief, as soon as they could find a nobleman whose high rank or age gave hopes that he would be acceptable to the spirits. They thought it meant prosperity, and it did. The tribes with great chiefs were undoubtedly more prosperous and wealthy. To a great extent they had great chiefs because they were wealthy, and they were wealthy because they were energetic, and so rose among their neighbours. Then they sought to ennoble themselves by alliances with the reigning families of states of higher rank. The prosperity that followed must have been in part the consequence of the energy that made them aspire. On the other hand, there is no doubt that present divinity evoked an enthusiasm which acted as a tonic, and braced men to greater efforts. These they made without strain because they enjoyed it. But the Fijians have no theoretic psychology, and so they look for the reason elsewhere. We do not accept their interpretation of the facts; but do we really understand much better than they do how monarchy works? Read our economists and sociologists, and see.

An interregnum invariably followed the death of a chief, for the new one might not be installed until the funeral ceremonies for his predecessor had been completed; these might not be for months. With us it does not matter whether a king has been crowned or not: he is king just the same, but in Fiji the consecration is a real thing, and if no one has been consecrated there is no king. When at last a chief is consecrated he is often not consecrated to full rank straight away. Thus the people of Yavulu in the island of Kandavu have a chief entitled Lord of the Windward.[9] If he dies they instal his successor under the title of Lord of Yavulu. If his chieftains see he is bad he remains Lord of Yavulu; but if he is good they consecrate him to the full dignity of Lord of the Wind-

9. *Tui Natheva.*

ward. By good and bad they do not mean virtuous or wicked, efficient in ruling or incompetent, but simply that the land prospers under him or not. A test is available immediately after his installation. At the conclusion of the ceremonies the people go snake hunting and fishing. If there is a good catch he is a good chief.[10]

The Jukuns suggest to us a reason why an interregnum must follow on the demise of a king. His death "is kept a close secret, and is not, in fact, revealed until many months afterwards, when the body is formally buried . . . The palace officials . . . assemble every morning as usual and are served with beer, and one of the officials, viz. the Ajifi, personates the king."[11]

In this case the burial is delayed, it would seem, because, as "the personification of the life of the crops, he cannot be buried during the dry season. Otherwise the crops would die for ever. He is usually buried at the beginning of the wet season when the bulrush-millet crop has attained a height of about one foot."[12]

Properly speaking then there is no interregnum in our sense of the term: there is a king all the time, the dead king. He reigns, but does not govern, but then he never did govern.

To understand how a dead man can reign we have to go back to our principles of ritual. We insisted again and again that the principal need not be a man, or even a living being: it may be a stone, an image, the corpse of a whale; it may even be, as with our philosophers, an Idea. The king is the principal of the national cult, and he continues to be so as long as he is above ground. While he reigns there can be no other king.

The same idea was dying out in Medieval England. The new king dated his reign from the funeral of his predecessor. The clue to this custom is given by private law. Possession (*seisin*) of an estate is not vacant until the dead owner's body is carried out for burial. The theory is borrowed from Roman

10. Hocart, *Mana; Mana Again; Natural and Supernatural,* etc. in Man, 1914, 46; 1922, 79; 1932, 78.
11. Meek, 168.
12. Meek, 169.

law that "a man can not lose possession until he has given it up both *animo* and *corpore*."[13] The dead king then does not surrender his kingdom till he is buried. Only the interval has been very much shortened, because the king no longer merely is, but does. The body is therefore only kept above ground a few days, but during that interval there is no king's peace. That does not matter much as long as the king's justice is exceptional, and the judicial routine is carried out by local and seignorial courts; but when it becomes the sole justice of the realm[14] even breaks of a few days are intolerable, so they ultimately disappear, and the kingship, as opposed to the king's person, becomes immortal: *Le Roy est mort, vive le Roy*. But it is the kingship that matters, not the king. As long as there is one, it is not essential he should be in the country or have reached an age when he can govern, and not be governed. He may be away for years, fighting against the Saracens; or he may be a boy nine years old: the kingdom carries on quite happily because there is a king's peace which need not be enforced by the king himself, but by his deputies.[15]

The Igbo theory of kingship requires an interregnum of not less than seven years after the death of the king. It may extend to twenty. If a people can carry on for seven years without a king there is no reason why they should not carry on indefinitely. But doubtless it is with most people as with the Fijians: they are quite content without a king until times are bad, and then they look for a cause and find it in the lack of a king. Also snobbery plays a part: to be without a king is to be in a position of inferiority in relation to neighbours.

In Tibet there is a necessary interregnum of at least nine months, to allow the late Dalai Lama to be reborn. A kingless period is therefore an integral part of the theory of kingship.

In Ancient India, as in Fiji, the throne might remain vacant many years for lack of a qualified candidate, that is, qualified not by a talent to govern, but by ritual fitness. One almost

13. Pollock and Maitland, II, 61.
14. Below, p. 140.
15. Pollock and Maitland, I, 522.

universal qualification is to have a queen. India limited the choice of a queen to one of royal lineage. If the heir had not a wife of the required rank he might remain uncrowned, contenting himself with the title of Governor.[16] It is best of all to have a king; but it is better to have none at all than one not ritually qualified, as witness the experience of Santanu. He usurped the throne that belonged by right to his elder brother Devapi. In consequence it did not rain for twelve years. Santanu then wished to consecrate his brother; but Devapi refused, and asked to become his younger brother's chaplain, to sacrifice for him. Apparently by his sacrifices he put things right, though the text does not say so.[17]

The Odyssey gives us a picture of a kingdom without a king. The people miss him because he was kind and just. His household suffers because the pretenders are eating up his patrimony; but otherwise society seems to function as usual.

It is abundantly clear that the king's *raison d'être* is not to coordinate, but to be head of the ritual. Lest however I should be accused of reading into the people's mind what is not there I shall quote the opinions of the Fijians themselves. "Of old," said a Lakemban elder, "the Lord of Nayau did not go to the wars, but the young men went. He was old and white-haired and stayed at home, and would say, 'Do this and that; get a kava bowl from Kambara.'[18] He did not go about at night. In the daytime he went a little with his chieftains to plant; he then came back and kava was made with the nobles from Tonga. This was done every day, and a feast was brought daily from Lakemba." Why did they want a chief if he spent most of his time drinking kava? Again ask a Fijian. One tribe was without a chief; it was run by the

16. *Mhvs.* VII, 46 ff.; VIII, 17. Cf. *Kingship*, 101 ff.
17. *Nirukta*, II, 10.
18. This is a good illustration how the mere knowledge of the grammar is inadequate. To understand the bearing of this statement we want a knowledge of the customs. The Lord of Nayau would requisition bowls, canoes, etc., for ceremonial presentation to noble visitors from Tonga, Mbau, and other great countries with whom he had ties of kinship, or who were suzerain; in other words to states with whom he was on terms of interchange of offerings.

chieftains, the heads of clans. The people decided to have a chief. To govern them? No, the reason they gave was "that he might face the feasts." That is, they wanted some one to receive their offerings, or, as I have expressed it, to be the principal. Offerings involve two parties that "face each other"; in the state ritual the chief is one party and faces the feast. The Fijians had invisible gods, sometimes present in the priest or in an animal; they preferred a god always present, one they could see and speak to, and the chief was such a god. That is the true reason for a Fijian chief's existence: he receives the offerings of his people, and in consequence they prosper.

The Jukun king "is not, and apparently never was, expected to be a leader of victorious armies, but he is expected to secure in his time a regular succession of rich harvests, and by his ability to do so is adjudged to be a true son of god."[19]

To be principal in the ritual is not to be purely passive. He must, as we have repeated again and again, be identified with that which he controls, and being so identified he has to behave as he wishes it to behave. If he is a lion he must behave like a lion triumphant. If he is the thunder he has to split the clouds and shed rain. If he is the sun he has to mark the orderly procession of the seasons. If he is the world he has to hold an even and normal course. He must see that the other participants in the ritual play their proper part in the cosmic drama, since they also are priests, that is minor gods.

The most important function of an Aranda headman is "to take charge of what we may call the sacred store-house . . . in which, concealed from view, are kept the sacred objects of the group."[20] In the performance of the ritual it is he who "takes the leading part; he it is who decides when it is to be performed, and during the celebration the proceedings are carried out under his direction, though he has while conducting them to follow out strictly the customs of his ancestors."[21]

19. Meek, 347.
20. *Arunta*, 9 f.
21. *Ibid.*, 11.

When several camps are met together for the performance of great ceremonies, one headman controls the whole assembly of some hundred natives or more. He consults the other headmen about the ceremonies.

The principal is by the very nature of things an authority on custom, since he has to know custom if he is to see that it is observed.

Fijian chiefs were great sticklers for etiquette. They were quick to resent offences against their dignity and unseemly behaviour in their precincts, such as walking with swinging arms through the village green. There was one who would throw stones at any lantern carried alight through the village, though the enforcement of customs was generally left to the young men of the "Border."[22] These may seem petty matters; but they are fraught with great possibilities. The Fijian chief has only to extend his precincts and interpret widely the traditional rules of ceremonial behaviour in order to acquire a criminal jurisdiction, and increase his interference with the life of his subjects. He has not done so; others have transformed the regulation of ritual into government.

The Polynesian chiefs have gone a step further in that direction than their Fijian neighbours. They are taboo, that is sacred, and this sanctity is communicable, just as life is, and all other qualities. By sanctifying anything they brought it within the sphere of ritual, that is their own sphere. This was certainly not done suddenly, but by persistently extending the applications of taboo, as we shall see our English kings extend their peace.[23] In Hawaii they extended taboo so far that it became a burden and had to be abolished.

Man deals with new situations by extending old customs. When families or clans cease to be able to solve their own problems and have to call in a social physician, they turn to the king or some other principal in the ritual. He extends his ritual prerogative to cover the case if he can.

22. Above p. 106 and below p. 181 f.
23. Cp. *Progress of Man* chap. XV and p. 269 f. The really fruitful homology
    Polynesian king's taboo = English king's peace
has generally been missed.

The Winnebagoes supply us with an instructive example. The chief "must be a man of well-balanced temper, not easily provoked, and of good habits. The one sacred object he possesses is his pipe. If he saw a man, woman, or child passing by, he was to call them in and give them food to eat, for they were his brothers and sisters." He "is a peacemaker, and if two members of the tribe ever quarrel he is supposed to intercede. If in a quarrel a person should be killed, the chief would go to the murderer and tell the latter to permit himself to be tied up. If the murderer consents to do so, then his arms are tied behind him and the chief walks in front of him carrying his sacred pipe." When they got to the hut of the murdered man's relatives "the chief would extend the stem of his pipe toward them. They might refuse to accept . . . , but if any member were to take a puff from it, then the murderer would be forgiven and turned free."[24] In short the chief can only settle a murder case by using his position as keeper of a sacred pipe and of an open table, by inducing the injured party to smoke that pipe and so put itself in communion with the culprit.

The Omaha chiefs had to use their supernatural power to keep order. "A disturber of the peace within the tribe or one whose acts were offensive to the chiefs was sometimes punished by the concerted action of" the society to which they belonged, "the members fixing their minds on the offender, placing on him the consequences of his actions so that he was thrust from all helpful relations with men and animals. Misfortune and death were believed to follow as a result of this treatment."[25] The real king of the Omahas seems to have been the sacred pole; the people said "it held the tribe together; without it the people might scatter."[26] But a pole has no ambition; it is not always trying to enlarge its sphere. That explains why in the evolution of the state king log has given way before king stork.

This gradual extension of the king's sanctity can be followed

24. Radin, 209.
25. *Omaha*, 497.
26. *Ibid.*, 229.

in our English records over many centuries. We have seen that in Anglo-Saxon times his opportunities for intervening were very limited indeed.[27] Gradually the king's jurisdiction spread, till it penetrated everywhere, as it does now; but it was not extended in response to a demand on the part of the people that the king should put an end to an anarchic state of nature; it was extended by extending the king's sanctity. He, or his justices, used the sanctity of his residence in order to bring the whole country under his justice. In Cnut's time the king's peace "only covered deeds of violence done to persons, or at places, or in short seasons that were specially protected by royal power."[28] Other persons as well as the king have their peace; "if it is broken compensation must be paid to them. The church has its peace, or rather the churches have their peaces, for it is not all one to break the peace of a 'head-minster' or to break that of the parish church. The sheriff has his peace . . . nay every householder has his peace; you break his peace if you fight in his house . . . . The time has not yet come when the king's peace will be eternal and will cover the whole land." The opportunities for extending the king's peace were numerous. For instance "in Normandy the sanctity of the house extended over a distance of four perches from its walls. Then in Normandy the plough was sacred; an attack upon a man while at the plough was an offence against the duke. . . . Offences against the duke's money, and offences against his writs of protection, were pleas of the sword." When from Henry II's day we hear that homicide, mayhem,[29] robbery, arson and rape belong to him, we may infer that the duke of the Normans, like the king of the English, has been making good some new and far-reaching claims.[30] There were also included offences against people traveling to and from court, and on the king's highway.

Eventually the king became supreme judge in all matters throughout the land.

27. Above p. 132.
28. Pollock and Maitland, II, 449.
29. Maiming.
30. Pollock and Maitland, II, 453; 455.

The germ which thus expands into law is the king's imitation of the universe, and more particularly of the sun, which is the life of the universe. This is nowhere more explicit than in India. There that regularity, that normality of the universe which produces good crops, fat cattle, peace and contentment, is expressed by the word *dharma* which means etymologically "support," "upholding." It describes the way in which animals, men, or things are expected to behave; it is natural law, civil law, custom, order, right, justice, religion. Everything is subject to *dharma*.[31] The sun is sometimes identified with *dharma* because it regulates the seasons, sometimes it is considered to be regulated by it. Among the gods Varuna is the one who lays down ordinances for the universe, and so is entitled "Lord of Right."[32] The king on his accession becomes to his people as Varuna is to the gods; he is Varuna; so he becomes "Lord of Right" also. "For," says the text, "whoever is Lord of Law, he is the supreme dignity; for he who attains the supreme dignity, to him they come in law."[33] "The king," it is said elsewhere, "is upholder of ordinances: for he is not versed in any kind of speech, nor in any kind of deed, but only in that which he may rightly speak, rightly do."[34] He is not an administrator, but a judge; for he has not only to observe the law, but see to it that his people do. The story of the King of the Kurus shows how vital the good conduct of king and court was to the welfare of the people.

The god did not rain in the kingdom of Kalinga, and a famine arose, and fear of pestilence through lack of food. The people from all the kingdom gathered together, and came to the capital, and made an outcry at the king's gate. The king standing by the window heard the noise and inquired the cause. They told him why and entreated him, "Make the god to rain, O Great King!" The king asked, "What did the ancient kings do when the god did not rain?" "They gave alms," was the reply, "they kept the sabbath, made vows of virtue, and retiring to the royal chamber lay seven days on a grass mat.

31. Cp. Chinese *tao*.
32. *Dharmapati.*
33. *Sat. Br.*, V, 3, 3, 9.
34. *Sat. Br.* V, 4, 4, 5.

Then the god rained." The king did so, but still there was
no rain. Then they said, "Dhananjaya, King of the Kurus,
observes the Law of the Kurus; therefore in his kingdom the
god rains every fortnight or ten days. That is the power of
the king's merit." So the King of Kalinga bade them bring
home written on a plate of gold the law of Kurus which
Dhananjaya observed. Now the law of the Kurus consisted
of five commandments: "Thou shalt not kill; thou shalt not
steal; thou shalt not commit adultery; thou shalt not lie; thou
shalt not drink intoxicants."[35] These not only the king observed
faithfully, but his mother, his chief queen, his younger brother,
the viceroy, the chaplain, the brahman, the land-surveyor, the
councillor, the chief merchant, the collector of taxes,[36] the
prime minister, the porter, the courtesan. One and all however
disclaimed faithful observance of the law. Each one alleged
some petty and unintentional breach which weighed on his
mind. Thus the king thought he *might* accidentally have shot
a fish with an arrow. The tax collector was afraid he *might*
have cheated a taxpayer of one grain of corn by oversight. The
deputation noted all these scruples on a golden plate, and,
returning to their king, told him all. "The king abiding in
the Kuru law fulfilled the five commandments. Then the god
rained in the whole kingdom of Kalinga."[37]

The story has been edited by Buddhists, and so it has taken
on that purely moral tone which is characteristic of that religion. It has purged old legends and ceremonies of their ancient material associates. Thus *dharma* becomes simply virtue,
goodness, religion, or more narrowly still, the Buddhist religion. Yet, as we have seen, it continues to express its ideals
in the old solar phraseology. Buddha is still the Sun of
Righteousness.[38]

Hinduism marks a ritualistic reaction against Buddhism, yet
it does not go back to the old naturalism of the Vedas. It

35. These are taken from the *Abhidhanappadipika*, No. 783. Cp. *Digha*,
II, 172 ff. (*Kingship*, 23).
36. *Donamapako*, lit. one who supervised the measuring of rice for the
revenue.
37. *Jataka*, II, 366 ff.
38. *Dharmasurya*.

remains moral, ultra-moral. The king has therefore to be a model of self-control and at the same time a punctilious observer of ritual prescriptions. The ideal king "has his senses under control"; he is "conqueror of his senses";[39] he is "pious, versed in the scriptures, eloquent, doer of meritorious deeds, drinker of *soma*, maintainer of a sacred fire, free-handed giver, warrior, just ruler." In the forefront of meritorious deeds are "the rites of the royal consecration and the horse-sacrifice accompanied by gifts to the priests."[40]

That is as far as the Indian conception of kingship has evolved. That conception does not lie so very far behind us in Europe. In this twentieth century our European kings are required to belong to the state church, and to attend its ceremonies.

Modern Egyptian kingship has reached much the same point as the Indian. Regular prayers and citations from the Koran are still weighty titles to popular favour for politicians as well as for kings. The verb *hakam*, "to judge," also means "to rule."

Homeric Greece takes us right back to a much earlier stage which has as yet diverged but little from the Vedic. Homer's *dike* expresses much the same as the Vedic *dharma:* it is *dike*, that is the natural law, of mortals when they die to be reduced to shadows, of old men to doze after a bath and a meal, and of kings to do and say nothing lawless among the people. By upholding *dike* or *themis* the king bestows prosperity on his people.[41] As elsewhere the conception of right became increasingly moralized, but at the same time the kings decayed and became extinct so that *dike* became entirely divorced from monarchy.[42]

The Omaha take us back once more to the older point of view. "Wakonda," says Miss Fletcher, "stands for the mysterious life power permeating all forms and forces and all phases of man's conscious life . . . Old men have said, 'Wakonda causes day to follow night without variation and summer to

39. Kautilya, I, 6 f.—*Nala*, I, 4.
40. *Nala*, XII, 37; cp. 32.
41. *Odyssey*, XI, 218; XXIV, 255; IV, 690; XIX, 109 ff.
42. For the Hebrew conception, see *Labyrinth*, 76 ff.

follow winter. We can depend on these regular changes and can order our lives by them. In this way Wakonda teaches us that our words and our acts must be truthful, so that we may live in peace and happiness with one another. Our fathers thought about these things and observed the acts of Wakonda and their words have come down to us.' Truth in word and action was fundamental to the scheme of ethics taught by the Omaha. As applied to action, it involved the idea of honesty and of faithfulness to a duty laid upon a person, whatever its nature, whether of a scout, a runner in search of a herd of buffaloes, or the performance of a rite by its proper custodian."[43]

To return to the old world, Jukun prosperity depends to some extent on the king's good behaviour. He is required to conform to a certain pattern of conduct; but failures in the supply of food may be due to the delinquencies of his subjects as well as his own. If he dies (even if he has been secretly murdered as the result of famine) "it is commonly said that he has forsaken the world and gone back to the heavens in consequence of the wickedness of men."[44] He represents, among other gods, the sun, and the sun is specially connected with right conduct. In the course of one sun cult the priest prays, "Let no man nurse evil in his heart, and let no woman be double-minded towards her husband. For such conduct is displeasing to the Sun, and the Sun will take the lives of those that behave in this way."[45]

The Igbo king too "is most intimately connected with agriculture: he ensures the fertility of the crops: he ritually clears a piece of land when the farming season begins, he also declares the number of months in the year by confirming what has been decided upon in each town as the number of months for that year." "One of his duties on taking up his post is to re-establish ritually the four market days."

Where law in society is but an imitation of law in the world, it is a natural consequence that the king is responsible for

43. *Omaha*, 597.
44. Meek, 131.
45. Meek, 187.

145

the calendar; for the calendar does not merely record the seasons of the year: it actually regulates them, as we shall find people still believing in England.[46] The calendar is thus part of the Right which it is the king's duty to uphold. It was so in Rome. Numa, the second king, at the bidding of the nymph Egeria, "instituted the rites that were most acceptable to the gods, appointed to every god his priest. . . . And first of all he divided the year into twelve months according to the revolutions of the moon," and added intercalary months to square the solar year with the lunar.[47]

It was as supreme pontiff that Caesar reformed the calendar. We shall find reason to believe the pontiff was once a king. A fixed Easter is still awaiting the assent of the Holy Father.

The sun determines the seasons. The king as sun determines them.

If any one wishes to find the earliest evidence of this connection of the sun with right, and of the king with the sun, he had best seek in the Near East. In Egypt the sun-god Re is entitled "Lord of Judgment." At the other end of time our Hymn Ancient and Modern No. 60 still hails "the Sun of Righteousness."[48]

In England the king's control over the elements is not as marked as in the East, yet it has survived to a greater extent than is commonly realized. We speak of "King's weather." A lady tells me she heard people talking as if the beautiful weather that marked every royal procession of the 1935 jubilee was a sign that God approved of King George V. "So it is," said a young lady who heard me repeat this.

Since almost all the power has passed to the ministers and other officials, so has all the praise or blame. The third paragraph of the Proclamation of November 21, 1818, addressed to the Kandyans of Ceylon ran: "Under this mild administration on the part of the British Government the Country appeared to rest in Peace; Cultivation was increased and divine Providence blessed the exertions of the labourers and re-

46. Below p. 147.
47. Livy, 1, 19, 6.
48. The Arabic name *Shams-ed-Din* means exactly the same, and so translates also literally the Sanskrit *Dharmasurya*.

warded them with plenteous crops." Later Disraeli out of office could write, half-seriously, to his queen: "I always feel that I did not bring your Majesty good fortune, and there must be something unlucky in a Minister who had to encounter six bad harvests. Certainly I might say, with a greater man, 'I was defeated by the elements.'"

No longer ago than March 7th, 1934, the following words were heard in the House of Lords:—"There are very many of the older people who are firmly convinced—and who knows whether they are right?—that the drought of last year and the floods of previous years are entirely due to the imposition of summer time. If that was the result of summer time I shudder to think what the result of this change of the clock would be." (Referring to the proposed 24 hour system.) To interfere with the calendar is still to upset the order of the seasons.

This belief is not to be brushed aside as a silly superstition confined to silly folks. It still has considerable influence on politics and through them on the whole nation. In 1927 the then Prime Minister complained "there were plenty of political cheap-jacks prepared to guarantee a change in the climate to suit every farmer, a change in the world markets to suit every seller."[49] Meteorological promises are scarcely worth making nowadays: we are no longer an agricultural population, and only worry about the weather insofar as it affects cricket or tennis. Besides we know too much about winds and rain to expect a government to control them. Unfortunately we know too little about human nature to recognize the limitations of a government in the matter of commerce and industry. Poor crops therefore no longer decide the fate of kings in Europe, but bad trade may overturn a government. It is the good old idea of supernatural efficacy confined by the progress of industry and of physics to trade. It is the righteousness of kings put into commission and industrialized.

It is not only this old Europe which carries on traditions as old as our long barrows or older. Look at America, a country

49. "Chacun s'en prend déjà au gouvernement de toutes les misères. Les plus inévitables sont de son fait; on lui reproche jusqu'à l'intempérie des saisons." De Tocqueville should have said "still," not "already" (*L'Ancien Régime*, Book II, chap. 6, end).

which has cut itself adrift from tradition, or thinks it has, which is always giving the lead in modernity to the obsolete nations of Europe. During the crisis it became clearer than ever "how this promise of uninterrupted prosperity and intolerance of certain sects were the forces which gave Mr. Hoover his great majority. . . . And we can see, now that the depression has come, that if Mr. Smith had been elected the Democratic Party would have been well-nigh ruined. The American people would have been told, and would have believed, that a Democratic Administration spelt business failure."[50] The defeat of that party in 1928 proved for it a blessing in disguise: the Republican party now bears the blame for a crisis which most thinking people know would have come anyhow, because it is not the doing of any government, but of the nations themselves. "The longer," says one of the thinking people, "the longer the various governments endeavour to fight such forces of nature, the worse the present confusion must become. No doubt the economists are aware of this, but the peoples do not understand that they are expecting their rulers to perform miracles."[51] They do not call them miracles because they believe they are possible. They only call it a miracle when they do not believe in it, as when an African king makes rain.

When all is said and done, however, the English kingship was from the first very much sublimated. The connection with nature was cast into the shade by a coordinating function which owed its rapid development to the traditions left behind by the Roman Empire; function outshone imitation. Already in the Middle Ages the king was less the representative of any prototype in nature than the upholder of the peace, an arbitrator when that peace was threatened, and a wielder of the sword against those who broke it. They were the king's enemies, whether within or without, whether malefactors or foreign foes. He was more of a judge than of a warrior, though it may not seem so in our histories. William of Normandy has gone down to posterity as the Conqueror, yet "it is as

50. *The Times*, 6th Nov., 1930.
51. *The Times*, 10th Oct., 1933.

supreme judge hearing and deciding the causes of the weak against the mighty, the stern punisher of all violence that his courtly chroniclers love to paint him."[52] The best kings took their judicial duties seriously. Henry the Second "was at heart a lawyer, quite competent to criticize minutely the wording of a charter, to frame a new clause and give his vice-chancellor a lesson in conveyancing; quite willing on the other hand to confess that there were problems that he could not solve." He took an active part in administering justice. "Even when he had appointed judges to hear a cause they would advise the successful litigant to wait until a judgment could be given by the king's own mouth." "All who had a good cause wished it might come before the king himself."

Louis the Saint's chief titles to fame are his inflexible justice, his zeal for the sacraments, and two crusades against the enemies of Christ. "Many a time," says Joinville, "it happened that in summer he went to seat himself in the wood of Vincennes after his mass, and he leant against an oak and made us sit round him. And any who had business came to speak to him without let of usher or other people. And then he asked them of his own mouth: 'Is there here some one who has a case?' And those got up who had a case. And then he said: 'Be silent all, and you will be dealt with one after another.' And then he called my lord Perron de Fonteinnes and my lord Geoffrey of Villette, and said to one of them, 'Dispatch me this case.' And when he saw anything to amend in the words of those who spoke for him, or in the words of those who spoke for others, he himself amended it with his own mouth."[53]

The Middle Ages were as convinced as the Indians that upon the justice of the king his stability depends. A greyfriar preaching before Louis the Saint at Hyères declared that in all his reading "he did not find, either among believers or among unbelievers, that any kingdom was lost or changed its lordship but by lack of justice. 'Therefore let the king who is on his way to France,' he concluded, 'take good care

52. Pollock and Maitland, I, 73.
53. Joinville, XII, 59.

that he do good justice and prompt to his people, whereby
Our Lord may suffer him to hold his kingdom in peace all
the course of his life.' "[54]

If he did not do justice, rebellion became lawful. The rebels
would be doing the work of God. That is a point of view
which it is hard for the twentieth century Englishman to understand. The theories of divine right propounded in the seventeenth century may be extinct, but they have done their
work; they have left behind an abhorrence for all rebellion.

Our twentieth century government commands. It is not left
to the discretion of the subject what his relations to the state
shall be; he cannot make terms. The state has an absolute
and indefeasible right to order his life. We are so used to
this unconditional obedience we are apt to assume it is natural,
the only form of social organization that has ever been. But
the power of early medieval kings was almost as conditional
as that of a Fijian king; only it did not depend as there on
kinship, but on ancient tenure, on terms made between the
king and his vassals. "In the really feudal centuries men could
do by a contract, by the formal contract of vassalage or com-
mendation, many things that can not be done now-a-days.
They could contract to stand by each other in warfare 'against
all men who can live and die'; they could (as Domesday Book
says) 'go with their land' to any lord whom they pleased;
they could make the relation between king and subject look
like the outcome of an agreement; the law of contract threatened to swallow up all public law. Those were the golden
days of 'free,' if 'formal contract.'" To give a concrete instance: after the siege of Exeter in 1136 Stephen spared the
garrison because they had never sworn fealty to him. Even
when a vassal had sworn allegiance that allegiance was qualified by a condition: "If a lord persistently refuses justice to
his man, the tie of fealty is broken, the man may openly defy
his lord, and, having done so, may make war upon him." Since
then the qualifying condition has been done away with, at
least in theory; for in practice political agitators are treated
with great leniency; but "a right, or duty, of rising against

54. Joinville, XI, 55.

the king and compelling him to do justice can no longer be pleaded in the name of the law."[55]

The common notion is that the doctrine of Divine Right, as held by the extremists of the seventeenth century, was the last kick of medievalism. That is the opposite of the truth: it was the first effort of the modern spirit. In the Middle Ages allegiance was conditional as it was in Fiji, ancient Ceylon, Jukunland, and other homes of divine kingship. A king is not necessarily absolute, nor his authority unconditional, because he is divine. Unconditional allegiance grew on the ruins of the medieval nobility. The struggle round this new growth was to decide not whether it should be fostered or destroyed, but who should gain possession of it, the king and his court party, or the parliament. In England Parliament won, and it now claims obedience as unconditional as ever was claimed by the most fanatical devotees of Divine Right. To the monarchy was left the consolation prize of unconditional succession: no matter if the heir be an infant, an invalid, a madman, or a buffoon, he succeeds, a great departure from the original theory of divine kingship.

It is only the formula that shocks us in the claims put forward on behalf of the Stuart kings; we have accepted the substance; and that is where parliament proved cleverer than the court: it wrapped up absolutism in more acceptable words.

That is the story of all struggles between parties. They ride different formulae into power, but the results are the same, because the factions are the sport of the fates which they profess to control.

We look at the formulae put forward by parties and miss the facts. The French Revolution was a great factory of formulae that have little relation to facts, about liberty and the rest. To it we owe largely the common delusion that most of the world outside Europe is enslaved by tyrants exempt from all law and morality. They can, it is alleged, do just as they please, even to marrying their own sisters, and eating their own subjects.

Nothing can be farther from the truth. To be a god does

55. Pollock and Maitland, II, 505, note 5; 506.

not necessarily mean to have more licence, but rather to have more duties: *divinité oblige*. The whole object of a god-man is that he should regulate the world by his own regularity. He has to keep all the observances prescribed by tradition. The more complicated the state becomes, the more complicated his daily routine. In a country like India every hour of the twenty-four is assigned, at least in theory, to a particular task.[56] The slave of etiquette and ceremonial cannot be the master of his dignitaries, so his power passes to them. The Jukun chieftain, who is a reproduction on a small scale of the king, lives "a life of constant anxiety and hedged in by innumerable taboos," he is "the slave of his position." So much so that it is difficult to find candidates.[57]

We derive false ideas from books of travels and missionary reports which dwell on the sensational, and omit the dull routine. We read of kings as prompt to cut off the heads of their subjects as was the Queen of Hearts, and we conclude that if they can do that they can do any thing. That does not follow at all: it may be lawful for a king to put to death, yet not lawful to omit one tittle of the ritual. A Fijian chief had a good deal of latitude in the matter of life and death, and occasionally ate his own subjects just to "learn them." On the other hand, it was fatal for him "to eat badly," that is to keep everything for himself and not share; or "to enter houses," that is pursue other men's wives. Cannibalism was the prerogative of the king and his old men; it was part of the ritual; but meanness was a sin, for it was the essence of chieftainship, as we shall see, to be liberal. Even the right of life and death had its limitations. A late Lord of the Reef, for instance, when put out of humour by one of his chieftains, would beat his serf unmercifully, "For," he explained to him, "I may not beat a chieftain of the land, but I can do what I like with you, even kill and eat you." The superficial observer notes the wilfulness of the act; he does not find out that this wilfulness is authorized by custom.

56. Kautilya, I, 19.—Quaritch Wales, 42 ff.
57. Meek, 324.

If we hear of a king of Ceylon or of Siam putting a man to death, because, in trying to save the royal person from drowning, he laid hands on the sacred body, we think that king an ungrateful monster; but he has no choice; it is custom that puts the culprit to death, not the king. We are told that the barge of a Siamese king once grounded. This meant death for the steersman; but the king was in a compassionate mood, and had an image executed instead. The steersman however was so worried about his fault that he importuned the king to enforce the penalty, and the king had to yield.

The Jukun king is a god. We think of a god as omnipotent; but like the divine chiefs of Fiji he "was judged by results. If the harvests were good the people were prepared to put up with a moderate amount of tyranny. But excessive tyranny would evoke a demand for his death whether the harvests were good or bad. He was so surrounded by taboos that it was never difficult to discover some breach of taboo which could be interpreted as a repudiation on his part of the gods whom he was supposed to represent, and a consequent repudiation of him by the gods. On this account the king is compelled to give due consideration to the advice of his coun- selors. . . . The very sacredness of the king's personality operated as a factor in the curtailment of his power. No man could approach him directly. Anyone who had a complaint or who was in a position to give first hand information could only approach the king through a chain of officials."[58]

Non-Europeans are just as convinced as we are that a king exists to uphold the Right. A Sinhalese king of the third cen- tury B.C. is thus admonished at his consecration: "Taking thy stand upon the laws rule with even law . . . If thou carriest out thy rule in accordance with our words, well. If not may thy head be split into seven parts."[59] The Igbo king was bidden at his consecration "to rule his town and people well and properly as was done by preceding kings; to rule with truth and justice." Admonitions to rule well appear in coronation

58. Meek, 333 f.
59. *Mhvs. Tika* on *Mhvs.* XI, 27–33 (p. 213 of Sumangala's ed., Co- lombo, 1895).

rites the world over.[60] The constitution is no new thing: it is the very essence of kingship.

In fine, the king begins, like every other personage in the ritual, and so in the state, by being in charge of certain departments of nature. We have reason to believe his first role was to be the sky. But the heavenly bodies process round the earth with a regularity that marks the times of the year. The king, as sky, must likewise beat time to his little universe represented by his acolytes in the ritual. We know that at one time he was first and foremost the sun which came to be recognized as the supreme regulator of the world. Thus this solar nature of the king emphasized still further his regulative function. This function comes more and more into the lime-light, while the object out of which it arose falls into the background, till at last the function alone becomes the mark of the king. He is no longer the sky, sun, or bull, except in metaphor and emblem; he is only the authority on Right.

This function proves so useful that it is extended. Limited at first to the ritual and the seat of ritual it gradually spreads to the whole of the king's realm and the whole life of his subjects.

It should give us confidence in our conclusions that this evolution from representation to function is definitely proved in language.

Linguists distinguish *semantemes,* words that stand for things, such as *sun, moon,* etc., and *morphemes* which indicate relations, for instance, *in,* the *s* of our plural, etc. The semantemes are the bricks, as it were, the morphemes the mortar. Now semantemes are constantly becoming morphemes, the names of things become the signs of relations or modes. Thus a word which once meant a *body* has dwindled into our adverbial suffix *-ly.* The same duty is performed in French by the suffix *-ment* which once stood for a thing, the mind.

The same has happened in writing. The reader will find plenty of instances in any history of hieroglyphics.

Our comparative analysis of institutions seems then to have converged with the work of linguists on to an important pro-

60. *Kingship,* chap. VII.

cess in the evolution of thought and its expression. Man, it would seem, begins by putting together representations (a mode of thought we revert to in dreams). Gradually he disentangles relations and modes, and gives them separate expression. In order to express them he has to use existing material, which consists of representations. These are purged of all substance, so that they may serve only to bind the representations into a well-ordered whole.

11· War

Heaven thunders forth its victor cry.
Hymns A. & M.

THE KING is not only the sun; he is commonly associated with the thunderbolt and the eagle. He is frequently the thunder-god. But the character of the thunder-god is very different from that of the sun-god. He is sudden, irregular, violent, cataclysmic; he smites and consumes. It follows that the king, when thunder-god, must be violent and aggressive.

The Fijian and Jukun facts do not help us much in this direction, but they must nevertheless be recorded.

In Fiji the High Chief did not go to the wars. He was generally an old man, because young men were thought to cause trouble. The younger members of his family, which might number fifty or more souls, took an active part in wars, and often originated them by their arrogance and quickness to take offence.

In wartime the Jukun king "remained at home. If his own city was attacked he only appeared if the fight was going against his own people."

In Eddystone Island it is exactly the opposite. The chiefs are mainly concerned with raids and not with agriculture. Their spirits after death became spirits of war, not gods of crops.

Indian evidence is full. The king is thunder-god and warrior. He is a warrior because he is a thunder-god. He is the thunder-god before all things.

"Defence of the people, bounty, sacrifice, also study, emancipation from the senses" the Creator assigned to the royal caste. Protection of the "four castes" involves war with his neighbours: "The king challenged by others, equal, greater, or less, protecting the people, should not desist from war, but remember the royal duty. Never to cease from battle, to protect the people, to hearken to the priests, is the highest happiness of kings." A fitting end for a king is "to seek his

156

death in battle after handing over the kingdom to his son."[1]
In Hindu India war has become the sport of kings.

This warlike character can be traced back to Vedic times,
where it is clearly connected with the king's impersonation
of Indra, as his law-giving powers belong to his impersonation
of Varuna. For Indra "is primarily a god of the thunderstorm
who vanquishes the demons of drought and darkness, and sets
free the waters or wins the light. He is secondarily the god
of battle who aids the victorious Aryan in overcoming his
aboriginal foes."[2] Since the king is equivalent to Indra, he
is, like him, a fighter of demons in the first place, and a slayer
of earthly foes in the second. Thus we are told that even as
Indra and the Fire-god[3] by a certain offering smote the fiends
and gained that universal conquest which now is theirs, so
the king by the same offering smites the fiends and gains the
victory.[4] In other words, by the ritual the king as Indra routs
the powers that menace life and prosperity. But how do we
pass from this to the routing of human enemies? Ritual exclusiveness is carried far in India: not all the community is admitted to it. Those who are admitted to it are identified with
the gods. Serfs and foreigners are identified with the giants[5]
who seek to destroy the efficacy of the ritual or quest of welfare. The king defeats these foes of prosperity either in their
sacrificial bodies, such as a piece of lead,[6] or in the bodies
of the heathens, by rites or by war. So much are the non-
initiated identified with the rivals of the gods that it is difficult
to say whether a hymn celebrates a ritual victory of Indra,
or an actual battle led by Indra in the flesh. Hymns can be
understood either way, because the words for heathens also
mean demons, and the fortresses are not necessarily built of
earth or stone, but may be invisible barriers. Probably such
hymns cover both cases, and anyhow the question has little

1. Manu, I, 89; VII, 87 f.
2. A. A. MacDonell, *Vedic Reader* (Oxford, 1917), 41.
3. The Fire-god is to the priesthood as Indra is to the nobility, a slayer
of demons. Above p. 56.
4. *Sat. Br.*, V, 2, 4, 13.
5. Above p. 118.
6. *Sat. Br.*, V, 4, 1, 9. Cp. *Kingship*, 210 ff., and *C.J.Sc.* I, 135 ff.

importance, for the victories of Indra and the king are primarily victories over the powers of darkness, physical darkness menacing the radiance of the sun. Whether the forms and bodies of the giants, or demons, are objects used in the cult, or human bodies, is a secondary matter, just as among the gods it is a secondary matter whether they are represented by a bunch of grass or by a human principal.[7] The essential is the Giant and the God; the forms and bodies are merely ways of getting at them. The king can defeat the demons with a sword; he can also defeat them with dice. A game of dice is still played in Tibet between the Dalai Lama as representative of the Buddha, and the King of the Demons, represented by some man. The Dalai Lama always wins.[8]

The enemies of prosperity may be internal or external. There can be no distinction in a society loosely knit together, where allegiance is conditional, and a subject can lawfully wage war against the king, and may even wrongly oppose him without being wicked. The king's enemy is whoever seeks to defeat the king in his quest of prosperity, whether from within the tribe or from without. Foreign warfare and ritual contests with subjects are not distinguished. Later in Hindu India defence and police are distinguished; fighting foreign kings and protecting the people against bandits are treated as separate duties of the king; but it is to the army that he still entrusts the execution of both.[9] India makes it clear that his policing duties are not derived from his upholding of the law, but from his defence of the realm against the assaults of the powers of evil. We have already had hints of this in other countries, and shall meet with more evidence as we go on.[10]

When the Fijians learned from our missionaries to call their old gods devils they also called the heathens devils, and a great war was waged between the Christians and the devils. Contrariwise in parts of Vanua Levu they call the old gods "heathens."[11]

---

7. *Sat. Br.*, I, 8, 3, 11; III, 4, 1, 17.
8. C. F. Koeppen, *Die Religion des Buddhas* (Berlin, 1857-9), III, 315.
9. Manu, VII, 88 ff; 144.
10. Above pp. 106, 107, and below pp. 181, 186.
11. *Itheni.*

In Homer's time Greece had already reached the stage at which India arrived later. The royal caste was a fighting caste. The king might be a judge, but his great glory was to fight. At least, that is the impression left by the *Iliad;* but allowance must be made for the fact that warlike deeds make a better theme for an epic than the routine of peace: literature has ever preferred the sensational. It is only later evidence that makes us realize how primarily ritual the king was. The connection of ritual and warfare can be recovered also from the myths.

$$\text{Zeus} = \text{Indra;}$$
$$\text{Giants} = \text{Asuras.}$$

The Greek thunder-god has adversaries like his Indian counterpart, and we may conclude that ritual contests were once waged in Greece between the impersonators of the gods and those of the Giants, as they are in our earliest Indian literature. The Homeric king was still representative of the thunder-god.[12]

Similar contests were waged in Egypt between Horus and Set, in Persia between gods and demons, in Scandinavia between Thor and the Giants. The same conclusion must be drawn.[13]

The Germanic nobility, like the Homeric, was essentially a fighting caste, and its traditions were continued in the Middle Ages. It found its Iliad in Malory's Morte d'Arthur. The romances on which it is founded still preserve the memory of the fight against the powers of evil. Legends such as that of Parsifal are more concerned with the quest of prosperity through the defeat of hostile influences, than with purely physical prowess.[14] In the XIth century the old idea of fighting evil in the person of the infidel broke out with greater force than ever, and sent expedition after expedition to the Holy Land. St. Louis, the leader of two of them, gave it as his advice that only very good scholars should dispute with the Jews,

12. I can produce no evidence of a thunder-god among the Arandas; but the Dieris have a god whose voice is thunder. Howitt, 538.
13. For Hebrews see *Labyrinth*, 94 ff., 107 ff.
14. Jessie L. Weston, *From Ritual to Romance*, Cambridge, 1920.

but the layman "when he hears the Christian law defamed should not defend the Christian law save by the sword with which he should smite the belly within as far as it will go."[15]

It was partly in order that he should smite the devil worshippers for the glory of God that the king was crowned. Before he was anointed they prayed to God that "armed with the helmet of Thy protection and ever protected by the invincible shield and surrounded by celestial weapons may he successfully obtain the triumph of a desirable victory over the enemies and strike the terror of his power into the infidels. . . . By Our Lord who by the power of the cross destroyed hell, and having overthrown the Devil's kingdom ascended as conqueror to heaven."[16] The primeval imitation is still there, only slightly dimmed. The principal imitates the God whom he represents, and as that God smote the Devil, so does he smite the infidels who worship the Devil: "Armed with the protection of the Holy Trinity may he, an invincible soldier, continually conquer the armies of the Devil." When it is prayed that he may defend the "fortresses of God," it is as hard as in the Vedas to say whether these fortresses are material or spiritual. The fact is, they are both, for the material and the spiritual cannot be separated. The progress of science has not abolished the fact that if a man does evil and is only to be restrained by force, force must be applied. If you hate evil you must smite those that stand for evil.

New faiths are now arising which threaten to divide Europe once more into good and wicked, believers and unbelievers. Only those faiths no longer rally round the king, but round a new figure that has supplanted him, the Leader.

It is he who is now the war-maker. The king, if he does survive at all, has lost that attribute. It was the last to survive. During the Great War the sovereign of Russia, the most archaic state in Europe, actually took the field as commander-in-chief. Except on very special occasions, the king's ceremonial dress is still that of a warrior.

That warlike function arose out of the representative·charac-

15. Joinville, X, 53.
16. E. S. Dewick, *Coronation Book of Charles the Fifth of France* (Publ. Henry Bradshaw Soc. No. 16), London, 1899.

ter of the ritual leader. He was the thunder and the eagle.[17] He behaved as both, and it was to behave as both that he was appointed. The objects have dropped out, leaving only the character, aggression. The only trace of the king's original department in nature is now to be found in imagery and emblems, such as the imperial eagle and thunder of the French.

We are now in a position to sum up the development of the king's chief attributes thus:—

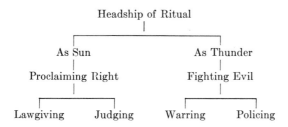

The character of warrior is entirely at variance with that of a maintainer of law and order. How came these opposite qualities to be united in the same person? The next chapter will give the answer: they were originally vested in two different persons one of which has swallowed up the other as part of the general process of absorption and centralization. India will supply a technical term for the one, law-king, the other we shall have to distinguish as executive or war king.

17. Tree: oak in the oak region — A comparative analysis will probably show that Horus was originally a thundergod who has lost his connection with thunder, because in Egypt there is no thunder that counts. He is solar; but so is Indra, and so are all gods eventually.

12· The Church and the State

Render therefore unto Caesar the things
that are Caesar's; and unto God the things
that are God's.

AN ARANDA ceremony for increase generally has two chief performers. In Strehlow I count 31 cases out of 52. The circumcision ceremony has one operator and one assistant. Various
duties are constantly carried out by pairs of men: two mother's-elder-brothers go with invitations for the initiation ceremony, and escort the candidate; two mother's mothers wipe
out the design painted on the novice's back; two father's-
brothers receive the blood of circumcision and subincision,
and so it goes on.

The Aranda myth is merely a record of ancient ritual performances. It does not come therefore as a surprise that the heroes, the ancestors who performed the ritual, constantly go
about in pairs. Unfortunately we do not know enough about
the chieftainship to understand this undoubted dualism.

The Winnebago chief "could not lead a war-party" and
no one might be killed in his lodge.[1] There was besides a
chief over half the tribe, the lower half. This second chief
was appointed from the Water-spirit clan, the leading one in
the lower half. Unfortunately again we know next to nothing
about the functions of this clan and its chief, only that it was
"connected with the passage of streams, etc."[2]

The Yuma of California have a non-hereditary chief who
was "an authority to whom appeal might be made on any
matter of dispute, but more significant as an embodiment of
spiritual power than as a law-giver or executive." He did not
go to war. "The control and direction of warfare lay, therefore, in separate hands . . . the war leader." The war chief
alone covered his body with black paint. The first chief "often
advised him not to be so restless."[3]

1. Radin, 57; 209.
2. Radin, 201; 241 ff.
3. Forde, 133 ff.

162

The Golden Bough[4] has a long list of dual kingships and gives at length an account of the Natchez who had a chief called the Great Sun, and also a war chief. There were sporting contests between their followers.

Dualism is the essence of the Fijian state and ritual. There was a saying that all things must go in pairs or the sharks will bite. It was also laid down that every chief has his second. This rule is borne out by practice. It is usual for a tribe to have two chiefs. Their relative positions vary. In Lomaloma, for instance, each one presides over his own half of the tribe; one takes precedence of the other, but is not over him. They inform each other of their wishes, and assent to each other. Sometimes they are so unequal that we should not recognize the second chief as such, but that he bears the title borne by the second chief in other tribes. Probably the commonest form is that one is chief over all, and chief of the senior half, the other chief of the junior half, both being in the relation of senior and junior, rather than of superior and subordinate. Each chief has his own court, his own herald, his own war chief, his own carpenter, and so on.

It is difficult for us to conceive of a government with two heads; but Fijian chiefs, I repeat, do not govern in our sense of the word. Their functions are those of principals in the ritual, and so not open to controversy; and it never occurs to a Fijian there might be any: they just "assent to one another" as a matter of course.

The senior chief usually bears the title of *Tui*, which we translate "King," if he is big enough. The junior chief is often called "God of War,"[5] in a few cases *Sau*, that is prosperity. They are sometimes distinguished by Europeans as the sacred and the secular, or the spiritual and the temporal, chiefs. But that is misleading. The Fijians make no distinction of spirit and world, of Church and State: society is an organization for prosperity, and that prosperity is to be achieved by the due observance of certain rules, and various functions in that quest are assigned to various dignitaries. Both chiefs are sacred, though one is usually more so than the other.

4. III, chap. on *Taboo* (1911).
5. *Vunivalu.*

The title of the second chief makes it clear that he is specially concerned with war. In Rewa they say "war is his part." That title is however restricted to one part of Fiji where cannibal warfare was most eagerly prosecuted. In other parts there is no indication that war is his special function. His essential characteristic, I think, is that he is the active partner. At feasts, for instance, it is often to him that the food is brought first, for him to control and then bring before the supreme chief who is purely passive. He who acts holds the power. Accordingly it was not infrequent that the junior chief was the real master, leaving to his senior no more than a sacred precedence. Thakombau, the so-called King of Fiji, was really the second chief of Mbau; but a series of able and ruthless holders of the office had raised his line to primacy in the whole of Fiji, while the incompetent Kings of Mbau lapsed into insignificance. In Lakemba the King has disappeared, evidently to Tonga, where the title is now found. The Sau is supreme; but in rising to the post of first chief he has also risen to its inactivity. It is beneath him to command, and so some one has to "carry the sovereignty," that is to give orders on his behalf, while he himself "just abides."[6] Only this office has not yet become hereditary, but is held by the most energetic and self-assertive of the chief's younger kinsmen.

This shifting of functions may explain the anomaly that the Winnebago chief is the head of the Thunder-bird clan, and yet a peacemaker. The peacemaking sky or sun king is extinct; Winnebago myths and the institutions of other North American tribes prove that he once existed. The thunder chief has moved up into his place and has become the peacemaker; a third chief has stepped into the vacant second chieftainship.

Thus the pattern of society survives revolutions. The individuals may change, but their arrangement remains. That is a process equally common in the human body and the body politic. Tissue often perishes, and its place is taken by other

6. *Tiko nga.* The British Government has made the chief Governor of the province, so that he is executive. The "carrier of the sovereignty" (*thola sau*), has in consequence disappeared.

164

tissue which takes over the functions of that which has disappeared, for instance the horny beak of the tortoise: it has not evolved out of teeth, but has stepped into the vacancy left by vanished teeth. We shall come across more instances in social evolution.

We can trace the elimination of the first King in Tonga, for it happened since our discovery of those islands. The king was too sacred to have any power. It was the Haʻu (the same word as the Fijian Sau) who had the say. Eventually he abolished his superior and assumed the title of King, which he bears to this day. The tendency is for the Prime Minister of European introduction to move up into the *position* of the Haʻu, not into the *title*.

In Japan there arose a great Mikado who was able to recover the power his predecessors had lost to the Shogun; but his descendants seem to have lapsed into the position of constitutional monarchs.

Several tribes of New Guinea' have a chief of the right and a chief of the left. This latter can be described as executive chief since he enforces the orders of his colleague. He is connected with war, and is often, though not always, called warchief. In one tribe weapons of war were always taken to his hall, not to the other chief's. Strangers who set foot in his hall were killed. The chief of the right appears as a peacemaker among the Elana and Roro tribes. To stop a fight it was sufficient for him "to get between the combatant lines, scatter lime from his gourd, and wave the leafy crown of a dracaena." The halls of these tribes are divided into right and left; the chief of the right sat on the right, the chief of the left on the left.[7]

The senior Abô is the Jukun "king's vis-à-vis. That is to say he is the representative of the people in their relations with the king, who is the representative of the gods. Though he is debarred from attaining to the kingship himself, he has a court of his own, which is only inferior to that of the king.

7. C. G. Seligman, *The Melanesians of British New Guinea* (Cambridge, 1910), 28 n., 216 ff., 227, 229, 338, 342.

He receives his food ceremonially like the king." He has his own royal priest,[8] and a second in command, the junior Abô, "who also has his own court and receives his food in ceremonial fashion . . . He might be called upon to act as leader in war. But normally he never left the capital, being the king's principal counsellor. He is the prime mover in all matters."[9] Thus in Nigeria, as in Fiji, big fleas have little fleas.

They are right-hand and left-hand chiefs since in one section of the Jukuns the principal chief takes the right-hand sector in a hunt, while his second takes the left.

The Yorubas serve our turn better than the Jukuns. They have a supreme king whom they speak of as 'the king terrestrial.' He is descended from the thunder-god and ritually closely connected with him, as comparative evidence demands he should be. The 'king celestial' is subordinate to him, but at the sky festival it is the supreme king who "occupies a humiliating position as one whose conduct is under review" by his celestial vassal, who can move the deposition of a king for exceeding the law. The sky-king is then a repository of law, as he should be according to our information elsewhere, and can rightly be termed a law-king. His fee is a horse: this connection of law-king and horse we also find elsewhere. He is chosen by the supreme king from among five families; on the other hand he has a voice in choosing that supreme king, but his choice is much more limited. Thus the law-king is more loosely hereditary than his colleague. We shall see that generally throughout the world he is by far the more liable of the two to lose his hereditary character. The greatest law-kings in the world are in fact completely elective. This may be because as upholders of Right they so readily become the champions of the people against the hereditary rulers.

The Yorubas thus bring out certain points which are fundamental to the theory of dual kingship, and so must be underlined:—

8. *Ajifi:* he it is who pours libations on the chief's behalf over the royal graves, or in front of the symbols of the deities present in the king. He seems to correspond to the Indian Brahman.
9. Meek, 334 f.

166

1) The celestial king is a law-king.
2) He is connected with the horse.
3) His heredity is less well defined than his colleague's.
4) The terrestrial king is a thunder-king.[10]

In West Africa the village reproduces the dualism of the court. In each Yauri village on the Upper Niger "there are two complete organizations, the Village headman and his elders, and Balkeri or Head Farmer and elders, the men of property in the village." The elders of each headman bear titles similar to those found in the house that rules over the whole country. Of the two the higher is "little more than a 'post office' for the conveyance of orders from higher authority. . . . Anything whatever connected with turning out men for labour must be done through" the Head Farmer. If he is disloyal the village head is powerless.[11]

We have had a great deal of evidence from India about the two aspects of the king. It remains to find them there embodied in separate persons.

In Nepal there is a King of Kings and a Great King, who is, in British official documents, termed Prime Minister. This gives a wrong idea of his true rank, title, and function. He is really a king of lower degree; but the real ruler of the country.

Next door to Nepal, in Bhutan, there was until recently a law-king and a king of the gods.[12] By law I translate the Indian *dharma* which we have learnt to know. The law-king then is a king of order, right, custom. His title is the title of the god Varuna in the old Brahmanic religion. The title "King of the Gods" on the other hand belongs to Indra, the fighting god.

We have now become accustomed to the idea that the world of the gods is but a reflection of the world of men, and vice-versa; because the men who take part in the ritual are one with the gods: what they do, it is the gods that are doing it. If then we fail to find in India proper dual kingship actually

10. *Yorubas*, 34 ff., 44, 48, 70 f., 152, 178 ff., 190.
11. P. G. Harris, *Notes on Yauri, J.R.A.I.*, 1930, 297 f.
12. *Dharmraja* (Skt. *dharmaraja*) and *Debraja* (Skt. *Devaraja*).

in being, we must turn to theology for evidence. There we find a constant contrast between Indra and Varuna, a contrast that must reflect a dualism in the world of men such as we have found in Bhutan. Only in the earliest prose writings the same king can be consecrated by two different ceremonies as Indra and as Varuna, thus uniting both gods and the functions of both in one person.[13] We now understand how the Indian king comes to combine the contradictory attributes of upholder of order and leader in conflict. The active king has apparently swallowed up the quiescent king.

The same contrast exists among the ancient Teutons between Odin and Thor. Here however the dual kingship persisted till quite late. Gibbon thus describes it among the Burgundians:—"The appelation of Hendinos was given to the king or general, and the title of Sinistus to the high priest of the nation. The person of the priest was sacred and his dignity perpetual; but the temporal government was held by a very precarious tenure. If the events of war accused the courage or conduct of the king, he was immediately deposed; and the injustice of his subjects made him responsible for the fertility of the earth and the regularity of the seasons."[14] Here again the second king is not only responsible for war, but for the crops also.

Homer's catalogue of ships shows that the dual monarchy existed in Greece.[15] It survived in Sparta, though the differentiation of function seems to have been lost. One king held the cult of Zeus of the Sky, the other of Lakedaimonian Zeus, apparently a terrestrial aspect of that god.[16] Generally however the executive king seems, as in India, to have absorbed the law-king, an absorption reflected in heaven; for Zeus is both a thunder-god and an upholder of custom. This latter function should belong by rights to Poseidon, the nearest Greek equivalent of Varuna.

13. Hocart, *Two Vedic Hymns*, C.J.Sc., I, 133; where this dualism makes quite straightforward a hymn which has baffled scholars ignorant of social organization and theory.
14. *Decline and Fall*, III, 36.
15. *Iliad*, II, 512; 517; 620; 678. — *Odyssey*, XI, 260 ff.
16. Herodotos, VI, 56.

Athens preserved the dualism of function better than Sparta, though they abolished monarchy altogether; but the archons carried on the duties of the kings. The first archon gave his name to the year and supervised the calendar, as befits a king who is responsible for the regularity of the seasons; he supervised the family, protecting parents and widows, orphans and heiresses, dealt with divorce and ensured the continuity of houses. He had jurisdiction in all that concerned individual and family rights. The second archon was called king and had jurisdiction in matters of ritual, and handled cases of homicide. His queen represented the God's wife in the sacred marriage of Dionysos.[17] He is not concerned with war, but he is with homicide, a breach of the peace.

The two consuls attest the former existence of dual kingship in Rome. In fact it runs through the whole Roman administration. It is not however in the consuls that we have to seek for the true representatives of the old dual monarchy, but in the High Pontiff and in the King of Rites. The first is summed up by Festus as "the highest judge of things appertaining to ritual and sacred ordinances, and punisher of transgressions by private persons and magistrates."[18] He was in charge of the calendar. The King of Rites was inferior in rank. He it was "who performed the rites which the kings were accustomed to perform." He was the executive in ritual matters.[19] This dualism was revived in the late empire by Diocletian, who took the title of Jovius, and bestowed that of Heraclius upon his associate Maximian. "Whilst the motion of the world (such was the language of their venal orators) was maintained by the all-seeing wisdom of Jupiter, the invincible arm of Hercules purged the earth of monsters and tyrants." So Gibbon.[20] Like all historians who trace a single stream of direct evidence, he missed the point of the institutions he was describing. The comparative historian knows it was not venal flattery, but the revival of a world-wide dual kingship.

17. Gilbert, I, 241.
18. S.v. *Maximus Pontifex*. (p. 113, 19-21 Lindsay). Cf. Livy I, 20.
19. Festus, s.v. *Sacrificulus Rex*. (p. 422, 11-13 Lindsay). Cf. Livy, II, 2.
20. *Decline and Fall*, III, 36.

Strabo[21] describes that institution among the Getae who had reached the Danube from the Black Sea. "It is said that one of the Getae, Zalmoxis by name, was slave to Pythagoras, and learnt something from him about the heavenly bodies, and also from the Egyptians, having wandered as far as that. When he returned to his country he was sought after by the rulers and the people, because he could foretell the astral movements. At last he persuaded the king to take him as partner in the government, as able to expound the signs from the gods. At first he was only made priest of the god most honoured amongst them, but later he was addressed even as god, and, having occupied a cavernous place inaccessible to others, he lived there, seldom meeting with the outside world, except the king and his own attendants; and the king was confederate, as he saw the people paid much more attention to him than before, as carrying out his commands according to the advice of the gods. This custom persisted even down to our times, as some one was always found of such character who was available as counsellor to the king, but was called God among the Getae. Even the mountain was supposed to be holy, and so they addressed it."

I have quoted Strabo at length because he is typical of the rationalistic historian. He did not believe in divine kingship, and made no effort whatever to understand it. To his self-satisfied Reason it seemed nothing but nonsense, and not to be explained but as an imposture practised by the priests upon a simpleton mass, a type of explanation as popular nowadays as it was in late antiquity. After the manner of the pure historians, those who will accept nothing but direct evidence, he liked to derive institutions from local accidents, even from such accidents as lies. A comparative survey satisfies us that the dualism of law-king and executive king did not originate among the Getae, but was inherited by them from a past so ancient that Pythagoras seems as of yesterday by comparison. Of course the Getae must have adapted it to their own genius, and given it its local colouring. The form it takes among them can be closely paralleled by our own scriptures, particularly

21. VII, 3, 5.

by I Kings, xix, the story of Elijah's sojourn in the cave of Horeb, "the mount of God."

The relations of Samuel and Saul, and of their successors are very much the same as existed between Zalmoxis and the Getan king, or between the two chiefs of the Yuma: a prophet designated by the deity, not by birth, declaring God's will to a more or less hereditary king, who has all the power of command. To this dualism of monarchs there seem to correspond two types of gods, the Baal, or Lord, and the Moloch, or king.[22]

Isaiah paints an idyllic picture of a King of Righteousness. It is evident that when he dreamed his beautiful dream the King of Righteousness had ceased to be a living institution, a real every day thing like Zalmoxis; for you cannot idealize what is daily before your eyes; a valet does not idealize his master. By the time of Isaiah the law-king had become the ideal of a nation enslaved and broken, which found in ideals an escape from reality. The Indians did the same. In the general despondency that marked the decadence of the old Brahmanic culture, they too transfigured the Lord of Right into spiritual saviour.

Buddhist scriptures are full of Messianic ideas. Male children are born from time to time whom signs designate for a great career, either the imperial dignity, that is the overlordship of the kings of the earth, or else the dignity of seer, of Buddha, that is "one who knows." He has the choice between what we should call a temporal and a spiritual empire; but we must always bear in mind that the spiritual and the temporal have never been as completely and artificially severed in India as they have been in Modern Europe. Emperor

22. It may be questioned whether it is right to call the law-giver "king." It is possible that title properly belongs to the executive variety. In India *rajan* is applied to both, but then India has very much confounded the two. In Athens *basileus*, in Rome *rex*, are reserved for the republican representatives of the second king. Future research may show that *rajan, rex, basileus, melech, king*, belong to the executive king; another series represented by *pati, pontifex*, and other words, to the law-giver. It might be more correct to speak of prophet and king, only the word prophet has such narrow associations.

171

and Buddha both uphold the moral law. The difference is that the emperor enjoys a splendid court and the wealth of the earth; the seer must lead a life of renunciation.[23] A prince of the Sakya tribe is said to have chosen renunciation. He became the last Buddha, till the next one appears. His installation as seer, his illumination, as it is called, follows very closely the lines of a Vedic king's consecration, except that his is a solitary installation: he does not receive it at the hands of priests and subjects, because the doctrine is anti-priestly and highly intellectual in its origin, and so undemocratic.[24] Like a Vedic king he practises austerities first, then takes his seat on a throne at the foot of a ficus tree,[25] he fights and overcomes the demons, and enters into a union with the Earth-goddess; then preaches the law. He becomes entitled King of Right.[26] But observe the difference: in Vedic ritual everything is literal: the fight is with the demons of real darkness, the darkness that blights the crops and living creatures, and the aim is progeny and food. The demons that assail the candidate for Buddhahood are the passions which cloud the understanding, and keep from it that light of truth which brings release from evil. The law is not the tribal law on the observance of which depends the natural and the social order, but a universal rule of conduct ensuring spiritual welfare and final escape from death. Yet that new law has palpably grown out of the old: for it is constantly compared with the sun, and is represented by a wheel, only that wheel is no longer the sun disc timing the universe, but a doctrine regulating the life of the individual. That is the philosophy: in practice the calendar still goes by the Prophet's career: his birth, his illumination, his retreat, his death, are important landmarks in the lunar year.

23. *Anguttara*, I, 76. — *Digha*, II, 16; 172 ff. — *Kingship*, 22 ff.; 20 ff.
24. Buddhism is usually reputed democratic because it is antipriestly, as if the priesthood was necessarily undemocratic. The intellectuals always think themselves democratic because they want to impose their culture on a populus that does not want it. The true democratic spirit consists in trying to understand their point of view and respecting it. The Buddhist *philosophy* has never taken hold of the people, though they may repeat its *formulae* by heart.
25. Above p. 97.
26. Hocart, *The Temptation*, C.J.Sc., I, 113.

The Buddha founded a spiritual state running parallel to the temporal. Mr. S. Parananvitana has shown that the Buddhist Church copied very largely the organization of those tribes that were ruled by *sanghas,* that is councils, such tribes as the Sakyas, the Mallas, the Licchavis. The Church is itself called a *sangha,* and the Buddha bears the title of King of the *Sangha,* King of the Church we should say. He has under him a general, not of soldiers, but of the faith.

The Buddhist scriptures are quite definite that Gautama, the last Buddha, was not a unique phenomenon. Such seers had appeared periodically before him, just as judges and prophets kept appearing in Israel. Outside India, in Tibet and adjoining countries, there is still a never-failing succession of them, designated by signs, even like the fabled Buddhas of old. Evidently Gautama was merely the last of a long series in India; he was the last because he came at a time when the institution was dying out, or was being driven into the mountainous country to the North and East. When an institution dies, when it is no longer before the eyes, imagination begins to play with the facts, years can be lengthened into aeons, principalities into worlds, everything can be magnified for the glory of the last of the line, whose reign is unending, because there is no successor. Thus an everyday institution, a petty sovereignty entrusted with the regulation of tribal custom, perishes in the flesh only to be reborn in the mind as a universal ideal, a spiritual monarchy overflowing all national boundaries. The Man becomes an Idea.

Thus in India we can almost see the Church growing out of one side of dual kingship, out of the King of Right and out of his court. A parallel evolution took place in Palestine at a later date. The same institution, exposed to the corroding action of decadence, underwent a similar transformation. The fleshly was eaten away and the spiritual shone forth.

Those who make of Jesus a naive pretender to the Jewish crown, a well-meaning, but misguided agitator, do not realize that the King of Righteousness is much older than the Christian era. His kingdom had already been sublimated into a Church five hundred years earlier in India. The royal pedigree, the signs at birth, the fasting, temptation and victory, the first sermon, the new commandments, the council of disciples, were all anticipated by Buddhism.[27] Christ was not the first Prince of Peace, Sun of Righteousness, Law's Great Maker, "True day dispersing shades of night," shedding the rays, not of the sun, but of the Spirit, not on nature, but "on every thought and sense."[28] When Christ spoke of the Kingdom of Heaven and of the Law, he was speaking a language familiar to the East, and which could never be taken as a claim to the executive throne.

Early Christianity, like early Buddhism, set little store by ritual: right living alone counted for salvation. Both religions began by attacking the old ritual; both however soon evolved a ritual of their own in opposition to the old one. Both thus found themselves in conflict with the powers that be, Buddhism with the Brahmans, Christianity with the Roman state. A complete divorce between Church and State resulted. But such a divorce was unnatural and could not last long. When Christianity captured the government, Church and State became united again as a dualism. Western Europe eventually acknowledged a spiritual head, the Pope, and a temporal one, the Holy Roman Emperor. The Pope still proclaims the moral law and regulates the calendar. The Emperor was more short-lived. He failed to maintain his supremacy over other kings, though the ambition to recover it has been a constant disturber of the peace of Europe. Thus the old dualism is obscured by the fact that to one King of Law there corresponds a multitude of executive kings.

Still, in the Middle Ages the old dualism is fairly well preserved, especially in the proceedings against heresy: the Church judged and the State executed. A strict line of demarcation never existed, because it is impossible. The king had his law as well as the Church; yet this law, under Henry the Second at least, was administered mainly by prelates of the Church.[29] The Pope excommunicated, the king outlawed. Ex-

27. *Kingship*, 121 ff.
28. *Hymns A. & M.*, 60; 71; 2.
29. Pollock and Maitland, I, 132 f.; 154.

174

communication is "an ecclesiastical outlawry; and, like temporal outlawry, though once it was the law's last and most terrible weapon against the obstinate offender, it is now (XIIIth century) regarded as a normal process for compelling the appearance in court of those who are accused. Indeed as regards the laity, since the spiritual courts can not direct a seizure of body, lands or goods, those courts must, if mere citation fail to produce an appearance, at once have recourse to their last weapon. Then, as ordained by William the Conqueror, the lay power comes to their aid. If the excommunicate does not seek absolution within forty days . . . , the ordinary will signify this to the king; a writ for the arrest of the offender will be issued, and he will be kept in prison until he makes his submission."[30] On the other hand outlawry might be described as a temporal excommunication; for the outlaw suffered a kind of spiritual death. "If the king inlaws him, he comes back into the world like a new-born babe, *quasi modo genitus,* capable indeed of acquiring new rights, but unable to assert any of those he had before his outlawry."[31] The spheres within which the temporal and the spiritual exclusion from communion with the living were applied, were not strictly separate. Excommunication could be used for purposes which we should call temporal. Thus St. Louis and his advisers debated before Damietta how they could prevent the plunder from being dissipated. The most effective measure they could think of was to threaten excommunication against anyone who did not bring it to the legate's house.[32] On the other hand the king also enforced his justice by making use of his sanctity. "Breach of the king's peace was an act of personal disobedience, and a much graver matter than an ordinary breach of public order; it made the wrong-doer the king's enemy. The notion of the king's peace appears to have had two distinct origins. These were, first, the special sanctity of the king's house . . . ; secondly, the special protection of the king's at-

---

30. *Ibid.,* I, 478.
31. *Ibid.,* I, 477.
32. Joinville, XXXVI, 167. — Above p. 139 ff.

tendants and servants, and other persons whom he thought fit to place on the same footing." Thus there is no fundamental distinction between the criminal and the infidel: both are the king's enemies, because the king stands for God. If the wrong-doer refuses to submit he is outlawed, and "outlawry involved liability to be killed with impunity. It was no offence to the king to kill his enemy, and the kindred might not claim wergild."[33] So impossible is it to distinguish really between the temporal and the spiritual, between infidelity and criminality, between the enemies of God and the enemies of man. No wonder the Pope had his armies as well as the king. He has just recovered a minute fraction of his temporal dominions.

Since the Middle Ages it is the temporal that has been encroaching on the spiritual. The State has gradually annexed education, the supervision of morals, the celebration of marriage, the provision of burial grounds. It lays down rules of conduct which it enforces with the threat of physical coercion. The Church continues to affirm the ancient rules of conduct, but has no means of enforcing them except its ascendancy over the minds of men. Conflicts ensue in the nation, even as they do in an individual who allows his personality to develop in two opposite directions.

The divorce of temporal and spiritual is unnatural; for both are rules of living, and there cannot be two sets of rules. Their separation means that society is trying, like Dr. Jekyll, to divide its life into two unconnected halves, one of which it calls religion, the other the world. We are now assisting at a reaction against this unnatural cleavage. Europe is demanding a State that will regulate the whole life. The State seems to be superseding the Church, but only by itself becoming a religion.

How did the dualism arise, and how is it so persistent?

We are not yet in a position to answer the first part of this question. We may however have some hints where to look for the answer. The law-king must in many cases, if not always, keep away from death, or at least bloodshed. Of the Jukun king we are definitely told he may not "look upon

33. Pollock and Maitland, I, 45; 49.

a corpse, for he has no part in death."[34] Being the principal in the quest of life, the repository of life, it is only natural he should avoid contact with the negation of life. There is a constant inconsistency between the rites of peace, which brings life, and those of death-dealing war. Of this opposition the Omahas yield a good example:— "Marriage with a man either on or about to go on the war path was not permitted; such a union was looked on as a defiance of natural law that would bring disaster on the people for the reason, it was explained, that 'War means the destruction of life, marriage its perpetuation.' "[35]

The Arandas too evidently consider manslaughter a complete reversal of the natural order of things. After a death (probably only that of an important person), they have to go and take lives. Sometimes they will massacre a whole camp with wanton bloodthirstiness. Before setting out on a killing expedition they have intercourse with those very women whom it would be death to possess in normal circumstances. A state of war confounds all the rules of peace.[36]

The spiritual judge in Medieval England might go through the form of requesting that the life of the victim whom they were handing over to the temporal authorities might be spared. This was in order to avoid blood-guiltiness. An ordained clerk might not even attend a surgical operation.[37] In the Great War he was often forbidden to fight for his country.

This opposition between order and bloodshed may explain why the maintenance of law and the slaying of those who transgress the ritual are vested in different persons. The upholder of the law must be serene; the conqueror of evil must use violence. Hence two different persons are required, one to set the course for the stars and men, the other to rout the forces of evil in nature and man.

However this differentiation came about, it fitted in with mental facts. The temperament that excels in judgment and

34. Meek, 129. The prince born to be Buddha was not allowed to see death.
35. *Omaha*, 325.
36. Strehlow, IV, 2, 6.
37. Pollock and Maitland, II, 476; 545.

177

serenity is not the one that shines in action, and vice-versa. The first requires self-control and leisurely reflection, and freedom from passion; the executive must be capable of quick decisions, and not too much burdened with scruples. Power always inclines to the man who acts, and acts swiftly. The tendency therefore is always for the executive king to squeeze out the law-giver. As, however, the king of righteousness loses power over things, he may enlarge his empire over the hearts of the people. Unsoiled by the dust of the world, he becomes an ideal figure which attracts to itself all the hopes of a people weary of the insolence of a fighting monarchy. The qualities that make a successful man of action are precisely the most dangerous when all checks are removed. The Fijians had a saying, "This state is going to ruin, because it is ruled by a man with all his teeth."[38] They distrusted the young and impetuous, and valued the mild and understanding rule of an old man, though in war he was no use. We have learnt by bitter experience since 1918 that the best war ministers do not make the best peace ministers, and mankind is oftener at peace than at war. The world has often had to rue that the necessities of troublous times have placed the man of action on a pinnacle of unrestricted power. Then the people turn from the arrogance of civil power to the humility of a spiritual king, who, having no power can do no wrong. Thus his very powerlessness becomes a source of power. Secure in the devotion of the masses he can often defy the secular authority, may defeat and supplant it, only to yield in his turn to the temptations of power.

In this their latest form the two kingdoms, spiritual and temporal, bear no trace of their original spheres, save that we still speak of a kingdom of heaven. The phrase takes us back to the earliest origins, to a sky king who is responsible for law and order in the world, and to an earth king who executes the heavenly law among men. We are however anticipating evidence still to come. The present chapter does not take up the tale so far back; it only recognizes two kings both belonging to the upper sphere: a sky or sun king who sets

38. *Lau Islands*, 51.

the example of orderly existence, and a thunder king who punishes breaches of the law.

Being the active party the second king frequently usurps all power, and eventually abolishes his partner: but he cannot abolish the dualism of war and peace. Thus the dualism in the state goes on as before; only the personages have changed places in the social plan.

13· The Commander-in-Chief

Behold, the ark of the covenant of the Lord of
all the earth passeth over before you in Jordan.
Joshua, iii, 11

BESIDES THE specific ceremonies in which the Aranda have
two chief performers I count three cases in which there are
three, one old and two young. In the final initiation there
is a camp chief supported by two others chiefs whom he en-
joins to watch the novices.[1] Evidently in Aranda ceremonial
3 = 1 + 2. This is reflected in the myths: the actors are often
one old man and two young ones. In one case we are told
their relationship: they are two brothers and their grandfather.

We must be content to note that two and three are found
side by side, and pass on to the Winnebago for more light.
They are, as we saw, divided into two; but the lower half
is again divided into two, so that they can at one time say
they are divided into two, at another into three, without con-
tradicting themselves.[2] The lower half reproduces the structure
of the whole. The Water-spirit clan which led the upper section of that half provided a chief for the whole, while the
Bear clan was chief over the lower section. Though ranking
below the Water-spirit clan it is said to have been the most
important next to the Thunder-bird clan, that of the chief
over the whole. They "are the soldiers or sergeants-at-arms
of the tribe. They have complete control of everything concerning discipline. Whenever the Winnebago are travelling
or moving, the Bear clan lead, and whenever they decide to
stop, there the leader would put his stick in the ground and
the other Bear clansmen would do the same, arranging them
in a row pointing toward the direction in which they were
going. The main body of the tribe would follow at a certain
distance. No member of the tribe would dare pass ahead of
the row of sticks." They burnt down the house of any one who
broke the rule. "They never jest and their word is command.

1. Strehlow, IV, I, 39.
2. Radin, 185 f.; 241.

If it is not obeyed, their next move is to punish. . . . when they are not on duty they are the same as other people."[3]

The description "soldiers" is somewhat misleading, for, in a community where everyone fights, there are no soldiers and no civilians. As a matter of fact the Winnebagoes have another clan which is termed the Warriors. The essential function of the Bear-clan is to take the lead in war and maintain discipline, as understood by the tribe.

Another Winnebago custom worth noting for future use is that whenever a war-party camps, two fires are placed on either side of the war-leader, a pair for each half of the tribe. We are not told if they are made on the spot or carried from home.[4]

It appears to have been common for a North American tribe to have its sacred pole carried in front of it as it moved in search of a new home.[5]

Similar functions to those of the Bear clan belong in Fiji to a clan or a group of clans which are designated "The Border."[6] They go ahead in war, they are strong men, and the nobles, when hard pressed, rely on them as their last resort. Some of them do not plant, but eat from the fields of the nobles. It is they who punish disrespect for the chief, and so form a kind of police. In the village of Tumbou in Lakemba they occupy a position similar to that of the Bear clan among the Winnebagoes: they are a clan, not the leading one, in the inferior half of the village. Sometimes however the whole of the inferior half, sometimes its upper section, is reckoned as Border. In the tribe of Rewa the war-chief is said to "be on the border": war is his part, and at feasts he receives the head of the pig or the fish, the invariable portion of the Border. Here he is none other than our second or executive king. Elsewhere the two are distinct. One reason for this fluctuation is that the function is all important: there are certain things that some one has to do; and there are certain rules which

3. Radin, 266.
4. Radin, 166.
5. E.g. J. R. Swanton, *Source Material for the Social and Ceremonial Life of the Choctaw Indians*, B.A.E., Bulletin 103 (1931), 22.
6. *Mbati*.

decide who is to do them; but those rules are not rigid; for the persons designated by their descent may be extinct, or unfit, or otherwise debarred, and then some one else has to fill the gap. Then again offices may split up into two, or two may be fused into one, according to the increase or decrease of population, or to meet other changes.

The function of vanguard in Fiji is certainly not based on tactical considerations: there is no battle array, for there are no pitched battles. Warfare consists in ambushes, in surprise attacks on sleeping villages, or in keeping the enemy cooped up in his fort. Besides it is the privilege of the Border to go in first at javelin matches,[7] and that shows clearly that the essential part of their duties is to go ahead, to lead, whether it be in war, matches, or feasts; and that is doubtless why they get the forepart of the pig. In javelin-throwing matches the first man of each team to throw is called "the spirit of the javelin game." He is then the representative of the spirit in a game which is very much controlled by spirits. Every man has his own peculiar spirit that helps him in the game.[8] The Border is sometimes called "The spirit battalion," literally "the spirit face of the army," or else "the face of the spirit." Like all other office-bearers they are essentially priests. They owe their rank to the fact that in the cosmic ritual different parts have to be taken by different families.

We have further proof that the vanguard is not tactical in the fact that they assail not only external enemies, but also those subjects of the chief who offend against him. In fact it is impossible to draw a line between enemies and offenders, since most wars are between suzerain and vassals, and many were large-scale assaults on a community guilty of some breach of etiquette. Vanguard and police can thus not be differentiated.

In Rotuma certain families led the war dance and went ahead in war. They wore a conical hat in the dance, whereas the rest, chiefs and commoners, had a semicircle of feathers radiating round the head.

7. *Tingga.*
8. *Lau Islands,* 91 f.

In those tribes of New Guinea which have a chief of the right and a chief of the left, the war chief may be the same as the second, but he may be a third chief.

Athens conformed to the threefold pattern. Next to the name-giving archon and the king archon came a third personage known as Polemarch, or Army-leader. At the time of the Persian Wars he only held an equal vote in war-councils with the generals, but in battle-array he took the right wing, the post of honour, and it was on him the battle line was formed.[9] Later however he lost all military command, but conducted certain sacrifices and arranged the funeral contests for those who died in war. He had jurisdiction over aliens and freedmen, and in suits where the defendant was a foreigner.[10] The essence of his function then was not war, but dealings with those who did not belong to the Athenian communion; for since Church and State were one, to be a citizen was to belong to the communion. War was only one side of his relations with the foreigner-infidel, one way of dealing with those that did not belong to the cult. As the city was sacred, the office of one who had dealings with the excommunicate naturally lay outside the city, while the other two archons had their offices by the ceremonial centre of the city, the *agora* or meeting place.

There appears to us in early Indian writings an "army-leader."[11] He belongs, not to the aristocracy, but to the lower half of the community, the *sudras*. He appears as the first of a list of court officials who come into the royal consecration at one point, but whose contact with the holy rites has afterwards to be atoned for, because they are "unfit for sacraments," connected with darkness, and by introducing them to the sacrament the king has entered darkness, just as the sun enters darkness when overcome by the powers of darkness.[12] The true nature of the army leader is made clear by the original text which describes his portion in the ritual. The king "having produced fire from two sticks, passes over to

9. Herodotos, VI, 109; 111.
10. Gilbert, I, 242.
11. *Senani*, from *sena*, army, and *ni*, to lead.
12. *Sat. Br.*, V, 3, 2, 1.

the house of the Army-leader. He strews for Fire-of-the-front[13] a rice-meal cake on eight potsherds. For Fire is the front of the gods; the army-leader is the front of the army. Therefore it is for Fire-of-the-front."[14] The army-leader represents Agni, the Fire-god, but one particular aspect of that god, which is known as Agni-of-the-Face, or Front, or Army. He is among men what the fire god is among the gods, the one who goes in front. He is not necessarily the commander-in-chief, as the title is often translated, but the one who goes in front of the army. The reason why he goes in front is made clear by another passage in which we see a tribe migrating with the sacrificial fire leading the way; nor may the priests cross a river not previously crossed by the sacred fire.[15] We know also that fire was carried in front of the army. Evidently the sacrificial fire must precede a tribe or household on the move, as it preceded the Israelites in the desert. Some one has to tend it, some one who is the impersonation of the fire god in so far as that god goes before the moving community. That man is the army-leader. His other duties merely flow from his essential function of priest of that aspect of the god.

He who marches in front of the army tends to control its movements. The rest have to follow him, and he has power to commit them to battle. The army-leader does in fact develop into a commander-in-chief. Unfortunately the stages of this evolution are scarcely known, because Orientalists are immersed in grammar and literature, and are not much interested in social organization. Until a new generation arises which prefers the fundamentals of life to the frills, we must be content to note such facts as come to our notice by accident.

In later times than the Vedic the title seems to be more commonly "Lord of the Army."[16] This office is frequently given in Ceylon to the king's sister's son.[17] As it became increasingly the custom for the king to marry royal blood, it

13. *Agni anikavat. Anika* = face, front, army (as with us).
14. *Sat. Br.*, V, 3, 2, 1.
15. *Sat. Br.*, I, 4, 1, 16.
16. *Senapati.*
17. *Mhvs.*, VI, 15; XI, 20; 25; XXXVIII, 81; *Jataka*, VI, 545.

is evident that the office was in time appropriated by the royal caste. Their part seems to gain in importance in Ceylon as times goes by, and successful lords of the army occasionally made themselves kings.[18] The commander of the vanguard is the second most important personage in the kingdom of Siam, and his Sanskrit title is "Great Sub-king."[19] The Europeans call him the Second. Next in importance, but a long way behind, comes the commander of the rear-guard. The commander of the vanguard was chief councillor and was usually the eldest son. The office has thus in Siam been definitely annexed by the royal family.

This is another case of the shift of function. The executive king has, as we saw, swallowed up the law-giver, but in doing so he has succeeded to his limitations. He requires a lieutenant, and that lieutenant is naturally the man who once came third, and so moves now into the second place: the commander of the vanguard becomes the young and active second king.

We can now go back to our Arandas and notice a custom which escaped us before, because we had not the necessary preparation. When a fighting force of theirs is two or three days out from camp, they make an earth mound, and place upon it a stick representing the man to be killed. The mound therefore seems to represent a burial mound, the grave of the doomed man. In front of this they place a fire with a special name; behind it sit two or three men entitled "those in front." The front is presumably the direction of the march, though we are not told so, nor whether this vanguard is hereditary, or how chosen. They are said to know everything and be able to teach. Spencer and Gillen take this to mean that they are merely the men who have done it before; but this does not follow. The people who are said to know are often those who have inherited the rites. That is the case in Eddystone Island. Here is an example how insufficient is grammar by itself to give the meaning: the customs have also to be known.

The Jukuns have an official who is described as "leader in

18. *Mhvs.* LVI, 7.
19. *Maha Uparaja.* Quaritch Wales, 52.

185

war," and as "commander-in-chief," but details are lacking.[20]

Medieval England had two army-leaders, the constable and his junior, the marshal. An episode of the reign of Edward I clearly proves that they were not commanders of the army, but king's serjeants who went in front. In 1297 Roger Bigod was marshal and Humphrey Bohun was constable. When "Edward proposed to the barons singly that they should go to Gascony whilst he took command in Flanders, he was met by a series of excuses. The Marshal and the Constable . . . . pleaded that their tenure obliged them to go with the king; if he went to Gascony they would go with him . . . . From threats Edward turned to prayers; . . . surely the earl Marshal would go; Bohun might feel a grudge for his late imprisonment and fine. 'With you, O king,' Bigod answered, 'I will gladly go: as belongs to me by hereditary right I will go in front of the host before your face.' 'But without me,' Edward urged, 'you will go with the rest.' 'Without you, O king,' was the answer, 'I am not bound to go, and I will not go.' Edward lost his temper: 'By God, earl, you shall either go or hang.' 'By God,' said Roger, 'O king, I will neither go nor hang'."[21]

We have seen that the king's state is reproduced by vassals and by vassals' vassals, as far down as it is possible to go. We are not surprised then to find petty local officers bearing the same title as the leader of the king's vanguard. These local constables that appear in the XIIIth century had to head the hue and cry.[22] The criminal, be it remembered, is the king's enemy, and not fully differentiated from other king's enemies.

The Lord High Constable has long ceased to exist, except as the puppet of a day. He is appointed by the Crown for the day of the coronation only. "When he has delivered the regalia to the Lord Great Chamberlain he has only to walk in the procession on the right of the sword of state. But until the Champion's service was dispensed with, he rode into the banquet on the champion's right, with his ancient partner,

20. Meek, 339.
21. Stubbs, *Constitutional History of England* (Oxford, 1875), II, 132 f.
22. Pollock and Maitland, II, 582.

the Earl Marshal, on the champion's left, a survival of their old association on the field of battle."[23]

Now it is this champion who bears "the only standard that has come down to us without a change from the Middle Ages." The Constable and the Marshal then form escort for the sacred emblem, the emblem of Saint George, who is no other than Marduk, Indra, Thor, the dragon-slayer in Christian guise.[24] The English survival of the army-leader still guards the English survival of the demon-fighting god.[25]

In England the constable has not developed into a commander-in-chief, as in India, but has petered out. More fortunate than his English colleague the Constable of France became commander-in-chief in the absence of his king, as Bohun and Bigod might have been, but for the English reluctance to go on foreign wars. Nevertheless the French constable later became even more extinct than ours. The Marshal of France became the title of the highest military officer in the kingdom. Our Earl Marshal is merely a ceremonial dignitary. The title of field-marshal however has become the highest in the British army.

These high destinies could not be suspected from the beginnings. The constable is merely the *comes stabuli,* companion of the stable or chief groom. The word marshal can be traced to old Teutonic where it means horse-servant.[26] To the present day the French call a farrier *maréchal-ferrant.* Europe and India thus supply us with a case of parallel evolution: the army-leader in both cases begins as a menial in the king's household, and ends by being a high office of state held by some great nobleman. That not seldom happens, for power goes to the man at headquarters. The king's servants rise with the king, and royal slaves have often become kings over the heads of noble governors of provinces.

As usual, the king's vassals copy his royal state. Every village headman in Fiji has his leader of the vanguard. In England

23. Round, 76 ff.
24. Round, 388.
25. Above p. 56.
26. *Oxford New English Dictionary,* s.vv. — Round, 371.

every battalion now has its bearer of the palladium, the some-time ensign, now less picturesquely called second lieutenant. We can now suggest the following pedigree of the office of army-leader:

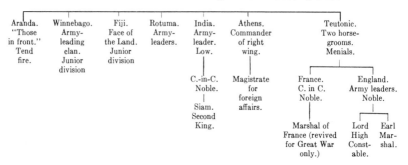

Custodian of the Palladium Going before the Moving Tribe

Aranda.	Winnebago.	Fiji.	Rotuma.	India.	Athens.	Teutonic.
"Those in front." Tend fire.	Army-leading clan. Junior division	Face of the Land. Junior division	Army-leaders.	Army-leader. Low.	Commander of right wing.	Two horse-grooms. Menials.
				C.-in-C. Noble.	Magistrate for foreign affairs.	France. C. in C. Noble. — England. Army leaders. Noble.
				Siam. Second King.		Marshal of France (revived for Great War only.) — Lord High Constable / Earl Marshal.

Wherever fire is of any importance for the attainment of welfare, it leads. The man in charge of it must be identified with it according to the fundamental principle of ritual. We have definite evidence that he was so identified in Ancient India; there is a suggestion of identity in our title ensign: we lack evidence elsewhere. In Fiji he impersonated the spirits. As usual, the object has gradually retired in favour of the function to which it gave rise, that of leading, later of commanding.

If there is an office which seems imposed upon society by what we men of the twentieth century recognize as utility, it is that of commander-in-chief. It would seem that the neces-sities of war must automatically bring him into existence, and so are sufficient to account for him. Yet we have seen that the institution is vastly older than the art of war. What use indeed can it be to peoples who have no wars, but only man-hunts, of which the object is not to subdue or destroy the enemy, but to kill at least one man as a sacrifice?[27] On the other hand it is very useful to have the ways purified, that is freed from death, before the advance. The sacred fire drives

27. Cp. *Progress of Man*, 271. Besides a small community can ill spare men to do staff work; they would be defeated by those tribes who put every man in the front.

away the demons as it goes forward. There must be someone to tend that fire. He is not chosen because he is doughtier than the rest, or more skilled in tactics, but because he is the hereditary proprietor of the god. His position demands greater courage and involves more risks. Doubtless an inadequate leader would be discarded, and the next best from the point of view of heredity put in his stead. For the rule of succession only tends to rigidity when an office is shorn of power like our kingship. Where it is a live one, enbued with power and responsibility, the rules of succession are tempered with expediency, sometimes by murder. Thus an office once created tends to select men of a certain stamp. In this way a post once assigned to the owner of the rites has in India passed into the hands of a class bred for war. In Europe it is theoretically any one who displays the greatest genius for the art of war, though that is seldom the practice.

The vanguard existed before its tactical advantages were known. By existing it gave opportunities to discover these advantages. Thus a non-tactical formation has developed into a tactical one. Those nations who, like the Greeks, the Romans, and ourselves, have been quickest to perceive its possibilities have thereby attained to an enormous military preponderance over those who have failed to do so, engrossed as they still are in the ideas that originally gave rise to the institution.

14· The Priest

*Zadok the priest and Nathan the prophet have
anointed him king.*
I Kings i, 45

ONE IMPORTANT principle of ritual we have not formulated
so far, though its consequences have already appeared; it is
that no man can perform the ritual for himself.

In Aranda initiation ceremonies the central personage is
very dependent on the good offices of others, even for services
he could easily do for himself, so far as physical possiblity
goes. Thus he may not just make himself a girdle and tie it
on himself: his father or some one qualified to play the father,
must provide it, and the mother's brother, or an equivalent,
must tie it on.[1] The conclusion of a ritual brings out most
clearly this differentiation of function. After the dance is complete, the performers take off their ornaments and present them to members of the other half of the community.
For the Arandas, like the Winnebagoes, are divided in
two.[2]

The Fijian principal cannot carry out the ritual for himself.
He just sits. The directions are given, the prayers and formulae
spoken, by another personage whom we have learnt to know
as the "Face of the Land." We have tried to express his duties
as those of a herald, or master of ceremonies, or better still
of a chief's priest.[3] His special province is the word; he is
the man who prays. Hence, next door to Fiji, in Tonga, he
is called *matapule*, from *mata*, face, and *pule*, to pray. In Fiji
we saw that the herald is identified with the sacred land, the
tumulus of the tribe, which is at once grave and temple-plinth.
So it is in Samoa: the heralds are there called *tulafale*, which
means "plinth of a house."[4] They are identified with the tumu-

---

1. Spencer and Gillen, *Native Tribes of Central Australia*, 75. — *Arunta*,
I, 181.
2. Strehlow, III, 1, 13 — Spencer and Gillen, *Northern Tribes of
Central Australia*, 290.
3. Above p. 106.
4. They are usually described as orators because they do all the talking;

lus on the familiar principle

worshipper = cult-object.

Passivity is always a handicap to the retention of power. In Fiji the chiefs have retained their power because warfare was a great passion, and the younger nobility was turbulent and flourished in war. If the first chief lost power therefore, it was not to the man who spoke, but to the man who acted. It was the war-chief therefore who was the high chief's serious rival. The herald enjoyed considerable prestige and might have considerable influence; but his prestige was that of the man who sat next to the chief, and was so closely associated with him that he alone of all the dignitaries might eat of the chief's leavings. He took a leading part in the election of the chief, and in his consecration. Sometimes he also buried him, though that duty often devolved on another official. The heralds were sometimes known to be the junior branch, while the chiefs represented the senior branch of the family. It was recognized that the duties of a herald were similar to those of a younger brother.[5]

The Samoans are fluent speakers, delighting in oratory, but an oratory which requires a very special training and tradition. A Samoan speech is not easy to follow, it is so full of an imagery that has to be learnt. The art is the speciality of the heralds, and as these speeches are more important and involved than in Fiji, so the heralds are more considerable people. On the other hand the nobility has lost much in influence owing to the perpetual feuds between rival claimants to titles. These rivalries placed great power in the hands of the heralds who awarded the titles,[6] who consecrated the chiefs, and who had to receive rich offerings in return; for it is another principle of ritual that it is reciprocal, that no man can receive the benefits of it without conferring some in return. The Samoan

---

but all these local terms obscure the fundamental identity: Fijian *mata ni vanua* = Tongan *matapule* = Samoan *tulafale*. — *Lau Islands*, 54. — C.J.Sc., I, 175 ff.

5. Hocart, *Fijian Heralds and Envoys*, J.R.A.I., 1903, 109.
6. Cp. our College of Heralds.

heralds have made full use of this principle. Hence in Samoa power has passed largely into the hands of the men who speak, especially those who are nobles as well as heralds:[7] they are the virtual rulers of Samoa. The insignia of the heralds are the fly-whisk, and the staff, on which they lean when they speak.

The triumph of the priesthood has been even more complete in India. The reason lies in the Indian character. It is not warlike as a whole, but it revels in speech.[8] The result is that the possessor of the word has by 800 B.C. attained to a power even greater than in Samoa. He is called a Brahman from *brahman,* prayer, mental worship, the ritual word generally. It is the name of a god, since the word is divine, like any other cult-object. The word has become so powerful that the priest has been able to assert his independence of the king. He consecrates the king and proclaims him to the people in these terms:— " 'This is your king, O Kurus (or whatever the name of the nation); Soma[9] is the king of us priests.' He makes this world tributary[10] to him, but exempts the priest; therefore the priest is not tributary, for he has Soma as king."[11] That is a very common device, to appeal from a real to an ideal king. It is very convenient, since, having no other mouthpiece than his prophets, God cannot contradict them. It is a device not peculiar to priests, but common to all those who seek to impose their ideas on the people. Some call the idea God; others call it Right, Justice, Conscience, Humanity: it all comes to the same thing.

The special insignia of the Indian priest is the staff, as the sword is the king's. One of the offices the priesthood holds is that of chaplain to the king, *purohita,* the Indians call it, that is "placed in front." The priest always goes before, he speaks the opening prayer, all ritual proceedings begin with

---

7. There are *ali'i tulafale* and *tulafale ali'i.*
8. The Indians were already scientific grammarians some 600 B.C.
9. The god and beverage of immortality.
10. *Adya,* lit. "eatable," that is "liable to provide food." This liability to feed or not is a marked feature of Fijian society. Above p. 181; below p. 211.
11. *Sat Br.,* V, 3, 3, 12.

the priestly god Agni.[12] The chaplain is the spiritual adviser: that gives great opportunities of power. Since the Indian king is essentially a sacrificer, his specialist in ritual procedure must inevitably become the most influential person in the kingdom: he directs the policy, since policy is to a great extent the application of rules laid down by the priest for the attainment of prosperity. The chaplain's opportunities are amusingly illustrated by one of the Buddhist birth stories.[13]

Once upon a time, when Brahmadatta reigned in Benares, his chaplain was tawny and had lost all his teeth. This chaplain's wife was carrying on an intrigue with another brahman of like physique. Since he could not break it, he resolved to destroy his rival, so he went to the king and told him the southern gate of his city was ill put together (that is without the correct rites) and was unlucky: it must be pulled down, and a new one built of lucky timbers after making a sacrifice under an auspicious constellation to the spirits that guarded the city; the victim must be a tawny toothless brahman of pure blood on both sides. The king agreed, but the fool could not refrain from boasting of it to his wife. She warned her leman, who escaped after spreading the news, so that all those who had the same peculiarities fled the city. Being the only one left who fulfilled the conditions the king's chaplain was seized for execution, but his pupil managed to secrete him away. Thus a chaplain could have public buildings pulled down and rivals executed, if he only was astute enough.

The state has need of welfare, and he who possesses the secret of welfare has the state in his hands. To cut a long story short the chaplain develops into a prime minister, keeper of the king's conscience, director of policy. To one of these priestly prime ministers is assigned a treatise on statecraft which in its cynicism anticipates Machiavelli.[14]

This prime minister is not to be confused with the executive

12. *Rgv.* I, 1. — *Ait. Br.*, I, 1.
13. *Jataka*, IV, 245 ff.
14. The *Arthasastra* of Kautilya. Much time has been wasted in discussions whether this is really the work of a prime minister of Asoka of that name. Who cares? The only thing that matters is the evidence it gives for the evolution of society.

king, as is so often done. The executive king is in India of royal blood. The prime minister belongs to the priestly, not the royal caste. He is the mouth, not the arm. Rather he steps into the place left vacant by the law king. As a specialist in the word he is the repository of tradition and custom, and it is from the brahmanical caste therefore that there issue those treatises on custom of which The Laws of Manu are the best known. Yet the position of the prime minister is somewhat different from that of a law king. As a subordinate he is lower than his sovereign; as a god he is higher. You can see him on the Indian stage, seated below the lofty throne where the king richly clad dominates the scene. Nevertheless the king pays obeisance to the chaplain who is the power *beneath the throne.*[15]

The pedigrees of some brahman families have been preserved: among them are descendants of younger brothers in royal families.[16] This is no doubt the general rule, for the chaplain of the gods is a cadet among the gods.[17] We have had the exception that proves the rule, the story of Devapi and Santanu, in which the younger brother becomes king and the elder his chaplain by a complete reversal of natural laws.[18]

When we turn to Greece our first impulse is to identify the *hiereus* with the Indian brahman, because he is attached to a temple, and conducts the worship, so we call him priest. But so are many other dignitaries in India who are not brahmans. In fact every head of a group conducts the ritual of that group. The brahman is merely the priest *par excellence,* because he holds the word.

In order to identify two offices, to trace their descent and kinship, to prove that they are homologues, we cannot be content with superficial resemblances, but must probe into the innermost structure. I have already suggested that the Greek equivalent of the brahman is the *kerux* or herald. Here is the comparative anatomy of brahman and herald:

15. Cp. Manu, XI, 32.
16. Muir, I, 227; 231 ff.
17. *Pancavimsa,* XVII, 11, 14, quoted by A. Weber, *Indische Studien,* X, 108.
18. Above p. 137.

BRAHMAN	KERUX
1. Agni = Hermes (p. 17).	1. Hermes = Agni (p. 17).
2. Hereditary.	2. Hereditary in Sparta, and in Eleusinian mysteries. Herodotos, VII, 134.
3. Speaks introductory prayer.	3. Speaks introductory prayer at an assembly before a host sets out. Thucydides, VI, 32. Plutarch, *Dion* 13.
4. Insignia a staff.	4. Carries a staff which in an assembly he places in the hands of a member to give him the speech.
5. Intermediary between gods and men, kings and men.	5. "Messenger of Zeus and men"; messenger of kings. *Iliad,* 1,320 f.
6. Man of peace, does not bear weapons but "speech is the sword of the brahman." Manu, XI, 33.	6. Peacemaker. *Iliad,* VII, 272 ff.
7. Inviolable. The killing of a brahman is the greatest sin. Manu, XI, 90.	7. Inviolable. Pausanias, I, 36, 3; III, 37, 6. His murder is expiated. Herodotos, VII, 133–136.
8. Carries out the sacrifice for the principal.	8. Assists the king at a sacrifice. Pours water over the hands. This function is distinctly more menial than in India. *Iliad,* III, 116 ff.; XVIII, 558; *Odyssey,* I, 146.

There are heralds not only in the state but in Eleusinian mysteries and at temples.[19]

The divergent evolution of brahman and *kerux* brings out the different character of the two peoples. The Greeks were never so interested in words as in thought and action; they did not make as good grammarians as the Indians, but more lucid thinkers. Their insatiable curiosity undermined tradition and revolutionized the ritual. Thus while the brahman was

19. Gilbert, I, 195. — Daremberg et Saglio, s.v. *praeco.*

mounting to superiority over the king, the herald was sinking from the honourable heredity which he still held in Homeric times, to the despised station of paid public crier.[20] Athens came very near to the spirit of the modern state.

In Jukunland we get right back once more to the ritual state, that is a state organized to woo prosperity by processes of a non-mechanical order.

It is a Jukun rule that "when a minister of a household cult offers a sacrifice, he must always be accompanied by others."[21] Thus even small family cults are not solitary, but more than one must take part (where two or three are gathered together, etc.). In the royal cult "the king is not himself the officiating priest of the public cults."[22] The chief priest in Kundi is drawn from a family which is descended in the male line from a former king, whereas the kings are descendants of his sister's son. He does not wear a gown round his neck, but binds his loins with a cloth; he does not wear a cap or straw hat, or mount a horse.[23] Unfortunately we hear no more of this particular chief priest. We are unable therefore to analyze him and see how far he may correspond to the Face-of the-Land, or the brahman; we must be content with a general idea of priestly functions as opposed to those of principal. From concrete cases it appears that the king or the chief, as in India, provides the offerings, while the priest offers them, makes libations, in short is the active partner. In Wukari there is a family of which the head elects the king and consecrates him, and "also instructs him in the ritual which must be observed by kings."[24] He is a teacher like the Indian chaplain. There are besides attendants who "as ministers of the god-man may be regarded as priests. . . . They are usually uterine relatives of the king or chief." The chief of one of them "pours libations on the chief's behalf over royal graves, or in front of the secret, sacred symbols which are the outward signs of the deities who are ever present with the chief." Another goes to fetch

20. Gilbert, I, 219.
21. Meek, 321.
22. Meek, 132.
23. Meek, 36.
24. Meek, 66; 135 ff.

water with a stick in his hand, the symbol of his office. Here too then the staff seems to be connected with priestly duties.[25]

The absolute power of a Jukun king "is curtailed by the necessity of living in accord with the priests of the more important cults. . . . A priest who has charge of the skull or hands of a former king has only to threaten to expose these sacred relics in order to compel the king to toe the line. The exposure of the relics would cause the king to sicken and die. To offend the priest is to offend the spirit or deified ancestor whom the priest represents, and if a drought ensues, the cause of the drought can be readily ascribed to the king's contempt of the priest of one or other of the innumerable cults."[26]

Levi was the third son of Jacob. The royal dignity did not fall to the descendants of the eldest, but to those of the fourth. This was however felt to be an anomaly and was explained as the effect of a curse on the eldest.[27] It is quite in accordance with the universal principles of ritual, that sin, which is ritual transgression, should disqualify from office. Do we not unfrock priests who break vows of chastity or purity?

The Levites lived not in a compact territory, but dispersed in townships. The point of this is not clear as long as we think of Judaism in its later form of extreme monotheism concentrated in one temple. We know however that in earlier times the Hebrews had local cults all over the country.[28] When there were local cults their services were required all over the country, so their residences had to be dotted all over it, even as the brahman, barber, washerman villages are in Ceylon.

Heredity has never been absolute, except in those offices that have ceased to function. As long as the principal or the acolyte is a real power, he has to be equal to his task. The standard may not be an exacting one, but there is a limit below which the rightful successor may not fall, or he is passed over. Let increasing stress be laid on personal qualities, and

25. Meek, 154 f.
26. Meek, 333 f. If power is curtailed it cannot be absolute. Absolute power has never existed: it is no more than a fiction put forward by those whose interests it would serve to make it a reality.
27. *Genesis*, XXIX, 32 ff.; XXXV, 22 ff.; XLIX.
28. E.g. *Genesis*, XXVIII, 18; XXXIII, 20; XXXV, 7.

an elective monarchy or priesthood results. Buddhism did so, and moreover made celibacy, which had been the exception,[29] into the rule. The Buddhist Church began as an anti-brahmanical movement. The final result was the usual one, that the Buddhist priests stepped into the shoes of the brahmans. They now conduct a ritual which is transparently brahmanic in origin, and stand in the same relation to the throne in Ceylon as the brahman in India. In Tibet their chief has supplanted the king, and is now law-king by title.

The Pope has all the insignia and pomp of royalty, and ranks above kings, even emperors. As in Tibet, the priest has become law-king, a development we may represent thus:—

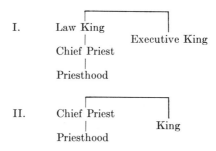

In England the Pope's authority has been abolished, and the king restored to theoretical headship of the ritual. Compulsory celibacy has also been abolished. The priesthood became a career for younger sons. Nobility and priesthood thus returned to their old relationship of senior and junior lines. Nevertheless the priesthood ranks ceremonially above the nobility, since the king has ceased to be the first of the nobles, and has been exalted into a caste by himself

It will be seen that the line of demarcation between king, especially law-king, and chief priest is a fluctuating one. They are easily confused.

29. E.g. Vestal virgins. — Meek, 280.

The official of Kundi whom Mr. Meek calls chief priest is known as "the *king* of the corn and rains." As in Fiji the head of every household conducts the household ritual. Thus the same man may act as priest in the royal consecration, and be principal in the cult of the family of which he is the head.

The same is true in India. The brahmans have special priestly gods, Agni, Brihaspati, Mitra; and are principals in their own cults. The priest has, like the king, to be consecrated into whatever rank he is to hold, and then he is principal. There is a consecration called *vajapeya*, in which either king or priest can be principal according as the object is to raise the one or the other to a higher rank.[30] On the other hand the brahmanic theory is that the king when sacrificing has, for the time being, a priestly character; for the royal weapons such as the sword, bow and arrow cannot encompass the sacrifice; only the priesthood can succeed with the weapons of the priesthood which are the potsherds, the winnowing basket, the black antelope skin, etc. "Therefore one of the royal caste when sacrificing, sets aside his own weapons, and with the weapons of the priesthood, in the form of a priest, becoming a priest, approaches the sacrifice."[31]

We can now understand how it is that Indian gods can worship one another, and make offerings to one another,[32] a practice so abhorrent to our ideas of divinity, with its rigid hierarchy. We must get rid of the late rigidity if we would understand earlier notions of divinity. Gods are not placed in a fixed order of superiority any more than men are: the leading part may be taken by different gods on different occasions.

The King of Ceylon had his own daily ritual; but he also used to act as priest for a greater king than himself, the Buddha.[33]

The medieval theory of the temporal king's part in the ritual was not unlike the brahmanic theory I have just quoted. When

30. *Sat. Br.*, V, I.
31. *Ait. Br.*, VII, 19.
32. Above p. 93.
33. *Temple of the Tooth*, 11.

the Pope delivered to the future Emperor the imperial raiments, he was supposed to make of him a priest; but the ecclesiastical theories tried to keep the emperor's sacerdotal rank as low as possible, fixing it at sub-deacon.[34]

We thus see how vain it is to try and define the terms "priest," "king," in fact any titles. You cannot define what is in a constant state of flux; priest passes into king, especially law-king, such as the Dalai Lama and the Pope, and king may be assimilated to priest. Nevertheless the two *functions* can generally be distinguished in full rituals, and the *personages* to whom they are severally assigned are fairly constant.

In India and in Greece the priest-herald represents the same sacrificial fire as does the army-leader, only in a different connection. He leads off all ritual and is the opener of ways. The Indian chaplain is in fact entitled "placed-in-front." We may conjecture that priest and army-leader are offshoots of the same office, that one has specialized in peace ritual, the other in the ritual that brings the tribe or nation into contact with strange peoples who follow other cults, or with strange lands not made prosperous by the correct rites. We may even suggest as a clue for further research, that one was originally the priest who opened the peaceful proceedings of the law-king, while the other preceded the executive king in his advance against the infidels. However that may be there seems to have a splitting up of an office in this manner:—

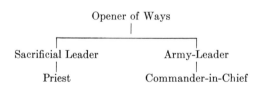

This is confirmed by the fact that in Fiji herald and army-leader are not always clearly distinguishable. The head of the "Border" in some tribes has duties which the herald fulfils elsewhere. In Natewa the herald and the chief of the Border, or leader of the van, are one and the same.

34. Bloch, 200 ff.

In Fiji fire plays no part whatever in the ritual, and it would seem then that this splitting up of the original office into two is older than the vogue of fire in the ritual. It would also follow that the connection of priest and fire is not the most fundamental part of his character; what is most permanent is his association with the staff and the word. He *is* the word, and it is as officer in charge of the word that he develops into the priest, the king's specialist in words.

The priesthood has followed the same course as other dignities. The priest begins by representing a thing. This representation gives him certain duties. In our state the duties alone are remembered; the original identity is forgotten; but fortunately it is preserved by others, such as the Indians.

Vassals copy the style of the king. They must have their chaplains, just as they must have their barbers, bakers, and so on. Thus the priesthood permeates the whole of society. Inevitably as its numbers increase, and the population also, all but the highest grades lose touch with the king. From being royal it becomes national, like our army, our navy, our parks, and so many other institutions. The higher ranks do however remain very much in touch with the throne, and in this respect the priesthood has been more fortunate than the crafts which have lost all royal or manorial connection.[35]

Like all other professions the priesthood has specialized more and more, and so branched off into cleric, judge, teacher. These different branches may become antagonistic to one another, as are priest and professor in our midst. In the East there is no such antagonism; there is not even much differentiation.

35. Dr. Perry points out to me that the connection survives in our "by appointment to H.M. the King," abroad "fournisseurs de la Cour."

15˙ The Revenue

The Lord loveth a cheerful giver.

THE OBJECT of the ritual is to make the macrocosm abound in the objects of men's desires. But the spirit of the macrocosm resides in the king, and so prosperity is to be attained by making that microcosm prosperous and bountiful. A poor king is a contradiction in terms. All nations like their kings to live in splendour, and to be liberal. We do so, we do not quite know why. It is a habit. Our kings are far away, and their liberality reaches but a small circle. Therefore many people seeing no advantage in monarchy would like to abolish it. That idea would not occur to a Fijian, because the chief is close to his people, and his liberality permeates the whole of the realm. Wealth flows in to him, but it flows out as rapidly. Meanness is a cardinal sin; and the chief who did not share used very properly to be knocked in the head, until we came on to the scene and allowed selfishness to be practised with impunity. "Of old," said a great nobleman to me, "the Lord of Nayau was as our father. If people wanted manufactured goods they went and begged of him." There were still chiefs who practised the old chiefly virtues, in spite of our individualistic gospel. The Chief of Mba drew a large income from a share in all rents. The people knew exactly when the rents were due, and they came one after the other with requests. One would come and squat down humbly inside the door. "What is it?" asked the chief. "It is I, Sir." "Well." "I have come, Sir. A small need of mine, Sir. I have no clothes, Sir. I have come to ask for a shilling, Sir, to buy a new cloth, Sir." Then the chief would, without rising from his mat, shuffle up to his box, take out a sovereign, and toss it carelessly to the applicant with the words, "Here is a shilling for you." That was the grand old manner, and it won the hearts of the people. The Fijians had not yet learnt the monstrous doctrine that a man can do what he likes with his own. In the old days when such a chief died men would come and gash themselves, saying, "This is the return for the food you gave me on such and such a day."

The Winnebagoes expected the same of their chief. "If any person came to borrow some object from him, he would tell the man that since he was without this particular thing, to keep it and use it for all time."[1]

Indian kingdoms had at an early period grown too big for the benefits of the king's wealth to be so directly felt. Yet they expected, and still expect of him a glittering pomp, and a life of pleasure. Buddhist scriptures describe with admiration a king as "foremost among those who enjoy pleasures."[2]

This splendour provides the hard-driven peasant with an escape from drab drudgery, giving him glimpses on which to build day dreams of tinselled glory. Our idealists may frame for him ingenious constitutions worked out from the first principles of the political philosophy prevailing at the time, but the people merely read into this new hocus-pocus their old conceptions of the state. I once presided at an election under such a paper constitution. It was in a village lost in the jungle. I was puzzled how the villagers would vote since they had not the vaguest notion what a vote meant. I asked the headman. "They will vote for X," he replied, "because he is the wealthiest of the candidates." They did.

Here the reader may think: "The king must be wealthy; therefore the people provide him with wealth. They do so by imposing taxes. It is all very simple, and we do not want any more complicated theory of the origin of taxes." Only we have undertaken not to guess, but to dissect the body politic, and to base our conclusions on the facts of its comparative anatomy.

To begin with, a Fijian chief is not provided for in that way. He has to get his wealth partly by sheer work. It was always insisted upon that to be a chief was hard work, because without work he could not feed the people and make gifts. At every turn he had to give: if they built him a house he had to make offerings in return, and, unless the offerings were

1. Radin, 209 f.
2. *Anguttara*, II, 17. — *Mhvs.*, XXXVII, 53.

lavish, he became unpopular, and might even be murdered. He alone might eat turtle, but every turtle took a bite out of his fields and his treasures: offerings had to be made to the fishermen on requesting them to go fishing, then on untying the rope round the turtle's neck, on setting up a turtle cage, on enlarging the cage: it was tipping all the way. There were no salaries, no share of rents, such as now come automatically to the chief, be he lazy or industrious. Instances were quoted of men who were too lazy to face the trouble and so had declined the proffered chieftainship. The chief's wives were another source of wealth; for they made bark-cloth, mats, oil, and they fished. Yet another source of wealth was wide connections. A nobleman who could trace his descent through the females to a subject village had influence in that village; he could commandeer their services, though, of course, they would get their own back by requesting favours. But the more kinship subject villages could claim with him the wider his influence, and influence brings wealth. A chief might be weak and poor if his connections were with foreign parts rather than inside his own dominions.

Prof. B. Malinowski has described a similar state of affairs in the Trobriands. The chief is apparently not provided with a revenue. His wealth depends mainly, if not entirely, on the number of subject districts represented among his wives. A man has a call on his wife's kinsmen: so the chief has a call on every part of his island from which he has taken a wife. The subjects evidently derive some benefit from the alliance, for they always see to it that they are represented in the harem.[3]

The Winnebago chief too depends much on his kinsmen. "All the relatives he has are to look after his possessions and keep him well supplied, for he was supposed to give away constantly."

Evidently the idea of providing the king with a revenue

3. *The Sexual Life of Savages,* (3rd ed., London, 1932), 110 ff. I regret that in my *Progress of Man,* in attempting to condense too much I described this work as "highly coloured," overlooking the bad connotation; all I meant was the amount of colour made it difficult to pick out the essential and very accurate facts.

in order that he spend it on the people who gave it him, is by no means as obvious as it seemed at first.[4] In fact put that way it seems rather absurd: why not keep it and spend it yourself? Exchange of gifts no doubt is psychologically more stimulating than selfish buying for oneself; but in order to make that psychological discovery you must have had experience of gifts. How did man get that experience, and how did revenue originate?

We must go back as usual to first principles, to the equation

principal = objective.

If the objective is food the performers cause it to multiply, so that they may have plenty to eat. It is part of the performance to eat the first instalment of that food. The principal is the first to partake. We have called this communion.

We have already seen how the Aranda headman partakes first of the animal or plant with which he is identified.[5] Unfortunately we do not know what happens in the case of artefacts. In addition to this portion at the ritual he is at all times entitled to a share of the young men's quarry. If an unmarried man kills a kangaroo, for instance, he must hand over the back half and the tail to his headman. It is only when he is married that he may retain it.[6]

There is no storing among the Arandas "except for a few days in preparation for a feast."[7]

In the Koryak whale ceremony the principal is an image, so the image eats first.

What will happen in cosmic rites? If we pin our faith to the logic of ritual, we shall expect that, since the king is everything, he will have a share of everything. And so it is.

When the crops mature in Fiji the first-fruits are brought to the gods at the temples and to the chief at Big House.

4. The Moslems seem to have arrived before us at this conception of taxes as a contribution. See Taha Hussein, *La Philosophie Politique d'Ibn Khaldoun* (Paris, 1918) 117.
5. Above p. 44.
6. Strehlow, IV, 2, 3. The reason why the married man can retain it cannot be discussed here. I hope some time to deal with it in a sequel on the family.
7. *Arunta*, 14.

Until that is done no one may eat. It is exactly the same principle as in Aranda-land, only the chief covers the whole ground, not one particular species. Whatever feast is held the chief gets the first share. If puddings are made, as soon as they are ready, one is taken to Big House as "tip of the oven." Then the feast as a whole is carried to the village green, and offered to the chief. He does not however retain it, but receives the first and best share, including the back of the pig, and certain "chiefly" fish, and the rest is distributed among the people. Ships were made for the chief, and there was much ceremony. On completion, the ship was offered up to the chief as he sat at kava by presenting him with the bailer in the same manner as any other offering, whether of food or of manufactured stuff. All these presentations were not pure gain: he had to make abundant gifts in return.[8] It is evident however that in the long run more comes in to the chief than goes out, since he lives in state and has the best of everything. However, the people get their reward in the shape of increased prosperity. The chieftainship braced the Fijians to greater efforts than they would endure for the sake of private gain. A Fijian will put his back into his work when striving to shine in the eyes of the great man. Personal devotion and love of display are two powerful incentives with him, the words "chief" and "state ceremonial" act like magic; and he understands enough about human nature to take full advantage of these traits.

Unfortunately the White Man had not the same understanding. The man who in his own country would have stoutly opposed any proposal to curtail the royal ceremonial looked upon it in Fiji as sheer waste. The pomp of his own country benefitted at most a few select shopkeepers and dazzled an infinitesimal portion of the population; in Fiji the whole people had the thrill of working for it, and of joining in the event. He could not see that; he could only see that it did not produce money or articles of export. He put the damper on the ceremonial, and thereby damped the enthusiasm which had sustained the people in their efforts. They were left without an aim in life beyond eating and drinking; they reduced their

8. Above, p. 108. — *Lau Islands,* 129.

output of work to fit the contracted aim; fields, ships, houses, everything dwindled with the dwindling pomp.

To return however to the olden times. The chief had another source of revenue worth mentioning, though a small one. When any one offended against the chief by insolence, or a breach of etiquette, he had to make a propitiatory offering just as he would to a god. It was said that sometimes a great man would refuse to put aside his anger until he had been offered what he coveted, perchance a young girl.

Fijian feasts are of two kinds, cooked and raw, and custom prescribes which should be used on each occasion. Cooked food has to be consumed without delay in the tropics. Of raw food some, like taro, does not keep; yams will keep for months; a live pig or woman indefinitely. Thus the yams could be put into store, the woman into the harem.[9] A certain reservoir could thus be created upon which the chief could draw to meet the many demands made upon him. Manufactured articles can be stored best of all. The chief did actually possess a "state basket" in which were kept valuable ornaments and whale's teeth. His wives also kept him supplied with mats and cloth. Thus he had the embryo of a treasury: offerings that came in did not go out at once, but formed a fund for use as occasion required, to present as tribute to a suzerain chief, to accompany a request for help against enemies, to reward workers, to offer to the relations of a dead man, or as counter-offerings for gifts presented in honour of his own dead, for weddings, and so on.

The Fijian term for the annual offerings to the chief has been used by the British Government to translate our word tax. It was rightly perceived that Fijian tribute and British taxation are akin. But it is a far cry from the Fijian system to ours. A tax is a compulsory national subscription to defray the cost of running the State. We no longer pay taxes to the king, but into a common fund, which was once the king's, but is so no longer, and from it are defrayed common expenses. Such a conception is fairly recent, and is foreign to most peoples who have not come under European influence. I doubt

9. E.g. *Lau Islands,* 129.

whether the Fijians have grasped it even now. I have heard them call the taxes we impose on them "the price of our bodies," in other words the ransom they pay for the right to live.

It makes little difference however whether the principle is understood or not; to understand taxation is not necessarily to like it. Taxation is unpopular. We pay our taxes as a duty, and bare duty is not inspiring. We pay them grudgingly, and would gladly omit them, if our consciences or our fear of the law allowed us. It is partly that they are now grinding: but even in moderation we do not like them. Tribute, on the contrary, was paid by the Fijians gladly. Perhaps we may understand why if we examine ourselves. We do not as a rule enjoy dropping money into a collecting box; we have to order ourselves to do it. The money leaps out of our pockets at a charity bazaar, where we combine pleasure with the satisfaction of doing good, and the approval of all concerned. A Fijian offering to the chief is even better than a charity bazaar: it combines a trip to town with glimpses of royalty, a display of food and manufactured articles, dances, a hearty meal, flirtations. Added to all this is the expression of loyalty to the father of the people, the hero-worship.

That hero-worship seems to be the main condition of willing giving, for people will go on paying without demur to a potentate so far removed that the payment cannot be the occasion of a festival. It may seem strange to us, with our utilitarian upbringing, that men should be willing to give to a distant great man, receiving nothing back in the shape of roads or other public services; yet object to taxing themselves for their own good; but the fact is they do. We are told that in the Roman Empire "the residents of a *civitas* were practically exempt from the payment of municipal taxes. Local taxation could not be introduced, because the tax was a sign of servitude. Rome could exact tribute, because she was mistress of the world, but for citizens of a municipality to pay taxes to a government which they themselves had established was out of harmony with their way of thinking."[10] Utility did not influ-

10. Abbot and Johnson, *Municipal Administration in the Roman Empire*, 138.

208

ence them, but only the pride which would submit to being taxed by the divine ruler of the world, but not by equals.

This personal element may explain why the Koryaks "were not on the whole opposed to the fur-tribute which they considered an offering to the Czar."[11]

I have been told the following story which illustrates the importance of the personal element. When the taxes were first imposed upon a certain Sudanese tribe none of the officials who collected them remained long enough to collect them twice. The people paid readily. Then came an official who stayed a second year. His second demand was refused. On inquiry they gave this reason: "We willingly made a gift to your predecessors, and to yourself. But now you come and ask for a second one. That is not fair." A gift to a great man seemed to them quite natural provided it was done in moderation.

The same type of offering seems to exist among the Jukuns as in Fiji. Thus if the king visits the house of a subject he receives from the householder the gift of a goat "to wipe out the footprints" of the king.[12] As in Fiji it is not all one-sided. There are occasions when the king makes gifts. Thus the new king, after he has been anointed with butter and honey, has to pay toll to the guards before he may enter the royal palace.[13]

At the great festival of Puje "every Jukun householder provides, as he is able, corn to be converted into beer and food for members of his household and his guests. He is expected also to send to the palace as many bundles of corn as he can spare in order that the king may be able to entertain the numerous visitors." This beer is a ritual beer, required for libations, and the very brewing of it is a ritual.

The chieftains of the king are entitled to similar perquisites. Thus a chieftain receives at harvest time "gifts of corn from the whole community, gifts which may be regarded as tithes

11. Jochelson, 12.
12. Meek, 129.
13. Meek, 134. It must be remembered Mr. Meek uses "household" of a group of houses with a common enclosure, a "compound" as they would call it in the East. It corresponds thus to the Fijian clan.

on the land paid to the gods and ancestors as landlords." Like a Fijian chief, he is entitled to first-fruits and a share of offerings for "he exacted tribute in kind, bundles of corn from all at harvest time, and gifts of beer on the occasion of any religious celebration. . . . He claimed a share of all major game-animals killed by hunters." He received gifts from persons seeking office.[14]

This system of first-fruits and tithes extends right down to the head of the household. He is in charge of the cult: his every meal, if he is an important head, is a ceremonial in which he begins by making an offering to the ancestors. He is therefore to the household what the king is to the nation. Now every meal cooked for the married men of the household is taken to him first, and he makes a point of eating from it before returning it to its owner. Thus he takes the first-fruits even as does the chieftain.[15] Mr. Meek gives an instance of a grown-up married man, who farms on his own account, yet "gives a small proportion of his crop to his father at harvest in recognition of his father's duty in providing the libations of the family cults."[16]

Thus the head of any cult, from the national head to that of the household, is entitled to first-fruits. He also receives contributions towards the sacrifices, naturally, since they are on behalf of all the people to bring prosperity to all.

Another source of the king's revenue was fines:— "He exacted a penalty of seven slaves from any household a member of which had been responsible for causing a virgin to be enceinte. He could sell into slavery all relatives of a person who had been guilty of witchcraft." As upholder of order in nature and society it is natural he should receive the atonements for breaches of that order.

The Egyptian god Amon declares that he has given the future queen "all life and satisfaction, all stability, all joy of heart . . . , *all offering and all bread.*" The potter god who fashions her repeats his instructions: "I have given to thee all health, all lands; I have given to thee all countries, all

14. Meek, 323, 333.
15. Meek, 293.
16. Meek, 104.

people; I have given to thee *all offerings,* all food."[17] Of course, all these things belong to her, since the king is everything, and this was a queen in her own right, like Queen Victoria.

The kings of Sparta were entitled to the following perquisites:— "On military expeditions they might use (for sacrifice) as many sheep as they wished, and of all the victims they received the skins and the backs."[18] So much for the military side. In addition the following are accorded to them. "If a public sacrifice is held, the kings are the first to sit down, and they are first to be served, receiving each twice as much as the other guests; and to them fall the first libation and the skins of the victims."[19]

The Greek word for a tax is *telos*. The fundamental meaning is end, completion. We cannot see how the idea of taxation can be derived from that meaning until we discover another sense, that of rite. A rite, such as a wedding, is a completion.

We saw that in Vedic India the various ranks of society paid tribute except the priests.[20] The word I there translated "tributary" means really "eatable." The lower orders supply the nobility with food. Considered from a ritual point of view, the third caste, that of the farmers, exists for that purpose, "The noble is an eater," says one text, "the yeomanry food." And again, "Whatever belongs to the yeomanry, the nobleman has a share in it."[21] The farmer is described as "another's tributary, another's food, to be oppressed at pleasure."[22] Now the word for tributary in this case is *balikrit*, literally, a provider of offerings. The term *bali* covers our words "oblation," "tribute," "tax." The Indian tax was then of the same nature as an offering of food to the gods or to birds.

We can now understand a curious episode in the history of British Ceylon. The fishermen used to pay a tithe of all their catch to the Government. The sentimentalists however would not leave well alone, but released the poor oppressed

---

17. Breasted, *Records,* II, 200–203.
18. The back as in Fiji.
19. Herodotos, VI, 56 f.
20. Above p. 192.
21. *Sat. Br.,* VI, 1, 2, 25; IX, 1, 1, 18.
22. *Ait. Br.,* VII, 29.

fisherman from this burden. But the poor fisherman was anxious to pay his tithe, and, since Government would not take it, he transferred it to the Church. The fishermen evidently looked upon the tithe as an offering which ensured prosperity. There are, or were, two institutions which gave prosperity to Ceylon, the Church and the State. If one withdrew, there remained the other.

As the sun comes increasingly to lord it over the world the Indian theory of revenue becomes solarized. "As the sun for eight months draws water with his beams, so let the king draw taxes,[23] for that is the function[24] of the sun." On the other hand "as Indra rains down for the four rainy months, so let the king rain down favours on his kingdom, carrying out the function of Indra."[25] This is no mere metaphor: the king is the Sun, he is Indra. In drawing taxes and in spending them he is merely carrying out the primeval principle of creative imitation, behaving as he wishes the departments of nature to behave. His showers, so far from being metaphorical, were enacted: on state occasions, the king showered precious stones on his subjects, seven or nine kinds is the consecrated number.[26]

This is no theory of compulsory subscription to a common fund for carrying out undertakings of public utility, but a theory of royal generosity copied from the generosity of sky and sun. A great deal of the wealth collected is lavished, not on social services, but on largesses, which, like the rain, fall indiscriminately on the good and the wicked; nor is it converted, as most of our revenue is, into a different form of wealth; it returns to the people in the form in which it came.

Part of it however does return in a different form as security; and a definite interdependence is recognized between taxes and public benefit. Manu makes the collection of revenue conditional on the king affording protection to his people. For, he argues, the king who gives security is performing the equivalent of a sacrifice; therefore he is deserving of worship.

23. *Kara* means both ray and tax.
24. *Vrata:* ordinance, religious duty, vow, etc. Function and duty are not yet distinguished in India.
25. Manu, IX, 304 f. In *Rgv.*, I, 57, 1 rain and generosity are equated.
26. *Jataka,* I, 387, cp. III, 311. — *Epigraphia Zeylanica,* II, 117 f.

(This does not seem to follow until we remember that the worshipper becomes the god.) By protecting his people he becomes entitled to a sixth share of the virtue of his people; by failing to do so he takes a sixth share of their sin. Therefore the king who receives tribute, taxes, tolls, presents and fines[27] from his subjects without affording them protection goes to hell.[28]

This reciprocity is no new feature: it is insisted on in Fiji; it lies at the basis of all offerings, since offerings are made with a view to benefits. Only in India this reciprocity has acquired a wider extension and a more definite mechanism than in Fiji. It is no longer a simple matter of redistributing the offerings, but of giving the people something in exchange, something different and intangible. The older process continues as a largesse, but the social services are beginning to crowd it out. In England we have gone still further: of the largesse there remains little beyond the Maundy money and a few such survivals.

There are other relics of the old taxation in our country, and, as in Ceylon, there are two bodies that receive it. But the State under the pressure of wars, of an increasing demand for a safe existence, of private greed and public extravagance, has increased its demands to an incredible degree, and has so transformed their character that taxes are hardly recognizable as the same in origin as the royal offerings. A Fijian chief gets the first and lion's share of any offerings brought by other communities, equal or vassal. Our duties on incoming goods have taken on an entirely new character: they are no longer a royal perquisite, but a commercial weapon; they do not enrich the king, but the merchant. We have here the whole spirit of the age.

The Church, as usual, more conservative, preserves the original dimensions and character more faithfully. First, there are voluntary offerings, such as there have always been, offerings in emergencies, rites carried out to obtain health for the sick, rain in times of drought, safety at sea, and also thanksgivings for all these benefits. Prevention however is better than cure,

27. *Bali, kara, sulka, pratibhoga.*
28. Manu, VIII, 303.

and it pays to make offerings regularly to insure against these calamities; and there is the future life to insure also. Besides this the Church has fixed assessments that are not voluntary: they are called tithes. As long as belief was unimpaired this burden was cheerfully borne. As disbelief spreads, the tithe comes to be looked upon more and more as an unjustifiable burden, because the farmer cannot see that he gets any benefit out of it: he no longer believes firmly that he is throwing his bread upon the waters and that it will come back to him. A financial depression heightens the sense of waste and extortion, and a tithe-war is the upshot.

Our whole treatment of such problems is thoroughly unpsychological. The human being is completely ignored. National and ecclesiastical revenues are now a matter of figures worked out with science, but without understanding. We have lost the secret, which many despised savages have preserved, of making it a joy to pay taxes. We have eliminated the personal element, and think ourselves mightily superior in that we have done so. It is that personal element which has been the success of monarchy in the past; and it is because it has lost that personal touch that it has disappeared from Europe; for the surviving monarchies are really hereditary republics as mechanized as the acknowledged republics. There is no one to whom one can give, and no one from whom one can receive: just a vast automatic machine into which the money must be dropped, and from which some may be returned. The modern state does not love a cheerful giver, nor produce a grateful receiver. Yet there is no sound basis for a revenue but a giving that is willing because it is sure of its reward and recognition.[29]

29. The barber-surgeon of a Delta village in Egypt receives from every person in the village 4 okes of wheat and 4 of maize twice-yearly. This is only custom, yet he says he has no difficulty in collecting it. Government taxes must have force behind them. An "advanced" institution does not necessarily function better than a "rude" one.

We grudge our income-tax but we subscribe willingly to jubilee and other funds on behalf of which monarchy makes a *personal* appeal.

16˙ Public Works

*And Solomon determined to build an house for
the name of the Lord, and an house for
his kingdom.*
II Chron., ii. 1

WHAT ARE the public works of an Aranda community? What we call economic activities seem to be left entirely to private arrangement. The public activities are ritual, that is they aim at promoting the life, the welfare, of the community by joining together in creative imitation. Public works are by consequence such as form a necessary part of that creative imitation: a shed representing the chrysalis of a grub,[1] a mound which is required for a snake ceremony,[2] a ditch, a ceremonial pole, all works of a very temporary description, and made specially for the ceremony.

The Winnebagoes have public works of a more permanent type. They have temples which, for some reason, it is the habit to call lodges.[3] They are places of ceremonial even as temples are. There are different kinds according to the rite: ceremonial lodges where the great ceremonies are held; sweat-lodges where ritual steaming takes place; menstrual lodges for the isolation of women during their periods. Unfortunately we have no details how the work of construction was initiated or organized. We are merely told that it was in the hands of the women, and that it does "not seem to have been restricted to any special class of women except in the construction of ceremonial lodges, in which only women who had passed their climacteric could participate." There are no revenue offices, no administrative buildings, no shops.

The same is true of Fiji: since they have no trade, apart from ritual exchanges, no roads, no police, no army or navy, nothing of what is implied in our word government, they require no buildings from which all these activities must be directed. Since every man is in direct touch with the soil and

1. Above p. 43.
2. Below p. 226.
3. This multiplication of terms is the curse of human history, for it obscures fundamental identities.

with the fish-teeming sea, there is no need of roads and other arteries of supply. The Fijian equivalent of our government is, as we saw, not concerned with directing what does not exist, but with organizing action to promote welfare. Public works are therefore connected entirely with that promotion of welfare which we have called ritual. The chief summons his people to build a temple, or his own house, he being a god; he orders his carpenters to cut a sacred canoe in honour of some deceased nobleman, and his lieutenant arranges for the people to supply food for the carpenters, and to prepare the feasts that mark each stage, from the cutting of the tree to the final launching. The chief's field is also planted by his people, or sometimes by half his people, the other half feeding those that do the work. Not until the advent of the European was a road made. It was made by a Tongan tyrant who had brought from missionized Tonga crude notions of European government. The workers however were not the people but prisoners of war. For the people to provide their own roads was out of the question.

Like the Fijian chief the Jukun king could command his people to till the royal fields and to repair the palace.[4]

In India the list of public works is longer because ritual has developed so, and has greater requirements. To temples and palaces are attached bathing pools, monasteries, alms-halls, hospitals, and other works of religious merit. He who is anxious that the rites conducive to prosperity should be duly performed must also provide the means and remove all obstacles. The renown of certain places of worship attracts pilgrims from afar, Kings of Celyon accordingly record it among their good deeds that they have made easier the ascent of Adam's Peak, that religious beacon of three religions, Buddhist, Hindu, Mohammedan.

The purely moral side (perhaps we should say individualistic side) has been very much developed by theoretic Buddhism. Doing good on one's own, regardless of social claims, is the chief way to salvation. The king's activities therefore tend to embrace anything that conduces to the interest of

4. Meek, 332.

his individual subjects, for instance roads as an avenue of commerce. The increasing size of the cities up to the twelfth century called for a public system of transport to feed the city population.

However moral and individualistic a religion may become it never completely loses its original character of a seeking after worldly and public prosperity. The king is responsible for the crops; he must keep them supplied with rain, or in default of rain, with running water. From early times therefore the king was connected with irrigation. Canals are among the works carried out for the kings of Egypt. "Labour ye for him," says a papyrus recording the benefactions of Ramses III, "labour ye for him as one man in every work; drag for him monuments, dig for him canals, do ye for him the work of your hands, that ye may enjoy his favour, in possession of his provision every day." The king of Egypt also digs a great well in the land of Ayan.[5] The kings of Ceylon, living in a country that was not irrigated by nature, devoted more labour to irrigation even than to temples. Both monastic lists and royal inscriptions enumerate the reservoirs they dug among the meritorious works of kings.

It would be an error to put such works in a category by themselves as "utilitarian" in opposition to "religious" works such as temples. Temples are just as utilitarian as dams and canals, since they are necessary to prosperity; dams and canals are as ritual as temples, since they are part of the same social system of seeking welfare. If *we* call reservoirs "utilitarian" it is because *we* believe in their efficacy; *we* do not call temples so because *we* do not believe in their efficacy for crops. What *we* think has nothing to do with matter, but only what the people we are studying think. It is true that reservoirs do not fit into the Buddhist system which is concerned with individual behavior: but they do fit into a much older theory of life, the cult of the cobra kings, water-deities which Buddhism has incorporated because its individualism could not displace the communal pursuit of fertility. The sluices of the great reservoirs of Ceylon were placed under the protection of these

5. Breasted, *Records*, IV, Nos. 412, 406.

cobra kings who were specially connected with the supply of waters.[6]

The Romans carried far what it is usual to call the secularization of public works. The phrase is unfortunate. It suggests that public works were taken out of one pre-existing compartment labelled "religion," and transferrred to another equally ancient compartment labelled "utility" or "reason." It would be more exact to say that a primitive undifferentiated quest of life, using indifferently every means at its disposal for securing life, has split up into various specialities: one relying on purely mechanical means, the other on mental action. This narrowing down of aims is unnatural if pushed beyond a certain point. Then collapse ensues. The Roman Empire collapsed like so many others before it, and for the same reason. The Middle Ages brought Europe back to a more primitive condition which it is customary to call barbarism, but which it would be more accurate to describe as an undifferentiated quest of life in which mechanism, art, soul-healing, etc., are not separated into mutually exclusive compartments. The organism is much smaller, and so does not require this differentiation.

When Medieval kings and feudal lords endow abbeys, church schools and colleges, they are blamed for mixing religion in all their doings, as if there were originally two separate elements, the civil and the religious; then men allowed the religous to get into the civil, as water gets into the wine. That is a complete reversal of the facts. The comparison is rather with a composite like air, which originally exists in a homogeneous and healthy mixture, but can be analyzed into its component elements, which are very little use alone, or even harmful. The church was not then, as it is now, a place where men go to be reverent once a week: it was the hub round which the quest of life revolved. There was not an agriculture and a religion, once separate, but which got entangled by accident. Agriculture and ritual were like the fresh milk before it has been separated into cream and skim. "The present age," says a leader in *The Times*, "is in the not ad-

6. Cp. Ph. Vogel, *Indian Serpent-Lore* (London, 1926), espec. chap. VI.

218

mirable position of having allowed its daily life to get out of touch with its religion, or its religion out of touch with its daily life." But there are plenty of survivals which point to a time when "the life of Nature and the operations of farm and garden were connected with the services of the Church . . . . The calendar of the Church was the calendar of the farmer, the labourer, the sportsman. They knew nothing of 'quarter-days': they knew of Lady Day, Midsummer Day (St. John Baptist), Michaelmas, and Christmas, which divided the year in four equal parts, each marked by its own particular farming operations. When 'parson's reading Genesis'—from January 2 onwards—was the time to sow broad beans, and Good Friday was the day to put in potatoes. For in those days the Church kept count of the seasons, marking them with her regular procession in the liturgy; and men and women . . . knew very well what psalms, what lessons, what epistles and gospels were to guide not their souls only but also their hands."[7] No wonder public works were dedicated to that which really mattered, life, while such accessories as rapid movement, museums, and schools were neglected.

As long as the tribute to kings and gods is mostly of a perishable nature it is impossible to accumulate a treasury sufficient to defray the cost of labour. Voluntary paid labour cannot exist; it must be compulsory; public works must be built by public work. We call such labour statute-labour; the French have a neater expression *corvée;* our army retains it under the name of fatigue. The Sinhalese call it "the king's work."[8]

We must not be misled by the word compulsory into imagining a kind of conscription. In a society like the Fijian there is no law defining the chief's right and threatening penalties against defaulters, because the idea of defaulting does not occur. Good breeding requires that the chief's wishes should be obeyed. They are obeyed as are those of the captain of a team, or of the committee of a club, because it would simply be bad form to refuse. Of course, there are men who do not play the game and cheat or slack, but that is low. Besides,

7. See a correspondence in *The Times,* beginning 14th August, 1933, on "The Countryman's Calendar." Leading article, 23rd August.
8. *Rajakariya.* Cp. Medieval *regale servitium.*

if the chief is good it is fun to obey. The thatching of his house will be a great event, what with the running to and fro, the passing up of the thatch, the shouting and singing, the competition in speed, and all the time a fine feast a-cooking. Rumours of its size will be circulating among the workers: the elders have assigned so many pigs and so many yams per clan, and the women have been fishing. Then, at the end of a busy and merry day the food-carriers file in, and the long-drawn out pleasure begins of seeing the food piled up, counted and recounted, proclaimed, leisurely divided. Trouble only arose if the requisitions for public labour were too frequent and interfered with cultivation, or if the chief were mean and did not warm up to the largesse as much as his subjects to the work. Then ca'canny would be resorted to. The British administration has abolished open disobedience, but it has provided a new weapon: the mean chief can be pilloried in the correspondence pages of the Native Gazette. One correspondent years ago complained that his people had been summoned to build the house of a chief or a nobleman. He let the workers see an ox, and let it be understood that it would be killed to feast them. Hence great enthusiasm. "Their souls waxed hot" over the work, and they sat down at the end with watering mouths. Alas! when they uncovered the pots there was nothing in them but rice, and not one piece of meat. Was not that a caddish trick?

The labour is not exactly a labour of love, for there is an eye on the reward; but it is willing; for it is not routine, and the reward is immediate. Something of this happy blend of compulsion and willingness was preserved in Ceylon of the first century B.C., if we are to credit the annalist. When the national hero, King Dutthagamani, began work on his colossal memorail to the Buddha, the Great Tope, "he announced, that no work was to be done on it unpaid. At each gate he had 16,000 pieces of money placed, very many garments, ornaments of various kinds, solid food together with drink, fragrant flowers, sugar, and so on, and the five perfumes for the mouth. 'When a man has done as much work as he wishes, let him take as much as he wishes,' he said. Those in the king's service accordingly distributed these. A certain monk wishing to join in the building of the tope brought a lump of clay prepared by himself to the site of the shrine, eluded those in the king's service and gave it to a mason. As the latter received it he detected it by its appearance. Then arose a hubbub." The matter was reported to the king. He outwitted the monk by getting an overseer to present him with three vases of jasmine flowers. The unsuspecting monk accepted, and so was paid for his labour.[9] The reason for this strange contest between a king who insisted on paying, and labourers who insisted on not being paid, was that the king wanted to keep all the merit of this great work to himself. Every brick laid free was so much transferred from his spiritual credit to another's. The people were equally eager to increase their credit balance of merit, theoretically for salvation, but what the people really want is health and progeny.[10] There is something to be said for a view of life which makes men so anxious to serve the public free.

This view of life is still at work. On pilgrimage days long files of humble villagers come up to buy bricks according to their means, and carry them up long flights of wooden steps to the bricklayers, in order to share in the merit of restoring the ruined tope of Dutthagamani.

The medieval villein rendered service in kind; but that service had lost all connection with the ritual, naturally, since the ritual is no longer the lord's, but belongs to the Church. The service consists mainly of work in the lord's field. "Let us take one out of a thousand examples. In the Abbot of Ramsey's manor of Stukeley in Huntingdonshire the services of a virgater are these:— From the 29th of September until the 29th June he must work two days a week, to wit on Monday and Wednesday; and on Friday he must plough with all the beasts of his team; but he has a holiday for a fortnight at Christmas and for a week at Easter and at Whitsuntide . . . Between the 29th of September and the 11th of November he must also plough and harrow half an acre for wheat, and for sowing that half-acre he must give of his own seed

9. *Mhvs.*, XXX, 21 ff.
10. Above p. 78.

the eighth part of a quarter. . . . : and on account of this seed he is excused a day's work. At Christmas he shall give three hens and a cock or four pence and at Easter ten eggs." Remember that the egg has from ancient times been connected with the creation, and still figures in our version of the old creation ritual, the festival of Easter. This payment of eggs is thus the relic of an Easter offering. We need not go into all the details of the services, but note that commonly "at harvest time there are also some 'boon days'; at the lord's petition or boon the tenant must bring all his hands to reap and carry the crop and on these days the lord often has to supply food; at Stukeley it is bread, beer and cheese on the first day, meat on the second, herrings on the third.[11] The medieval custom seems to have been much more one-sided than the Fijian.

In Lakemba it was sometimes arranged that the Northern half of the island should dig the chief's fields or build his house, while the Southern half fed the workers with a feast and made them the usual offerings of manufactured articles. In this custom we have a starting point for the commutation of labour into contributions of stuff or money. In Fiji it is not yet commutation, because the people are not divided into a small band of builders or tillers, and a vast mass who get off the corvee by contributing the pay of that small band. The division is part of that ritual dualism of society of which we have already had indications, and which we shall have to discuss systematically in chapter 20. Let that twofold divison of society break down, let whoever has the means cross over from the working side to the contributing side, and whoever cannot afford it join the workers regardless of territorial divisions; then we have commutation.

Increasing complexity of technique and increasing specialization gradually make statute-labour obsolete by driving out the amateur. Currency makes possible its disappearance. It allows each man to be credited with whatever labour he does for others, and to offer that credit to the state in lieu of labour. In the Middle Ages "we may see the process of commutation

11. Pollock and Maitland, I. 366 ff.

in all its various stages, from the stage in which the lord is beginning to take a penny or a halfpenny instead of each 'work' that in that particular year he does not happen to want, through the stage in which he habitually takes each year the same sum in respect of the same number of works but has expressly reserved to himself the power of exacting the works in kind, to the ultimate stage in which there is a distinct understanding that the tenant is to pay rent instead of doing work"[12] I have myself paid for some years my annual rupee in lieu of labor on the roads of Ceylon.

The change from statute-labour to payment is necessarily slow. The old system in its most primitive form was distinctly pleasant, and as long as conditions remained the same, there was no need to change it. The change is a necessary evil forced upon society by specialization. Sometimes it is forced upon one people by the advent of another which is highly specialized. The change may then be exceedingly rapid, because it is a choice between quick adaptation or extinction.

I was the witness of such a rapid adaptation in Fiji. The inhabitants of the Windward Islands had asked Government to establish a school, and had agreed to support it. The Government, obsessed with the idea that the Fijians are lazy, insisted that the people should support their school in the good old way by supplying food and free labour. Unfortunately it could only see one side of the good old way, the contributions and the labour; it forgot the compensations, the feasts and the gifts. Had it commandeered the labour and the yams by a special envoy bearing whale's teeth, had it awaited the freights of yams with feasts, with bales of cloth and mats, and with dances, had it fed the staute-labourers in chiefly wise, liberally, and with ceremony, had it done all this, all might have been well, and the change over might have been slow. As it was, it merely gave orders on foolscap, and expected to receive without giving. It did not realize that, so far from upholding the good old custom, it had carried out a revolution: it had substituted a one-sided take for a balance of give and take. The people wished to adapt themselves to this revolution.

12. *Ibid.*

They wanted to use those means of adaptation which the foreigner himself had introduced to them; that is they wanted to commute statute-labour and levies in kind into cash payments, into rates. They wished this because there was no alternative. The new statute-labour, as conceived by Government, might keep some of the form of the old public works, but none of the spirit; it abolished the old elasticity and reciprocity. The people wanted to compensate one change by another. They argued that during the time which they spent on collecting and transporting yams, or in working without pay, they could cut copra to a value far exceeding the value of their services. They could out of the proceeds pay school rates enough to feed the school and to pay hirelings, and still have money left over to buy bread, and butter, and tea, and some of the corrugated iron required to roof their houses. They could in this way save their society from the dislocation with which it was threatened by the tying down of their labour to unprofitable work; labour and commodities would continue to circulate with all the freedom of the old days. They resorted to the usual weapon of ca'canny, and won; for a determined people will always defeat the most autocratic ruler.

In Modern Egypt the *corvée* had become so unpopular that it could only be enforced by flogging. Yet it was often imposed for vital purposes, not merely for building the chief a fine house. "The people of Egypt could not live unless they were supplied with water to irrigate their fields. The water could not be placed on the fields unless the mud, which the rise of the Nile leaves at the bottom of the canals, was annually removed . . . But the majority of the people were blind to their own interests . . . They now learnt that they were not, under any circumstances, to be flogged. In that case, they said, we need not, and we will not remove the mud."[13] The Powers of Europe had to surrender to this fact, and the *corvée* was abolished, except for guarding the banks of the river during the floods. Yet these same people will repair their village mosque without any compulsion from government; in fact, the mosque might fall down for aught the government knows.

13. Lord Cromer, *Modern Egypt*, 408 ff.

So far is it from true that man acts always from calculations of interest. Political theories and experiments based on that assumption must end in nothing. The fact is that man is an animal so constructed as to react in certain ways to certain situations, even though he sees it means failure or death. Perhaps it is that some great scheme, in which he is only a pawn, sometimes requires that he shall fail or die.

17· Temples

And the blue sky my fretted dome shall be.
S. T. Coleridge

AMONG THE public works of the Australian Blacks we noticed a long mound which the Warramunga fashion for their snake cult. It represents a sandhill by the side of which the snake stood, and the body of the snake is drawn upon it.[1] We also noticed a long low hut which represents the chrysalis of the grub which is the objective, totem, if you prefer, of the Aranda grub cult, the dancers representing the grub itself.[2]

In the lodge built for the grizzly-bear dance of the Winnebagoes there was placed a mound of earth which "is supposed to represent a bear's cave, the four points of the cross representing the entrance to the cave, and the four lines running to the centre, the paths along which the grizzly-bear travels when he scents a man. The place in the middle is supposed to be the habitation of the bear himself."[3] In the dance, as usual, "the dancers are supposed to imitate the motions and the cries of the grizzly-bear." They will take tobacco from the mound. "They believe that they are representing the bears when they do this."

Thus in specific rites, besides having a representation of the objective or god, they may also provide a representation of its abode. The sea, the abode of the whale is represented, for instance, in the Koryak whale festival.[4] We have seen that cosmic rites do not change the fundamental features and principles of ritual. We shall expect then to find in them also an abode of the god. But the god in this case is a spirit of the sky, of the earth, or of the whole universe; therefore his abode will be the sky, or the earth, or the whole universe. So it is.

The Pawnees adjoin the Sioux to the South, but speak a

1. Spencer and Gillen, *Northern Tribes of Central Australia*, 234 ff.
2. Id., *Native Tribes of North. Aust.*, 76; *Arunta*, I, 151.
3. Radin, 347.
4. Above, p. 52.

different language. One of their great ceremonial leaders informs us that for the great Hako ritual a dwelling is necessary. "Such a place is necessary for all ceremonies. We are now to set aside a place where we shall put the sacred articles we are to prepare and make it holy. We are not thinking of the holy place where we shall lay the sacred articles, but we think of all that holy place will mean. It will represent the place where new life will be given. . . . The earth lodge with its domeshaped roof is likened to the stretch of land bounded by the horizon and roofed by the dome of the sky . . . the sacred fire must come in a place set apart for it. . . . We make the fire in the centre of the lodge where all within can share its benefits."[5] If the lodge is the world it follows the fire is in the centre of the world.

At a later stage of the Hako ritual the priest draws a cricle which he explains thus:— "The circle represents a nest, and is drawn by the toe because the eagle builds its nest with its claws. Although we are imitating the bird making its nest, there is another meaning to the action; we are thinking of Tira'wa making the world for the people to live in. If you go on a high hill and look around, you will see the sky touching the earth on every side, and within this circular enclosure the people live. So the circles we have made are not only nests, but they also represent the circle Tira'wa atius has made for the dwelling place of all the people. The circle also stands for the kinship group, the clan, and the tribe. The down represents the light clouds near the dwelling place of Tira'wa—the dome of the sky over the dwelling place of the people—and it stands for the protection of Tira'wa. When there is no down to be had, white ashes may be used."[6] Here then

circle = nest = world = community.

It is clear that the Winnebagoes share the Pawnee view; for the posts "were always painted blue to symbolize the day."[7]

The Fijians are not much given to explore the foundations

5. *Hako,* 33 f.
6. *Hako,* 243 f.
7. Radin, 105.

of their customs. Everything is simple, even their thought. In regard to their temples we only know this much, that the chief is called "the prosperity of the land," and it is consistent with this, that, in Vanua Levu at least, the sacred plot or mound where the god abides is called "The Land," as if it were a condensation of all the land. In Tonga the king is the sky, and so is his tomb.

The roof of a cosmic temple is the sky. In the Gilbert Islands the sky is a roof. "The Gilbert navigator regards the night-sky as a vast roof . . . His whole terminology of the skies follows consistently upon this fundamental idea. He calls the eastern horizon *te tatanga ni mainiku* (the roof-plate of the east), and the western, in a similar manner, *te tatanga ni maeao* (the roof-plate of the west). The meridian is *te taubuki*, the ridge-pole." So the whole conception is worked out in detail. "The navigator sits in imagination beneath this immense framework, upon which the stars themselves form the ever-shifting thatch. It is by reference to the purlins that he expresses the altitude of a heavenly body above the horizon, while the rafters afford him a rough measure of declination."[8]

The sacred mound in Vedic ritual is the universe, the bottom of it is the earth, the top the sky, and the intervening part the atmosphere.[9] I have discussed the matter at length in my *Kingship,* chapter XIV. The full theory is stated in one of the latest ritual books, but it evidently was already in existence at the time *Rigveda* I,164,35 was composed: "This altar is the furthest border of the earth, the sacrifice the navel of the world." In I,59,2 the sacrificial fire is the navel of the earth. When the theory of elements came into vogue this parts of the mound were each identified with an element. This "elemental tope" reached Japan.[10] To the present day when they build a fasting hall[11] in Siam "they seal up in the foundations

8. Arthur Grimble, *Gilbertese Astronomy,* Journ. Polynesian Soc., 1931, 197.
9. *Sat. Br.,* XIII, 8, 1, 17; 5, 2, 2; 1, 1, 13. Cp. VII, 5, 1, 1 ff.
10. James Troup, *On the Japanese Sotoba,* Journ. Roy. Asiatic Soc. 1919, 137. — Rémusat et Klaproth, *The Pilgrimage of Fa-Hian,* (Calcutta, 1848), 92.
11. *Uposathaghara.*

a spherical stone which symbolizes the world."[12] I have seen
Buddhist pictures of the God Sakra (the same as Indra) cast-
ing out the Giants from heaven: Heaven is just the upper
storey of a wooden palace. Thus the world is a house, and
the god's house is the world. These pictures are popular pictures. The Buddhists of Ceylon crown their colossal topes with
the figure of a sun to each of the four quarters, and above
that place the abode of the gods.[13] Canopies inlaid with stars
were held over royal persons in life and in death. These were
sometimes called sky-canopies.[14] In the Indian world too

mound or temple = world.

The same holds good in Persia. Porphyry[15] tells us that
"Zoroaster first constructed among the hills near to Persia
a natural cave flowery and provided with springs, to the honour
of Mithra, creator and father of all. The cave bore the likeness
of the universe which Mithra created, and the things inside
according to their proportional distances bore symbols of the
cosmic elements and regions. After this man Zoroaster, it became the custom among others also to confer the initiation
by means of caves, whether natural or built." The Parsees
of Bombay preserve to the present day the cosmic temple
of Zoroaster. In their temples "the fire-room is built as a dome,
recalling the dome of heaven."[16] I have seen a cave such as
Porphyry decribes. It is at Attanagala near Colombo, and recently restored. The roof is painted with a cloudy sky, the
sun and the moon, and under it a Sinhalese legend is represented. In this case the cosmic theory has probably degener-
ated into a mere play of fancy.

Plutarch tells us:— "Numa is said to have built the temple
of Vesta in circular form as protection for the inextinguishable
fire, copying, not the figure of the earth as being Vesta, but

12. L. Fournereau, *Le Sian Ancien* (Ann. du Musée Guimet, XXVII
& XXXI), I, 101.
13. *Mhvs.*, XXXVI, 65.
14. *Jataka*, I, 57; cp. 178. — *Thupavamsa*, 21. — *Daladasirita*, p. 56,
par. 5, *ahasvitana*. Cp. French *ciel-de-lit*.
15. *De Antro Nympharum*, 6.
16. *Zend-Avesta*, I, 61.

of the whole universe, as centre of which the Pythagoreans believe fire to be established, and this they call Hestia and the monad."[17] The ancient, like the modern historians always wanted to trace everything to a definite man and place, thinking they had explained a custom by assigning it to some creator. They forgot to explain how the idea had got into the head of this genius. *Ex nihilo nihil fit.* The cosmic temple is much older than Pythagoras; it never began, but gradually grew out of something that was there before.

In the life of Romulus, 11, Plutarch informs us that "a circular ditch as dug round what is now the Comitium, and first-fruits of all which are by custom used as being good, or by nature as necessities,[18] were placed therein. And finally they brought a little portion of earth, each from his land of origin, and threw it in and mixed it all together. They call this pit the same name as the seat of of the gods, namely *mundus.*" This word means both world and the sacred pit, and is sufficient in itself to attest that the Romans looked upon this sanctum as a miniature of the world.

The Egyptian temple "was built in the semblance of the world such as the Egyptians knew it. . . . The pavement, of course, represented the earth. . . . The roof, vaulted in Abydos, flat everywhere else, answered exactly to the idea they had of the sky. Each received a decoration appropriated to its meaning." For the minute consistency with which the idea was carried out I refer the reader to Mr. G. Maspero's description of which I have only quoted the gist.[19]

The rationalizing historian can, of course, point to the dome of Ste. Marie in Brussels, all studded on the outside with stars; or to the high vault of New York Central Station twinkling at night with electric stars, and ask triumphantly: "Will you maintain that these architectural heavens are anything but a play of fancy, but pure art?" Certainly, modern buildings may imitate the heavens with no further purpose than to

17. *Numa*, 11. Cp. Dionysius Halicarnassensis, *Ant. Rom.* II, 66.
18. The ancients knew the distinction of instinct and intelligence, or congenital and acquired, only they used different expressions.
19. *L'Archéologie Egyptienne* (Paris, 1887), 88; English trls. (1895) 90; — Cp. J. Capart, *Egyptian Art* (London, 1923), 107.

please; but we have no right to conclude that it was always so. Numerous cases have been produced of utilitarian designs degenerating into ornament, but the reverse process has yet to be found. As utilitarian I should certainly reckon a design that is part of a scheme to secure life.

Our present age may look upon a dome as nothing more than a pleasing design; but earlier, in the Byzantine churches, "the fixity of the scheme followed from its close association with the rite. Each part of the church had its own significance, with which its decoration was brought into accord. The central dome represents the heavens. At the summit is Christ, Pantokrator. . . While the *dome* and the *bema* represent the suprasensible, the remainder of the church stands for the sensible world . . . . The pendentives, by which dome is joined to the arches beneath, have the Evangelists, whose word joins earth and heaven." And so on with much detail which I omit, "The principles are constant from the eleventh century and are those followed by the writers of the Painters' Guides. Nothing is admitted to a chief place which has no relation to the ritual."[20]

In the thirteenth century William Durandus, a Provencal, "begins his *Rationale de Divinis Officiis* with the chapter on the church building, and thus shows with deliberate intention that an understanding for the Christian liturgy, for the innermost and intimate life of the Church is not possible without a complete explanation of the place in which the liturgy takes place, and to which it is bound as the soul to the body."[21] Let us go to the fountain head, to Durandus himself:— "Our first task is to consider the church and its parts. It must be noted that of the churches one is material, the one to wit in which the divine offices are celebrated; the other is spiritual, being the congregation of the faithful, that is the people assembled by its ministers. . . . For as the material church is built of stones joined together, so also the spiritual one is joined together out of various men. . . . The material church

20. O. M. Dalton, *East Christian Art* (Oxford, 1925), 243 f.
21. Joseph Sauer, *Symbolik des Kirchengebäudes und seiner Ausstattung in der Auffassung des Mittelalters* (Freiburg i/B, 1902), 106. Cp. my preface to *The Temple of the Tooth*.

typifies the spiritual as will be explained in the section on its consecration. Again the Church is called in Greek catholic, that is universal, because it is set up or spread over the whole world." Then again:— "The material church in which the people meet to praise God, signifies the Church which is built in the heavens of living stones."[22] Then Durandus proceeds to carry out his symbolism with a minuteness and a subtlety which soon palls on the plain common-sense of the unspecialized layman. It is too much the work of a specialist absorbed in his one thesis and ready to force the facts into it.

The old symbolism still plays a part in discussions of ecclesiastical architecture. In a recent newspaper correspondence on the position of the organ and rood in a cathedral the general standpoint was modern, that is aesthetic; but one divine contended:—"In Gothic churches the *pulpitum* was meant to be surmounted by a great Rood and not primarily by an organ. . . . The mystical meaning of the interior arrangement of the church thus became explicit: the nave represents this present life, the chancel Heaven, and the Rood, towering above the partition between proclaimed that only through the saving Death of Christ can man pass to his perfect consummation and bliss, both of body and soul."[23]

This symbolism is not a popular idea at the present day. It never was, if by popular we mean that it was discovered by the people. All theories are conceived and worked out by thinkers; the only question is whether those thinkers are in touch with the people and so able to lead them, or whether they are so specialized that their ideas die with them. A theory can only be called popular in the sense that it affects the life of the people at large, as opposed to one which falls on the rock and never germinates. Much of Durandus is of the latter kind, but the fundamental equation

temple = world

22. Guilelmus Durandus, *Rationale Divinorum Officiorum* (Naples, 1859), chap. I, paras. 1; 2; 9. — Translation by J. M. Neale and B. Webb as *The Symbolism of Churches and Church Ornaments*, Leeds, 1843.
23. N. P. Williams, *The Times*, 23rd July, 1932. I am indebted to him and to Mr. H. G. Richardson for references to medieval literature.

has, as we have seen, influenced the architecture of peoples from Europe to America, and so has every right to be called popular. It can also claim a remote antiquity since it is common to peoples of such widely different types of culture.

In the form in which it appears in St. Paul, as

$$\text{congregation} = \text{God}$$

it has had effects on the body politic. "The idea of the Church as the mystical body of Christ has had an important influence on the growth of the law of corporations."[24] We can recognize it in the theory that the dean and the chapter are as man and wife; "the chapter is *covert* by the dean as the wife is *coverte* by her husband."[25] For Christ is the spirit and the Church is the body, and so are husband and wife.[26]

"You said at the beginning," a critic may object, "that in cosmic rites

$$\text{principal} = \text{universe.}$$

You now say

$$\text{shrine} = \text{universe.}$$

Therefore

$$\text{principal} = \text{shrine.}$$

This is too absurd."

Absurd or not the inference is drawn.

At the very outset we saw that in all rituals there may be more than one thing equivalent to another, and in particular it may happen that

$$\text{shrine} = \text{principal} = \text{objective (god or totem).}$$

To refresh our memories I will quote further passages from the brahmanic books. On the one hand we have such statements as that "the fire altar is these worlds (earth, air, sky)";

24. Pollock and Maitland, I, 495.
25. *Ibid.*, 491.
26. Cp. *Kingship*, 106 ff. — Anatole France, *Le Lys Rouge*, ch. XXIII (new ed. p. 276). — Jeremiah, III.

and on the other hand we are told that the altar is the sacrificer's "divine self," as opposed to his "human self," viz. his body. It is not due to the liturgist getting lost in his equivalences and forgetting what he had said before, for in two successive verses we are shown how the altar and its ritual can be equated on the one hand to the world, on the other hand to the man.[27] Actually the altar is constructed in the shape of a bird, not of a man.[28]

A similar view of the mound seems to have been held by the Winnebagoes or their predecessors in their land: for in their territory are found mounds, some shaped like men, others like birds and other animals.[29]

St. Paul gave the idea what is called a "mystical" turn, or, it is more likely, accepted a current mysticism:— "Know ye not that ye are a temple of God, and that the Spirit of God dwelleth in you? If any man destroyeth the temple of God him shall God destroy, for the temple of God is holy, which temple ye are." And again:— "Or know ye not that your body is a temple of the Holy Ghost, which is in you, which ye have from God?"[30] Durandus agrees:— "Verily, Man, if he has an altar, a table, a candlestick, and an ark, is the temple of God. . . . The altar is our heart, etc."[31]

The Pawnees are hardly less elaborate than Durandus in the instructions of their creator to their Adam and Eve:— "I will now show you how to build a lodge, so that you will not be cold or get wet from rain. Go and get timber. Cut ten forked sticks and set them in a circle. Cut some poles to lay across the forks. Four of the upright forks must form a parallelogram, with the longest sides extending east and west. The posts that are set in the ground to uphold the lodge

---

27. *Sat. Br.*, VII, 3, 1, 13; IX, 3, 4, 12; X, 1, 2, 2 f. — "As large as the Vedi (altar), so large is the earth," *Sat. Br.*, III, 7, 2, 1. — Cp. M. A. Canney, *The Magico-Religious Significance of Sand*, Journ. Manchester Egyptian and Or. Soc. XIX, p. 40. Also his *The Primordial Mound*, ibid. XX, 25.
28. *Sat. Br.*, VIII, 1, 4, 8 f.
29. Radin, 94 f.
30. I *Cor.*, III, 16; VI, 19.
31. *Rationale*, II, 6.

represent the four gods who hold up the heavens in the north-east, northwest, southwest, and southeast. There are minor gods between these, with powers that connect the power of one god to another. There is also an outer circle of many gods, and you shall cut poles to represent them; their power extends from one god to another. The south side of the lodge will be for the men, for the men will be strong, and so they must be on the right. The north side shall be for the women, for they are not as strong as the men and so must be on the left. The entrance of the lodge shall always face the east, for the lodge that you are to build shall breathe as if human. Five posts are on the south side, representing the five branches of man, two legs, two arms and head. The five forks at the north stand for the five branches of the woman. You shall net willows together. These shall be thrown upon the east side of the posts that stand for the gods in the heavens. These netted willows represent the ribs of the gods that the posts represent. When the lodge is complete, dig in the centre for the fire-place and I will give you fire-sticks so that you can make your fire. These fire sticks belong to the sun."[32]

The analogy of body and temple is carried out in the Hako ceremony, for they paint a child with various colours which represent the dawn, the sky, "dwelling place of" the mighty power. "The lines forming an arch across the forehead and down each cheek of the child represents the dome of the sky, the abode of" the mighty power. "The line from the middle of the forehead, the centre of the arch, down the ridge is the breath of Tirawa'atius. It descends from the zenith down the nose to the heart, giving life to the child."[33] In other words the child becomes the dwelling of the Pawnee Holy Ghost, and this is achieved by painting a dome on his face. The chief difference between St. Paul and the Pawnee is that we *are* temples by birth, but the Pawnee child has to be *made* into a temple. That is one of the most fundamental differences between Christianity and most religions, that Christians are

32. George A. Dorsey, *The Pawnee Mythology*, (Carnegie Institution, Washington, 1906), Part I, 14.
33. *Hako*, 227 f.

born with souls and immortality: others have to acquire them. Hence the ritual has become superfluous in the eyes of many Christians, since it no longer does anything.

The Pawnees did not adopt this equation *man* = *temple* just to satisfy a mystic longing, but for the severely practical purpose of obtaining life. Every step in the applying of red paint, for instance, brings nearer "the coming of the new day, the rising sun, the vigour of life."

Since temple and man are interchangeable they are treated alike in the ritual. They are consecrated in the same manner. Another way of putting it is that either can be principal in the ritual.

The brahmanic altar is baptized and anointed with ghee even as a man is.[34] Moses was bidden to make "an holy anointing oil" and to "anoint therewith the tent of meeting, and the ark of testimony."[35]

Durandus invokes this as a precedent for consecrating the church, and proceeds to expound the rites in detail. They are made up of the same episodes as the consecration of a human being: circumambulation, baptism with holy water. Durandus is well aware of the identity. First he compares the consecration of the temple to the sacrament of marriage, "It suggests at once the betrothal of the Church, and of the faithful soul. For a house not consecrated is like a virgin promised to some man, but not yet endowed nor united in the union of the flesh by the commerce of wedlock; but in the consecration it is endowed, and is changed into the proper spouse of Jesus Christ." Then again he compares it with baptism.[36]

In Fiji beneath all the variations of rituals we always recognize the same fundamental structure. Unfortunately we know next to nothing about the consecration of their temples; but what we do know is not peculiar to them. Human victims are slain and eaten just as for the consecration or funeral of a chief.

The consecration of a ceremonial lodge of the Pawnees re-

34. *Sat. Br.*, III, 5, 1, 35; 2, 4 ff.; 11 ff.
35. *Exodus*, VI, 1.
36. *Rationale* VI.

duces itself to circumambulation outside and inside and then a ceremonial smoking.[37] Tobacco smoking has become the cardinal feature of North American ritual; it overshadows, or even supersedes, the lustration, the unction, and the liquid or solid communion of other peoples, for it has the advantages of all.

The short and the long is that all rituals are but one at bottom, variations of a simple theme according to the particular object in view.

The temple building has had the same career as the personages in the ritual, naturally since it is merely, like them, an abode of the god. It begins by being the abode of a thing, and derives its characteristics from that thing, so far as is compatible with the laws of gravity.[38] The function however acquires an ever greater voice in determining the form, till few of us now think of the temple as a replica of the world, but all think of it as a place for worship.

37. *Hako*, 97 ff.
38. *Progress of Man*, pp. 38 f., chap. VI.

18· Idols

*Plus ça change, plus c'est toujours la
même chose.*

THE MOST important cult-object of the Arandas is called
tjurunga. It is made of wood or stone, is cigar-shaped, only
flat, covered with designs which allude to myths concerning
the divine ancestors. Some small wooden ones have a hole at
one end for a string by which they are whirled to produce
a loud hum. These are the bull-roarers so famous once among
anthropologists, more for their strangeness than for any light
they have shed on the history of thought. "The bodies of
the totemic forefathers," says Strehlow, "are supposed to have
changed into such *tjurunga*. . . . The *tjurunga* passes as the
common body of the man and of his totemic ancestor. But
it also connects him with his totem itself. . . . If the *tjurunga*
is rubbed with fat and red ochre, creative forces go forth from
it, which work upon the totem." "Each man has two bodies,
one of flesh and blood, and one of stone or wood." Carried
in battle a *tjurunga* gives a man strength. The Blacks are very
definite that the *tjurunga* is not the seat of the soul or life.[1]

These amulets are kept in caves close to the camp in charge
of the headman. The Arandas recognize these caves as their
equivalent of the Christian church, and they are right.

The Fijians have cult-objects about the nature and workings
of which they hold very precise views. A man may possess
a club in which there resides a spirit. Such a club he will
call the *mbure,* that is temple, of the spirit. He makes no distinction then between an idol and a temple: they are both
dwellings of the spirit. I was once myself the owner of such
a shrine, besides being a shrine myself. I was initiated into
the banned cult of the "Children of Water." A kava ceremony
was held according to ancient rites revised. A libation of kava
was poured out for the Twins, the chief deities of the cult.
Then we all drank in turn. Then a spirit embarked on one

1. Strehlow, IV, 2, 5. — *Arunta*, 227.

238

of us, and he began to quake, his eyes rolled up, and he cried out, "It is I! It is I!" "I" being no longer the man of flesh and blood, but the familiar spirit speaking through his mouth. I tried hard to be possessed, but never succeeded in working up a fit. However the medium professed to be satisfied, and declared that "The-Tunderbolt-crashes" had embarked upon me, and would be my guardian spirit. Then he took my ebony staff and anointed it with kava so that it should become the shrine of "The-Thunderbolt-crashes." Thus I can truly say that my stick and I were embodiments of the same spirit, and so functionally equivalent.

In the New Georgian group of the Solomon Islands the ceremonial has died out, and shell money is used to house the spirits of the dead. Those spirits were also housed in their own skulls, or in default of that in an upright stone, a kind of diminutive menhir, very rarely in an image of human form.

In the snake-clan feast of the Winnebagoes "shortly before the feast begins the host takes out a bundle containing four skins—a yellow-snake skin, a rattlesnake skin, a blowsnake skin, and a bull-snake skin. In honour of these he gives his feast and makes his offerings."[2]

Among the cosmic symbols of their Hako ceremony the Pawnees have two feathered stems, one male, one female. One part of the female is painted with blue "the colour of the sky"; a groove in it is painted red: "This groove is the path along which the spirits of all the things that are to be put upon this stick of ash may travel as they go forth to give their help during the ceremony." The rest is painted green which represents vegetation, "the covering of mother-earth." Thus this stem represents the world, yet only one half of it: the night, the moon, the north, and stands for kindness and helpfulness. "It is the mother." The other stem is "the male, the day, the sun, and the south"; "it is inclined to war to hurt some one."[3] Thus each side represents one side of nature, corresponding more or less to the two sides represented by the two kings.[4] Together they make up the whole world. Thus

2. Radin, 325.
3. *Hako*, 38 ff.
4. Above chap. 9.

in a cosmic rite the cult-object, as well as the temple, represents the world. This is inevitable since it is an *alter ego* of the principal.

To the Jukuns "the physical body of a man is known as *adi,* and when it is born into the world it is accompanied by a separate spiritual individuality known as the *dindî.*" Some neighbours of the Jukuns prepare figures of the dead so that the *dindî* may enter them; "but among the Jukuns rounded stones, pieces of old corn-rubbers as a rule, are used instead of figures. In some Jukun communities, however, the *dindî* of the dead chiefs are believed to reside in the wooden images which represent them, or in the skull, hand, or other part of the body, which has been preserved. In all cases where material objects are used in shrines as emblems of deity the objects are considered sacred, because they are regarded as embodying the *dindî* of the deity."[5]

We referred in the first chapter to the Koryak fire-board.[6] It is the most important among the images in the shrine attached to the house on its left side. It is the deity of the household fire, the guardian of the family hearth. It is roughly shaped like a man, "It is adorned with a collar made of sedge-grass which is used in all sacrifices. This collar serves the charm in lieu of clothing. It is 'fed' from time to time by smearing its mouth with fat." It is called "father": as usual the ancestor is the god. Like a human being it is clothed and anointed. The figure is very crude in spite of the fact that the Koryaks can produce quite good carvings. Compared with these the "images of their anthropomorphic 'guardians' appear like the products of a backward tribe." It is not lack of skill then, but some unknown reason for not letting their idols be too like the human form.[7]

We saw that the Indian fire-altar is supposed to represent a man. Besides that they place inside the altar a gold man. This gold man is, like the altar, identified with the Fire-god, Agni, on the one hand, and with the sacrificer on the other.

5. Meek, 202.
6. Above p. 21.
7. Jochelson, 565 f., 33 f.

"He is made of gold, for gold is light, and fire is light; gold is Life (*amrita*) and fire is Life."[8] Such a gold man was found in excavations at Taxila, and I saw one by the kindness of Sir John Marshall. It is a tiny gold sheet cut out in the semblance of a man, roughly like the Koryak fire-board.

Like the Koryak fire-board, the Indian altar is merely the most important among cult-objects. The bunch of sacrificial grass (corresponding to the Koryak sedge-grass), the sticks planted round the altar, the ladle, even the verses that are sung, are all "forms of the sacrament."[9] That is they are material presentations of the sacrifice, just as the *tjurunga* of the Aranda is a material presentation of the god (so-called totem), and, like it, is the common body of the god and the man. Thus the sacrificial grass is both the god Indra and the sacrificer himself.[10] Most of these 'forms' make no attempt to imitate the human shape. It is not till later that objects shaped like men or animals, especially like men, become favourites.

When and where and how these images of man originated it is premature to speculate. A special faculty called anthropomorphism has been invented to account for them. Why not then invent a theriomorphic faculty? an astromorphic, a pyromorphic, a potamomorphic one to fit each case, and finally an ananthropomorphic one for cases where there is definite avoidance of the human form? The human form is but one particular device among many, and many peoples, such as the Fijians, do not think of it. They find their clubs quite as effective.

The human image appears as early as the Upper Palaeolithic.[11] It is impossible to account for those figures except as having a ritual purpose; for Upper Palaeolithic Man could draw animals with wonderful truth and life; but of man himself he has produced mere indications, or even grotesque caricatures; exaggerations that suggest he was avoiding the true human form, even as the Koryaks appear to be doing.

8. *Sat. Br.*, VII, 4, 1, 15.
9. *Sat. Br.*, IX,, 5, 1, 48.
10. *Sat. Br.*, I, 8, 3, 11; III, 4, 1, 17. — C.J.Sc., 1, 139.
11. Marcellin Boule, *Fossil Men*, 298 ff.

In periods covered by records we do not meet with more and more images as we travel backwards in time, but quite the contrary. Herodotos[12] says of the Persians, "It is not their custom to set up images and shrines and altars, but they impute folly to those who do, because, I take it, they do not, like the Greeks, believe the gods to be of human form." India is now a stronghold of idolatry, but it was the Hellenistic school that introduced in the first century A.D. the figure of the Buddha which became an object of worship. Before that his image was left out of set purpose, and his presence indicated by non-human symbols such as a tope, a sacred tree, a foot-print. Some Indian tribes are still without idols. Buddhism carried the worship of images to Tibet, where it now flourishes, to China and to Japan. Now let us turn westward. Varro declares that the ancient Romans had served the gods more than 170 years without images.[13] They had to import their types. Tacitus and Caesar comment on the absence of idols among the Kelts and the Germans.

The area in which idols came into real vogue (I do not say originated), and where accuracy in rendering the human figure was first really striven after, can be narrowed down to the Eastern Mediterranean. It is to the Mediterranean peoples they always seem to have appealed most, even to the present day; but it is also that race that has bred the fiercest opponents of idols, possibly because excess produces reaction.

Even where idols of human form are most popular however, they do not seem to occupy the first place in the affections of the people. The image of the Buddha in Ceylon ranks a long way after the sacred tree, the sacred tooth, and the tope. The Hindus are far more addicted to images, yet the phallus is the commonest symbol of Siva. In Southern Europe the images usually gravitate round the Host.

It is not natural then for man to represent his gods in human form. In fact the difficulty is to explain how he came to do so. I do not offer to solve the problem. This much seems certain, the vogue of human idols grew with man's conceit of

---

12. I, 131.
13. In St. Augustine, *De Civitate Dei*, IV, 31.

himself as the lord of creation, tending to reject all kinship between himself and brutes.

However popular the human form may have become it has never been sufficient to make a statue into an idol. Nor is the material any more sufficient, or both combined. Whether he use gold, or bronze, or wood, the form of man, or beast or plant, the sculptor can never produce more than a statue. To make of the statue an idol it is necessary to consecrate it. "Before the Eyes are made," says Knox,[14] "it is not accounted a God, but a lump of ordinary Metal, and thrown about the shop with no more regard than anything else. . . . The Eyes being formed it is thenceforward a God. And then . . . it is dedicated by Solemnities and Sacrifices." We see the reason in William Ward's account how a Hindu statue is turned into a god. The evening before the consecration of a statue of Kali, "the person at whose temple this image is to be set up, brings together twenty-two different things. . . . With all these the officiating *bramhûn* touches the forehead and other parts of the image, repeating *muntrus*. This is called *udhivasu*, or inviting the goddess to enter the image and receive worship. The next day the business of giving to the clay eyes and a soul comes on. . . . No one reverences the image till this work is done." Ward also describes the rite of "breath-giving": "The officiating bramhun touches with the two fore-fingers of his right hand the breast, the two cheeks, the eyes, and the forehead of the image. When he touches these places he says, 'Let the soul of Doorga long continue in happiness in this image.'"[15] The Cambodian ceremony, which is allied to the Indian, begins by sprinkling the statue with water; then water is poured on its head. Next the critical ceremony of the opening of the eyes is performed. The Commandments are recited. Children representing the gods come and sit down before it, just as court dignitaries representing the gods attend the king at his consecration. The

14. Robert Knox, *An Historical Relation of Ceylon*, 82. (The references are to the pagination of the edition of 1681, which is given in the margin of the reprint of 1911, London).

15. *Account of the Writings, Religion and Manners of the Hindoos* (London, 1811), IV, 125; 364.

fight which the king wages with the demons is here represented by the placing of candles on the altar, accompanied by the recital of Buddha's victory over the Devil.[16]

At the British Museum are to be seen idols from the Belgian Congo which have been coated with clay to bring them to life.

This process of giving life to a statue is alluded to in Revelation XIII, 13 ff.: "And he had power to give life unto the image of the beast, that the image of the beast should both speak, and cause that as many as would not worship the image of the beast should be killed."

All these rites differ only in the degree of complication, not in principle, from the Fijian consecration of a staff or club.

We can now see how unfair are the continual gibes of the iconoclasts that idolaters worship stocks and stones. "He planteth a fir tree," says Isaiah XLIV, 99 ff., "and the rain doth nourish it. He burneth part thereof in the fire; with part thereof he eateth flesh. . . . And the residue thereof he maketh a god, even his graven image." The apocryphal Epistle to Jeremy is one long tirade upon this theme. Christian Fathers repeat the same arguments in different words. It is all very unfair, but typical of the rationalists of all ages. No one ever worshipped the material; only the life that has been fixed in it by the consecration. The image is only reverenced for the power that abides in it.[17]

Of that we have had ample evidence. We may therefore be content here with one more witness. "It must be again emphasized," says Mr. G. T. Basden, "that no object is itself worshipped by the Ibos; it is sacred only as the habitation of a spirit. It has only that relative sanctity to which it is entitled as the shrine or home of a certain spirit. Very seldom are the objects themselves called upon by name; the petitions are invariably addressed to the Igaw-maw, i.e., the spirits."[18]
Mr. Jeffreys fully endorses this view from his own experience.

---

16. A. Leclère, *Cambodge: Fêtes Civiles et Religieuses*, (Paris, 1917), 374.
17. Cp. Apuleius, *Asclepius*, 23-4.
18. *Among the Ibos of Nigeria* (London, 1921), 218.

Idols, he says, "are not worshipped in themselves . . . though prayers appear to be addressed to them when these cult objects are in use."

After all this is fundamental to all rituals, even to all religions, except a few highly abstract and dying ones, which have been reduced to the contemplation of a sublime idea. The aim of all *practical* religions, those that count, is to bestow life on matter so that it may benefit the community. Even the Quakers, those most consistent of anti-ritualists, await the coming of the spirit to rest on individuals for the spiritual vivification of the community. There is no difference anywhere in the principle. There are variations in aims, whether the life is conceived as vigour to win in battle, or success in cultivation, or recovery from lowered vitality, or mental health. Yet it is not these essentials that men quarrel about, but the seeming unessentials such as the form of the vehicle, whether man or animal, image or aniconic symbol, or complete absence of anything material. Why have they quarrelled so violently on these details? To answer that question we must rapidly review the most notable of those quarrels.

Akhenaten, king of Egypt about 1375 B.C., is the first champion (of whom we have any record) to enter the lists against the worship of images and against local cults. For a multitude of gods in human, semi-human, or bestial form he substituted a single symbol of a single god, "the splendour which is in the disc of the sun" represented by the solar disc with rays ending in hands. These hands hold various symbols including that of life. Akhenaten has, on account of his monotheism, been acclaimed as the "first individual in history," the first to think for himself, and to free himself from the priestly yoke. As a matter of fact Akhenaten was anything but the friend of freedom. The despotic tendencies of his religion are clearly indicated in his hymns: "There is no other that knoweth Thee, save thy son Akhenaten." Under Akhenaten, says an admirer, "the theological theory of the state is simply that the king receives the world that he may deliver it to the god. . . . Thus theological thinking is brought into close and sensitive relationship with political conditions. . . . It can be no accident that the notion of a practically universal god arose in Egypt at the moment when he was receiving universal tribute from the world of that day."[19] In other words the king is the sole exponent of the Supreme God's will. The truth is that this king's heresy was merely the culminating point of the concentration of all life, and so all power, in the person of the king.

Iconoclasm and centralization went hand in hand in Palestine. Local idols meant power dispersed; a central cult in Jerusalem meant power concentrated at headquarters. We now know that the centralizers pursued their aim with no more regard for truth than any political faction of the present day. They are said to have emended and expurgated the ancient records so that it should appear their faith was the original one, and polytheism a degeneration. The Hebrew rationalists ignored everything in the ancient records that did not fit in with their conception of the rational man. Fortunately for us they accidently left in hints of image worship in ancient Palestine; for instance, the brazen serpent.[20]

The Early Christians were opposed to the cult of idols. It is perhaps more than a coincidence that their first imperial convert, Constantine, tried to arrest the process of decentralization begun by the pagan Diocletian; and that after him the return to decentralization and to images went on side by side. For as Christianity spread from the cities to the country it weakened in its hostility to images. Like all parties it reintroduced what it had destroyed, only under another name: it substituted the word image for idol. "An image is the semblance and impression of things that are and subsist. But an idol is the figment of things that are not, and do not subsist."[21] Thus the iconoclastic principle was surrendered. All objection was waived to the worship of images as such, but only in so far as they represented beings that do not exist. Of course, no one worships beings he does not believe in. A further distinction was made that, if images and crosses are placed in Christian churches, it is not that they are regarded as gods, but as mementoes. The implication is that in idols it is the

19. Breasted, *History*, 359.
20. Cp. *Myth and Ritual*, ed. S. H. Hooke, Oxford, 1933.
21. Vacant, s.v. *Images*, VII, 789.

statue that is worshipped. This, we saw, is quite an unfair presentation of the case: the idol is merely a carrier of divinity.

By the eighth century everything was as it had been before in the Byzantine Empire. Again the attack upon images was led by the centralizing Emperor Leo III, and carried on with greater animosity by his son, Constantine Kopronymous "who was an apt pupil of his father in the lessons of autocratic government and the assumption of imperial supremacy in ecclesiastical affairs."[22] Bury's portrait of him may be quoted, for he recalls Akhenaten by his fanaticism, and is typical of the iconoclast in all ages. He "won the reputation of being addicted to free theological speculation. He forbade the prefixion of the epithet saint to the names of men; he would not permit anyone to speak of St. Peter, but only the apostle Peter. He bantered his courtiers unsparingly when they displayed traits of superstition or an inclination to practise austerities, which he deemed unjustified by reason. If one of his nobles slipped and fell in his presence and happened to employ such an expression as 'Virgin, help me,' he was exposed to the Emperor's smiles or sneers."

Iconoclasm came later to the West, just at the time when autocracy was rising on the ruins of Feudalism. A renewed attack on idols was later made by the atheists of the French Revolution who proclaimed France "one and indivisible," and who prepared the way for the extreme centralization of their country. For atheism is but the left wing of monotheism.

In order to understand the past we should never miss an opportunity of observing the present. About 1912 the age-long conflict between rationalism and polytheism was being waged in Fiji, and is perhaps still being waged beneath the surface. Nominally the Fijians were free to choose their own religion, but in practice heathenism was banned, for it was linked with nationalism. Methodism meant allegiance to a single God who was in the hands of the European, both as regards doctrine and administration of the Church. It was a loyal religion. The cult of the Children of Water meant that every man had

22. J. B. Bury, *A History of the Later Roman Empire from Arcadius to Irene* (London, 1887), 461.

his own tutelary spirit to which he looked for earthly prosperity. If tolerated it would have meant also the revival of all the local cults, the spiritual autonomy of Fiji, and an attempt to translate it into temporal independence.[23] The worship of numerous spirits housed in sticks or clubs, and domiciled in Fiji, was incompatible with the centralized rule of the Colonial Office.

How much idolatry can divide the Neapolitans will show. During an epidemic of cholera "all the hundreds of churches of Naples were open the whole night, ablaze with votive candles and thronged with people. All their hundreds of Madonnas and saints were hard at work night and day to visit the dying in their respective quarters. Woe to them if they ventured to appear in the quarter of one of their rivals! Even the venerable Madonna della Colera who had saved the city in the terrible epidemic of 1834, had been hissed a few days before at Bianchi Novi." Do not extol to an inhabitant of Anacapri the patron saint of Capri: "As to his miracles you could count them on the top of your fingers, while San Antonio, the patron saint of Anacapri, had done over a hundred."[24]

The struggle between idolaters and iconoclasts is then at bottom a struggle between local autonomists and centralizers. The idol begins by representing things and persons, and as things and persons have their individuality, so have their cults. As the world absorbs its constituents, the idol comes to represent the world, or rather the Lord of the World. From being the animating principle of the world it is but an easy step to becoming its guiding principle, one might almost say its functioning. The idol then becomes superfluous, in fact hampering, since it directs the mind to the thing and away from the abstract function. It is therefore either done away with entirely or survives only as a symbol, which is often a geometric figure like the cross, swastika, or triangle, in order to

23. I published a native essay on this heathen revival in the *Hibbert Journal* X1 (1912), 85. Since then the second part of the essay has come into my hand in which the nationalistic sentiments are more outspoken.

24. Axel Munthe, *The Story of San Michele*, chaps. VIII & I.

avoid all concrete suggestion. The prayer-niche of a mosque has ceased to represent anything at all; it has nothing left but a function, which is that of indicating the direction of Mecca.[25] When this stage is reached all the cults are standardized, since there are no local habitations and names. Under these conditions a few can dictate the religion of millions, because it is mass-produced with no regard for local needs and traditions. You cannot standardize the ideas without standardizing the behaviour. Centralization of cult thus always goes with centralization in the state.

25. Prof. K. A. C. Creswell informs me it is now definitely established that the concave *mihrab* is by origin the Christian apse received with reluctance by Islam. The Byzantine apse helped to give direction, but it was still representative.

19· The City

Zion, City of our God.
Hymn A. & M.

WE HAVE seen that king, priest, animal, tree, corpse, idol, all represent things it is desired to control. So do the temples and palaces in which these cult-objects or principals are housed. So does the city in which stand the temples and palaces: it is sacred in the same sense as they are, that is they are equivalent to that on which the life of the people depends. Only the city never stands for anything specific; it is never less than the whole world, and its parts are the parts of the world, not this or that species.

That is indeed the purpose which has brought cities into existence, though not the one which has caused the modern state to retain them in spite of all their drawbacks. The modern state must have villages, towns, cities, because it must have centres of distribution and coordination; but it would be a mistake to refer this function back to the origin of cities. In many communities there is no need for any centre of distribution because there is very little to distribute or coordinate; nevertheless such people congregate into cities, or what has all the characters of a city, though we may not call it so. They do not congregate so for the same reason as we do now. Then are we to suppose that it is inherent in human nature to shun isolation and to live in villages and towns? Facts do not bear this out. Many peoples, even highly evolved ones, prefer to live each on his own land, notably the Channel Islanders, except for a few towns, most of our farmers, and the Sinhalese.

It is not manual work that concentrates men into villages: the Fijian prefers the inconvenience of living away from his fields to that of being remote from the centre of chiefly doings. We, on the contrary, balance the advantages of the periphery, with its green grass and trees, against those of living at the centre over office or workshop, and choose the first.

Population first condenses round the centre of ritual, not round shops. In the West of England they talk of "church towns," not of "shop towns," although church towns are shopping towns, because the church is the primary fact. Ritual is vastly older than shops; even kings are. On the other hand, the true centre of a highly specialized nation like ours is the Exchange, not Buckingham Palace, because transport and distribution have become vital in an overcrowded country, and so they determine everything. Administration and play have broken away more recently than trade from kingship, and still have their centres near the palace, in Whitehall and in Piccadilly.[1]

The condensation round a headman is called a village, if it is stationary, a camp, if mobile. Round a king or a cathedral it is called a city. In ancient India there is the *pura* in which the king resides; anything outside it is a *grama*.[2]

In Eddystone the chief is not the centre of a cult. Feasts are not brought to him, and he does not hold daily court with chieftains. There are gods and they are tribal; but they do not figure in the routine of life. They are only resorted to when the crops fail and there is famine in the land. There is no constant worship of gods, visible or invisible, to keep the people in close contact with chief or central shrine. Therefore there are no clans and no compact villages. The cults that punctuate the year, that intervene on all the common occasions of sickness, of fishing, hunting of man or beast, are family cults addressed to the spirits of deceased father, mother, or other kinsfolk dwelling in their skull-house beside the hamlet.[3]

Our authorities are not quite agreed as to the shape of an Aranda camp: Spencer makes it round; Strehlow makes the married men's camp oblong with the long axis east and west; east of it lies the camp of mateless men, and west of it that

1. The palace is still the play centre for a set that is nothing more than a survival.
2. In Ceylon they distinguish the *nuvara* (Skt. *nagara*) and the *gama*.
3. I am describing the state of affairs before the advent of the White Man. Now there is peace the people have moved down from their hillsides to the shore, leaving their skull-houses behind.

of mateless women. Both agree that the camp is divided in two: east and west according to Strehlow, north-west and south-east according to Spencer.[4] Residence is not a matter of choice, but of descent. The two halves do not however form different classes of society, for the whole camp is one big family, and all its members are related. An individual finds in his own side his paternal relations, his mother's relations on the other. Each side is again divided into two, making altogether four divisions which Strehlow places N-E, S-E, S-W, N-W, but Spencer, N, E, S, W. Membership of these subdivisions is also decided by descent.

The camp of the Loritjas, westerly neighbours of the Arandas, completely reverses the positions, turning the whole camp married and mateless, east to west.[5]

At a great annual festival a fire is lit at each of the four cardinal points.[6]

A Winnebago village is circular. According to one account it is divided exactly like the two halves of an Aranda camp, only the orientation is N-E and S-W. So the members of the senior division say. The junior division draws a plan in which this twofold division is obscured. We lack the clue which would help us to reconcile these apparently conflicting statements, though I feel sure they would be reconciled if we only knew more. However that may be the senior division is split up into four, the junior into two, each of which seems to be divided into two and again into two.[7] The number four plays a very important part in Winnebago ritual.

The Ponka divide their camping circle into two, East and West; but both moieties are again divided into two, making four quarters, as among the Aranda, not three. These quarters are necessarily orientated N-E, S-E, S-W, N-W, and are called respectively Fire, Wind-makers, Earth, Water.[8] From which it would appear that the American Indians subscribe to the

4. *Arunta*, 500.
5. Strehlow, IV, 2, 12.
6. Strehlow, IV, 1, 42.
7. Radin, 321. — Hocart, *Winnebago Dichotomy*, Man, 1933, 169.
8. J. O. Dorsey, *Siouan Sociology*, 15th Annual Report, B.A.E., 1893/4, pp. 230 ff.

doctrine of four elements. This must then be far older than the Greeks, unless we suppose the Greek theory found its way to America.

The Omaha camp is also circular and in that circle each clan has its fixed position according to the point of the compass.[9] On the one side are the sky-people, on the other the earth-people, so that the whole makes up the world. It is so also among the Winnebagoes.

We possess a detailed description of what an Indian city should be like somewhere about the 3rd century B.C.[10] It is attributed to a brahman; but there are ancient sites and modern cities enough to show that his plan was not pure priestly fantasy, but was actually put into practice.[11] The author allows the king's citadel to be "round, long, or square." In practice the square seems to have been the commonest. There is one main street running north and south, and one main street east and west, so that they form a cross, and there is a gate at each of the cardinal points. The rule is there should be three "king's streets" each way, making six in all with three gates on each side, or a total of twelve. Outside each gate was a "gate-village," or suburb.

Local usage varied considerably as regards orientation; but orientation there must be. In India the king's palace usually faces East, as the residence of the god should do. In Kandy, Ceylon, it actually faces West, but then so does the adjoining Temple of the Tooth. The palace is either in the centre or in the eastern quarter; Kautilya places it north of the centre. He assigns the royal caste to the East, the mercantile to the South, the artisans to the West, and the priests to the North. The city was sacred, and therefore outcastes were not allowed to reside within, but occupied the suburbs or hamlets beyond. The cemetery lay outside the city, which is not the place for death, but for life, for the gods, as represented by the king, the priests, and the idols. The site has been carefully chosen

9. *Omaha*, 42; 58.
10. Kautilya, book II, chaps. 3 f.
11. I have discussed the archaeological evidence in *C.J.Sc.*, I, 150; II, 86.

as one occupied by deities that make it lucky.[12] The gates
are sacred, as we saw in the story of the tawny brahman:
they are repositories of welfare.[13] It is true the artisans, who
represent the Giants, powers of darkness, are assigned a place
within the city, but on the other hand they are required in
certain episodes of the ritual, and they represent gods as well
as Giants.[14] They have a very different status from that of
the outcastes: they are respected members of the community,
holding court offices, and in this way are able to enjoy considerable influence at court. As attendants on a god the gate-
keeper, the charioteer, and the rest are not mere menials, but
men of consequence.[15]

The square city or citadel is to be traced across Farther
India to China. The forbidden city of Peking is a square city
with four gates facing the four cardinal points. A wide paved
strip runs through the centre from south to north: along this
are placed the halls of ceremony in a row, "The southern
half of the Forbidden City was designed for great ceremonials,
when the Son of Heaven received his officials in state, and
the northern half was used for the daily interviews at dawn,
when ministers in constant communication with His Majesty
entered by the north gate." The entrance to the inner quad-
rangle is called "Gate of the Sun at its Zenith." "Upon the
solemn occasions when it is opened, a bell is sounded as the
Son of Heaven passes under the central arch, thus announcing
to the people of the Capital the fact that the Imperial sun
is actually in the ascendant." On the east side is a sundial
signifying that "as the sundial is useless when obscured by
clouds, so the Imperial Sunshine is without effect if clouds,
that is evil counsellers, are allowed to intervene between the
King and his people."[16] That detail alone stamps the official
religion of China as a moralizing one. It is an urban religion
concerned with conduct, and losing interest in the natural phenomena on which the daily bread of the agriculturist depends.

12. *Digha*, II, 86 f.
13. Above p. 193.
14. *Kingship*, 114.
15. *Mhvs.* XXXV, 51. — *Nala*, 15; and the story of the Kuru law.
16. Ayscough, 111.

In a strictly agricultural ritual the clouds are not evil always, but only when they obscure the face of the sun too much. A moralized ritual makes a strict opposition between the always and entirely good and the always and entirely evil. This moralizing tendency, runs right through the interpretation of the plan of the city. Moral maxims are hung about the throne such as, "Sincerely hold fast the perfect mean." This perfect mean represents the orderliness of the older agricultural religion, the absence of any excess in nature.

The outline of a village in Ontong Java is determined by the beach which hems it on three sides; for Ontong Java is an atoll, the largest in the world, a little to the north of the Solomons. The skeleton of the Indian plan however is there: a cross formed by a long narrow street and a short broad one which runs nearly east and west; but the orientation seems to be determined by the shape of the land, rather than by the compass, for the long arm is parallel to the long axis of the land. The centre of the cross is called *malae*, the common term in Polynesia for a village green or sacred enclosure. The short arm divides the village into two, North and South. The temples stand on the green, and in each angle of the cross stands a club for men, not like our clubs just a place for talk and pastimes, but a ceremonial necessity. The cemetery lies outside to the north or land side.[17]

Many, if not most, Fijian villages have moved since the coming of the White Man. The old villages were squeezed into the smallest possible space, so that they could quickly be palisaded when there were rumours of war. It does not seem that they aimed at any fixed plan, but fitted the village to the ground. The village was commonly divided into two, the Water or Sea people and the Land People. The boundary was sometimes, if not usually, a stream. The village had its green. It was not merely an open place; it was the scene of festivals. Now what we said of the medieval church is even truer of the Fijian green; for a Fijian festival is neither religious nor secular, public nor private, economic nor aesthetic,

17. H. I. Hogbin, *The Social Organization of Ontong Java*, Oceania, I, 399.

because all these specialized activities have not yet been analyzed out of the undifferentiated life of the community. A festival rolls into one a visit of condolence after a death, an exchange of commodities, an international conference, offerings to mutual gods, strengthening of family ties, banquets, ballets and concerts, a fair, sight-seeing, news spreading, and what not. None of these aspects can be separated from the rest. It is dangerous therefore to describe the village green as sacred, because the urban mind immediately enters it on that score in the column "religion"; but there is no religion in Fiji, only a system which in Europe has split up into religion and business. If we use the word sacred then, it must be on the understanding that it means merely that the green was the chief place in which men sought the all-round welfare of the tribe. It was bordered by the temples and the houses of the chief and great noblemen. In it were held all the outdoor ceremonies. It had its officials, the Lords of the Green. The common people had to go through humbly with folded arms.

We pick up the square city again in South America.[18] Those who will not at any cost allow that American civilization has any kinship with that of the Old World may object that these square sites in America are not cities, but ceremonial enclosures. Such objectors have completely missed the point of an Indian citadel: it is the place of temples and of gods, and is only inhabited by those who have a place in their cult. There is no differentiation into ceremonial and non-ceremonial. Later indeed such a specialization does come in; the secular becomes less particular about conforming to the shape of the universe, and more about defence and convenience; while the spiritual, freed from all considerations of defence or communications, can be stricter in applying cosmic theories. Sinhalese monasteries about the IXth century are able to conform to the ideal plan much better than the cities: they are often square with two streets in the shape of a cross, four main gates, and a rigorous orientation.[19] As for Angkor-Vat and simi-

18. P. A. Means, *Ancient Civilizations of the Andes* (New York, 1931), 125.
19. *C.J.Sc.*, II, 10 ff.; pls., XLIII, LXIII.

lar Cambodian sites, they are as ceremonial as any American site and as square.

Egyptian towns were called the House of Osiris, or of Bast, or whoever the patron god might be. To the Egyptians therefore they were primarily the residence of the god. The hieroglyph for a city is a circle enclosing a cross of St. Andrew.[20]

An Igbo town had four markets.[21]

The Greeks were evidently influenced by the necessities of war rather than of the sacrifice. Citadels like the Acropolis were shaped by the rock on which they were built. So, after all were Sigiriya and Yapahuva in Ceylon. Man at his best is not a pedantic adherent of rules. He does not cling to the square shape when that shape is obviously dangerous tactically. He is always ready to compromise between the different demands of his nature. It is only when he becomes decadent that he sacrifices his existence to a principle. The acropolis may be formless but it is more than a mere fortress; it is a place of temples, and especially of the chief cult. Outside it, in the city, lies the public square, the *agora*.

If we approach the study of that square with ready made divisions of life into trade and religion and politics and war, we shall never understand why the *agora* is at once a market place, a place for ritual, and for political assembly. Our experience however in other parts of the world will enable us to conceive of a state of society in which all these occupations are not yet differentiated, that is assigned to different men, places, and times, but where the same men may worship the gods by an exchange of goods. The Greek city is sacred.[22] That does not mean, as it would with us, that all self-interest, all base desires, all evil thoughts are excluded in order to make up for their concentrated pursuit outside. It is not a place where you must be utterly good as a change from being utterly selfish at home and in the shop. It is merely a place where the gods reside, in other words, where the life of the people

20. Moret, *Nile*, 50; 41.
21. The four animals of the Lango (above p. 54) seem a relic of the four quarters. In India each quarter has its animal (*C.J.Sc.*, II, 13). Cp. the four beasts of the Apocalypse.
22. *Odyssey*, IX, 167. — Theognis, 605.

is concentrated. The life of the tribe requires an exchange of commodities as well as the production of them, so it is not surprising that the exchange takes place in a square surrounded by temples. Nor is it surprising that affairs of state are discussed there, since affairs of state are questions of succession to the throne, public games, and all matters concerning the gods. We learn from Homer that both nobles and commons attended the assemblies.[23] We are not told whether the artisans and serfs were excluded; presumably they were excluded, for it was the case in Thessaly, and after centuries of democracy Aristotle still advocated "free public squares," not free in the sense of being open to all, but "kept pure of all merchandise, and which no craftsman or peasant or any such person is to come near unless summoned by the magistrate."[24] As a philosopher he gave the sacredness of the public square a new basis, an intellectual one: the sheep and the goats were no longer the ritually qualified and the ritually unqualified, but highbrows and labour.

We learn from Plutarch that Romulus made a circular ditch round what was later known as the Comitium, or place of assembly. The Capitol, on the other hand, being a place of refuge in war, conformed to the shape of the rock on which it stood. It contained the temple of the chief deity.

Our cathedrals and churches are now mostly swamped by seas of dwelling houses and mercantile offices, and it is difficult to realize how great a part of the city they once were. Our markets too have dwindled in importance and we have now to go to the continent to see them held beside the church. It would be considered unbecoming in this country of reverence. We no longer have one centre for every kind of activity, but a separate one for each, theatre, club, school, exchange, picture gallery, learned society, town hall, church or chapel.

Of a square city after the Eastern pattern we seem to find no trace in Europe. Yet there have recently been revived in Ferrara medieval games with all their medieval trappings. We are told that in accordance with the old custom there were

23. *Basileis* and *demos*. *Odyssey*, II, 1 ff.; XI, 14; *Iliad*, II, 198.
24. Aristotle, *Politics*, IV, 2 (= Tauchnitz, VII, 10).

four races, and in the last of them there were eight horses, one for each ward, and one for each suburb. The reason is there were once four wards in the town and without it four suburbs, each with its colours and banners.[25] We are not told what was the shape of the town, but the arrangement is thoroughly Indian.

Not only the camp of the Arandas, but their whole territory is divided into four. It is impossible from Strehlow to make out the orientation of the districts. All we know is that in each one the chieftainship was reserved for one of the four sections of society represented in the camp.[26] This fourfold division of the land has therefore the same basis as that of the camp into four.

In the Indian world the whole country was, like the city, divided into four quarters, sometimes with the king's country in the middle, making a total of five.[27]

There are traces of this fourfold division even in this country. If a theft has been committed the medieval appellor "ought at once to raise the hue and cry, he ought to go to the four nearest townships, 'the four quarters of the neighbourhood' and proclaim his loss." Again after a crime "the justices turn to the representatives of the four vills that are nearest to the scene of the misdeed and take their oath." Pollack and Maitland suggest that reference is made to the four townships because "they are the four quarters, east, west, north and south of the neighbourhood." There is definite evidence that the number four was associated in the medieval mind with the four quarters. If a man were expelled from his land he had four days to eject the usurper. He might "ride one day east, another west, another north, another south, to collect friends and arms, and must perpetrate the re-ejectment on the fifth day at the latest."[28]

In a twelfth century coronation four barons carried four lighted candles before the king.[29] This number four occurs

25. *The Times*, 6th (?) June, 1933.
26. Strehlow, IV, 1 f.; I, 6.
27. *C.J.Sc.*, I, 105; 177.
28. Pollock and Maitland, II, 160 f.; 644; 50; 590.
29. Round, 326.

too often in the Middle Ages to be accidental: the township sends to the court of law four good men; we hear of four coroners, and so on.[30] Indian and North American evidence teaches us to interpret these four barons as survivals of the impersonators of the four quarters round the king who is the impersonator of the whole world.

It looks as if the city is the land in brief. If the city is the earth in little there must be a spirit of the city as there is of the earth.

Of this belief I have so far only found traces in Europe and in Asia. Cities of ancient India, Greece, Italy had their goddesses, Athene, Roma, or whatever the name.[31] Rome was a goddess, and, like other city goddesses, was often represented wearing a crown in the shape of battlements. The Buddhist art of North-Western India used the same emblem.[32]

The earth is impersonated by the queen, the consort of the sky. It follows the city too must be impersonated by the queen. This conclusion has been drawn by Assyria. A stele shows us Assurbanipal's queen wearing a mural crown.[33] The vase of Berenice figures "that queen, wife of Ptolemy Euergetes, under the features of Good Fortune," the city-goddess of Antioch "with the dish and the horn of abundance."[34] Imperial Rome remembered, relearnt, that the queen was the city. "On the great cameo of Vienna the goddess is represented at the side of Augustus."[35]

Since the goddess Cybele wears a mural crown we must conclude she was not merely the earth, but the earth as concentrated in the city.[36]

If cities are represented in the shape of a divine woman

30. Pollock and Maitland, I, 610; 664; cp. 111; II, 581. — Round, 72; 349. — Cp. the old 4 faculties of our universities.
31. Tacitus, *Annals*, IV, 56; Livy, XIII, 6.
32. Foucher, I, 360.
33. Bruno Meissner, *Babylonien und Assyrien* (Heidelberg, 1920/5), 77.
34. Daremberg et Saglio, s.v. *Roma*, 877b. Cp. *Encyclopedia of Ethics of Religion*, s.v. *City*, 681a.
35. Daremberg et Saglio, s.v. *Fortuna*, 1266b.
36. Daremberg et Saglio, s.v. *Cybele*, 1687.

it is not the memory of a play of fancy but of a reality, of a queen crowned with battlements, who sat enthroned beside her heavenly spouse. It may be doubted whether there ever has been a fancy that was not originally a reality.

In conclusion, we start with a camp or city, round or square, which is a miniature of the earth, and so must have four quarters like the earth. This little earth is also impersonated by the queen, the consort of the sun-god on earth, namely the king, who dwells in the East.[37]

Strategic necessity, or the ground, eventually destroys the shape of the city, but the fourfold division lives on longer, and longest of all the sacredness of the city's centre and enclosure. In England the capital has long ceased to represent any thing; it is just the nerve-centre of the country.

37. A casual remark that the Aranda sungoddess belongs to the eastern division of the camp suggests a city in which the positions are reversed, in which there is an earth-god living in the western quarter. *Arunta*, 496 f.; cp. Strehlow, I, 1, 16.

20* Heaven and Earth

Le Ciel a visité la Terre.
French Hymn

IN CHAPTER 12 we had to report the existence of societies of which all the members were apportioned among two chiefs. The existence of two kings is commonly known as the "dual kingship." The technical term for the division of the people into two is the "dual organization." The two phenomena are one and the same among those communities that seem to pre-serve best the original scheme: society has two heads because it has two bodies, like Siamese twins. But the history of the bodies is not that of the heads, and so it is convenient to retain the two terms, and necessary to discuss the institutions in separate chapters. We saw that, as the functions of the two kings were emphasized, their spatial boundaries faded and they became distinguished only by functions and by rank. The territorial division of the people has persisted much longer, kept alive by a sporting antagonism which may degen-erate into real enmity. We shall see that in South India the lowest classes still carry on ritual feuds, while the king and priest, once rivals, preserve a lofty neutrality. In England the dual organization has followed the dual kingship into oblivion; and has only left local survivals among the common folk, and a habit of team games among all classes. The only dualism that remains is double-mindedness, allegiance to two sets of ideals which are often quite contradictory, the world and the kingdom of heaven.[1]

We have already had frequent references to a division of the people into two. That division is a necessary consequence of the impersonation of things. If men are identified with things both in heaven and on earth, and never combine the two categories in one person, then it will be possible to divide all citizens into earthly and heavenly. That is actually done.

1. For a guide to the dual organization see W. J. Perry, *The Children of the Sun*, chaps. XVIII–XX.

As the impersonation fades and the function shines forth more
and more, that dualism must become obscured. It is on the
whole best preserved where the representative character of
the actors in the ritual drama is best preserved, for instance
in Australia and in America. It has faded most where the rulers
are thought of as functionaries with duties, not as representatives of things.

With this sketch map before us we can now proceed to
explore the jungle of facts.

Most of the Aranda facts have already been mentioned. The
two halves of society are orientated East and West. The eastern half is known as the big men and the water-dwellers, the
western as the small men and the land-dwellers. We shall
call these divisions moieties, following the practice of most
anthropologists, and we shall distinguish the two as A
and B.

The two moieties are two sides of a big family; for they
keep intermarrying. Each man's moiety is his father's people,
the other his mother's. It is from his mother's moiety he takes
his wife.

Intermarriage is not the only form of interaction. Neither
moiety can carry out the ritual without the assistance of the
other. Here are further instances in addition to those already
given.[2] Performers are usually adorned by their sister's sons
who belong to the other moiety, since a woman finds her husband in the opposite moiety.[3] If a man dies his daughter's
son, necessarily a member of the other moiety, must gash himself on the shoulder. If a child dies its mother and other
women of her generation and moiety gash themselves. They
belong to the other moiety, since a child follows its father.
In the case of a man again, a senior member of his own side
and generation and a mother's brother from the other side
fix the dead body in position. At circumcision the father provides the girdle, the mother's brother (of the opposite moiety)
puts it on. The operator is generally a man of the opposite
moiety, but father's brothers, therefore of the same moiety,

2. Above p. 190.
3. Strehlow, III, 1, 2.

receive the blood in a shield.[4] We are unfortunately not told what relatives bury the dead.[5]

Thus every duty is assigned by rule either to a paternal or to a maternal kinsman, and within each group it is generally narrowed down to a particular generation and line of descent. It becomes clear then that the rule by which a man must marry a woman of his mother's moiety and of one particular section within that moiety, is merely one particular case of a general interplay. For it appeared at the very outset of our inquiry that formal carnal intercourse was a necessary part of ritual. Normally a man's partner is a woman of his own generation, on the other side; but there are occasions where it is not so. Thus before going on a foray it is the duty of the warriors to have connection with women of their own moiety. The reason given is that "their bellies may be inflamed with rage."[6]

There appears to exist between Aranda moieties a friendly hostility which we shall find to be characteristic of the relations between the two sides the world over. Spencer and Gillen describe, without understanding it, a mock preparation for fight. It is evidently not real, since it takes place whenever two friendly camps meet, and this regulation quarrel is not between the two camps, but between the two moieties represented in both camps. The points quarrelled about are ritual omissions.[7]

Among the Dieris of South-Eastern Australia A initiates B and B initiates A.[8]

Of the Winnebago moieties which form the two sides of the village, one is called "those who are above," the other "those who are on earth." Quite consistently moiety A has birds as clan animals and leaves its dead on a raised platform, while B has all land animals and buries its dead in the ground. The sky people rank above the earth people; but precedence was evidently not always as fixed as it appears to be now;

4. Strehlow, IV, 1, 23; 26.
5. Strehlow, IV, 2, 16 ff.
6. Strehlow, IV, 2, 6. — Above p. 177.
7. *Arunta*, II, 507.
8. Howitt, 512.

for a myth relates that the animal ancestors of the two sides played a game of lacrosse against each other to decide where the chieftainship should lie. The sky people won and have held the chieftainship ever since.

The chieftainship, as we saw, is essentially an office of peace. The vanguard in war belongs to the other side. Certain functions are thus fixed absolutely on one side or the other, and are not reversible; others are reversible and can be performed by one side or the other according to the side from which the principal is drawn. Thus only A will provide a chief, only B a public crier. When they are on the war path A always has its fire on the left, B on the right. On the other hand, A will bury a man of B, and B a man of A. B supplies the bride if the bridegroom is of A, but A if the bridegroom is of B. Some functions then are absolute, others relative.

The two moieties play lacrosse against each other with much ceremonial.[9] They put up two champions to vie as to who shall eat fastest an equal amount of food.[10]

There is one important difference between the Aranda and the Winnebago systems. In the first there are two moieties in a peculiar relationship to one another. That relationship subsists only between those moieties, and not between the subdivisions of the same moiety. A1 is not to A2 as A to B. Among the Winnebagoes the subdivisions of the same moiety can perform for one another duties such as one moiety performs for the other. Thus B is divided into B1 and B2: a man of B1 may bury a man of B2, and vice-versa. B1 and B2 are again subdivided into smaller divisions that may bury one another.[11] However much we may dislike technical terms we may find it convenient to describe this dividing and subdividing as *dichotomy*.

The principle upon which Omaha society rests has been expressed for us in terms of European thought as follows: "An invisible and continuous life was believed to permeate all things, seen and unseen. This life manifests itself in two

9. Radin, 185; 190; 183; 120 f.
10. Radin, 430.
11. Hocart, *Winnebago Dichotomy*, Man, 1933, 169.

ways: First, by causing to move—all motions, all actions of mind or body are because of this invisible life: second, by causing permanency of structure and form, as in the rock, the physical features of the landscape, mountains, plains, rivers, lakes, the animals and man. This invisible life was also conceived as being similar to the will power of which man is conscious within himself—a power by which which things are brought to pass. . . ."

"Human conditions were projected upon nature, and male and female forces were recognized. The Above was regarded as masculine, the Below feminine; so the sky was father, the earth, mother. The heavenly bodies were conceived as having sex; the sun was masculine, the moon feminine, consequently day was male and night female. The union of these two forces was regarded as necessary to the perpetuation of all living forms, and to man's life by maintaining his food supply. This order or method was arranged by Wakonda[12] and had to be obeyed if the race was to continue to exist. . . ."

"Myths relate that human beings were born of a union between the Sky people and the Earth people; and, in accordance with this belief, the union of the Sky people and the Earth people was conceived to be necessary to the existence of the tribe. There was a teaching among the old men that the division of the tribe into Sky people and Earth people was for marital purposes. . . ."

"The duality in the tribal organization was further represented by two principal chiefs, one standing for the Sky people and the other for the Earth people."[13]

All the rites entrusted to the Earth people "have a direct relation to the welfare of the people." The ceremonies connected with the warrior as the protector of life and property of the tribe were in charge of the clan of wrath, "whose place was at the eastern end of this division and at the southern end of the opening, or 'door,' of the 'tribal circle' viewed as when oriented. The rites pertaining to the people's food supply—the hunting of the buffalo, the planting of maize, the

12. Above, p. 144.
13. *Omaha*, 198.

protection of the growing crops from the depredations of the birds, and the fostering help of wind and rain—were in charge of four other *gentes*[14] of this division, each gens having its special share in these ceremonies. Besides these rites which bore directly upon the food supply, there were other duties which were concerned with the governing power and the maintenance of peace within the tribe." The Sky people "had charge of those rites by which supernatural aid was sought and secured. The rites committed to the gentes composing this division were all connected with the creation and the maintenance on the earth of all living forms. . . . Thus the belief that by the union of the Sky people and the Earth people the human race and all living forms were created and perpetuated was not only symbolized in the organization of the tribe, but this belief was kept vital and continually present to the minds of the people by the rites. . . . No tribal ceremony, negotiation, or consultation could take place without both divisions being represented; no council could act unless there were present one chief from the Sky division and two from the Earth division. In this connection an old Omaha man . . . said, 'the Sky division represented the great power, so that one chief from that side was enough, while two were necessary for the earth division.' "[15]

As among the Winnebagoes, A ranked higher, and B was divided in two; A was male and North, B female and South; but the heavenly regions seem again to have been divided into male and female, since the sun is male and the moon female. The two moieties played a game of ball against each other. It "is said to have had a cosmic significance and the initial movements of the ball referred to the winds, the bringers of life. It was played by the two divisions of the tribal circle as representatives of the earth and the sky." There was an invisible but well known line dividing the camp between the two moieties. If any boy attempted to cross that line a fight ensued. "While the old men of the tribe generally

14. What I call clans.
15. *Omaha,* 198.

punished boys for fighting together, these juvenile combats over the line were not objected to by the parents and elders."

The Osage likewise camp in a circle with the war moiety to the east or right, and the peace side to the west or left; but they are also divided into three, two of the divisions being in the right side, which is the war side, while the left is the peace side. When children are ill their parents apply to the other moiety for food.

The Incas were divided into Upper which sat on the right in assemblies and feasts, and lower which kept the left. Each division had its chief, but the chief of the right was chief over all. Each was subdivided into eight, whereas among the Winnebagoes it is four on one side and eight on the other. The division into right and left persists to the present day in certain esoteric societies in Bolivia. The right hand party dances to the south of the square, the left hand one to the north. "If either division encroaches on the space allotted to the other, bloody battles follow. Everywhere the same antagonism was met with, and among the Incas culminated in civil war."[16]

The Water side of a Fijian village has considerably outdistanced the Land side, at least among the bigger tribes. The widening of the interval between the two can be traced directly in the traditions of Lakemba,[17] and also by the circumstantial evidence obtained by comparing tribes in various stages of this process. The chief of A is chief over all; but the chief means much more than among the Winnebagoes, especially among the High Fijian coastal tribes. There he is exalted to such a height that the Land necessarily sinks in the balance. Further the ambition to rise among nations caused nobilities to seek alliances with other nobilities abroad, instead of taking wives from the Land. Thus the nobility from being merely the leading clan of the tribe were tending to become a closed caste seeking mates within its limits. In short, the Fijians were evolving from a dualism of Water and Land

16. R. E. Latcham, *The Totemism of the Ancient Andean Peoples*, J.R.A.I., 1927, 78 ff.
17. *Lau Islands*, 236; 41.

into one of Nobles and Commons, the latter including the master of ceremonies.

Yet another factor that obscures the dual organization in Fiji is the passion for dichotomy. Every unit is divided in two, and again in two, right down to the clan, which normally consists of two "edges of the oven," as they are called, a senior one and a junior one. The subdivisions are to one another as the whole is to another whole, so that the simple Australian scheme of two sides has been much confused. It is not a plain case of A marrying B, but of A1 also marrying A2, and A1*a* marrying A1*b*, and so on, until a real relationship is reached which is too close to allow of marriage. Even that obstacle can be set aside for reasons of state. Descendants of two brothers may be joined together in matrimony, if three or four generations apart. The two branches would then from being related as brothers come to be related as two intermarrying groups.

There is much more than intermarriage involved however. Supposing M and N are such groups: if a member of M dies, the people of his group will, at the close of the mourning, take off their clothes to the people of. N; that is, on the appointed day, they will discard their tattered mats, wrap themselves round and round with cloth, and take it off in presence of their kinsmen of N as a gift to them in addition to many other gifts. Besides they beg freely from one another, and those who are reckoned of the same generation will plunder one another, use abusive language to one another, and generally behave as insolently as possible, yet at the same time be the best of friends. In fact a man's proper "pal" is his cousin on the other side, his cross-cousin, as it is agreed to call him. Intermarriage is thus merely one item in the prescribed behaviour; there are other items. Fijians never call such groups intermarrying ones, but refer to them as "two sides,"[18] and in describing their behaviour intermarriage is often the last thing they refer to, if they refer to it at all. We can only conclude that intermarriage is not uppermost in their minds.

18. *Veitambani.*

These reciprocal functions are described by the Fijians as
veinggaravi, literally "facing one another," hence "waiting
on one another." We may translate it "mutual ministration,"
and I propose to use this phrase to express these reciprocal
duties wherever we meet them.

It is obvious that when a village is full of pairs of "sides,"
when A1*a* is paired with B, with A2, with A1*b*, etc., the behaviour I have described can only be carried out in moderation. Life would be intolerable if a man's house was continually
invaded by all the people who intermarried with his. It would
grow stale if he could not go out without being playfully called
a cad by most of the people in the village, or if a woman
was liable to have her hair pulled daily by her numerous male
cross-cousins. The mutual behaviour of sides is therefore best
observed, not in the village, but in the relations between tribes
that seldom meet. Then the behaviour is, if anything exagger-
ated. One tribe visiting the other will plunder it on a grand
scale without opposition or resentment: abuse will be bandied
about in good humour; and hoaxes are permissible. All this
is sanctioned by the god; and if you ask why they act in this
way they will seldom base it on marriage; generally they tell
how the gods of the two tribes tricked one another or abused
one another; since then their descendants are cross-cousins
and do the same.[19]

Such is the form of behaviour that prevails in the East of
Fiji. On the main island, especially in the hills, the plunder
is less in evidence, but the rivalry more so. "Two sides are
lands that vie with one another. It is a disgrace that the report
should go forth that they have been overwhelmed or weak
in war, or in exchanges, or in eating, or in drinking. It is better
they should die in battle than run away, it is better they should
be poor than that their contribution of stuff to the potlatch
should be small, it is better that their bellies should be burst
and their stomachs rent than that food and water should be
left; it must all be eaten up."[20] In other words, if two tribes

19. Hocart, *The Fijian Custom of Tauvu,* J.R.A.I., XLIII, 101. — *More
about Tauvu,* Man 1914, 96. — *Maternal Relations in Melanesian Ritual,*
Man, 1924, 132 and other articles there referred to.
20. *Native Gazette,* 1896, 172.

are related as cross-cousin to cross-cousin, neither can suffer itself to be outmatched in anything; even eating becomes a competition. The horseplay between men and women is very rough and obscene. The sexual relationship is there, yet it does not seem to be what impresses the Fijian most, for it is not included in definitions such as the above.

The behaviour is essentially ritual, and it would seem that originally it was only indulged in on the formal occasion of a ceremonial visit of one group to the other. The informal joking and cheating of individuals is probably an extension.[21]

All these functions of the sides are interchangeable; that is if the principal belongs to A, then B are the recipients of certain gifts; but if the principal belongs to B it is the other way round. Thus if a man of A has died, it is to B the clothes are taken off, and vice-versa. But there are functions which are definitely fixed on one side or the other, because the principal is always the chief, and the chief is fixed in the highest division of A. In the state ritual, as opposed to family ritual, the parts played are therefore not reversible: the master of ceremonies is always on the chief's side, the Land Chief and the Border, probably also the Lord of the Green and Sir Crier,[22] on the other. It is not clear where the chief's buriers belong: they may be of the other side, but in some cases they are the heralds and so not in B but of A2, which is to A1 as B to A. The same applies to king-makers. Dichotomy has obscured the original rule. In house-building the Land takes the landward side, the nobility and heralds the seaward side.

The two sides of a village differ in manners. The noblemen are gentle, the landsmen are loud. These landsmen act as a police and punish rudeness to the chief. The difference in manners is not one of breed, since the two sides intermarry, but, like the varying manners of our public schools, is the result of behaving as tradition expects.

The ritual interdependence of the two sides is even more evident in parts of New Guinea than in Fiji. Father Guis says

21. Cp. Hocart, *Chieftainship and the Sister's Son in Fiji, American Anthropologist*, 1915, 641.
22. *Ro Kathikathi.*

that "the young men of a Mekeo village may only marry the girls of their allied village. . . . By these words it is understood . . . a village that in every contingency and under all circumstances acts with another. For example, the folk of Beipaa feed pigs and bring up dogs, but these pigs and dogs are not for them; they are for the village of Amoamo," their vis-à-vis,[23] "and in return the pigs and dogs of Amoamo come to Beipaa. When a death occurs at Beipaa a feast is given which is eaten by the folk of Amoamo, and when one of the latter dies the reverse takes place."[24]

In New Guinea we found chiefs of the right and chiefs of the left. We also found some tribes with a war chief distinct from the chief of the left, so that both the dual and the triple system seems represented in that island.[25]

Our information about the social organization of the Koryaks is most unsatisfactory, but our experience in Fiji will enable us to find traces of the dual organization in the myths. I have reconstructed from scattered fragments the following pedigree:—[26]

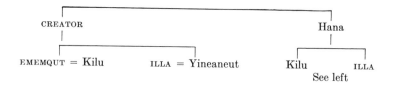

It was evidently the custom for the children of the brother to marry the children of his sister, just as it is the custom in Fiji and so many other places. The same behaviour exists between these cross-cousins as in Fiji: they cheat one another and are rivals. Though this cross-cousin marriage is no longer practised, yet the brother of a married woman will court her husband's sister, a relic of that system.[27]

23. Corresponding to the Fijian *veitambani*.
24. Seligman, *Melanesians*, 363.
25. Above, pp. 165, 183.
26. Males in capitals, females in small letters.
27. Jochelson, 140; 146; 156 f.; 750.

Cross-cousin marriage has almost disappeared among the Jukuns, but is still practised, a relic of the dual arrangement of kin. Another relic is the joking relationship between a man and his wife's younger brother, a woman and her husband's younger sister, who would be cross-cousins in a country practising cross-cousin marriage. The wife's brother is treated as female, the husband's sister as male, a sexual inversion which is rather symptomatic of the dual organization.[28] We came across a trace of right and left in the hunt.[29]

Close to Jukunland, the Ashanti still practise cross-cousin marriage, and the institution is common in Africa.[30]

So far our African evidence is limited to the division of kin into intermarrying groups which have ceased to be well defined. For a well marked division of the people into two we have to turn to the Gallas of Abyssinia. Their clans are arranged into two divisions which can only marry into one another. Each moiety is divided into right and left, which therefore do not coincide with the moieties but with subdivisions of the moieties. One clan of each moiety is "central" and acts as witness at weddings and other important transactions.[31] This looks like a transition to a threefold division.

The division into right and left is found in India. Unfortunately it is obscure, partly because it exists only in a state of survival, partly because European investigators have not known what to look for. They do not, for instance, give us a complete list of the castes and their distribution among the two sides, nor do they locate their facts accurately.

We are told that the left-hand group "comprises the Vaisyas or trading class, the Panchalas or artisan classes, and some of the low Sudra castes. It also contains the lowest caste, namely the Chucklers or leather-workers, who are looked upon as its chief support. To the Right-hand faction belong most of the higher castes of Sudras. The Pariahs are its chief sup-

28. Meek, 71; 116 f.
29. Above p. 166.
30. R. S. Rattray, *Ashanti Law* (Oxford, 1929), 304.
31. Alice Werner, *Some Galla Notes*, Man, 1915, 10. Why are we not told exactly what the "transactions" are?

port. . . . In the disputes and conflicts which so often take place between the two factions it is always the Pariahs who make the most disturbance and do the most damage. The Brahmins, Rajahs, and several classes of Sudras are content to remain neutral."

If we inquire why these frequent quarrels we are told that "perhaps the sole cause of the contest is the right to wear slippers or to ride through the streets in a palanquin or on horseback during marriage festivals. Sometimes it is the privilege of being escorted on certain occasions by armed retainers, sometimes that of being accompanied by native musicians at public ceremonies." One great feud once arose "simply from the fact that a Chuckler had dared to appear at a public ceremony with red flowers stuck in his turban, a privilege which the Pariahs alleged to belong exclusively to the Right-hand faction."[32] In short these disputes turn upon what we saw to be the whole basis of caste, namely the ritual. It is the acknowledged right of each side to punish breaches of the ritual rules committed by the other side. Thus the Beri Chettis, merchants, are with the Kammalans the leaders of the Left in one area. They set up the usual banana stumps at their weddings with this difference that the stumps may not touch the ground; otherwise the Pariahs, who are of the right, will come and cut them down. Yet the Pariahs are very low, and the Chettis very high, being a branch of the farmers or third caste.[33] But right is right. This is one of the many facts which paint the Indian caste system in a very different colour from that of the mud with which superficial observers and sentimentalists have daubed it.

An intelligent native of Travancore told me that in his country the farmer caste[34] was divided into those who wear the end of their cloth tied up on the right and those who wear

32. Abbé J. A. Dubois, *Hindu Manners, Customs and Ceremonies* (ed. H. K. Beauchamp, Oxford, 1897), 25 ff.
33. Edgar Thurston, *Castes and Tribes of Southern India* (7 vols., Madras 1901 et sqq.), s.v. *Beri*, 1213.
34. *Vellallan* in Tamil country. They claim to represent the ancient Vaisya.

it on the left. They can intermarry. He added that if breath be taken in through the right nostril at conception the child will be a male; if through the left a female. He thought therefore the left-hand people are descendants in the female line. The division into right and left, male and female, not only ranges the castes into two groups, but cuts the castes in two also; another case of dichotomy though much decayed.

In South India and Ceylon Brahmins wear the sacred thread on the right-hand side; Valluvar and potters on the left. Both claim to be Brahmins, the Valluvar as teachers, astrologers, and intellectual workers for the lower castes; the potters because, as Brahma fashioned men, so they fashion pots.[35]

Throughout the right and left country and beyond it, for instance in Ceylon, reigns the kinship system which we have learnt to know as the cross-cousin system, in which a man marries his mother's brother's daughter or his father's sister's daughter.[36] With it goes the usual behaviour of cross-cousins, free exchange of obscenities without ill-feeling. This kinship system and the grouping into right and left have however no longer any connection, since Right and Left do not intermarry; on the contrary, there is the greatest exclusiveness. The system does divide into right and left, male and female, within the caste where there is intermarriage, as among the farmers of Travancore.

It is however, to ancient Northern India I want to come, since it is there mainly that we have become familiar with ritual theories. We have already seen how those ancients divided society into aristocracy and serfs, and how this division persists in Ceylon to the present day.[37] The aristocracy is divided into three by a process of dichotomy. About the divisions of the serfs we have scanty information. On the strength of this classification they hold one fourth of the city. There is another arrangement possible which is followed in rare cases. Thus at one point of the creation ritual there is a procession

35. Above p. 115.
36. For a guide to the cross-cousin system see my *Progress of Man*, (London, Methuen, 1933), chap. XXI.
37. Above p. 114.

of three animals. "The horse relates to the Nobility, the ass to the Farmers and Serfs, the he-goat to the Priest." Here the farmers and serfs are jointly represented by a single animal. In another passage the nobility and the farmers are contrasted with one another as male and female.[38]

The antiquarians, accustomed as they are to the fossils of extinct societies, imagine everything to be as cut and dried in nature as the dead specimens in their texts. They cannot imagine them as what they once were, living organisms, continually changing and adapting themselves, ever in a state of transition between two states. Opposite statements therefore appear to them merely as breaches of logic, and as destroying one another; and they welcome these contradictions as an excuse for dismissing priestly books as having no relation to reality. Those, on the other hand, who make living societies the basis of their study learn that a perfectly consistent picture cannot be true, because one system appears before the old one has decayed, so that the old and the new always overlap. The new cannot wait till the old is gone before it makes itself ready to take its place. For the student of living forms therefore a contradiction points to a change-over.

We were actually able to watch such a change-over in Fiji. We could arrange the same tribe into Sea-folk and Landsfolk, and at the same time see it re-sorting itself as nobility and commons. In India we have just traces of an old system:—

This system seems to survive in Tamil country underneath the later classification, for the farmers are leaders of the Left, and the serfs are distributed among both sides. The kings and priests seem to have withdrawn from the feuds, as being too

38. *Sat. Br.*, VI, 4, 4, 12 f.; II, 5, 2, 36.

low for their refined notions. A re-grouping seems to have taken place, thus:—

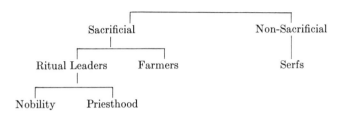

It has already almost obliterated the older system in the ancient ritual books, and is the only one recognized in Ceylon at the present day.

Under this scheme the sacrificial castes are the Gods, the non-sacrificial the Giants. It is among the divinities that we have to look for the ritual rivalry of the two sides. The Gods and Giants are perpetually striving for sacrificial victory. The Giants prevail for a time, but in the end are defeated. It would seem then that the preeminence of one side over the other was not fixed originally, but at one time depended on the issue of the contest. This would explain the curious fact that in Persia the relative positions of Gods and Giants are reversed. The Indian *deva* or God corresponds in status to the Persian *ahura,* the Persian *daeva* to the Indian *asura* or Giant.[39]

It is to the myths again that we have to turn for evidence of mutual ministration. "The Gods and Giants, both of them sprung from Prajapati, strove with one another. Then the Giants, even through arrogance, thinking, 'To whom now shall we sacrifice?' kept on sacrificing into their own mouths. They were defeated, even through arrogance. . . . But the gods kept sacrificing to one another; . . . the sacrifice became theirs."[40] For those who will not take the myths in evidence

39. The whole question is complicated by the fact that such great *Devas* as Varuna and Indra are also *asuras.* It is quite evident that there never was originally a hard and fast division. There are landsmen in Fiji who are also noble (*mbati turanga*), and in Samoa heralds who are nobles.

40. *Sat. Br.,* XI, 1, 8, 1 f.

there is the fact that the principal in the sacrifice cannot get on without the non-sacrificial castes, the charioteer, the huntsman, and the rest. That is still the case to the present day, for no Sinhalese village of farmers can get on without its barber and its washerman. To forbid the washerman to wash is tantamount to a sentence of excommunication on the village, for it means that no weddings, birth and puberty ceremonies, or funerals can be properly celebrated.[41] These functions are not reversible: the farmer never shaves the barber.

England is not the most favourable field in Europe for the study of social classification. "When compared with the contemporary law of France or at any rate of Germany, our law of status is poor: in other words, it has little to say about estates or ranks of men. Men are either free men or serfs; there is not much more to be said."[42] Down to the present day the boundaries between class and class are much less distinct among us than they are in Germany. The peerage melts into the commons, whereas the *Adel* cuts itself off from the *unedel*. In Anglo-Saxon times we find the freemen divided into two main groups, earl and churl.[43] There remains the clergy to place. As in Buddhist countries celibacy has forced it to draw on other classes; but we can deduce its original status from the law. Now "orders were regarded as conferring . . . a kind of nobility. There was a special scale of *wergild* for the clergy; but it was a question whether a priest who was in fact of noble birth should not be atoned for with the *wergild* appropriate to his rank, if it exceeded that which belonged to his ecclesiastical rank; and some held that for the purpose of *wergild* only the man's rank by birth should be considered."[44] The Clergy then formed a branch of the nobility, yet was quite distinct from it. "It is an estate of the realm."[45] We thus arrive at a scheme somewhat like this:—

41. I have a record of a headman who about 1927 brought a refractory village to heel by such an interdict.
42. Pollock and Maitland, I, 407.
43. Ibid., I, 34.
44. Pollock and Maitland, I, 34.
45. Ibid., I, 439.

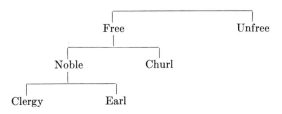

This classification long continued to be reflected in Parliament thus:—

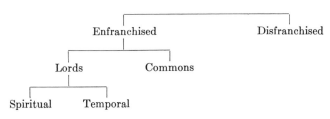

The French before the Revolution kept their lords spiritual and lords temporal in different assemblies, making three. Thus two easily passes into three by dichotomy of one moiety. On the other hand, three readily shrinks back to two by the lapse of one subsection, or its fusion with another. Most parliamentary systems have eliminated the clergy and so gone back to simple dualism. Germany supplies a good instance of elimination. The Holy Roman Empire had a threefold diet with the lines drawn a little differently to what they were in France:— 1) Electors; 2) Princes and Prelates, 3) Commons. The Empire of 1871 had Princes and Commons only. In Italian cities the executive powers were entrusted to the three consuls chosen from the three orders of captains, valvassors, and commons;[46] but traces of a fourfold division existed in Ferrara: each of the four wards had its farmers (*masari*), knights, pages, and halberdiers.[47]

The dual organization survives in England in that degeneration of ritual which we call pantomime: fairy queens and godmothers always enter from the right of the stage, demons, ogres, and wicked giants from the left.

46. Gibbon, V, 307; 303.
47. Cp. above p. 258.

At this point I may be allowed to revert to parallel columns in order to give a bird's eye view of the facts. We shall look for the following items on each side of the community:—

1. Division of the world.
2. Orientation.
3. Right and Left.
4. Rank.
5. Manners.
6. Peace and War.
7. Light and dark.
8. Seasons.
9. Male and Female.
10. Mutual Ministration: general.
11. Mutual Ministration: intermarriage.
12. Mutual Ministration: burial.
13. Antagonism.

Now let us dissect each example:—

I. ARANDA:—

	A	B
1.	Water	Land
2.	East	West
3.	———	———
4.	Big	Little
5.	———	———
6.	———	———
7.	Light	Dark
8.	———	———
9.	———	———
10.	Yes.	
11.	Yes.	
12.	Take part in each other's funerals.	
13.	Put-up rows.	

II. WINNEBAGO:—

	A	B
1.	Sky	Earth
2.	S-E	S-W

3. Left   Right
4. Nobler   Lower
5. ——   ——
6. Peace   War
7. ——   ——
8. Summer   Winter
9. ——   ——
10. ——
11. Yes.
12. Yes.
13. Rivalry in games.

III. OMAHA:—

1. Sky   Earth
2. North   South
3. ——   ——
4. Nobler   Lower
5. ——   ——
6. ——   ——
7. Day   Night
8. ——   ——
9. Male   Female
10. ——
11. Yes.
12. ——
13. Hostility, rivalry.

IV. OSAGE:—

1. ——   ——
2. East   West
3. Right   Left
4 ——   ——
5 ——   ——
6. War   Peace
7. ——   ——
8. ——   ——
9. ——   ——
10. Yes.
11. ——
12. ——
13. ——

V. INCAS:—

1. ———   ———
2. East   West
3. Right   Left
4. Noble   Lower
5. ———   ———
6. ———   ———
7. ———   ———
8. ———   ———
9. ———   ———
10. ———
11. ———
12. ———
13. Hostility amounting to civil war.

VI. FIJI:—

1. Water   Land
2. Seaward or Landward or leeward
   Windward
3. ———   ———
4. Noble   Common
5. Gentle   Rough
6. ———   Vanguard
7. [In Vanua Levu some tribes are divided into "red" (that is light coloured) bodies and black bodies].
8. ———   ———
9. Male and Female in one case of intermarrying tribes.
10. Yes.
11. Yes.
12. Receive each other's offerings at funerals.
13. Cheating, joking, and rivalry.

VII. BANKS:—

1. ———   ———
2. ———   ———
3. ———   ———
4. Higher   Lower
5. Gentle   Rough
6. Peaceful   Quarrelsome
7. Sun-born   Night

282

8. ——————   ——————
9. ——————   ——————
10. ——————
11. ——————
12. ——————
13. Hostility

VIII. KORYAKS:—

Traces of hostility, cheating, and intermarriage.

IX. JUKUN:—

Traces of right and left, of dichotomy, of joking and inter-marriage.

X. SOUTH INDIA:—

1. ——————   ——————
2. ——————   ——————
3. Right   Left
4. ——————   ——————
5. ——————   ——————
6. ——————   ——————
7. ——————   ——————
8. ——————   ——————
9. Male   Female
10. Traces of mutual ministry in the services of low castes to high, and of gratuities of high to low. Not reversible.
11. Intermarriage between castes generally gone, though it still survives.
12. Washerman, barber, and tomtom beaters officiate at funerals; the barber is "as a priest" on the cremation ground.
13. Hostility.

XI. ANCIENT INDIA:—

1. Sky   Subterranean[48]
2. East   West
3. ——————   ——————
4. Noble   Common
5. ——————   ——————

48. In Buddhist pictures the world of the Giants is below ground; it can be seen on the plate facing p. 179 of my *Kingship*.

6. ———   Army-leader
7. Light   Dark
8. ———   ———
9. Male   Female
10. Low castes necessary to the ritual. The principle of mutual ministration laid down as rule of sacrifice.
11. ———
12. ———
13. Hostility. Rivalry. Cheating (in myths).

The blanks do not mean that the thing is not there: it may have been missed by the observer. Spencer and Gillen completely missed the characters of the two Aranda moieties and we owe our knowledge of them to Strehlow. We might not know the Winnebago moieties are connected with summer and winter, were it not that this connection exists elsewhere in North America. That knowledges keeps our eyes open for any evidence, and makes us notice that the lower moiety of the Winnebagoes holds winter feasts at night, while the upper moiety holds summer feasts by day.

This bird's eye view shows that the most persistent feature of the dual organization is not intermarriage, but mutual ministration. This feature is so persistent that it outlives the dual organization. There seems to be no getting rid of it except by getting rid of the ritual.

It will be seen in these tables that the place of sky and earth is among Fijians and Arandas taken by water and land, or earth. Among the coast people the word water refers to the sea, and the term for water people were better rendered "seafolk." Now the Arandas believe in waters above the firmament.[49] The Indian word for ocean means both the waters above the firmament and those that encircle the earth.[50] An Egyptian text says, "The water of life which is in the sky, it comes. The water of life which is in the earth, it comes."[51] It is not surprising then that Varuna, the great sky-god of ancient India, is also a water-god, and, now that he has been

49. Strehlow, I, 1, 1.
50. *Sanskrit Dict.* s.v. *samudra.* Cp. *Nirukta,* II, 10.
51. *Pyramid Text* 2063, quoted by Moret, *Nile,* 82.

supplanted in heaven by Siva, he confines his dominion to the Ocean. In the same way Odin is a sea-god as well as a sky-god. The ocean is merely a continuation of the firmament. The Fijians take no interest in the sky, and it does not figure in their ritual, or scarcely. They are deeply interested in the sea as teeming with fish and as highway from kinsfolk on one island to kinsfolk on another, and kinsfolk are people who supply you with such food or wealth as you may be deficient in. The sea therefore remains alone of the original sea-sky continuum.

If this conclusion is correct it follows that the Arandas derive their dual organization from a maritime people, or else that they formerly lived by the sea. Their own myths are explicit, for they tell us that originally the land was covered by the sea. The MacDonell range, right in the centre of Australia, rose above the sea. Upon its slopes were undeveloped men. Those who became moiety A lived in the water, while the future moiety B lived on the slopes. That is a good description of the relative position of sea-folk and land-folk on the main island of Fiji; but the Arandas are hundreds of miles from the sea, so the watery nature of A is now nothing but a memory, and plays no part in the life of the people. It does very much in Viti Levu.[52]

What system does the comparative method lead us back to? To a small society which is one big family, because all the members keep intermarrying so that every one is related to everyone else. This society falls into two groups, one associated with the sky, one with the earth. This not a mere philosophy, but the inevitable consequence of the very practical equation

principal = objective.

In cosmic rites the whole world is involved, but in two parts, sky and earth, because all prosperity is conceived to be due to the orderly interaction of sky and earth. The sky alone cannot create, nor the earth alone bring forth. Therefore in the ritual that regulates the world there must be two principals,

52. For instance round about Rewa the sea-folk may not eat fish in the presence of land-folk, or land-folk pig in the presence of sea-folk.

and they must be male and female, for the interplay of earth and sky is analogous to the intercourse of sexes. We should expect the sky to be always male, but that does not appear to be always the case; for in Egyptian myth it is the female. The Polynesian version is as we should expect and agrees with the general opinion of mankind: the sky is the male.

Traces of the sky-earth dualism linger in medieval England. In the XIIth century "the civil law might be the law of earth, *jus soli*," but canonical law "was the law of heaven, *jus poli*."[53] For the King is of the Earth, the Church is of Heaven, a point of view which takes us right back to what we take to be the earliest form of dual kingship, a sky-sun king who regulates, and an earth-king who executes. But this is only a reminiscence, a metaphor. Objects no longer matter, except as supplying images. What really distinguishes the two legal systems is not their localization in the universe, but the nature of the cases to which they apply.

Intermarriage is a constant feature of the dual organization. It means that every sky-man must marry an earth-woman, every earth-man a sky-woman. Consequently the sky-king must take an earth-woman to queen. We have had evidence, meagre, but sufficient, that the queen is the earth. It is unfortunate that this evidence comes entirely from countries where the dual organization no longer exists, so that a society in which the sky-king makes a relation of the earth-king his queen must remain a postulate for the time being.

Dichotomy has obscured this simple arrangement. It has led to the sky-king taking a consort from other subdivisions of the sky half. A Fijian chief's possible marriages will show how this works:—

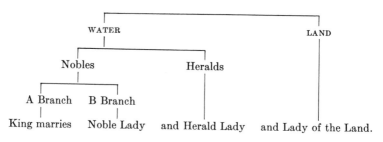

53. Pollock and Maitland, I, 112.

The dignity of Earth-queen is eventually transferred from the earth side to the solar side. In India the queen may be of solar lineage,[54] like the king, but she none the less represents the earth.

Into the dual organization there kept butting in another system, a threefold division. We have watched attempts to reconcile two and three in North America.[55] It should be noted that the Omahas divide the universe into three, heaven, air and earth, besides dividing it into two, sky and earth. In the threefold division sun, moon, stars, and birds belong to the sky; winds, rain, clouds, mist, forest animals are assigned to the air; hills, valleys, rivers, lakes, trees, grasses, and insects that creep among the grasses and burrow in the ground to the earth.[56]

Three occasionally turns up in that stronghold of dualism, Fiji. Thus Somosomo, the capital of the King of the Reef,[57] is divided into three. Some tribes have land and water with the nobles between and above them. The Tongans divide their main island, Holy Tonga, into Front, Above, Below.[58] The division is not accidental, for when they colonized Wallis Island they were at pains to reproduce the three districts exactly. Upolu, the king's island in Samoa, is also divided into three.

The boundary between three and four runs through Nigeria. To the north of that line, in Niger Province, Mr. P. G. Harris tells me "there was a system whereby the ruling house consisted of three branches which became chiefs of Nupe in regular sequence. Now I find that every Village Head has adapted the triple sequence as well."

The number three is all powerful north of that line and in Asia. We can more or less trace its invasion of India. There as elsewhere, two is the number of the parts of the world;[59] four is that of the cardinal points of the compass. Those two

54. *Suryavamsa.*
55. Above p. 180.
56. *Omaha,* 115 f.
57. *Tui Thakau.*
58. *Mu 'a, Hahake, Hihifo.*
59. *Rodasi* in the Vedic hymns; "this world" and "that world" in the Brahmanas.

numbers, especially four, are still full of vitality in the old ritual books; but between sky and earth a third region commonly appears, the atmosphere. Not that they knew anything of air as a gas, but they recognized a space below the firmament in which the wind blows and the lightning speeds, the first step in the discovery of air. Each of these three regions had its god. Brahma, for instance, "created the gods; having created the gods he set them separately in these worlds, in this world Agni, Wind in the atmosphere, in the sky even the sun."[60] At an earlier date the Rigveda describes how "the Maruts go along the sky, over the earth Agni, Wind here goes through the air."[61] Yaska expounds the doctrine thus:— "There are three deities, Fire, the terrestrial; Wind or Indra, the atmospheric; the Sun, the celestial." He points out these are not absolutely separable:— "Their community of abode and of use is to be noted. . . . Community of use is observed as in the common use of the earth by the cloud in company with wind and sun, of the other world (heaven) in common with Fire. It is like human society."[62] In other words each element has its own sphere, but its action extends to the two others; just as in human society you cannot keep functions absolutely separate.

Later the Hindus have, among other trinities, one consisting of wind, sun and moon. "These three gods support the whole of the three worlds."[63]

A different threefold division was current in Babylonia. The abode of the god Anu was the sky, of Enlil the earth, of Ea the ocean of fresh water beneath the earth.[64] The Greeks again differ slightly from the Babylonians for their triad was Zeus in heaven, Poseidon in the Ocean, and Aides "who rules

---

60. *Sat. Br.*, XI, 2, 3, 1.
61. *Rigveda*, I, 161, 14. Cp. *Rgv.*, I, 108, 9; VII, 104, 11; II, 27, 9; etc.; and W. Kirfel, *Kosmographie der Inder*.
62. *Nirukta*, VII, 5.
63. *Nala*, 24, 30 ff.
64. S. Langdon, *The Epic of Creation* (Oxford, 1923), 149 & note. — Sydney Smith, *The Babylonian Ritual*, J.R.A.S., 1925, 39. — Does the ocean below the earth explain why Varuna is also king of the dead?

among those below the earth."[65] As however Poseidon corresponds to Varuna, and Zeus to Indra, it seems likely that the
triad was originally Sky, Air, and Earth.[66] The Germans had
a triad Odin, Thor, Freyer.[67] The Egyptians were fond of
triads. The three divisions into which they divided the earth
correspond roughly to the words heaven, earth, and hell. On
the other hand they have a triad composed of the morning,
evening, and night suns.[68] It seems then to have been with
the threefold divisions as with the twofold: each division can
be again divided by the same number. Thus Agni is one of
a triad, but he himself has three aspects.[69]

The Roman Catholic Church divides itself into three, the
church militant, the church suffering, the church triumphant.
Thus it divides the world, as it does the deity, into three.
It is certainly not an accident that the papal crown is triple.
The connection with heaven and earth is here barely discerni-
ble: it has given place to a connection with actions and states
of mind.

In the few cases where we seem to catch the triple organization in the act of forming itself it is by the splitting of
one of the components into two. That is so among the
Winnebagoes.

This raises the question whether this dichotomy is traditional or innate in man, whether it is merely an old habit
persisting age after age, or whether it does not lie deeper
in human nature, as a law which it obeys in common with
the rest of nature. Arteries, nerves, growing shoots, single cells
all multiply as a rule by dichotomy.

Perhaps it is a law of nature, but that is not sufficient to
explain the dual organization, for dichotomy need not produce
a pair, except fleetingly as a first step. In the end it may produce any pattern threefold, fourfold, fivefold or more. Nor
does it explain the curious interaction of the moieties; in fact

---

65. *Iliad*, XV, 187.
66. Common elements of Poseidon and Varuna.: ocean, horse, trident.
67. Grimm, *Teutonic Mythology*, (trsl. by Stallybrass), 113 f.
68. W. Budge, *The Book of the Dead* (London, 1923) ch. XV, p. 45.
69. Above p. 19.

it is this interaction which must explain the dual division; for men divide themselves into two groups in order that they may impart life to one another, that they may intermarry, compete with one another, make offerings to one another, and do to one another whatever is required by their theory of prosperity.

The pedigree of our own threefold division may be sketched in the following manner, provided we bear in mind that this sketch is not a final solution of the problem, but only points the direction in which a solution may be found.

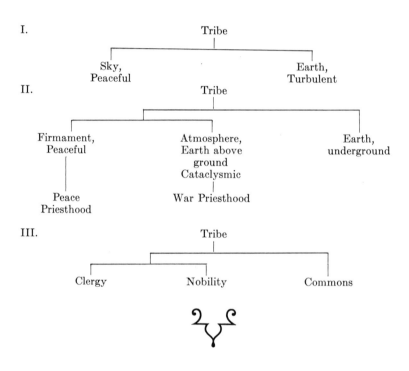

21· Summing Up

OUR SEVEN witnesses can scarcely be expected to give us more than the broad outlines of the story. We have tried from time to time to give a bird's eye view of the growth of the state by means of diagrams. Such diagrams however introduce a definiteness of detail which is certainly not in our evidence. It may never be there, for it is not the purpose of the comparative anatomy of society to reconstitute the past in all its details, but to sum up growth in formulae. In the present state of our science however diagrams such as we have used may be admitted as substitutes for general formulae; for they can bring out the general idea more vividly than pages of discourse, provided we look at the form, and do not take the details too seriously.

In chapter 9 we tried to express in this way the change from representative to administrative offices. We were at that time ignorant of the dual organization. In the light of subsequent evidence we can revise our formulation in some such manner as this:—

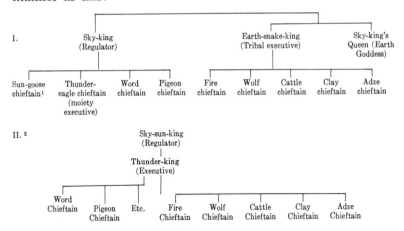

1. The goose is the sun-bird in India.
2. The fate of the earth-king is obscure. It has certainly varied in

291

III.

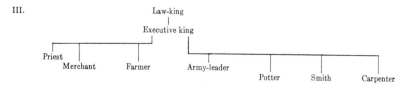

Gradually the high rise higher, the low sink lower, until the state is rearranged in a vertical hierarchy such as ours. The great height reached by our social edifice will be brought home to the reader if he will trace all the gradations of our state from king to able-bodied seaman, to private, or to mason in government employ; then compare them with the three or four storey society of Fiji:—

In the primitive scheme the royal family was of the same blood as the commons. It is hard for us to conceive of a king who is the cousin of his meanest subjects; yet such kings exist. The Lord of Nayau, chief of Lakemba, towered high above his subjects, yet nevertheless he claimed kinship with the lowest of his people. There was however a marked tendency for the royal families of the greater tribes to isolate themselves, and to seek mates from other royal families, and so to form a closed royal caste such as exists in India. By introducing monogamy and our snobbery we have hastened the process. We need not however go outside our own country to watch

different countries. Where the sky and light and their impersonator, the first king, have become identified with goodness, the earth and darkness with wickedness, it would seem that no one has aspired to be appointed devil. The office therefore remains vacant, except when it has to be filled on special occasions, like our coronation offices. Thus the *advocatus diaboli* makes his appearance periodically at a Tibetan festival (*Kingship*, 25). In the middle ages he declined into a part on the stage. Indian evidence, on the other hand, suggests he may be the brahman, who has been transferred to the higher side of society, the side of light and life. A great deal of detailed comparative work is required to settle this point.

this gradual isolation. Every school-boy knows that our kings used to marry English ladies. The royal family has now become a breed at the top of society, instead of a lineage in front.

As it rises, the royal family draws after it those offices that are the most necessary assistants in the work of commanding, such as the priest, the leader of the vanguard, the navigator. Those who are of no help in commanding, those who in the original scheme had charge of artefacts, all these sink and form a serfdom of crafts.

Yet the more these groups tend to fly apart the more urgent becomes the need for some binding agent to keep the community together. We have seen how the problem is solved: each king's officer or local chieftain has a court copied and reduced from the king's, and the servants of the king's servants have their own servants, and so right down to the bottom, so that the whole community is knit together by social ganglia, as it were, all linked together. The more specialized they become in the work of coordinating, the more they shed all those original characters, such as heredity, and naturalism, which are not relevant to coordination; at last they become scarcely recognizable as ministries, departments, county councils, town councils, provinces, sees, parishes, G.H.Q.'s, Army H.Q.'s, and so on, equipped with their clerks, technicians, inspectors, and all the apparatus of a modern state. The vast mass of the people, the professions, the traders, the manual workers are moved by the machine but are no longer parts of it.

The bigger Fijian states are already large enough to require some intermediary between king and people. Already such a function is appearing: the land-chieftain is often the one who "leads the commons" to the chief, though there is as yet little verticality in society, and the land-chief is leader in the sense of going in front, rather than of commanding. The ancient Indians lay great stress on the mediating functions of the fire-god and his representative, the priest. In later India the priest, as prime minister, is definitely a channel between the supreme power and the people. As the king keeps rising the links in the chain that binds him to the lowest must increase in number. Thus the conveyers of orders from above and of needs from below spread like nerves through the whole body politic. It is the men who think who are specially appropriate as channels of communication. They therefore tend to oust from the centre the men who work with their hands. A Fijian carpenter is the companion of his chief. An English carpenter belongs to the proletariat.[3]

Those that rise isolate themselves from those below, even as the king isolated himself from them. Snobbery, that most potent force in the building up of society, that great instrument of progress, converts every section into a breed. That is the stage reached by India.

There is no doubt these breeds differ very much in their attainments and characters: they are born different. But how has this come about? Originally they all intermarried, as they still do among the Arandas, the Fijians, the Winnebagoes. How could a start be made in breeding special abilities out of an undifferentiated society, where everyone is a kinsman to everybody? In our own society there are men born with a definite literary bent; others are born strategists; there are men who could never be anything but clerks, while others could never be happy or successful as clerks. There are no such strongly marked differences of vocation in a society like the Fijian, and it is difficult to see how such differences as exist can be perpetuated or intensified, as long as every class marries every other. Differences of function do exist, but they are not imposed by differences of temperament or ability: a herald is not a herald because his genius urges him into heraldry. How then can specialization of function give rise to specialization of natural gifts?

If it was a law of ritual organization that the men best fitted for an office should be appointed to that office, our question would soon be answered: social selection bred the types required for each work, just as we breed horses for the turf and for draught. Failing that, if the founder of the family owning an office had been chosen for his fitness, there would still be some social selection; but traditions generally have

3. The idea of a blacksmith being a high court personage tickles my Egyptian students.

it that, if a lineage is appointed to an office, it is in virtue
of seniority. Thus it has been the custom in some parts for
the senior line to receive the kingship, the second line the
priesthood. It is difficult to see how special abilities can ever
be bred under such conditions.

Nevertheless we can see in Fiji how specialization of function may lead to some specialization of congenital abilities.
Fijian society is not rigid: it can always be adapted to circumstances. Heredity might designate a man for office, yet character and intelligence might veto him. Instead of keeping to
hard and fast rules, as savages are supposed to do in books,
the Fijian in such a case overruled heredity. Thus the head
of Little House was master of ceremonies to the Lord of Nayau
by right. But that house had acquired an evil repute, as it
had caused the death of many a high chief; it had decayed
in character and numbers; and the few survivors in my time
were rather feckless, their head a bleary-eyed kava addict,
a great talker, but small doer. He was titular herald, but the
chief did not use him in that capacity; he preferred a descendant in the female line. This man however was shy and no
speaker, so he could only act where his deficiencies did not
matter; but on all great occasions a chieftain from the other
side of the village discharged the duties of herald. Thus it
was not self-assurance, memory, and the gift of speech that
gave rise to a herald caste, but the function of herald that
created a need for men of that type. As long as a house produced men in the least adequate it held the post; but if it
fell below the line some one more suitable was preferred. This
social selection applied specially to the priests of the gods,
for they had to be possessed, and it is not everyone who can
be. On the death of one therefore the next man in the order
of succession was tried, then the next, until a man was found
who could go into a fit.

On the other side of the globe, Jukun society displays the
same elasticity. "One of the kings of Kundi, being old and
near to death, summoned his son to hear his counsel. But the
son was negligent and went after his own pursuits. So the
aged king summoned his daughter's son and conferred on him
the royal insignia, saying, 'I make you king of all the land.

Go and abide in the town of your father.'" The king's son received the priesthood as a consolation prize.[4] It is even recorded that a high official set aside his sister's son, his natural successor as the head of the household, and before his death formally handed over the cults to a bought slave and a foreigner, and made it known to all his household he wished this slave to be his successor at the head of the family. His sister's son's conduct had ever been unsatisfactory, whereas this foreign slave had proved himself a man of personality and straightforward character.[5]

India has many tales of families being discarded from the duties that should have been theirs by descent. That is what outcasting amounts to.

Theoretically then, descent, not ability, is the qualification for office. But facts often resist theory, and unfitness is one of those facts. There are times when it cannot be ignored, and then social selection comes into play.

Social selection is more intense and earlier in the case of ritual leaders than in the case of lesser offices. For the position carries with it advantages that are coveted. It means wealth, since more comes in than goes out. It means what is even dearer to men than wealth, namely honour and power; for power goes to the man who has favours to dispense, whether it be food, crops, or lucrative appointments. The greater the power the greater the competition. The most glorious throne is also the most dangerous, and to hold it requires character, energy, and decision. The struggle for existence is fierce. The history of monarchies endued with power is one of constant intrigue and murder. It was commonly said in Fiji that of old the strongest were chiefs.[6] The records bear this out. There was a saying at one time: "Three chiefs are slain for every crop of chestnuts." The reason given why the nobles used to kill one another was that "the chief was like a god." The nobles were also the first to go over to inbreeding so that the selected qualities tended to perpetuate themselves.

4. Meek, 36.
5. Meek, 79.
6. The Fijians do not distinguish in speech between physical and moral strength.

Accordingly, a ruling breed seems to emerge before any professional one. Among peoples who have no very marked specialization in crafts an aristocratic type is often well in evidence. So it was in Lakemba. Some of it was no doubt the result of upbringing, and of having from childhood been in the centre of things. But the refinement of features, the slightly greater stature, and the greater intelligence and self-confidence could not be entirely explained in this manner.[7] There was breeding. The difference was small compared with the extremes to be observed in Europe, and it could not be great while the ruling class still intermarried with the commons.

Comparative evidence then shows that caste is older than occupation and is the cause of specialization in work, not the consequence. It has made necessary a certain specialization that was not there before. This specialization has broken up the caste system that gave rise to it. This effect is one that can be observed in Fiji at the present day. Young men are being drawn into the government and into the mission. They are selected, not by heredity, but on certain abilities, to specialize in certain types of work, instead of living like their forefathers the life of all round country gentlemen with certain duties at court. They drift away from their families, and get out of touch with village affairs. They can no longer officiate in the place assigned to their clan. They are scattered for the purposes of their work all over the country. In Europe too increasing specialization has broken up the old heredity.

In spite of the change in Europe from heredity to selection by ability, specialization of function remains ahead of specialization of abilities, in fact it has, if anything, increased its lead. As there is little specialization in the South Seas, there is little discrepancy between a man's work and his fitness for it. It is otherwise with us: a rivet-maker is far from being adapted to make nothing all day but rivets; still less is a cafeteria girl designed by nature to do nothing else but hand out knives and forks for hours on end. It follows that a very small

---

7. The Lakemban aristocracy came out 5 cm. taller, though the numbers measured are scarcely adequate, *Lau Islands*, 41.

part of their persons is exercised for one third of the day, and then it is exercised to excess. The greater remainder is left hungering for activity till evening. That is the tragedy of our civilization: our men and women have not yet been narrowed down by nature to fit the narrowness of their tasks. When the day is over, there does not follow a complete expansion of the personality, but only highly specialized activities of another kind, perhaps an orgy of an emotion which finds no satisfaction at other times. The pursuit of life is no longer a wide all-embracing exercise, but an alternation of limited reactions. There are morals and trade, which are allowed to have nothing to do with each other, there is pure music, pure dance, pure drama, pure painting, there is work and there is play.

This specialization is not all the result of unwilled adaptation, but of man's purpose. He wills a certain end, and in the pursuit of that end he is compelled to adapt his means, with the result that in the end he himself becomes adapted. If his end is wide, so are the means he adopts in its pursuit. If the end is a good life his daily round covers the whole of life. If he believes that life is best to be secured by reproducing in society the various departments of nature and living in accordance with them, he divides society into corresponding groups, and assigns to each the corresponding duties. These in turn tend to select certain types. As the population increases the competition for life becomes more severe. He who concentrates on his special duties to the neglect of more generalized activities surpasses, other things being equal, the man who spreads himself more, and so forgoes excellence in anything. Specialism is found to give a better *immediate* chance in the struggle for life, whatever, the *ultimate* effect may be. The purpose again sets the course, and leads to further specialization. Thus the will is ever ahead of nature, and steadily draws away from it.

Specialization and centralization go hand in hand; they are the aspects of the same process. The more specialized an organism becomes the more dependent it is on its neighbours, and the greater the number of specialists it has to cooperate with. As the organism becomes more and more complex the need for a coordinating system becomes ever more insistent, the nervous system in the human body, the administration in the body politic.

If the growth of a coordinating system can be watched as it proceeds under our eyes, if it can be traced further back into the ages with the aid of records and comparative inference, then there is hope that we may be able to discover not only what happened, but also how it happened. In other words, we may be able to trace the stages by which man has successively adapted himself to changing circumstances. It may be in the evolution of institutions that we shall find the key to the problem of adaptation of organisms generally. It may be we are more likely to discover the secret of adaptation and evolution by seeking for it in ourselves than outside human society among animals and plants.

The facts reviewed in this book have suggested that conscious purpose precedes the adaptation of behaviour, and the adaptation of behaviour is followed by adaptation of structure. A community wants something; it shapes its actions so as to achieve that something, and the result of its action is to alter its organization. It is not indeed government that man wants, for how can he conceive of a government except by experience of it? It is life he wants, and in the effort to live he does one thing after another till he eventually finds himself governed, that is specialized into producers and into regulators of those producers. He does not want a priesthood or a civil service to control him; he wants to control nature for his own benefit; but in the pursuit of this aim he places some members of his community into new functions which in turn produce a new type of man, no longer the all-round handy man, but the man who lives largely by thinking. The conscious purpose is the impulse that sets the whole machinery in motion with results that are not foreseen.[8]

8. Cp. my *The Role of Consciousness in Evolution*, Psyche Annual, 1934, p. 160.

Additional Notes

1. *Cult as Social Centre. P. 35.*

Dr. H. A. Winkler describes in his *Die Reitenden Geister der Toten* (Stuttgart, 1936) how a man possessed by the dead has become adviser, judge, physician, etc., to a group of Egyptian villages. He comments: "It is fascinating to observe this germ of a social centre in the first stage of its growth. Under special circumstances—especially when a really notable man bears it or stands in close proximity to it—this germ can develop into a powerful political centre" (p. 112). One thinks of the Mahdi, and many others.

Thus a humble villager working on the equivalence

$$\text{principal} = \text{god}$$

in its crudest form, possession, can acquire some regulative power over the activities of his community.

Note that the man is not one deity, but several. He is not all simultaneously, like the king; but the king too can be different deities in succession in different rites.

2. *Victim = god. P. 53.*

The prayers and actions that accompany the fishing ritual of Eddystone Island point to the same underlying theory as the Koryak whale ceremony. See a paper to be published in the *J.R.A.I.* on *Fishing in Eddystone Island*, end. The precise form here taken by the unfailing equivalences is

$$\text{fish, canoe, net, shrine, all} = \text{spirits of forbears.}$$

Evident the same doctrine is current among the Jukuns since *jǒ* means both god and offering.

3. *Acquiring the Gods of the Conquered. P. 99.*

When the King of Upper Egypt acquired sway over Lower Egypt he added the crown of his new dominions to that of his old one. These crowns were the visible forms of the goddesses of Upper and Lower Egypt. Thus the king in uniting the two lands united their deities on his head.

4. *The King a Slave of Ceremonial. P. 153.*

The excessive multiplication of offices round the king heralds the decline of monarchy. It means the king is becoming wound round and round with ceremonial. For the senseless inflation of his household and the stultifying effects of a meticulous ceremonial see H. Taine's *L'Ancien Régime*, book II, chap. ii, *La Maison du Roi*, and *Les Occupations du Roi;* also note 4 at the end of vol. I.

5. *The Herald's Staff. P. 195.*

Our own heralds carry sceptures or batons.

We shall probably have to recognize two homologies of brahman-kerux-face of the land in our country. A Germanic one has been overlaid and reduced to mere pageantry by another one from the East. The first one still gravitates round the king; the second one had already emancipated itself before it reached these shores.

We are all familiar with such duplicates in language. Compare Germanic *begin* and Latin *commence*. In such cases either the duplicates specialize in different directions like *chaise* and *chair?* or one drives out the other as *napkin* has done to *serviette*.

6. *Caste Born of the Sacrifice. P. 117.*

I take down the third volume of *The Mysore Tribes and Castes* (Mysore, 1930). I open it at random. It happens to be the article *Devanga*. The name of this weaver caste means "Limb of the god." A myth explains the name: they were born from the limb of the god. There is no reason to doubt the truth of the myth, since kings are gods, and heads of families derive their divinity from his.

For a Devanga to change his cult means to break away from the main body, and to form a sub-caste. That is natural, since a caste is a family with its cult.

7. *The Two Kings. P. 163.*

The people of Suva, Fiji, thus describe the functions of their two chiefs: "The Noble Lord of Suva remains idle, the God of War keeps working." They compare them to a provincial chief and a district chief under the British Government.

8. *Cult and Policy. P. 105.*

The following incident shows how international relations and cults are one in the mind of the Fijian. There is a god who has a temple in Mbau and one in Suva. "Mbau and Suva have gods in common (*kalou vata*, see *The Fijian Custom of Tauvu* in J.R.A.I.,

1913, 101 ff). The Suvan Envoys to Mbau are his priests. The ancients of the clan of Nandonumai begged of old for a lady of Mbau that she might come and wed in Suva. The lady was brought, and she came with this god. Those who brought him from Mbau are now his priests. This is how the nobles arose in Suva."

Compare *Genesis* xxxi, 19 ff., only there the gods are taken away by stealth.

The fashionable explanation is that religion has got into policy, as if Primitive Man was guided by Pure Reason at first, then allowed Religion to invade it like a disease. Apart from assuming the existence of a substance or force called religion that theory quite misses the point. The whole aim of policy is to fetch prosperity from abroad. The Fijians bring it in the shape of a prosperity-dispensing lady and her god. We fetch gold, rubber, tin, etc. Somehow the Fijian theory works, as witness the consequent rise of Suva, Namata, and other tribes that acted upon it.

9. *Monotheism and Centralization. P. 85.*

Heard at the Congress of Religious Faiths, July 1936: "One God must mean one Humanity. . . . The unity of mankind through attachment to the God that is above all."

10. *The Four Quarters. P. 254.*

The proclamation announcing the date of the King's coronation is read in London in four places, but these are now in a line, not at the cardinal points.

11. *Imitation. P. 75.*

In the stations of the cross the worshipper repeats the stages in the sacrifice of the God-man.

12. *Right and Left. P. 98.*

In the Christian Churches of the East the men sit on the right, the women on the left. This is still to be observed in Paris churches at funerals.

Appendix

In the parallel which I traced in *Kings and Councillors* between Agni and Hermes I drew on the results of my own examination of the original texts. In the following I have relied mainly on the data supplied in A. A. Macdonnell's *Vedic Mythology.*

Varuna	Poseidon
1. Dwells in the sky.	1. ———
2. All-seeing.	2. ———
3. Lord of Right.	3. ———
4. Eye is the Sun.	4. ———
5. King (râjan).	5. King at Athens (basileus).
6. Rainmaker.	6. God of growth.
7. Judge in underworld.	7. Infernal deity (Hesiod, *Theog.*, 732 ff.).
8. His animal is the horse; horse sacrifice.	8. His animal is the horse; horse sacrifice.
9. God of the water, especially the ocean.	9. God of the sea, also rivers and springs.
10. His weapon is the snare.	10. ———
11. ———	11. His weapon is the trident.
12. Supports the world.	12. Maintains and supports the earth.
13. ———	13. Causes earthquakes.

Indra	Zeus
1. ———	1. Dwells in the sky.
2. ———	2. All-seeing.
3. ———	3. Upholder of Right.
4. God of the atmosphere.	4. ———
5. King of the Gods.	5. King of the Gods.
6. Makes rain.	6. Makes rain.
7. ———	7. Infernal aspect.
8. Compared with a bull.	8. Takes the form of a bull.
9. Compared with an eagle.	9. His bird is the eagle.
10. The eagle brings him the draught of immortality.	10. The eagle brings him Ganymede, bearer of the cup of immortality.
11. His weapon is the thunderbolt.	11. His weapon is the thunderbolt.
12. Which is made by Tvastri.	12. Which is made by Hephaestus.
13. He defeats Urtra, a serpent.	13. He defeats Typhon, a serpent.
14. He fights Asuras and other demons.	14. He fights Titans and giants.

This appendix is reproduced by permission from A. M. Hocart, *Social Origins* (London: Watts, 1954), pp. 146–47.

INDRA	ZEUS
15. He smites mountains.	15. He casts enemies down from mountains.
16. He settles mountains.	16. Mountain tops dedicated to him.
17. He fights infidels.	17. Is the pursuer of transgressors.
18. He is a parricide (*Rgv.* QV, 18, 12.)	18. Precipitates his father into Tartarus.
19. Is the Helper.	19. Is the Saviour (Sotêr).
20. Is pre-eminent as drinker of soma.	20. Presides over feasts of ambrosia.

There is a close correspondence between Varuna and Poseidon, except that the latter lacks items 1–3, which the Greeks assign to Zeus. Transfer them to Poseidon and the parallel is complete. Varuna later followed the same deline as Poseidon, being ultimately confined to the ocean. Already in the earliest times "a few passages ascribe to Indra actions characteristic of Varuna." In Greece Zeus so encroached upon Poseidon that eventually a god Zeus-Poseidon was recognized in Asia Minor. Zeus becomes a complete autocrat because the Greeks unified the State to a greater extent than the Indians ever did. The process began before our records, and it is only comparative evidence which helps us to trace it backwards.

Similar parallels between Rê, Odin and Varuna and Horus, Thor and Indra could probably be worked out.

Index

Absolutism: totalitarian state, 100;
in England, 150; divine right,
151ff.; theoretic only, 153,
196–97; advance towards, 268
Absorption of gods, 83, 88–89,
168–69; by consecration,
93–94, 168; of cults, 107. *See
also* Centralization;
Monotheism
Abuse. *See* Joking relationship
Academics. *See* Universities
Administration, 31ff., 123, 293
Adultery: how punished, 131–32;
sun punishes, 145
Adversary. *See* Death; Demon;
Devil; Dragon; Serpent
Adze, cult of, 109
Agni, 19ff.; dragon slayer, 19, 57,
157; fire-altar, 64; army-
leader, 184; atmospheric,
288. *See also* Fire
Agora, sacred, 183, 257–58. *See
also* Green; Market
Ahura. See Giants
Ambrosia, 67. *See also* Beer; Kava;
Soma
Amrita, 67, 241. *See also* Soma
Analogy. *See* Metaphor; Organic
analogy
Anatomy. *See* Organic analogy;
Structure
Ancestor: god, 41–42, 61, 75–76
240; first man, 48; imitated,
48, 50, 52–53, 70; cult-object
is, 53–54. *See also* Creator;
God; Imitation
Andree, Richard, lxxiii–lxxiv
Angkor-Vat, 256
Animals: role, 51, 58; in Christian-
ity, 84; royal, 90–92, 96–97;
gods, 105; of land and air,
264. *See also* Bear; Bull;
Cattle; Cows; Dog; Eagle;
Elephant; Hawk; Imitation;

Animals:
Panther; Snake; Thunder-
bird; Wolf
Annexation, through gods, 98–99,
300
Anthropologists: before Hocart,
lxix–lxxv, lxxxiv; contempo-
rary, lxxv–lxxvii, lxxx–lxxxi,
lxxxviii–xc, xciv–xcv; French,
lxxxviii–xc; table of, lxx, lxxi
Anthropomorphism, 240ff.
Anvil worship, 113–14
Aphrodite, 70
Apostolic succession, 58, 74, 77
Archaelogy. *See* Palaeontology
Archon, 169, 183
Argus, 19
Ark, 180, 236
Army: as police, 158. *See also*
Army-leader; Police; Strategy;
Vanguard
Army-leader, 156–61; Agni and
Hermes, 18–20; English, 121;
and chaplain, 200–201. *See
also* Constable; Marshal; Pal-
ladium; Vanguard
Artefacts: in ritual, 42, 46, 62;
cult-objects, 54; gods, 54, 84;
anvil worship, 113–14. *See
also* Adze; Axe; Canoe; Car-
penter; Smith
Assembly: for festivals, 255–56;
people's, 258. *See also* Green;
Market
Asura. See Giants
Atheism, 247
Atmosphere: temple posts, 227–28;
social division, 287ff.; gods of,
287ff.
Atonement, 207
Axe, thunderbolt as, 56–57

Bali, 117, 211
Barber: Fijian, 107; Indian, 115ff.;

305

Barber:
Egyptian, 119; homologies, 125
Bard, 112
Bastian, Adolf, lxxii, lxxiv–lxxv
Bear: dance, 49, 52, 226; clan, 52, 226
Beer: food of gods, 71; supply of, 209
Bird: mound, 234; heavenly, 264. See also Eagle; Hawk; Thunder-bird
Birth, creation is, 45–46, 116, 301
Blacksmith. See Smith
Blessing, 49; meaning of, 50, 73; from king, 99
Body: a vehicle, 51ff., 93–94; duplicate, 95
Border clan, 106, 139, 181–82, 200, 271. See also Army-leader; Dual organization; Vanguard
Brahman: and Agni, 21; same as herald, 22, 194–95; potter is, 116, 192ff. See also Agni; Herald; Priest
Breath: is fire, 64; king is, 95 n
Brihaspati, 63; king, 89
Buddha: lion, 90–91; law-king, 77–78, 171–72. See also Buddhism
Buddhism: spread, 25; ethical cult, 73, 77ff.; ritual, 77ff.; monasteries, 256
Buffalo: dance, 48–50; clan, 103
Bull: is dragon slayer, 56–57; Buddha is, 78; Indra is, 90
Bull-roarer, 238
Burial: effect of, 135; human sacrifice at, 236; according to moiety, 264

Calendar: fixed by king, 145–46; by archon, 169; Buddhist, 172; church and agriculture, 219. See also Law; Sun
Camp, 251ff. See also City
Canoe, 42, 108, 206
Canopy, 229
Carpenter: Egypt, 120; England, 122; Fiji, 108ff., 117; India, 116

Caste, 102–27 passim; based on ritual, 63, 77, 116–18, 301; right and left, 273ff.; outcasting, 296; older than occupation, 297; orientation, 253; Egypt, 119–20; Fiji, 106ff.; Greece, 118–19; India, 114–15, 156–57; Nigeria, 110ff.; Persia, 118. See also Barber; Border clan; Carpenter; Drummer; Dual organization Musicians; Nobility; Potter; Priest; Royal officers; Serf; Smith; Vanguard; Washerman
Cattle: and Agni-Hermes, 19–20; Koryak, 21; creation of, 65. See also Bull; Cows; Reindeer
Cave: abode of prophet, 171; is world, 229; temple, 238
Celibacy, 25, 77, 198
Centralization, 81–85, 250–61 passim; growth of, 37–38; 92ff.; and specialization, 39–40, 298–99; and monotheism, 245, 302; in Fiji, 268. See also Absorption of gods; Annexation; Monotheism; Specialization
Chamberlain, 121, 124
Chaplain, 41–59 passim; at coronation, 93; brother, 137, 194; English, 124; Yoruba, 112. See also Priest
Cheating, 271. See also Dual organization; Joking relationship
Chief, 42, 86, 130. See also King
Chieftain: use of term, 61; priest, 113, 116, 182, 194; dualism, 167
Christianity: ethical, 174; contrasted, 235–36
Church: and state, 162–79, 262; spouse, 98, 233; peace of, 141; building and congregation, 231ff.; church towns, 251. See also Dual kingship; Law-king; Temple

Circle: camp, 251ff.; city, 253; and cross, 257
Circumambulation, 236
Citadel. See City
City, 250–61; origin of, xxix–xxxii; sacred, 169, 183, 253ff.; wards, 259, 279; epitome of land, 260; goddess, 260
Clan: absence of, 251; and moieties, 262–90 passim; Fijian, 22, 61, 104; Winnebago, 49, 103. See also Caste; Dual organization; Royal officers
Clerk: supplants noble, 121–22, 126, 191
Cloud: men, 42–43, 55–56, 83; dragon, 56; mountain, 56
Cobra-king, 91, 217
Colour: meaning of, 239; in dual organization, 282. See Light, and darkness
Commander-in-chief, 180–89. See also Army-leader
Commandments, five, 143
Communications, absence of, 215–16
Communion: theory of, 51; through fire, 20; by eating, 44, 48–49; daily meal, 210; Christian, 76; peace-making, 137–38; imitative, 205–6. See also Beer; Kava; Soma; Tobacco
Commutation, 222
Comparative method, lii–lix, 11–27 passim, 28, 34, 81
Comparative philology, lii, liv, lxv n, 15–16
Compass, points of. See Quarters
Conquest. See Annexation; Vassalage
Consciousness, and evolution, 298–99
Consecration: of elephant, 91; of priest, 199; of temple, 236; of idol, 239–40, 243; life-giving, 243–44. See also Royal consecration
Constable, 121, 123, 124, 186ff.
Consuls, 169

Conubium. See Dual organization; Intermarriage; Moieties
Cook, 116, 121, 125
Coordination, 30ff., 128–29; 148; centres of, 250; growth of, 293
Corvee, 219ff.
Cosmic rites, 60–71 passim, 142ff., 205ff., 239ff., 250ff. See also City; Temple
Council: old men, 130; chieftains, 137–38; in dual organization, 267
Court: copying of, 110, 112, 114, 122, 167, 186, 201, 287. See also Chieftains; Royal officers; Village; Vulgarization
Cows, are rain, 57
Craftsmen, 119–20; decline, 125–26, 292–93
Creation: nature of, 68; ceremony, 55–56, 59; myth, 67, 82; Easter, 221–22; by word, 45; by ritual, 45, 48; by procreation, 65ff., 265ff., 285–86. See also Sacred marriage
Creator, 50, 52; rainmaker, 56; Koryak, 84; Winnebago, 87; potter, 116 n
Cremation, 20
Crier: Winnebago, 103, Fiji, 107; Athens, 196. See also Herald
Crime: opposition to king, 158, 175–76, 182; breach of natural order, 210. See also Adultery; King's enemies; King's peace; Law; Police; Sun
Criminal jurisdiction, 139, 158. See also Crime; Police
Cross, 75, 226, 232, 253ff.; and circle, 257; stations of, 302. See also Quarters
Cross-cousin, 269, 272, 275. See also Dual organization; Intermarriage; Joking relationship; Moieties
Crown, 50; sun-disc, 64, 65; assumption of, 96; papal, 289
Crusades, 159. see also Demon; Heathen; War

Cult-object: nature of, 51; form of sacrament, 241
Customs duties, 213
Cybele, 260

Dalai-Lama, 136, 158
Dance, 43ff.; 48ff.; 182. *See also* Imitation
Darkness, 117; fight against, 158; serfs belong to, 183; not evil, 255. *See also* Dual organization; Giants; Heathen; King's enemies
Death: conception of, xxxii–xxxiii, xxxv; devil is, 48 n; god of quarter, 89; king, 89. *See also* Darkness; Demon; Giants
Decadence, 72, 297
Deer dance, 49
Demeter, 70
Demon: slayer of, 19, 48; heathen, 63; nature of, 117. *See also* Agni; Giants; Hermes; Indra; Zeus
Deva. See God
Devapi, 137, 194
Devil: is death, 48 n. *See also* Death; Demon; Giants
Dharma, 142ff.
Dice, 158
Dichotomy, lxxxvii–lxxxviii; examples, 180, 252–53; gives rise to three, 275, 279, 287 288–89; definition, 265. *See also* Dualism; Dual organization; Four; Three
Differentiation, 38ff., 217–18; of places of activities, 251, 258; absence of, 255–56, 257–58; of abilities, 294–95
Diffusion, 25–26, 81. *See also* Comparative method
Dike, 144
Ditch, 215, 230, 258
Divine right, 151
Diviner: Jukun, 111; Yoruba, 112
Dog: god, 105; king's, 107, 125
Dome, 227ff.
Dragon: Vritra, 19, 56; and St George, 187. *See also* Agni; Cobra-king; Snake;

Dragon:
Thunder-god
Dress, 43, 47, 196
Drummer: Yoruba, 115; India, 117ff.
Dualism, 162–79 passim; Fiji, 22–23; vis-à-vis, 62; male and female, 98; gods and giants, 117. *See also* Dual kingship; Dual organization
Dual kingship, 161, 162–79 passim, 198; Jukun, 111; Yoruba, 112; dual priesthood, 200; sky and earth, 240; and dual organization, 262, 266. *See also* Church and state; Dualism; Dual organization; Executive king; Law-king; War-king
Dual organization, 262–99 passim; sky and earth, 84–85; gods and giants, 117; summer and winter, 284; in camp and city, 252ff.; nobility outside, 273–74, 287; summary, 285ff. *See also* Cheating; Dualism; Dual kingship; Hostility; Intermarriage; Joking relationship; Land and water; Mutual ministration; Obscenity; Opposites; Rivalry; Sky and earth; War
Dugong, 46
Dumézil, Georges, xlix, lxxv–lxxvi, lxxxiii

Eagle, 227; Indra, 90; Zeus, 119; royal bird, 156, 161. *See also* Hawk; Thunder-bird
Earth: consort of sky, 66; god, 70; king, 70; queen, 79; absorbed by sky, 84–85; goddess, 260. *See also* City; Queen; Sacred marriage; Sky and earth
Earthmaker. *See* Creator
Economics, 35–36
Efficiency, 135
Eight: gods, 89; divisions, 252, 268; wards, 259. *See also* Four; Quarters
Elements: in tope, 228; four, 253

Elephant, king's double, 91
Elixir. *See* Ambrosia
Empire, 63
Endogamy. *See* Inbreeding
Enemies. *See* King's enemies
Equations. *See* Equivalence
Equivalence, xlvi–xlix, 41, 44, 50, 52–53, 55, 300; temple and world, 227–28; temple and man, 233; man and idol, 239; Egypt, 57ff.; India, 64; created, 69, 95; ethical, 76
Ethical rites, 76–80, 81–82; monotheistic, 89; reinterpretation of nature rites, 143, 172ff., 254–55. *See also* Buddhism; Christianity; Islam
Etiquette, royal, 152, 207, 300–301
Euclidean procedure. *See* Equivalence
Evidence, lxvi–lxviii
Evolution: social, lx, lxii, lxxxii–lxxxiii; of thought, lxxxvii
Exclusion from ritual, 42, 63, 114, 117, 157
Excommunicates: king's enemies, 157; serfs, 183; foreigners, 183. *See also* Heathen; King's enemies; Outcaste
Excommunication: and outlawry, 174–75; Ceylon, 278; outcasting, 296. *See also* Excommunicates
Executive king, 156–79 passim, 198, 301; not prime minister, 194
Eye, opening of, 243–44

Face of ritual, 106, 184, 186, 190–91, 200
Famine, 136–37
Farmer caste: India, 115, Syria, 121
Fealty. *See* Vassalage
Feast: contributions, 104; cooked and raw, 207. *See also* Communion
Fees, 108–9, 204, 206, 209–10
Fertility, xxxiv

Feudalism, 98–99. *See also* Caste; Royal officers; Service; Vassalage
Fire: Agni and Hermes, 17ff.; Koryak, 21, 240; god of quarter, 89; priestly god, 93; king, 89; in creation, 66–67; palladium, 184–85, 188; central 227–28, 229–30; altar, 240–41
First-fruits: to king, 44, 206, 210–11; to gods, 230. *See also* Communion
Five: quarters, 226, 259; days, 259
Flag: of St George, 187; of city wards, 259
Flood, 48, 76
Foreigner, excommunicate, 157, 183, 200
Four: ancestors, 50; animals, 50, 55; world stones, 56; fires, 181; snake skins, 239; in ritual, 252; in England, 259–60; divisions, 22–23, 279; distribution, 287. *See also* City; Dichotomy; Elements; Quarters
Function, 30; change of, 37, 165; differentiation of, 39–40; shift of, 164, 185, 188, 197, 200–201; overshadows representation, 85, 148, 154, 237, 248, 256, 261, 263, 286, 293
Funeral. *See* Burial
Games: javelin, 182; lacrosse, 265, 267. *See also* Rivalry
Gate: sacred, 193; position of, 254–55
Gens, 61, 110, 114. *See also* Clan
Giants, 117; serfs and heathen, 157ff., 254; excluded from ritual, 277; feud with gods, 277–78. *See also* Darkness; Demon; Dual organization; God; Heathen; Hostility; Serf
God: is life, 33ff., 95, 257; not omnipotent, 151–52, 153; is victim, 44, 67, 90, 300; is ancestor, 43–44, 50; is totem, 54; worshipper is, 75, 213, 233, 234, 240–41; animal, 104; royal, 92–93, 142;

God:
    priestly, 18, 195, 198–99;
    sacrificer, 277; no fixed order,
    199; versus giants, 277. *See
    also* Absorption; Agni;
    Cybele; Dual organization;
    Giants; Hercules; Hermes;
    Imitation; Indra; Jupiter;
    King; Life; Odin; Poseidon;
    Quarters; Queen; Thor;
    Varuna; Zeus
Gold: sun disc, 64–65; life and
    light, 241
Golden Stool, 94
Government: origin of, xxiv–xxviii,
    xxxv, lxi–lxiv; growth of, 30ff.,
    36ff., 293–94; absence of, 35,
    128ff.
Grave: temple, 105. *See also*
    Mound
Green (village), 107, 255–56;
    Lord of the, 107, 250. *See
    also* Square

Hako, 227
Harpoon, 46
Hawk: king, 91, 96; sun-bird, 96
Head: cult of skulls, 239, 240, 251
Headman. *See* Chieftain
Healing: revival, 75; by myth, 82;
    mutual ministration, 268
Heathen: demon, 63, 157ff.; crimi-
    nal, 176
Heaven. *See* Sky
Herald: intermediary, 20; same as
    Brahman, 21; Fijian, 105,
    190ff., 295; Tongan, 190;
    Samoan, 190–91; queen's,
    107; principal, 107; *See also*
    Agni; Brahman; Crier;
    Hermes; Kerux; Staff
Hercules, fighting god, 169
Heredity: in ritual, 52, 55, 58, 61,
    63; of serjeanties, 121; decay
    of, 73–74, 77, 195–96. *See also*
    Apostolic succession; Caste;
    Seniority
Heretic. *See* Heathen
Hermaphrodite, 98
Hermes: and Agni, 16ff., 57;
    dragon slayer, 19, 56–57

Highway, 141. *See also* Roads;
    Streets
Hinduism, 72
Historical reconstruction, lx–lxi,
    lxv–lxix, lxxvii–lxxxi, lxxxvi
Hocart, Arthur Maurice: criticism
    of, xiv–xvi, xxxvi, xli–xliv,
    xlvi, lii–liii, lx–lxi, lxviii; ob-
    scurity, xiv, xc–xciv; field-
    work, xv, xviii–xx, lxiii;
    importance of work, xv–xvii,
    lxiv–lxv; publications, xv, xx,
    xxi, xxiv; family, xvii–xviii;
    popularity, xvii, xxii; educa-
    tion, xviii–xx; in Fiji, xviii–xix;
    army career, xix; in Ceylon,
    xix–xx, xxii, xxxviii; and lan-
    guages, xix, xxii; academic
    career, xx–xxii, xc–xciv; mar-
    riage, xx; at Cairo, xxi, xxii;
    death, xxi; nonconformity,
    xxiii–xxiv, xxviii–xxix, xcii; .
    style, xxiii–xxiv; terminology,
    xxxiv–xli; method
    xxxviii–xxxix, xlvi–xlix,
    lxii–lxviii; premises, liii–lix;
    and other anthropologists,
    lix–lxii, lxix–lxxvi, lxxxiii–lxxiv,
    lxxxviii–xc
Hocart, Elizabeth Graham Hearn,
    xx, xxi
Hocart, James (father), xvii–xviii
Hocart, James (grandfather),
    xvii–xviii
Holiness, 73
Holy Roman Empire, 174
Homicide, and king, 141, 169,
    176–77
Horse: sacrifice, 63, 65, 83, 90,
    144; Varuna, 64, 303. *See
    also* Constable; Marshal;
    Master of Horse
Horus, 57, 91, 159
Hostility: ritual, 264ff., 273–74;
    281ff. *See also* Dual organiza-
    tion; Rivalry; War
House, 141
Hume, David, xxv–xxviii, xxxi
Huntsman, 125; Jukun, 111;
    English, 122

Hymns: creative, 67; Christian, 76; victory, 157. *See also* Word

Iconoclasm, 244ff.
Identity, 41, 43; theory, 51, 53, 65; healing by, 75; in Islam, 80; in coronation, 93; royal officers, 111–12; god and worshipper, 75, 212, 233, 234, 241. *See also* Equivalence; Imitation
Idol, 238–49; ithyphallic, 18; fire-board, 21; whale, 52; function of, 64; Buddhist, 77; consecration of, 238–39, 243–44
Image, 246ff. *See also* Idol
Imitation, 41ff., 46ff., 250; of Christ, 75, 232, 302; of Buddha, 78; of cobra, 91; of sky and earth, 262; by king, 138, 142, 145, 152; by vanguard, 182; in communion, 205; revenue, 212; public works, 215; temple, 226–27; gives place to function, 85, 148, 154. *See also* Cosmic rites; Equivalence; Identity; Sacred marriage
Immortality, 68; acquired, 236. *See also* Ambrosia
Inbreeding, of nobility, 268–69, 292–93, 296
Indra, 303–4; dragon-slayer, 56, 303; giant killer, 229; king of gods, 167, 303; thunder-god, 157, 303; sun, 94; atmospheric, 288; king is, 63, 93, 157; same as Zeus, 159
Infidels. *See* Excommunicates; Heathen
Insignia, 43, 90–91, 96, 192. *See also* Crown; Investiture; Sceptre; Staff
Intellectuals: hostility to ritual, 35; hostility to priests, 276; arrogance, 99, 192, 258; coordinators, 294; rise of, 123, 126, 294–95

Intermarriage: forbidden, 121; of moieties, 263, 269, 280ff., 284. *See also* Cross-cousin; Dual Organization; Mutual ministration; Sacred marriage
Intermediary: god, 19; herald, 195; land chief, 293
Interregnum, 134ff.
Inversion: ritual, 48; in war, 177; of sexes, 273
Investiture, 47; mace, 65. *See also* Crown
Io, 57
Irrigation, 217
Islam, 73, 80

Joking relationship, 269ff., 273, 280ff.
Jotun. *See* Giants
Judge. *See* King; King's justice; Law-king
Jupiter, law-god, 169
Jus Conubii. See Intermarriage
Justice, 128–55 passim. *See also* King's justice

Kangaroo, 41–42
Kava, 61–62, 104; king's daily, 137; to consecrate idol, 238–39
Kerux, 21, 194–95. *See also* Herald
Kin, 130. *See also* Cross-cousin; Dual organization; Inbreeding
King, 86–101, 128–79 passim; none, 50ff.; principal, 61, 63, 70, 74, 137–38; prosperity, 62; sky, 62, 79; sun, 79, 91, 97, 183; moon, 67, 70; thunder-god, 156–61 passim; Indra, 88, 93; breath, 94; various animals, 90–91; eagle, 156, 161; many gods, 70–71, 88ff.; microcosm, 67, 70, 83; divine, 74; higher than god, 61, 105–6; promotion, 134; and calendar, 146; as warrior, 144; as judge, 141, 143; as priest, 198–99; related to serfs, 292. *See also* Absorption of gods; Calendar; Dual kingship; Homicide;

King: King's enemies; King's high-
way; Microcosm; Prosperity;
Royal consecration
Kingmaker, 112
Kings and Councillors: subject
matter, xxiv–xxviii; reception,
xxix; method, xxxviii–xxxix,
li–lix; premises of, xxix–xxxv.
See also Hocart, Arthur
Maurice
King's enemies: internal and exter-
nal, 158; offenders, 182;
heathen, 148, 175–76; crimi-
nals, 148, 175–76, 186; ex-
communicates, 157; for-
eigners, 186. *See also* Crime;
Excommunicates; Heathen;
Police; War
King's highway, 141. *See also*
Roads; Streets
King's justice, 128–55 passim; imi-
tation of world, 142; exten-
sion, 138ff. *See also* Law; Sun
King's liberality, 140, 144, 152,
202ff., 212–13
King's officers, 143. *See also* Royal
officers
King's peace: extension, 139ff.;
breach of, 175. *See also*
Crime; Police
King's serjeants, 121ff., 186. *See
also* Royal officers
Kuru, 143

Land and water, social division,
263ff., 280ff., 285
Land tenure, 120ff.; and fealty,
150
Largesse, 212–13. *See also* King's
liberality
Law, 128–55; function of,
xxv–xxvii; imitation of world,
142; natural, 142ff., 265; civil
and canonical, 174–75, 286.
See also Commandments;
King's justice; Law-king;
Righteousness
Law-king, 162–79 passim, 142
161; priest as, 194, 198
Left. *See* Right and left

Levites, 197
Life: conception of, xxxii–xxxv;
object of ritual, 32ff., 48, 78;
substance, 32ff.; givers of, 51,
236, 267.; is light and gold,
241; water of, 284; from
heaven, 235; spiritual, 73, 77;
nirvana, 77; consecration
gives, 243–44; permeating all,
265–66; Omaha conception of,
266
Light: and darkness, 117, 158,
183, 280ff.; is life and gold
241. *See also* Demon; Giants
Locke, John, xxvi
Logic, 57, 74
Lord of Right. *See* Law-king
Louis X, 133, 149, 159–60

Mace. *See* Sceptre; Thunderbolt
McLennan, J. F., xciv
Malae, 255. *See also* Green
Male and female: essences, 79;
moieties, 280ff.; heavenly
bodies, 266; nobility and far-
mers, 275–76; pipes, 239;
right and left, 98, 235, 275.
See also Sacred marriage; Sky
and earth
Mana. See Virtue
Manu, law of, 194
Market: specialized, 258; four,
256; Igbo, 145; Athens, 183,
257. *See also* Green
Marriage: peace rite, 177; con-
secration, 236; and corona-
tion, 137. *See also* Intermar-
riage: Sacred marriage: Sky
and earth
Marshal, 122ff., 186ff.
Masks, 43ff., 53, 91
Mass, 76
Master of Horse, 112. *See also*
Constable; Marshal
Matangali, 104. *See also* Clan
Mata ni vanua. See Herald
Mauss, Marcel, lxxxviii–xc, xciii
Mbati. See Border clan
Mbota. See Barber
Messiah, 171ff.
Metaphor, role of, xliv–xlvi

Microcosm, 64, 67, 83, 102, 202; temple, 226–27; child, 235; born or made, 236; city, 250
Migration. *See* Comparative method
Milk, 57
Minister, 111
Miracle, social, 148. *See also* Virtue
Misrule, 178
Moieties, 250–90 passim; Winnebago, 162; use of term, 263; reversible duties, 265
Monastery, 256
Monasticism, 25. *See also* Celibacy
Monotheism, 75, 80; centralizing, 82ff., 245ff., 302; solar, 85, 98; and kingship, 89; growth of, 97
Moon: soma, 67; king, 70, 88; queen, 79; god of quarter, 88; one of trinity, 288
Morality: is repression, 144. *See also* Ethical rites
Mormons, 36
Mound, sacred, 106; is man, 190, 234; is world, 228–29, 234; snake, 215, 226. *See also* Grave
Mountain: is cloud, 56; holy, 170
Mundus, 230
Murder, 130–31, 140
Musicians, 112. *See also* Drummer
Mutual consent, 129
Mutual ministration: use of term, 273; general, 138, 263ff., 280ff.; reversible and non-reversible, 265, 270–71; Aranda, 190; Fiji, 222. *See also* Intermarriage
Mysticism, 234
Myth, 45; of flood, 48, 76; of whale, 52–53; creative, 66; based on reality, 94, 157, 159, 171, 229, 260, 277–78; Christian, 76; Buddhist, 78. *See also* Word

Navigator, 99, 108; admiral, 125
Nephew. *See* Uterine nephew
Nirvana, 77

Nobility: status, 114, 262–90 passim; fighting, 156ff., 159; related to serfs, 292; aloofness, 274, 287; exclusiveness, 278, 292; natural selection, 296; monopolizes office, 121–22, 184–85, 187–88, 268, 287; gives place to clerks, 123, 126. *See also* Church and state; King; Royal officers; War

Oath, coronation, 153
Objective in ritual, 46; *See also* Equivalence
Obscenity, 269–70, 275
Ocean: continuation of sky, 262–63, 284–85; sky god, 168; one of trinity, 287; *See also* Poseidon; Varuṇa
Odin, 168, 285, 289
Officials. *See* Royal officers
Opposites (ritual): Fiji, 138, 269–70; Aranda, 190; New Guinea, 271–72. *See also* Dual organization; Moieties
Organic analogy, xl–xlvi
Organization, based on ritual, 34ff., 39, 300
Orientation: by wind, 282; by coast, 255. *See also* City; Dual organization; Five; Four; Quarters; Right and left
Originality, need for, xcvi–xcviii
Ornaments, 45, 231
Outcaste; meaning of, 254; Ceylon, 114–15; Fiji, 117–18; outside city, 253. *See also* Excommunicates; Excommunication; Outlawry
Outlawry, 174–75

Palace: ritual centre, 251; position, 253. *See also* City; Temple
Palaeolithic, 81
Palaeontology, 12–13, 20, 24, 81–82
Palladium, 180–89 passim; fire, 19–20, 184; pole, 181. *See also* Army-leader; Flag

Panther, 91
Pantomime, 279
Parallel evolution, 187
Peace: various kinds, 141; special ritual, 200; female, 239; and war moieties, 239, 267ff. *See also* Dual kingship; War
Peacemaking: by chief, 140; by priest-herald, 195
Persephone, 70
Phallus, 18, 48, 242
Pipe, 140
Plundering, 270
Pluralism, 70, 86–101 passim; meaning of, 99; usual, 102; through consecration, 93. *See also* Absorption of gods; Monotheism
Pole, sacred, 103; king, 140; palladium, 181; god, 235
Polemarch, 183. *See also* Army-leader
Police: Fiji, 107ff., 125, 139, 181, 271; India, 158; Winnebago, 181; England, 186; public security, 212–13
Polytheism: decentralizing, 245ff. *See also* Idol; Monotheism; Pluralism
Pope: law-king, 174–75, 198; temporal power, 176; fixes calendar, 146; crown, 289
Poseidon, 168, 288, 303, 304
Potter: Jukun, 110; India, 116, 275; Fiji, 109; creator, 116, 210
Power, supernatural. *See* Virtue
Prajapati, 63, 87–88
Priest, 190–201; misuse of word 46; status, 276ff.; intermediary, 293; rival of king, 192, 245ff.; chieftains, 108ff., 113, 116, 182, 194; minister, 111; king's priest, 106; god, 63; insignia, 192, 195, 196–97, 199. *See also* Chaplain; Dual kingship; Prime minister
Prime minister: Tonga, 165; brahman, 193; pseudo, 167; junior branch, 191, 194, 197,

Prime minister: 198; male line, 295; king as, 194
Principal: definition, 42, 46; nature of, 52, 58, function, 51; king, 61, 63, 70, 74, 138; dead king, 135; priest or king, 199; herald, 107; God, 74; many gods, 63; idol, 77. *See also* God; Idol; King; Priest
Prophet, 169ff. *See also* Law-king
Prosperity: depends on king, 133–34, 136–37, 143–44, 145ff., 153, 228; and wealth, 202ff.
Provinces: four, 259; five, 259
Public opinion, 129ff.
Public square. *See* Green; Market
Public works, 215–25
Punishment. *See* Crime
Pura, 251
Purohita. See Chaplain

Quarters, of the world: gods, 64, 87, 234–35, 253, 288; eight gods, 89, 235; wind stones, 56; division of clans, 22–23; markets, 145, 257; provinces, 259ff.; cross, 226; in tope, 229; in camp and city, 251ff.; in coronation, 302. *See also* Five; Four
Queen: earth, 79, 97, 260, 286; moon, 79, 260; absorbed by king, 97; indispensable, 137; her herald, 107. *See also* Earth

Raglan, Lord, xxi, xxii, liii, xcix
Rain: is milk, 57; is semen, 66; fails through sin, 137, 142; largesse, 212. *See also* Prosperity; Rainmaking
Rainbow, 43
Rainmaking: Aranda, 42–43, 45–46; Lango, 54–55; New Guinea, 56, 73; caused by sun, 212
Rank: of kings, 162ff.; of moieties, 264ff.
Ratzel, Friedrich, lxxiii, lxxv

Raven, 52, 83–84
Rearguard, 185
Rebellion, 150
Rebirth, 46, 63; identification by, 65; of outlaw, 175
Reciprocity, 213. *See also* Mutual ministration; Opposites
Regalia: keeper of, 103; makers of, 112; discarded, 199. *See also* Crown; Sceptre
Reindeer, 21, 53
Religion. *See* Ritual
Representation. *See* Function; Imitation
Repression, 143
Revenue, 202–25 passim; organization, 104; imitative, 212–13
Right and left, 165–66, 183, 268ff., 279–81; male and female, 98, 235, 275, 280ff., 302. *See also* Dual organization
Righteousness, 128–55 passim; sun of, 72. *See also* Justice; Law; Law-king
Ritual, xxxiv–xxxv, xlix–li, lxiii–lxiv, 41–80 passim; organization, xxvii–xxxii, xxxv, 39–40; analysis of, xxxv–xl, xlix–li, lix, 42ff., 46; only one, 237; life-giving, 33ff., 245; use of word, 34; not religion, 35, 217, 256; undifferentiated, 256–57. *See also* Consecration; Equivalence; Face of ritual; Giants; God; Idol; Imitation; Inversion; Investiture; Myth; Sacred marriage; Temple; Word
Rivalry: of moieties, 163, 270ff., 281; games, 182, 264–65, 267; gods, 277; leads to war, 268
Roads, 217. *See also* Highway
Roof, 228, 230. *See also* Dome; Sky
Royal caste. *See* Nobility
Royal consecration: Hebrew, 34; Indian, 65, 93; Siamese, 95; English, 96, 123–24; French, 160; proclamation, 192, 302; presence of serfs, 183; offices,

Royal consecration: 186; queen necessary, 137. *See also* Absorption of gods; Investiture; Oath
Royal officers, 37–38, 102–27 passim; at coronation, 93ff.; king's serjeants, 121ff.; navigator, 99; priests, 108ff., 111–12, 116; serfs, 254. *See also* Army-leader; Barber; Carpenter; Caste; Chamberlain; Huntsman; Master of Horse; Musicians; Navigator; Potter; Smith; Steward; Undertaker; Washerman

Sacred: meaning of, 253–54, 256–57; taboo, 139
Sacred marriage, 46–47; heaven and earth, 66, 79, 84, 98; mystic, 236; with turtle, 109; with horse, 65; Indian, 65; Babylonian and Greek, 69–70; Christian, 76, 98; Buddhist, 78; Chinese, 79; Athenian, 170. *See also* Intermarriage; Queen; Sky and earth
Sacred thread, 275
Sacrifice: nature of, 52–53; human, 236; basis of caste, 116–17, 301. *See also* Ritual; Victim
Sacrificer, 62–63. *See also* Principal
Saint Louis, 133, 149, 159–60
Sambara, 56
Sceptre, 65. *See also* Staff
Seasons. *See* Summer and winter
Self-help, 31, 130ff.
Seniority: king and priest, 294–95; younger is priest, 191, 194, 197–98; and office, 137, 191, 194; departure from, 197
Serf, 115ff.; admitted to ritual, 117; slayable at will, 152; demon, 157; king's officer, 187; in city, 254; related to king, 292. *See also* Caste; Royal officers
Serjeanty, 121ff. *See also* Chamberlain; Constable; Marshal; Royal officers; Steward

Serpent, 56. *See also* Dragon; Snake

Service, 105; and caste, 114ff.; and land tenure, 121. *See also* Land tenure; Royal officers; Serf; Vassalage

Sex, 45–46. *See also* Male and female; Sacred marriage

Sister's son. *See* Uterine nephew

Siva, 285

Skull. *See* Head

Sky: king, 62, 70, 79; god, 70, 84, 87, 97; tomb, 228; roof, 222. *See also* Dome; Ocean; Sky and earth

Sky and earth, 262–90 passim; marriage, 66, 79, 84, 97–98, 260, 266; dualism, 178; father and mother, 266; functions, 266–67; symbol of, 239; in temple, 226ff.; in city, 253. *See also* Dual organization; Sacred marriage

Smith: hausa, 113, 132; India, 116; Egypt, 120

Snake: clan, 50, 104; offerings to, 239; brazen serpent, 246. *See also* Cobra-king; Dragon

Social contract, xxv–xxvi

Society as organism. *See* Organic analogy

Sodomy, 48. *See also* Inversion

Solarization: of revenue, 212; Akhenaten, 245. *See also* Absorption of gods; Sun

Soma, 67; king a drinker of, 144; king of priests, 192

Soul: catching, 33–34; among Jukuns, 240; of idol, 243

Specialization, lxii, lxxxii–lxxxiii, 31; and centralization, 39, 298; in ritual, 58, 200; encourages money, 223; excess of, 232, 297. *See also* Centralization

Specific rites, 41–59 passim, 58ff., 86; adze, 109; anvil, 113

Speech. *See* Word

Square: camp, 251ff.; city, 253ff. For public square *see* Green; Market

Staff: herald's, 192, 195, 301; priest's, 192, 195, 197, 201; connected with speech, 192, 195, 201; consecration of, 239

Statute-labour, 219ff.

Steward, 122–23

Stone: idols, 44, 56, 238; abode of spirits, 239–40

Strategy, 184, 189, 255, 257, 261–62

Streets: form cross, 253ff. *See also* Highway

Structuralism, lxxxiv–lxxxvi

Structure, conception of, xxxix–xli

Sublimation, 72–80 passim, 77

Substance, 33

Succession: unconditional, 151; of younger branch, 197; through females, 295; sin a bar to, 197. *See also* Seniority

Summer and winter, 284

Sun: fire, 20; gold disc, 64–65; god, 83; king, 79, 88; god of a quarter, 89; Indra, 94; eye, 91; animals, 97; of righteousness, 72, 78, 142, 143ff.; condemns adultery, 145; spiritual, 254; one of trinity, 288; monotheism, 245. *See also* Solarization

Syllogism, 64. *See also* Equivalence

Symbolism, xxix–xxxi, xlviii–xlix

Taboo, 139

Taxes, 202–25 passim

Temple, 226–36; clan, 104–5; state 105; Winnebago, 215; of the Tooth, 77; representative, 248; consecration of, 236; on public square, 255ff.; city place of, 250–60 passim. *See also* Dome

Thor, 168, 289

Thread. *See* Sacred thread

Three: worlds, 233–34, 287ff.; chiefs, 180, 183, 272; divisions, 114, 118, 180, 273, 275, 279, 287ff.; forms of the word, 66; through dichotomy,

Three:
275, 289; boundary of, 292. *See also* Dichotomy; Trinity
Throne, 94
Thunder. *See* Thunder-bird Thunderbolt; Thunder-god; Thunder-king
Thunder-bird, 87, 164, 180. *See also* Eagle
Thunderbolt, 56, 65, 87. *See also* Axe
Thunder-god, 56, 83, 119; king as, 156–61 passim; as peace-maker, 169; St George, 187
Thunder-king, 156–79 passim; as peace-maker, 164. *See also* War
Tithe, 209, 212, 214
Tjurunga, 238
Tobacco, 51, 140, 226, 237
Tooth of Buddha, 77
Tope, 228–29
Totalitarian state. *See* Absolutism
Totem, 54. *See also* God
Trade, absence of, 215
Treason, 133
Treasury, 207
Tree, 56; and king, 69, 70, 97; cross is, 75; Buddhist, 77
Tribute: food, 192n, 211; offering, 207, 211ff.
Trinity, 288–89
Truth, 145
Tumulus. *See* Mound
Turtle: dance, 49; rites, 109; fishing, 204
Tyranny, 153

Undertaker, 107, 110, 112
Universe. *See* World
Universities, xc–xcvii
Usurper, 137
Uterine nephew: clan, 107, 110; commander-in-chief, 184; priest, 196

Van Gennep, Arnold, xcv
Vanguard, 180–89 passim; Fiji, 107, 282; same as herald, 200. *See also* Army-leader

Varuna, 303–4; god of a quarter, 89; god of water, 89, 284, 303; horse, 64–65, 303; Lord of Right, 63, 142, 168, 303. *See also* Law; Ocean
Vassalage: cult of king, 99, 106; adopting god, 302; imitation of king, 110ff. *See also* Absorption of gods; Annexation; Court; Village; Vulgarization
Veda, 66
Vehicle (ritual): kinds of, 51; Fiji, 58. *See also* Identity
Victim: is god, 44, 52, 67, 75, 90, 300; is worshipper, 51, 75, 90. *See also* Identity
Victory, 49–50, 61, 73; spiritual, 77
Village: copies court, 110, 114, 167, 186, 287; opposed to city, 251, 253. *See also* Green
Virtue (supernatural power), 139–40
Vis-à-vis. *See* Opposites
Vishnu, 67
Vritra, 19, 56. *See also* Dragon
Vulgarization, 110, 114, 127, 165ff., 186–87; of court, 112 121–22, 293

Wake, Charles Staniland, xciv–xcv
Wakonda, 144–45
War, 156–61; ritual, 244; special ritual of, 200; breach of peace, 177; defence of people, 212; and king, 144; male, 239; in dual organization, 284, 268. *See also* Army-leader; Crime; Heathen; Hostility; Peace; Police; Rivalry
War-king, 156–79 passim, 161; head of vanguard, 181
Washerman: India, 120n, 125; Egypt, 122; England, 125. *See also* Chamberlain
Water: opposed to land, 263; god of, 89, 284, 303. *See also* Land and water; Ocean
Wealth, 202

Whale, 52, 95, 226
Wheel, 172
William the Conqueror, 148
Wind: king, 89; giver of life, 267;
  one of trinity, 288
Wolf, 52
Woman: necessary to ritual, 63;
  half of man, 63, 65, 98. *See
  also* Sacred marriage
Word, 45, 47; of power, 61, 66,
  192; three forms, 66; herald
  is, 106. *See also* Myth
World, 60–71; god, 63, 74, 83,
  88–89; ritual model of, 67.

World: *See also* Cosmic rites;
  Microcosm; Temple
Worship, 54
Worshipper: is god, 47, 75; is vic-
  tim, 51, 75, 90. *See also*
  Identity

Yang and Yin, 79
Younger brother. *See* Seniority

Zeus, 303–4; bird, 119, 303;
  thunder-god, 159, 168, 303;
  one of trinity, 289